PRAISE FOR *CONFORMING TO RIGHT REASON*

"Professor Brady has written an extremely impressive work that, in an exhaustive and precise manner, examines areas of Thomas Aquinas's thought that are of fundamental importance for contemporary ethics and moral theology. In a charitable but forthright manner he demonstrates that certain major figures in these fields have offered misreadings of Thomas as a basis for their own theories."

Kevin L. Flannery, S.J.
Pontifical Gregorian University, Rome

"In a fine display of Thomistic scholarship, Ryan Brady's *Conforming to Right Reason* sets forth the ends of the moral virtues and their importance for our lives, showing how natural reason and prudence as the 'charioteer' of the virtues direct our appetites and desires to virtuous ends. He guides us through from Aquinas's early to his late works on this question, helps to resolve long-standing puzzles, and shows commendable mastery both of the recent scholarship and the historic commentators in the Thomist tradition. Moreover, as a professional translator of Thomistic works from the Latin, his fluency in Aquinas's language and thought is simply outstanding. In an era where nonsense in the mind continually reinforces corruption in the appetites, work like Brady's is exactly what we need."

David Elliot
The Catholic University of America

"In this book, Ryan Brady accomplishes an impressive feat. He decisively contributes—offering a compelling solution—to a long-standing debate among interpreters of Aquinas with respect to the role of reason and the will in the judgments of conscience and prudence. Moreover, after decades of scholarly and pastoral confusion about conscience and morality, Brady's analysis of Aquinas is worth reading by anyone interested in thinking clearly about such matters. Thoughtfully engaging with many interlocutors from the past and the present, Brady defends the priority of intellectual judgement in pursuit of happiness and right action. Truth matters for the moral life!"

Michael A. Dauphinais,
Ave Maria University

"All too forgotten in discussions concerning knowledge of first moral principles, *synderesis*, the profound root of conscience, deserves a much more central place in scholastic discussions of moral epistemology. This is particularly true concerning our knowledge of the natural law, the content of which ramifies through all the various acquired moral virtues. If reflection on first principles is truly an office of wisdom, then reflection on our epistemological capacities for knowing such principles is also part of such sapiential meditation. Given that a small error in principles will lead to immense woe in later discussions and debates, assiduous attention should be paid to Dr. Brady's analysis in this text so that future debates concerning virtue ethics, moral epistemology, and human knowledge of the natural law might focus more on this important intellectual *habitus*, *synderesis*, without which no moral knowledge would ever be articulated by any human mind. No sound moral epistemology, whether in the order of nature or in that of the Christian life of grace, can fail to take into account the noetic phenomenon associated with our grasping of moral truths by way of *synderesis*. This text is to be highly recommended, and it is my hope that it helps to reorient contemporary debates around the truly central principles that dominate the whole of the various questions connected with the matters covered in this admirable volume."

Matthew K. Minerd
Byzantine Catholic Seminary of Ss. Cyril and Methodius

RENEWAL WITHIN TRADITION

SERIES EDITOR: MATTHEW LEVERING

Matthew Levering is the James N. and Mary D. Perry Jr. Chair of Theology at Mundelein Seminary. Levering is the author or editor of over thirty books. He serves as coeditor of the journals *Nova et Vetera* and the *International Journal of Systematic Theology*.

ABOUT THE SERIES

Catholic theology reflects upon the content of divine revelation as interpreted and handed down in the Church, but today Catholic theologians often find the scriptural and dogmatic past to be alien territory. The Renewal within Tradition Series undertakes to reform and reinvigorate contemporary theology from within the tradition, with St. Thomas Aquinas as a central exemplar. As part of its purpose, the Series reunites the streams of Catholic theology that, prior to the Council, separated into neo-scholastic and *nouvelle theologie* modes. The biblical, historical-critical, patristic, liturgical, and ecumenical emphases of the Ressourcement movement need the dogmatic, philosophical, scientific, and traditioned enquiries of Thomism, and vice versa. Renewal within Tradition challenges the regnant forms of theological liberalism that, by dissolving the cognitive content of the gospel, impede believers from knowing the love of Christ.

PUBLISHED OR FORTHCOMING

Reading the Sermons of Thomas Aquinas: A Beginner's Guide
Randall B. Smith

The Culture of the Incarnation: Essays in Catholic Theology
Tracey Rowland

Self-Gift: Humanae Vitae and the Thought of John Paul II
Janet E. Smith

On Love and Virtue: Theological Essays
Michael S. Sherwin, O.P.

Aquinas on Beatific Charity and the Problem of Love
Christopher J. Malloy

Christ the Logos of Creation: Essays in Analogical Metaphysics
John R. Betz

The One Church of Christ: Understanding Vatican II
Stephen A. Hipp

O Lord, I Seek Your Countenance:
Explorations and Discoveries in Pope Benedict XVI's Theology
Emery de Gaal

The Trinitarian Wisdom of God:
Louis Bouyer Theology of the God-World Relationship
Keith Lemna

One of the Trinity Has Suffered:
Balthasar's Theology of Divine Suffering in Dialogue
Joshua R. Brotherton

Vessel of Honor: The Virgin Birth and the Ecclesiology of Vatican II
Brian Graebe

The Love of God Poured Out:
Grace and the Gifts of the Holy Spirit in St. Thomas Aquinas
John Meinert

A Living Sacrifice: Liturgy and Eschatology in Joseph Ratzinger
Roland Millare

The Primacy of God: The Virtue of Religion in Catholic Theology
R. Jared Staudt

The Order and Division of Divine Truth:
St. Thomas Aquinas as Scholastic Master of the Sacred Page
John F. Boyle.

Conforming to Right Reason

Conforming to Right Reason

On the Ends of the Moral Virtues and
the Roles of Prudence and Synderesis

RYAN J. BRADY

Steubenville, Ohio
www.emmausacademic.com

EMMAUS
ACADEMIC

Steubenville, Ohio
www.emmausacademic.com

A Division of The St. Paul Center for Biblical Theology
Editor-in-Chief: Scott Hahn
1468 Parkview Circle
Steubenville, Ohio 43952

©2022 Ryan J. Brady
All rights reserved. Published 2022
Printed in the United States of America.

Library of Congress Cataloging-in-Publication Data applied for
ISBNs: 978-1-64585-162-2 hc / 978-1-64585-163-9 pb / 978-1-64585-164-6 eb

Unless otherwise noted, Scripture quotations are taken from The Revised Standard Version Second Catholic Edition (Ignatius Edition) Copyright © 1994 by the Division of Christian Education of the National Council of the Churches of Christ in the United States of America. Used by permission. All rights reserved.

Excerpts from the English translation of the Catechism of the Catholic Church, second edition, copyright © 2000, Libreria Editrice Vaticana—United States Conference of Catholic Bishops, Washington, DC. Noted as CCC in the text.

Cover design by Patty Borgman
Interior layout by Emily Demary
Cover image: *Prudence* by Piero del Pollaiuolo, 1470 oil on panel, Uffizi Gallery.

TABLE OF CONTENTS

Abbreviations xiii

Foreword by Steven A. Long xv

Introduction 1

Chapter 1: The Importance of the End 29

Chapter 2: On the Causality of the Intellect 99

Chapter 3: What Appoints the End? 183

Conclusion 235

Acknowledgements 241

Bibliography 243

Index 249

Abbreviations

ST	Aquinas, *Summa theologiae* (All Latin quotes from *ST* are from the Editio altera Romana [Rome: Forzani and Sodalis, 1894]).
SCG	Aquinas, *Summa contra gentiles*
In I–IV *sent.*	Aquinas, Commentary on Peter Lombard's *Sentences* (IV bks.)
The *Scriptum*	*In* I–IV *sent.* outside specific-text citation
In I–X *eth.*	Aquinas, Commentary on Aristotle's *Nicomachean Ethics* (X bks.)
In I–XII *metaphys.*	Aquinas, Commentary on Aristotle's *Metaphysics* (XII bks.)
In I–VIII *phys.*	Aquinas, Commentary on Aristotle's *Physics* (VIII bks.)
In I–III *de an.*	Aquinas, Commentary on Aristotle's *De anima* (III bks.)
In I–II *de interp.*	Aquinas, Commentary on Aristotle's *De interpretatione* (II bks.)
CT I–II	Aquinas, *Compendium theologiae* (II bks.)
Quolibet I–XII	Aquinas, *Quaestiones de quolibet* (XII bks.)
Super Rom/Eph/etc.	Aquinas, Commentary on Biblical Books
Leonine ed.	Aquinas, *Opera omnia iussu impensaque Leonis XIII P. M. edita* (Rome: Typographia Polyglotta S.C. de Propaganda Fide, 1882–) (Unless otherwise noted, as with *ST* above, Latin quotes of the works of Aquinas are from the Leonine ed. Latin of all of Aquinas's works can be found also at https://www.corpusthomisticum.org/opera.html.)

Cajetan commentary	Commentary on *ST* by Thomas de Vio Cajetan in the Leonine ed. vols. 4–12, cited by *ST* primary-text location and Cajetan's section number
Dominican Fathers trans.	Dominican Fathers of the English Province translations of *ST* (London: Burns, Oates, and Washbourne, n.d.) and *SCG* (London: Burns, Oates, and Washbourne, 1924)
	Unless otherwise noted (e.g., Dominican Fathers), all English translations are original (although other reliable translations can be found in the bibliography).
CCSL	*Corpus Christianorum Series Latina* (Turnhout: Brepols, 1953–)
NPNF1/NPNF2	*Nicene and Post-Nicene Fathers of the Christian Church*, 1st and 2nd series (New York: Christian Literature Company, 1899).

Foreword

THAT CONFUSION about the nature of practical reason and the moral life has affected Christian thought over the past sixty years is an object both of theological note (see *Veritatis Splendor*), and also of philosophy, history, and the sociology of knowledge. Without denying the influence of a variety of factors, greater or lesser departure from the patrimony of Saint Thomas Aquinas's moral theology is undeniably part of the story. But in addition to exogenous factors, undergirding such departure there also lie difficult systematic issues at the root of Thomas's teaching that even minds of distinction seeking to understand Thomas's teaching encounter. These difficulties, left untended, in critical respects have the potential to become seminalia for theological deconstruction and both the decohering of moral thought in its own right and of Thomas's moral teaching in particular. One of the most delicate of these issues regards correct understanding of the relation of synderesis and prudence, an issue that in many respects tracks Saint Thomas's similarly strategic teaching of the objective primacy of the speculative vis-à-vis the practical life. Ryan Brady's *Conforming to Right Reason* provides a serious account of the foundation of the moral life in natural intellectual knowledge of ends, and of the order of ends, as defining the nature of the moral good.

Regarding prudence and synderesis, texts of Thomas that seem contradictory require analysis. Saint Thomas writes at one point that prudence appoints the end of the virtues (*Summa theologiae* [*ST*] I-II, q. 66, a. 3, ad 3) while at another (*ST* II-II, q. 47, a. 6, resp.) he very expressly denies this very thing and holds that synderesis does this ("it does not belong to prudence to appoint the end to moral virtues, but only to regulate the means"[1]). His reasoning in question 47 of *ST* II-II makes very

---

[1] *ST* II-II, q. 47, a. 6, resp.: "Et ideo ad prudentiam non pertinet praestituere finem

clear that without natural reason appointing the end absolutely speaking, there would be no inclinations in need of perfection through moral virtue because we would be aware of no end to pursue. Moral virtue appoints the ends to the virtues not simply, but only insofar as the proximate end of the virtues is the right use of the means for the sake of the end, and so it is *this* right use of the means that constitutes the end that is appointed by prudence and by doing so assures motion to the end and so, further, "appoints" it. However, the means are means only in relation to the end, which must first be known if this is to guide action. Rational inclination—will—is always specified by intellect. Even when one wills abruptly to cease some consideration, this is always specified by some known object (unless we speak of subrational interruption, as when one suffers a heart attack or the roof caves in).

Nonetheless, in the twentieth century, minds of the eminence of Yves Simon have expressed themselves in a way that at least strongly suggests that they thought that prudence appoints the ends of the virtues absolutely speaking[2]—that the agent's attunement to the incommunicable

---

virtutibus moralibus, sed solum disponere de his quae sunt ad finem." See also ad 1 of a. 6: "Natural reason known by the name of 'synderesis' appoints the end to moral virtues, as stated above [*ST* I, q. 79, a. 12], but prudence does not do this for the reason given above."

[2] Yves Simon argues that, whenever "specific situations and specific regulations are involved, there is absolutely no possibility of preceding by logical connection" (*The Tradition of Natural Law*, ed. Vukan Kuic [New York: Fordham University Press, 1992], 155–56). Certainly the character of practical reasoning is not exclusively deductive in its provenance. But one might prefer the formulation not that "the connection between 'particular determinations' and universal norms is not logical, it is prudential," but that "the connection between 'particular determinations' and universal norms is not achieved merely through logical deduction, but through reasoning regarding natural teleology aided by prudential awareness of circumstances and pertinent individual dispositions." As Simon observes: "To know what I should do here and now, I must rely on the judgment of practical wisdom. And this judgment, reasoned as it may be, is ultimately determined not by the intellect but by the inclination of the will" (*The Definition of Moral Virtue*, ed. Vukan Kuic [New York: Fordham University Press, 1986], 96–97). But the will is a rational power. *De veritate* surely is correct to teach that when an agent determines an end for itself, this occurs through intellect: "ipsum agens determinat sibi finem, sicut est in omnibus agentibus per intellectum" (q. 3, a. 1, corp.). Not merely the logical, but the teleological order—which requires individual cognizance of circumstance and of pertinent dispositions—is decisive. To be sure, there is an incommunicable element of discernment of singularities of circumstance, but the order of this to the end is of principal importance and is not contrary to logic, nor does it annul the priority of knowledge of the end, but helps to make this knowledge effective and is judged in relation to the end. Prudence cannot, apart from natural knowledge of the end, proceed with the least moral adequacy. I believe Simon would acknowledge

singulars bound up with action is not only necessary for good action, but dwarfs the role of intellectual knowledge of principle in the moral life. Because of the genuinely high regard shown by Thomas (and Thomists) for prudence, in particular because of the conflicting texts in question, and perhaps somewhat aided by the "turn to the concrete" influential among many Thomists of the mid-twentieth century, the teaching that prior right apprehension of the end is necessary for the formation of the *habitus* of prudence has suffered a measure of neglect. Yet as Brady notes, from the first *Scriptum on the Sentences* to the *Summa theologiae*, there it is. In the *Scriptum*, he notes that what is necessary for moral virtue is the appointing of the end, the inclination to the appointed end, and the choice of the means.[3] Because the end is the first thing to be intended, and because intention presupposes the *ordinatione rationis ordinantis aliquid in finem*[4] (even though intention is an act of the will—*ST* I-II, q. 12, a. 1, ad 3), clearly the prior rational apprehension of the end enjoys ultimate primacy. Thus it is rightly said that the *intellectus est simpliciter prior voluntate* even though the will is prior *secundum quid*.[5] The act of appointing the end must precede the inclination toward the end. Once apprehended the known end can then elicit inclination and at times, further, elicit intention, thus moving one toward the deliberation and choice of means. In the *ST* I-II, q. 19, a. 3, ad 3, we find Thomas responding to the objection that as the will is mover of the reason, the goodness of the will does not depend on reason. He writes:

> The Philosopher speaks there of the practical intellect, in so far as it counsels and reasons about the means: for in this respect it is perfected by prudence. Now in regard to the means, the rectitude of the reason depends on its conformity with the desire of a due

---

this, and contradistinguish, while yet his formulations at times do seem to this author unduly to distance the will from its ineluctable intellective specification. The danger in these formulations of misprizing the strategic role of natural knowledge of the end for moral agency is not insignificant.

[3] See *In III sent.*, d. 33, q. 2, a. 3, corp., and the subheading in chapter 3 of the present volume particularly addressing distinction 33 (under the heading on the *Scriptum* and Capreolus).

[4] *ST* I-II, q. 12, a. 1, ad 3: "the decree of reason ordering something to the end."

[5] For this teaching that the intellect is simply prior to the will, see *ST* I, q. 82, a. 4, ad 1 (asserting that the intellect is higher and more noble than the will *simpliciter*), as well as *De veritate*, q. 22, a. 12, ad 1, and *De virtutibus*, q. 2, a. 3, ad 12, both of which hold that the intellect is simply prior to the will.

end: nevertheless the very desire of the due end presupposes on the part of reason a right apprehension of the end.[6]

This—even had Thomas never written the very clear explanation of II-II, q. 47, a. 6, resp. (which he did)—gives the clue to the twofold use of "appoint" that is implicitly involved in the dueling texts of Aquinas. In one way, the submarine commander who seeks to find a particular ship and destroy it "appoints the end" by knowing the importance of that ship to the enemy's war effort and realizing it would be good to deny the enemy its use. In another sense, the particular tactics on the final torpedo run, inclusive of the use of the periscope and the order to fire, bring "into focus" all the requisite means and so "appoint the end" in the sense of orchestrating all the means to the target.

Brady's analysis pellucidly explains the nature and role of synderesis and prudence in moral life as articulated consistently by Saint Thomas across different works and semantic formulations. He is keenly aware that the judgment that prudence presupposes is said to be made or brought about by the "speculative reason" (see *ST* I-II, q. 57, a. 6). The question he engages touches the speculative character of the apprehensions of synderesis, speculative because these apprehensions do not necessitate action although they provide the *ratio* for action *tout court* and so enter into the causal account of every human act (as opposed to "acts of man"). The *ratio* for action precedes action, and precedes the intention for action, and indeed precedes the desire which is at the font of intention (because knowledge is presupposed to desire). Hence, in terms of the ends of agency, the reason for such knowledge is not originatively action, even though this knowledge does supply the origins for practical agency. This of course does not deny that some things truly are human ends to which contingent singulars are orderable and thus practical objects, but the way that they are initially known (prior to desire and intention) is speculative and so practical only *secundum quid*.[7] Simi-

---

[6] *ST* I-II, q. 19, a. 3, ad 2 "Philosophus ibi loquitur de intellectu practico, secundum quod est consiliativus et ratiocinativus eorum quae sunt ad finem, sic enim perficitur per prudentiam. In his autem quae sunt ad finem, rectitudo rationis consistit in conformitate ad appetitum finis debiti. Sed tamen et ipse appetitus finis debiti praesupponit rectam apprehensionem de fine, quae est per rationem."

[7] Although ends are by nature principles of practical reason, our first knowledge of the end is prior to our practical reasoning. Thus, while this first knowledge is with respect to practical knowledge assuredly practical, in the mode of our initial knowledge it is simply rational apprehension, an apprehension of that to which human nature is ontologically ordained from its creation. Indeed, were human nature not so ordered, action

larly, the end as the *ratio* of action is both extrinsic to action and the very reason for it, and so the knowledge of it that precedes desire, intention, and action is not sought for the sake of the good of an action but is simply and purely knowledge. Hence, in the terms of the eleventh article of question 79 of the *prima pars* of the *Summa theologiae*, such knowledge is speculative while supplying the vertebrae of the moral life. As the pearl forms around the grain of sand, so practical agency forms around a prior *speculum*. It is in a sense accidental to any grain of sand that a pearl form around it: but it is not accidental to the pearl, *qua* pearl, that it forms around a grain of sand. Practical agency presupposes the knowledge of the end (which knowledge is practical by its nature *qua* end, while being speculative in its origin as knowledge prior to action and as not *hic et nunc* necessarily requiring action). Thomas's teaching on synderesis analogically reflects this priority of natural reason vis-à-vis the will.

Brady's work decisively refutes the famed claim of James Keenan that Thomas shifted his position to "voluntarism" in the *Summa theologiae*. Brady notes that, in Keenan's opinion, Aquinas eventually came to see the "truth" that the will is not only "the mover of all powers, including itself and the intellect," but that its self-movement "takes precedence over all other movements."[8]

While in *ST* I, q. 82, a. 4, ad 3, Thomas argues an intellectual apprehension precedes every motion of the will even though a motion of the will does not precede every apprehension, Keenan argues Thomas radically altered his position around the year 1270. Yet Thomas clearly teaches that:

> That which is first simply and according to the order of nature is more perfect. For this reason, act is prior to potency. In this way, the intellect is prior to the will as the mover is prior to the movable and as the active is prior to the passive; for the understood good moves the will.[9]

---

would be both impossible and inexplicable: effective teleology is presupposed to actual inclination; thus even evil action implies some—defective—motion to the end.

[8] James Keenan, S.J., *Goodness and Rightness in Thomas Aquinas's Summa theologiae* (Washington, DC: Georgetown University Press, 1992), 45.

[9] *ST* I, q. 82, a. 3, ad 2: "Ad secundum dicendum quod illud quod est prius generatione et tempore, est imperfectius, quia in uno et eodem potentia tempore praecedit actum, et imperfectio perfectionem. Sed illud quod est prius simpliciter et secundum naturae ordinem, est perfectius, sic enim actus est prior potentia. Et hoc modo intellectus est prior voluntate, sicut motivum mobili, et activum passivo, bonum enim intellectum movet voluntatem."

Keenan holds that "insofar as the will first exercises itself, it is not moved by an object"[10] and that "as first mover, the will's movement is independent of and prior to reason's presentation of the object."[11] He takes the later shift in Thomas's semantics—a shift from stressing that the intellect gives the end to the will, to the further minor precision that the intellect "specifies" the will as formal cause while the will acts as efficient cause in willing—to signify a radical shift that asserts the absolute priority and autonomy of the will. Granted that while the *voluntas ut natura* wills with a certain necessity, and the will in choice does not, nonetheless no act of the will is simply "unspecified" by the intellect. Further, that the will may instigate or interrupt cognition does not mean that this instigation or interruption is itself lacking specification by reason. Even the will no longer to think of something after a very firm judgment has been made is (if we speak of voluntary motion) specified by reason (e.g., "this is too taxing a judgment for me to act upon now" or "but this is contrary to other commitments and I refuse to think of it now"). To speak of will as unspecified by intellect is to speak of a non-willing because willing has an object and without some prior intellective specification the will as a rational power cannot be actuated. An act of the will lacking intellective specification is an act of the will that is wholly indeterminate. But what is wholly indeterminate can have no means, since it is impossible to determine means to something that is wholly unknown and unknowable. This is why even the natural willing of the end prior to determination of the means is consequent on knowledge, since elsewise "good" and "end" would have no signification whatsoever. The idea that Thomas would set this aside is cognate with the idea that he would set aside the metaphysical truth that being is not nonbeing:[12] it is simply an impossibility.

As noted, Keenan textually locates Thomas's putatively voluntarist shift regarding intellect and will as lying within the *prima secundae* of the *Summa theologiae*, thus occurring *after* Thomas's formal and extensive treatment of the powers of intellect and will in the *prima pars* as quoted above. Yet, textually speaking, it is also the case that Thomas does not observe any conflict between his earlier and later accounts, nor note any difference in substantive teaching (something which he is given to do when

---

[10] Keenan, *Goodness and Rightness*, 43.
[11] Keenan, *Goodness and Rightness*, 47.
[12] Of course there is no real relation between being and nonbeing, because things that do not exist do not have real relations, and nonbeing is not something that exists. But there is a real *distinction*, because by its real character, being is not nonexistent.

there is a significant rejection of a position, e.g., to take two examples: when in *ST* II-II, q. 8, a. 6, he rejects the summary account of the nature of the Gifts of the Holy Spirit that he provides earlier in I-II, q. 68, . 4; or in his clear shift of conclusions through several works regarding the *potentia generandi* with respect to the Triune God[13]). Thomas's treatment is precisely what one would expect it to be if the shift were a minor semantic shift for pedagogic purposes of clarification, rather than a strategic unsaying of his own extensive arguments to the contrary. Keenan appears not to see that the very sense in which the intellect specifies the will is precisely in presenting the object (which is the end) to the will, without which the will *cannot will*. The datum that the will may, under diverse intellectual specification, defer or terminate a rational consideration, is not to say that it ever operates without the direction of reason. The interpretation propounded by Keenan would render desire, volition, and intention to be objectless nullities wholly independent of reason, something Thomas simply does not hold. Having expressed the primacy of intellect clearly and strategically in that part of the *Summa theologiae* that most formally addresses the relation of intellect and will, it is noteworthy that Thomas himself does not treat his later and marginally different semantic as betokening a strategic shift from this teaching.

Brady's work manifests and explains the primary role of natural reason and its relation to the crucial but subordinate sense in which prudence "appoints" the end in the sense of judging the "proximate end"—that is, the means required to move toward the end (something that manifestly, as Thomas expressly says, presupposes *prior knowledge of the end*). This work serenely articulates the speculative unity undergirding Thomas's teaching as defining both his earlier pedagogically less precise formulation and his later more pedagogically precise semantic. Brady corrects the central deprivation of much contemporary moral theory: the loss of the primacy

---

[13] See John F. Boyle, "St. Thomas and the Analogy of *Potentia Generandi*," *The Thomist* 64 (2000): 581–92, which besides its primary object of understanding Thomas's teaching regarding the nature of the *potentia generandi* in God, and his discerning understanding of the nature of Thomas's analogical judgment, also manifests clearly the manner in which Thomas indicates major shifts of judgment when they formally dispose a question. But Thomas nowhere denies that in formal specification of the will the intellect gives the end to the will, and arguably the contrary view should be more denominated "irrationalist" than "voluntarist." On such an account, the source of every human agency would necessarily be all agent "push" prior to, apart from, and without any original knowledge, understanding, or contemplation. Whatever else may be said about such a teaching, it is not that of Aquinas.

and centrality of natural reason in the moral life. Students of Aquinas, and Catholic moral theologians in particular, will find in Ryan Brady's serious and intricate analysis a true vaccine against the theoretic disorders of voluntarism and nominalism in the moral life, and an instruction in the perennial and universal wisdom of the Common Doctor of the Church.

Steven A. Long

Introduction

THE ENDS OF THE MORAL VIRTUES are essential guideposts for Christians who are striving to attain to what the Second Vatican Council refers to as man's "most high calling" (*altissimam eius vocationem*) in §22 of its Pastoral Constitution on the Church in the Modern World, *Gaudium et Spes*—namely, eternal beatitude. They are so important, in fact, that prudence, though referred to as the "charioteer of the virtues,"[1] has to look to these ends as final causes of the activity it directs. Because the subject of the moral virtues is the appetitive part of the soul (the will or rational appetite being the subject of justice and the sensitive appetites being the subject of temperance and fortitude), appetites that are rectified by virtuous habits incline the prudent person toward the fitting end.[2] Appetites, for Aquinas, are "nothing other" than inclinations

---

[1] See: *ST* suppl., q. 2, a. 4, corp.; *In* II *sent.*, dist. 41, lec. 1, obj. 3; *SCG* III, ch. 35 (the charioteer image is, in fact, used throughout *SCG*). It is specifically the charioteer or driver of the moral virtues: As *De virtutibus*, q. 1, a. 6, corp., says, prudence is both *perfectiva* of the moral virtues and "the cause of all the virtues of the appetitive part, which are called moral [causa omnium virtutum appetitivae partis, quae dicuntur morales]."

[2] Aquinas says justice is in the will, temperance in the concupiscible appetite, and fortitude in the irascible (*ST* I-II, q. 61, a. 2, corp.). These appetites make up "the appetitive part" of the soul. Moral virtue, therefore, "is in the appetitive part; accordingly, it implies a certain inclination for something desirable [Virtus enim moralis est in parte appetitiva. Unde importat quamdam inclinationem in aliquid appetibile]" (*In* II *eth.*, lec. 1, no. 3). To ensure that the object of desire is something truly good, moral virtue must rectify the appetites. As George Reichenberg says, the moral virtues, "seated in different parts of the soul . . . rectify the will and sense appetites" ("The Intellectual Virtues (Ia IIae, Qq. 57–58)," in *The Ethics of Aquinas*, ed. Stephen J. Pope, Moral Traditions Series [Washington, DC: Georgetown University Press, 2002], 131–50, at 140).

of the desiring person, which means that rectified appetites are *rightly* ordered inclinations of morally virtuous people.[3] Since order implies an order to *something*,[4] the appetites must be ordered to something both good and perfective if they are to be rightly ordered—and this comes about thanks to reason.[5]

This book will investigate what the ends of the moral virtues are, their importance in the moral life of the Christian, and what it is that appoints them in view of two texts in which Thomas apparently gives two conflicting opinions.[6] In the course of this investigation, I hope to demonstrate that the appetites are, in fact, able to point to an end that prudence pursues[7] even while prudence retains its contact with higher principles than those indicated by the appetites alone. Although prudence is "not only in the reason"[8] and is moved by the appetite,[9] Cajetan argues it also depends upon the rectitude of the intellectual virtues,[10]

---

[3] *ST* I-II, q. 8, a. 1, corp.: "The appetite is nothing other than the inclination of the one who desiring towards that which he desires." The moral virtues, of course, rectify appetites (see, e.g.: II-II, q. 47, a. 13, ad 3; I-II, q. 58, a. 2, corp.; q. 58, a. 3, corp.).

[4] *ST* I, q. 42, a. 3, corp.: "The word 'order' is always used in reference to some principle."

[5] As *ST* II-II, q. 157, a. 2, corp., says, the very "*ratio* of moral virtue consists in the subordination of the appetite to reason."

[6] *ST* I-II, q. 66, a. 3, and II-II, q. 47, a. 6, in which he respectively says prudence appoints the end to the moral virtues and that the habit of the first principles of the practical intellect does but prudence does not.

[7] In *In* III *sent.*, dist. 33, q. 1, a. 1, qc 2, corp.), Thomas argues *ratio* can only be *recta ratio* (i.e., prudence; see *ST* II-II, q. 47, a. 8, corp.) inasmuch as *ratio* is conformed to upright ends (*rectos fines*). As a consequence, it can be said that prudence must look to the appetites it presupposes (which is indicated by *ST* II-II, q. 57, a. 4, corp.: "Prudence . . . looks to the appetite in such a way that it presupposes its rectitude." Thomas words this in a slightly different way in the commentary on the *Nicomachean Ethics* when he says the appetites must be rightly ordered for the very principles of prudence to be preserved (*In* VI *eth.*, lec. 4, no. 13). *ST* I-II, q. 65, a. 1, ad 3, says, "the appetite moves the reason in some way [appetitus movet quodam modo rationem]," and this seems to especially pertain to the deliberation prudence—or any deliberation about means, whether "prudential" or not.

[8] *In* VI *eth.*, lec. 7, no. 7: "Prudentia non est in ratione solum, sed habet aliquid in appetitu."

[9] That prudence, for Thomas, is moved by the appetite is clear from the fact that the will is an appetite and that the appetitive power moves the "commanding reason" (see *ST* I-II, q. 17, a. 2, ad 1). The third act of prudence, which Thomas refers to as right reason, is to command.

[10] See Cajetan commentary on *ST* I-II, q. 65, a. 1: "Prudence . . . is in the reason as moved by the appetite. . . . Although right reason about doable things [i.e., prudence] depends upon a twofold rectitude regarding ends (namely, that of the apprehensive part and that of the appetitive part), the rectitude of the apprehensive part is, nevertheless, not

among which he includes synderesis.[11] If he is correct, prudence is not solely reduced to "feeling it out" when it comes to discerning the right thing to do in any given situation; instead, one can also look to intellectual data provided by intellectual acts, habits, or virtues such as conscience, synderesis, or faith (all of which, I will argue, can be said to appoint the end in some way).

The appetites or inclinations of the moral virtues are crucial because they enable a person to perceive fitting ends. In his commentary on Aristotle's *Nicomachean Ethics*, Saint Thomas says:

> Two things are necessary in the work of virtue, one of which is that a man have a right intention of the end, which moral virtue brings about inasmuch as it inclines the appetite toward the fitting end. The other is that a man be well disposed in regard to the means: and prudence, which deliberates well about the means and judges and commands in regard to them, brings this about.[12]

From this quote, we might think that the appetites have a kind of priority because they relate to the end whereas prudence relates only to the means. This would seem especially reasonable since Aquinas even says in one place that "virtue principally consists in the inclination of the appetite."[13] If this is so, prudence must be subordinated to the moral virtues inasmuch

---

proper to prudence but to ... the intellectual virtues" (Leonine ed., 6:421 [no. 10]). Cajetan goes on to suggest that Thomas refrains from speaking about prudence's reliance upon the intellectual virtues (at least here) because the rectitude of the appetite is that which is proper to prudence and its starting point. For a discussion of Cajetan's understanding of the relationship of prudence to synderesis and the appetites, see the tremendous work of Dominic Farrell (to whom I am indebted for having provided me with a digital copy of his work), *The Ends of the Moral Virtues and the First Principles of Practical Reason in Thomas Aquinas* (Rome: Gregorian and Biblical Press, 2012), 103–9.

[11] Commenting on *ST* I-II, q. 66, a. 3, Cajetan says: "Synderesis is a virtue, because it is the understanding of principles" and "synderesis is the sufficing virtue in the apprehensive part in respect of the end absolutely" (Leonine ed., 6:433–34 [no. 12]).

[12] *In* VI *eth.*, lec. 10, no. 13: "Duo enim sunt necessaria in opere virtutis, (scilicet) quorum unum est ut homo habeat rectam intentionem de fine; quod quidem facit virtus moralis, inquantum inclinat appetitum in debitum finem. Aliud autem est quod homo bene se habeat circa ea quae sunt ad finem: et hoc facit prudentia quae est bene consiliativa et iudicativa et praeceptiva eorum quae sunt ad finem."

[13] *In* I *eth.*, lec. 16, no. 4: "Virtus consistit principaliter in inclinatione appetitus."

as they ensure the right appetites that prudence looks toward and presupposes in its attempt to order the means.[14]

In the final chapter of the present volume, we will see that Capreolus († 1444) wrestles with the related teaching found in the *prima secundae* of the *Summa*, wherein Thomas says that "reason, inasmuch as it apprehends the end, precedes the appetite for the end; but the appetite for the end precedes the reason reasoning (*ratiocinantem*) for the sake of choosing those things that are for the end, which pertains to prudence."[15] For Capreolus and other early commentators, passages like this suggest there is some kind of reason that *precedes* the appetite for the end. Nevertheless, texts from the Thomistic corpus that indicate that upright appetites regarding fitting ends (which appetites are brought about by moral virtue) precede prudence (which is essentially right reason regarding practical means) have understandably led more recent authors such as Yves Simon to focus on the role of the appetites and inclinations. The latter argues that the judgment of prudence, "as reasoned as it may be, is ultimately determined *not by the intellect* but by the inclination of the will."[16] Regardless of what Simon, who is generally extraordinarily perceptive, meant to definitively assert by saying this, some have taken him to be

---

[14] *ST* II-II, q. 57, a. 4, corp.: "Prudence . . . looks to [*respicit*] the appetite as presupposing its rectitude."

[15] *ST* I-II, q. 58, a. 5, ad 1: "Ad primum ergo dicendum, quod ratio, secundum quod est apprehensiva finis, praecedit appetitum finis: sed appetitus finis praecedit rationem ratiocinantem ad eligendum ea quae sunt ad finem, quod pertinet ad prudentiam: sicut etiam in speculativis intellectus principiorum est principium rationis syllogizantis." See the "Capreolus on the *Scriptum*" section in chapter 3 and John Capreolus, O.P., *Defensiones Theologiae, De Novo Editae Cura Et Studio Paban et Pegues*, vol. 5 (Turin: Cattier; 1904), dist. 36, q. 1 (p. 431).

[16] Yves Simon, *The Definition of Moral Virtue*, ed. by Vukan Kuic (New York: Fordham University Press, 1986), 96–97: "To know what I should do here and now, I must rely on the judgment of practical wisdom [prudence]. And this judgment, reasoned as it may be, is ultimately determined not by the intellect but by the inclination of the will" (emphasis added). In his work, *The Tradition of Natural Law* (ed. Vukan Kuic [New York: Fordham University Press, 1965; repr. 1992]), Simon similarly argues that, *whenever* "specific situations and specific regulations are involved, there is absolutely no possibility of proceeding by logical connection" because the answer to such questions is "not obtained by logical connection with principles"; for him, the connection between "particular determinations" and universal norms "is not logical, it is prudential" (155–56). All of this seems to be at odds with what Thomas says in a text of *De veritate*, q. 3, a. 1, corp., which indicates that, when an agent "determines an end for itself," this comes about through the intellect: "Ipsum agens determinat sibi finem, sicut est in omnibus agentibus per intellectum."

precluding the role of intellectual principles in the process of discerning the mean of virtue. Andrew Yuengert, for instance, comments on this quote by saying, "disagreements about prudence cannot be resolved by appeal to a set of principles," because there are "no endpoints to which prudence is affixed; one is always in the middle of it, discovering and practicing it on the way."[17] As Simon himself argues, Søren Kierkegaard's assertion that "truth lies in subjectivity" is accurate when it comes to judgments of the practical intellect, because the only knowledge that can be had there is "knowledge by inclination, subjectivity."[18] In explaining this latter principle regarding inclination (one he explicitly gets from Jacques Maritain in a section about Aquinas[19]), he suggests that, in regard to basic moral principles such as the one regarding lying, one has to feel or sniff out the truth about their goodness or badness because "strict logic" does not apply.[20]

James Keenan, S.J., also emphasizes the role of the appetites in the moral life, though his approach is significantly more radical than Simon or Maritain[21] inasmuch as he tends to subject all cognition to appetite.[22] Keenan's name in particular will come up frequently in the chapters to follow, due to how well versed and instrumental he is in regard to the

---

[17] Andrew Yuengert, *The Boundaries of Technique: Ordering Positive and Normative Concerns in Economic Research* (New York: Lexington Books, 2004), 99.

[18] Simon, *Definition of Moral Virtue*, 110–11.

[19] Simon, *Definition of Moral Virtue*, 108. He cites Maritain, *Man and the State* (Chicago: University of Chicago Press, 1951), 84ff. Page 91 of that work lists a number of quotes from Aquinas to back up the claim that, in Aquinas's account of practical knowledge, the foundation lies upon "moral regulations known through inclination" because "the very mode or manner in which human reason knows natural law is not rational knowledge, but knowledge through inclination" (91 and 93).

[20] Simon, *Definition of Moral Virtue*, 108–9. He says nearly the identical thing on 155 of *Tradition of Natural Law* (when he argues there is "no logical connection with principles" when it comes to particular "questions about the right and the wrong").

[21] Simon, of course, attributed his doctrine about "knowledge by inclination, subjectivity" to Maritain (see, *Definition of Moral Virtue*, 111), and James Keenan (*Goodness and Rightness in Thomas Aquinas's Summa theologiae* (Washington, DC: Georgetown University Press, 1992], 43) quotes Maritain to argue that Aquinas tended to emphasize the order of specification (which specification comes from the intellect) over the order of exercise (which is due to the will).

[22] In one place, Keenan seems to admit that the movement of the will is in some way "measured by its fittingness to reason," but since he unequivocally maintains the will's activity is prior to intention and takes precedence over all other movements (whether of the lower appetites or the intellect), it is hard to see how the will could be measured by reason in any meaningful way (see, *Goodness and Rightness*, 82, 142, 45).

contemporary debates over the role of the intellect in the moral life, his insightful analysis of certain points, his contemporary influence,[23] and his ability to poignantly express a moral outlook that, in my estimation, not only fails to properly evaluate the mutual complementarity of cognition and volition but also places an inordinate emphasis upon the role of the latter, thus departing from the standard evaluation of the Thomistic commentatorial tradition.[24] In this way, his positions serve as a fitting foil for an account of morality that is more rooted in the guidance of the intellect and which I hope to defend as both accurate in itself and in keeping with the generally consistent teaching of Aquinas.

As Thomas Hibbs demonstrates, Keenan tends to view the doctrine of Saint Thomas in a way that would "mark a decisive break from Aristotle's account of virtue as action in accord with right reason."[25] In Keenan's opinion, Aquinas eventually came to see the "truth" that not only is the will "the mover of all powers, including itself and the intellect," but its self-movement "takes precedence over all other movements."[26] On his account, then, reason as such (not only in regard to the means, and thus the *recta ratio* that is prudence) seems somewhat insignificant because, without the "antecedent willingness" of the will to move both itself and the reason, reason will be unable to "influence the will with its objects."[27]

Authors such as Keenan and Josef Fuchs (whom Keenan considered himself privileged to study under[28]) are referred to by Father Michael

---

[23] Keenan has especially been influential in regard to current debates over *Amoris Laetitia*. See, e.g., Keenan, "Receiving *Amoris Leatitia*," *Theological Studies* 78, no. 1 (2017): 193–212, and Richard A. Spinello, "Debate Continues over *Amoris Laetitia*," *Crisis Magazine*, May 25, 2017, crisismagazine.com/2017/debate-over-amoris-laetitia. Keenan's "Redeeming Conscience" (*Theological Studies* 76, no. 1 [2015]: 129–47) was also influential.

[24] See Daniel Westberg, "Did Aquinas Change His Mind about the Will?," *The Thomist* 58, no. 1 (1994): 41–60, in which Westberg observes that the more modern exegetical approach to Aquinas's writings regarding the relationship between the intellect and the will "is definitely not the standard, 'received' view of traditional scholastic commentators" (51).

[25] Thomas S. Hibbs, "Interpretations of Aquinas's Ethics Since Vatican II," in Pope, *Ethics of Aquinas*, 412–25, at 420.

[26] Keenan, *Goodness and Rightness*, 45. For instance, though in *ST* I, q. 82, a. 4, ad 3, Thomas argues an intellectual apprehension precedes every motion of the will even though a motion of the will does not precede every apprehension, Keenan argues Thomas radically altered his position around the year 1270. In chapter 2, I will endeavor to demonstrate he did not.

[27] Keenan, *Goodness and Rightness*, 50.

[28] See Keenan, *Goodness and Rightness*, xii.

Sherwin as theologians of "moral motivation."[29] They tend, like Simon and Maritain (though to a far more radical extent), to highlight the role of motivation in ethical theory.[30] Fuchs appropriated Karl Rahner's emphasis on human subjectivity and transcendence by putting forward concepts such as "basic freedom" and "fundamental option."[31] He also made a distinction between goodness and rightness[32] while claiming "that the influence of explicit Christian faith on morality is principally motivational"[33] because, in the end, whether or not one is right about some intellectual *datum* is of little soteriological import.[34] Keenan, for his part, wrote a book on the distinction between goodness and rightness in which he emphasized a level of human freedom that is "transcendental" inasmuch as the decisive moral factor is a kind of "moral motivation or moral goodness" that is not limited or boxed in, as it were, by intellectual rightness. Holding to a "sphere of motivation, which is antecedent to intention,"[35] Keenan argues that moral goodness consists solely of exercising oneself according to a natural instinct and that it need not be aligned with rightness.[36] Sherwin, who points out a

---

[29] See Michael S. Sherwin, O.P., *By Knowledge and By Love: Charity and Knowledge in the Moral Theology of Thomas Aquinas* (Washington, DC: Catholic University of America Press, 2005), 6.

[30] See chapter 1 of Sherwin, *By Knowledge and By Love*. For a potential link back to Maritain in both of these thinkers, see the following footnote 31.

[31] Fuchs himself attributes these concepts and terms to Karl Rahner, who Fuchs says borrowed ideas from Maritain (Fuchs, "Good Acts and Good Persons," in *Readings in Moral Theology No. 10: John Paul II and Moral Theology*, ed. Charles E. Curran and Richard A. McCormick, S.J. [New York: Paulist, 1998], 47; cited in Sherwin, *By Knowledge and By Love*, 6).

[32] See Mark Graham, *Josef Fuchs on Natural Law* (Washington, DC: Georgetown University Press, 2002), 70–74, 121–24, 137–39, 247. Keenan, *Goodness and Rightness*, 67, says, "Only one question, the question of moral motivation, concerns the fundamental, formal self-movement of the agent. This moral motivation gives moral significance to all right dispositions or actions, and it alone is the singular description of moral goodness." He cites Bruno Schüller here, who "continually returns to this fundamental level of the person in which the moral self-determination of the person logically precedes all other acting (see Schüller, "The Debate on the Specific Character of Christian Ethics," in *Readings in Moral Theology No. 2: The Distinctiveness of Christian Ethics*, ed. Charles E. Curran and Richard A. McCormick, S.J. [New York: Paulist, 1981], especially 214, and Keenan, *Goodness and Rightness*, 7, 14–15).

[33] Graham, *Joseph Fuchs on Natural Law*, 208.

[34] See Graham, *Joseph Fuchs on Natural Law*, 208, He more benignly says that, for Fuchs, rightness is not "the decisive soteriological issue," but the contexts suggest to me that its importance is practically null.

[35] Keenan, *Goodness and Rightness*, 125.

[36] "By exercising ourselves according to [natural] instinct we are good" (*Goodness and*

number of problems with this way of thinking and provides a masterful critique of it, explains that Keenan's understanding of goodness is ultimately "antecedent to and independent of practical reasoning."[37] As will be argued below, if it were true that "antecedent willingness" necessarily precedes reason[38] in a kind of "precognitive movement toward the good,"[39] there would be no reason to conform to reason's judgment, which would be rather subjective.

The present book is partially written for the sake of arguing that Aquinas was not what Tobias Hoffmann refers to as a "proto-Humean, subordinating reason to desire"[40] (which he would be had he thought the judgment of prudence to be in no way ultimately determined by the intellect and that moral ends are merely "posited by desire" rather than being

---

Rightness, 55). "Goodness describes striving and is antecedent to rightness" (*Goodness and Rightness,* 15). Thomas, for his part, argues that what makes man distinct from animals is precisely that they are able to rise above inclination: "The Philosopher [Aristotle] seems to touch upon a certain property of man in virtue of which he differs from the other animals. For the other animals are made to perform their actions by a kind of natural instinct; man, however, is directed to his actions by the judgment of reason" (*In I analyt. post.*, lec. 1, no. 1 [proem.]).

[37] Sherwin, *By Knowledge and By Love*. See pages 218–225 and elsewhere for Sherwin's analysis and critique of Keenan.

[38] Keenan, *Goodness and Rightness*, 50. Keenan also argues that "in contemporary moral theology, goodness is not consequent to rightness, but antecedent to and distinct from rightness" (7). For him, "insofar as the will first exercises itself, it is not moved by an object" (43).

[39] See Thomas Osborne, "Practical Reasoning," in *The Oxford Handbook of Aquinas*, ed. Brian Davies [New York: Oxford University Press], 276–86, at 279: "There has been some recent controversy over whether for Aquinas the will has some sort of precognitive movement toward the good. But Aquinas frequently reiterates Augustine's statement that 'nothing is loved unless it is known.'" Osborne cites many places including *ST* I-II, q. 60, a. 1, sc, and I-II, q. 3, a. 4, ad 4.

[40] This quote from Hoffmann was made as a characterization of a false understanding of Aristotle's teaching in the sixth book of the *Nicomachean Ethics*. Given that Aquinas essentially reproduces the Stagirite's teaching on this point, the quote works well as a characterization of a similarly false understanding of Aquinas's doctrine. See, Tobias Hoffmann, "Prudence and practical principles" in *Aquinas and the Nicomachean Ethics*, ed. Tobias Hoffmann, Jörn Müller, and Matthias Perkams (Cambridge: Cambridge University Press, 2013), 165. The Humean reference can be explained by John Cahalan's exposition of Hume's relevant thought: "Hume concluded that reason cannot dictate to desires about values since desires determine what things are values and what are not. When reason makes value judgments, it is a "slave" of desire; it only reports what desires do" ("Natural Obligation: How Rationally Known Truth Determines Ethical Good and Evil," *The Thomist* 66 [2002]: 101–32, at 101).

determined by reason). At the same time, the positions of Simon and even the theologians of moral motivation can be defended by appealing to certain texts in Aquinas (though those texts would often have to be taken out of context, in my opinion). They are at least *prima facie* plausible because the ends of the moral virtues, which are habits in the appetites and not the intellect, are the "principles of prudence."[41] Worded differently, "the subject of prudence is the practical intellect as ordered to an upright will."[42] Actually, without being ordered toward the ends of the moral virtues in one's appetites, prudence (which is always about means to an end)[43] would not have an end to strive for that befits a rational creature. In *ST* II-II, q. 47, a. 6, one of the two central articles of this work,[44] we read:

> Moral virtue makes the intention of the end right; prudence, however, the means towards this end [*quae ad hunc*]; therefore, it does not pertain to prudence to appoint [*praestituere*][45] the end to the moral virtues, but only to arrange the means [*disponere de his quae sunt ad finem*].[46]

An upright end, then, will begin to be sought only after one's appetites are pointing toward it. As Thomas says in *ST* I-II, "prudence is right reason about things to be done, and the starting-point of reason is the

---

[41] "The ends of the moral virtues are the beginnings [*principia*] of prudence" (*ST* II-II, q. 181, a. 2); "the moral virtues make man well disposed toward certain ends, from which the reasoning of prudence proceeds" (*ST* I-II, q. 65, a. 2, corp.).

[42] *ST* I-II, q. 56, a. 3, corp.: "Subjectum prudentiae est intellectus practicus in ordine ad voluntatem rectam."

[43] *ST* II-II, q. 47, a. 1, ad 2: "Prudence considers those things by which a person arrives at happiness. But wisdom considers the object itself of happiness"; *SCG* III, ch. 35: "Prudence makes a person well ordered regarding those things which are chosen for the end." Cf.: *ST* I-II, q. 58, a. 5, ad 1; II-II, q. 47, a. 15, corp.; II-II, q. 49, a. 6, corp.

[44] The other is *ST* I-II, q. 66, a. 3, which will be introduced below.

[45] This word has been translated very differently by various authors, and although it seems to me that "set up in advance" might be the best translation, I have decided to render it "appoint" lest the translation of this word (one that will appear frequently) seem too wooden. Roy Deferrari has "to determine or appoint beforehand, prescribe." (Roy J. Deferrari, Inviolata M. Barry, and Ignatius McGuiness, *A Lexicon of Saint Thomas Aquinas Based on the Summa Theologica and Selected Passages of His Other Works* [Baltimore, MD: Catholic University of America Press, 1948], 878). See the section "The Meaning of *Praestituere*," beginning on page 24, for a more complete explanation of this translation.

[46] *ST* II-II, q. 47, a. 6, sc.

end of the thing to be done to which end man is rightly disposed by moral virtue."[47] Among the appetites, the most noble one is the intellectual one known as the will, so as we might expect, it is most of all to it that prudence looks.

As Aquinas says in *De virtutibus*, the end of prudence is determined by the will: "Presupposing the end of the good that comes from the will, prudence searches for the ways by which this good might be perfected and preserved." Prudence is thus the habit of the intellect that "depends upon the will as that from which it accepts its principle; for the end in practical things [*operativis*] is the principle."[48] Moreover, even though prudence is seated in the intellect, it is dependent upon appetite on the level of exercise.[49] One might wonder, therefore, if the intellect is ultimately somewhat feckless in the process of pursuing moral goodness and, ultimately, eternal life.

The fact that prudence needs to look to the appetites (whether rational or sensitive) of the moral virtues to know the end calls to mind Maritain's reference to the "knowledge by connaturality" that results from listening "to the inner melody that the vibrating strings of abiding tendencies make present in the subject."[50] The image of there being a harmonious relationship between upright tendencies and the reason (with the latter being led forward by them in virtue of a kind of *manuductio*) is certainly not only striking but also likely to bring out an aspect of Aquinas's teaching regarding the role of affectivity that is sometimes overlooked.[51] For Thomas, in fact, prudence cannot even exist in an

---

[47] *ST* I-II, q. 65, a. 1, corp. Though I find this translation by the Fathers of the English Dominican Province to be inexact, I decided to go with it instead of my own clunky translation, which would be: "One is not able to have prudence unless he have the moral virtues, since prudence is right reason about doable things, which proceeds, as from principles, from the ends of those things to which one is rightly ordered by the moral virtues [cum prudentia sit recta ratio agibilium, quae sicut ex principiis procedit ex finibus agibilium, ad quos aliquis recte se habet per virtutes morales]."

[48] *De virtutibus*, q. 1, a. 7, corp.: "There is a certain habit of the intellect that depends upon the will as that from which it accepts its own principle; for the end in practical matters is the beginning; and thus it is with prudence."

[49] *ST* I-II, q. 9, a. 1, ad 3: "The will moves the intellect in regard to the exercise of the act."

[50] Maritain, *Man and the State*, 92.

[51] Clifford Kossel expresses well the value of being properly attuned to one's appetites: "Although reasons can be given for them, the final judgments of prudence cannot be demonstrated. This judgment is always about particular actions: this is the right time and place to eat, to preserve my life, or to risk my life for a friend or for the common good. If I have the virtues of temperance and fortitude, my reason will not be led astray

individual without upright tendencies because it looks to the appetites and presupposes their rectitude[52]—which can exist only thanks to the moral virtues. For this reason, Sherwin goes so far as to say there is a sense in which "the moral virtues provide the ends of practical reasoning,"[53] and Thomas himself indicates as much by saying the ends we are ordered to by the moral virtues are "that from which the reasoning of prudence proceeds."[54] Nevertheless, as important as the moral virtues and the rectified appetites necessarily associated with them are, it is not the case that they are themselves the charioteers (*aurigae*) of virtue.

Prudence, which "directs all the moral virtues,"[55] is their *auriga* and cannot, as a consequence, ever be left out of an account of moral virtue; indeed, as he says in *ST*, it is "placed in the definition of the moral virtues" precisely because "the moral virtues depend upon prudence."[56] Or, as he explains it in the *Scriptum* (on Lombard's *Sentences*), it is found in that definition because prudence "perfects the *ratio* of virtue in all the moral virtues" and is the "common rule of all the virtues."[57] Prudence, considered as an intellectual virtue (which it is, strictly speaking[58]) is superior to the moral virtues and makes the moral virtues to *be* virtues

---

by concupiscence or fear (IIa IIae, q. 47, a. 7). I can trust the inclination of virtue" ("Natural Law and Human Law (Ia IIae, Qq. 90–97)," in Pope, *Ethics of Aquinas*, 169–93 at 177).

[52] *ST* I-II, q. 57, a. 4: "Prudence . . . looks to the appetite as presupposing its rectitude."

[53] Sherwin, *By Knowledge and By Love*, 112.

[54] *ST* I-II, q. 65, a. 2, corp.: "Prudentia autem non potest esse sine virtutibus moralibus, inquantum virtutes morales faciunt bene se habere ad quosdam fines, ex quibus procedit ratio prudentiae."

[55] *ST* I-II, q. 58, a. 2, ad 4.

[56] "Prudentia ponitur in definitione virtutum moralium, ut patet in 2. Eth. (cap. 6.) et in 6. (cap. ult.), eo quod virtutes morales dependent a prudentia" (*ST* II-II, q. 23, a. 4, ad 2). Note that prudence is said to be in the definition of moral virtue because Aristotle "defines virtue through its being in keeping with right reason" (*De virtutibus*, q. 5 a. 1, ad 10; see footnotes 76 and 77 below).

[57] *In III sent.*, dist. 27, q. 2, a. 4, qc 2, ad 1: "Prudence . . . perfects the notion of virtue in all the moral virtues; and therefore right reason, which pertains to prudence, is placed in the definition of prudence, as is clear in the second book of the *Ethics* [2. 6.1106b]: 'Virtue is a chosen habit standing in the middle as determined by reason, as a wise man would determine it.' This is not to say that prudence is not a special virtue, but rather that it is the general measure of all the virtues."

[58] Although this is certainly the case, since its subject is the practical intellect, Peter Kwasniewski points out that "it is often grouped with moral virtues because of its inseparable connection to them, both in that it stands in need of them, and in that they stand in need of it. Cf. *ST* I-II, q. 58, a. 2, ad 4, and aa. 3–5; q. 65, aa. 1–2; II-II, q. 47" (Thomas Aquinas, *On Love and Charity: Readings from the "Commentary on the*

because it is rational *per essentiam* whereas the moral virtues are only so *per participationem*.[59] Virtue, of course, is a good quality of the mind[60] that is "determined by reason as a wise man would determine it"[61] (understanding "wise man" as referring to a prudent man).[62] In other words, since it is ordered to the individual's own good,[63] it must be instantiated in an individual prudent person, who ensures his appetites are conformed to reason in virtue of prudence.

Prudence is so vital that Aquinas insists in *ST* I-II, q. 66 (the other text that stands at the center of this book), that prudence "does not only direct the moral virtues in choosing the means [*ea quae sunt ad finem*], but also in appointing [*praestituendo*] the end."[64] Saint Thomas, therefore, said both that prudence does not appoint the end but merely pursues the ends pointed out by the moral virtues (in the text from *ST* II-II, q. 47, we encountered above) *and* that prudence does, in fact, appoint the end. In the latter text, he added that "natural reason, which is called synderesis" is that which "appoints [*praestituit*] the end to the moral virtues," the consequence of which is that it "moves prudence, just as understanding [*intellectus*] moves [the virtue of] knowledge [*scientiam*]."[65]

The most famous commentator of Aquinas, Thomas Cardinal Cajetan (1469–1534), suggested that the two texts appear to be "repugnant" to each other and added that the question of how to resolve the tension that occurs when trying to reconcile them is a "challenging question."[66] Bradley observed that Aquinas gets the notion that prudence is

---

Sentences *of Peter Lombard*," trans. Peter A. Kwasniewski, Thomas Bolin, and Joseph Bolin [Washington, DC: Catholic University of America Press, 2008], 156n260).

[59] See *ST* I-II, q. 66, a. 3, sc. Similarly, he says in II-II, q. 47, a. 5, ad 1, that the definition of moral virtue includes the intellectual virtue of prudence because the moral virtues are virtues inasmuch as they participate in intellectual virtue.

[60] This comes from the definition attributed to Augustine, which is found in *ST* I-II, q. 55, a. 4.

[61] *ST* I-II, q. 59, a. 1, corp.: ". . . determinata ratione, prout sapiens determinabit."

[62] *In I sent.*, dist. 46, q. 1, a. 4, expositio: "Taking 'wise man' for a prudent man, even as found in the definition of virtue that is posited in the second book of the *Ethics* where it is said, 'as a wise man will determine.'"

[63] *ST* II-II, q. 47, a. 11, corp.: "Prudence simply speaking . . . is ordered to one's private good."

[64] *ST* I-II, q. 66, a. 3, ad 3: "Prudentia non solum dirigit virtutes morales in eligendo ea quae sunt ad finem, sed etiam in praestituendo finem."

[65] *ST* II-II, q. 47, a. 6, ad 1 ("Virtutibus moralibus praestituit finem ratio naturalis, quae dicitur synderesis") and ad 2 ("synderesis movet prudentiam, sicut intellectus principiorum scientiam").

[66] Cajetan commentary on *ST* I-II, q. 66, a. 6: "A significant difficulty arises in the treatment of the author: how, namely, can it be true that prudence directs the moral virtues

always solely about means from Aristotle and that he often reiterates that teaching.[67] As a consequence, he suggests the text from *ST* I-II, q. 66, a. 3 (asserting prudence appoints the end) is the "one exception" to the norm, as it would appear to widen the berth of prudence and attribute to it an ability to deliberate about the ends themselves and not only about means. We will revisit this interpretation in chapter three. The question of how to save the appearances, as it were, and reconcile these two passages is so challenging to resolve that we will wait until that chapter to propose a definitive solution. For now, we can simply state the obvious: synderesis, prudence, and the moral virtues are all essential in the endeavor of attaining virtue.

Whether or not prudence can be said to pertain to no more than means (and to be consequently unable to appoint the end to the moral virtues), prudence and the moral virtues certainly presuppose each other. As Ralph McInerny says,

> As has often been pointed out, there is a virtuous circle here. The moral virtues presuppose prudence, prudence presupposes the moral virtues. At the least, this means that they are acquired simultaneously. As to their interaction, the following picture is urged upon us. The moral virtues ensure an appetitive ordination to particular ends constitutive of the ultimate end. Prudence or practical wisdom determines how the moral ideal can be realized here and now; that is, thanks to prudence, we deliberate, judge and command as to the means of realizing the end. It is here that the notion of practical truth makes its appearance. The judgment of prudence as to the means of realizing the end is said to be true, not by conformity with the way things are, but by conformity with the presupposed ordination to the end by moral virtue.[68]

---

even in appointing the end? . . . This seems to be repugnant to what was said in the *secunda secundae*" (Leonine ed., 6:433 [no. 11]).

[67] Denis J. M. Bradley, *Aquinas on the Twofold Human Good: Reason and Human Happiness in Aquinas's Moral Science* (Washington, DC: Catholic University of America Press, 1997), 206–7.

[68] Ralph McInerny, *Ethica Thomistica: The Moral Philosophy of Thomas Aquinas* (Washington, DC: Catholic University of America Press, 1997), 107. The "virtuous circle" teaching has its origin in Aristotle (*Nicomachean Ethics* 6.13.1144b36). John E. Naus also refers to it as a virtuous circle in *The Nature of the Practical Intellect according to Saint Thomas Aquinas* (Rome: Libreria Editrice Dell' Universita Gregoriana, 1959), 157.

Once one enters into the realm of the practical, the role of the appetites takes center stage, and so, if prudence is going to make a true judgment, it needs to be conformed not only to objective reality considered in abstraction from the individual, but to subjective inclinations as well. Virtue is always *quoad nos* in some way. Just as it would likely be foolhardy for a wounded man to rush into battle in the same manner as the ideally disposed soldier, any individual moral act must take individual dispositions into account[69] and, in a sense, be conformed to them. In McInerny's last line, which speaks of practical truth, he likely had *ST* I-II, q. 57, in mind:

> Truth is not the same for the practical, as for the speculative intellect. Because the truth of the speculative intellect depends on conformity between the intellect and the thing. And since the intellect cannot infallibly be in conformity with things in contingent matters, but only in necessary matters, no speculative habit about contingent things is an intellectual virtue, but only such as is about necessary things. On the other hand, the truth of the practical intellect depends on conformity with a right appetite. This conformity has no place in necessary matters, which are not affected by the human will but only in contingent matters which can be effected by us, whether they be matters of interior action or of the products of external work. Hence it is only about contingent matters that an intellectual virtue is assigned to the practical intellect, viz., art, as regards things made, and prudence, as regards things done.[70]

---

[69] *In II eth.*, lec. 7, no. 5, Thomas explains that virtue is concerned with the mean that relates to each individual, as opposed to a kind of objective or exact mean he calls the "mean of the thing" (*medium rei*).

[70] *ST* I-II, q. 57, a. 5, ad 3: "Ad tertium dicendum, quod verum intellectus practici aliter accipitur, quam verum intellectus speculativi, ut dicitur in 6. Ethic. (cap. 2.): nam verum intellectus speculativi accipitur per conformitatem intellectus ad rem; et quia intellectus non potest infallibiliter conformari in rebus contingentibus, sed solum in necessariis, ideo nullus habitus speculativus contingentium est intellectualis virtus, sed solum est circa necessaria: verum autem intellectus practici accipitur per conformitatem ad appetitum rectum; quae quidem conformitas in necessariis locum non habet, quae voluntate humana non fiunt; sed solum in contingentibus, quae possunt a nobis fieri, sive sint agibilia interiora, sive factibilia exteriora; et ideo circa sola contingentia ponitur virtus intellectus practici; circa factibilia quidem ars, circa agibilia vero prudentia" (Dominican Fathers translation).

In contingent matters, then, there really must be some kind of conformity to appetite. If those appetites have been habituated in the right direction through virtuous acts, prudent action will ensue through conformity to them. In any event, prudence is not only dependent upon right appetite, but vice versa. We have seen how McInerny described the virtuous circle. Aquinas also speaks about this *circulatio* that follows upon the fact that "the truth of the practical intellect is determined in comparison to upright appetite, while the rectitude of the appetite is determined by its consonance with true reason." In this passage (which comes from his commentary on the *Nicomachean Ethics*), however, he proposes a way out of that circle by locating its foundation in something more primary. He says:

> A certain circular course [*circulatio*] follows upon these [two kinds] of determinations just mentioned. It should, therefore, be said that appetite pertains both to the end and to those things that are for the end [the means]. The end, though, is determined for man by nature, as was related above in book III. Those things that are for the end, however, are not determined for us by nature. Rather, they are investigated by reason; it is manifest, therefore, that the rectitude of the appetite with respect to the end is the measure of the truth in the practical reason. And consequent upon this, the truth of the practical reason is in accordance with [lit. "toward"] upright appetite. The truth of the practical reason itself, however, is the rule of the rectitude of the appetite about those things that are for the end. And in this way, upright appetite is said to pursue whatever true reason says it should.[71]

---

[71] *In* VI *eth.*, lec. 2, no. 8: "Videtur autem hic esse quoddam dubium. Nam si veritas intellectus practici determinatur in comparatione ad appetitum rectum, appetitus autem rectitudo determinatur per hoc quod consonat rationi verae, ut prius dictum est, sequetur quaedam circulatio in dictis determinationibus. Et ideo dicendum est, quod appetitus est finis et eorum quae sunt ad finem: finis autem determinatus est homini a natura, ut supra in III habitum est. Ea autem quae sunt ad finem, non sunt nobis determinata a natura, sed per rationem investigantur; sic ergo manifestum est quod rectitudo appetitus per respectum ad finem est mensura veritatis in ratione practica. Et secundum hoc determinatur veritas rationis practicae secundum concordiam ad appetitum rectum. Ipsa autem veritas rationis practicae est regula rectitudinis appetitus, circa ea quae sunt ad finem. Et ideo secundum hoc dicitur appetitus rectus qui persequitur quae vera ratio dicit."

There remains a striking *circulatio* in Aquinas's explanation, but this circular course really pertains to means and thus implicitly follows upon intention of the end, which is necessarily preceded by former knowledge because, as Steven Long argues, "every practical ordering presupposes a prior *speculum*, like the bit of matter around which a pearl forms."[72] In other words, knowledge pertaining to some truth that is considered in a speculative mode may or not find its way into the order of means (regarding things like deliberation and consent) or into the fully practical realm of execution of what has been chosen as the appropriate means.

If that which is pondered becomes a matter of pursuit, any action that results is like a pearl that has been formed around a bit of matter; the "matter" need not have developed into a pearl, but once it does, the measure of the pearl's veracity, as it were, is the rectitude of the appetite (again, because the "rectitudo appetitus per respectum ad finem est mensura veritatis in ratione practica").[73] At the same time, prudence arranges the action, presupposing the end that has been determined naturally. The way Cajetan explains this is that prudence "depends upon the rectitude of both ends; namely, the rectitude of the apprehensive part and of the appetitive part," but since the former "is not proper to prudence, but common to itself and the other intellectual virtues," Aquinas sometimes neglects to mention it.[74]

ST I-II, q. 58, a. 4, is one of those texts where he does not neglect to mention the need for rectitude in the apprehensive part as a *sine qua*

---

[72] Steven Long, *The Teleological Grammar of the Moral Act*, 2nd ed. (Naples, FL: Sapientia, 2015), 76.

[73] *In* VI *eth.*, lec. 2, no. 1131: "The rectitude of the appetite in respect to the end is the measure of the truth in the practical reason."

[74] To be clear, the apprehensive part includes the reason. So the point Cajetan is making is that, even though prudence relies upon virtuously ordered appetites, it also relies upon intellectual virtue pertaining to first principles. Cajetan's comments were occasioned by the words of *ST* I-II, q. 65, a. 1, corp., in which Thomas said the right reason about doable things known as prudence "proceeds from the ends of these doable things, as from principles toward those things someone is rightly ordered to by the moral virtues." It is a subtle text, but it seems to be speaking about two sets of principles. Cajetan explains it as follows: "Although right reason about doable things depends upon a twofold rectitude regarding ends (namely, that of the apprehensive part and that of the appetitive part), the rectitude of the apprehensive part is, nevertheless, not proper to prudence but to . . . the intellectual virtues." Cajetan insists upon the need for this twofold rectitude even while observing that Thomas sometimes omits speaking about the requisite rectitude of the apprehensive part due to the fact that the rectitude of the appetite is that which is proper to prudence (Leonine ed., 6:421 [no. 10]).

non for moral virtue (and thus also for prudence, which requires moral virtue[75]). He says moral virtue requires *intellectus* about first principles in addition to prudence:

> Moral virtue can indeed be without some of the intellectual virtues such as wisdom, knowledge, and art; but it cannot be without understanding and prudence. Indeed, without prudence there is not able to be moral virtue because moral virtue is an elective habit; that is, one making a good choice. Now for choice to be good, two things are required:
> first, a fitting [*debitum*] intention of the end (and this comes about through moral virtue which inclines the appetitive power towards the good befitting reason, which is the fitting end);
> second, that a man rightly grasp those things that are for the end. And this is not able to happen without the reason rightly deliberating, judging and commanding, which pertains to prudence and the virtues annexed to it, as was said [*ST* I-II, q. 57, aa. 4–6]. Accordingly, moral virtue cannot exist without prudence—and thus it cannot exist without understanding [*intellectus*] either. For principles that are known naturally are known through the intellect, and it is equally necessary that this be so whether we speak of speculative things or practical [*operativus*] ones. Accordingly, as right reason in speculative things presupposes the understanding of the principles inasmuch as it proceeds from naturally known principles, so also does prudence, which is right reason about doable[76] things [*recta ratio agibilium*].[77]

---

[75] *ST* I, q. 22, a. 1, ad 3: "Prudence presupposes the moral virtues, through which the appetite is related to the good."

[76] *Agibilium* ("doable") is often found in this context (*recta ratio agibilium*). The most frequent translation is "right reason about things to be done." Because that may be taken as if there were a hortatory or jussive sense even though *agibilia* implies merely possibility, I translate it as I have here despite the clunkiness of the phraseology.

[77] *ST* I-II, q. 58, a. 4, corp.: "Virtus moralis potest quidem esse sine quibusdam intellectualibus virtutibus, sicut sine sapientia, scientia, et arte; non autem potest esse sine intellectu, et prudentia. Sine prudentia quidem esse non potest moralis virtus; quia moralis virtus est habitus electivus, idest faciens bonam electionem. Ad hoc autem quod electio sit bona, duo requiruntur: primo, ut sit debita intentio finis: et hoc fit per virtutem moralem, quae vim appetitivam inclinat ad bonum conveniens rationi, quod est finis debitus: secundo, ut homo recte accipiat ea, quae sunt ad finem: et hoc non potest esse, nisi per rationem recte consiliantem, judicantem, et praecipientem; quod pertinet ad prudentiam, et ad virtutes sibi annexas, ut supra dictum est [q. 57, aa. 4–6]; unde

Clearly, prudence and the moral virtues must have a kind of symbiotic relationship according to which each is dependent upon the other. So there is a subjective element requiring that prudence be informed by appetites. At the same time, if those appetites are to be consistently upright, they need to be informed and guided by prudence. Interestingly, though, understanding (*intellectus*) stands at the beginning of the circle and is presupposed to it.

By declaring that the moral virtues need *intellectus* in addition to prudence, Aquinas seems to be saying understanding provides the more remote ends (albeit not exclusively these), which are actually more foundational ones in the realm of morality. As Theo Kobusch notes, "in the realm of moral being, the final end assumes the scientific-theoretical status proper to first principles in speculative philosophy."[78] This is so because, in moral matters, the end is the first thing to be intended even if it is the last thing to be carried out.[79] The *final* end, therefore, must take on particular importance. It is the ultimate principle or *telos* at which one aims. So if there are *principia* provided by *intellectus* that are more remote than the particular ends the moral virtues appetitively point to, the more remote ones must be more foundational. As David Gallagher explains,

> In the order of intention, what is first is the last end, and the higher an end is on the chain of ends, the more priority it has. In the order of execution, by contrast, what is lower is what is first accomplished and only at the end of the activity is the ultimate goal achieved.[80]

Because general precepts pertaining to the natural law seem to have

---

virtus moralis sine prudentia esse non potest. Et per consequens nec sine intellectu: per intellectum enim cognoscuntur principia naturaliter nota, tam in speculativis, quam in operativis: unde sicut recta ratio in speculativis, inquantum procedit ex principiis naturaliter cognitis, praesupponit intellectum principiorum; ita etiam prudentia, quae est recta ratio agibilium."

[78] Kobusch cites *ST* I-II, q. 72, a. 5, which says, "The beginning of the whole order in morals is the ultimate end because its place in practical matters is the same as an indemonstrable principle in speculative ones"; see Kobusch, "Grace (Ia IIae, Qq. 109–114)," in Pope, *Ethics of Aquinas*, 207–20, at 210.

[79] *ST* I-II, q. 1, a. 1, ad 1: "Even though the end is last in execution it is nevertheless first in the intention of the acting person." See also: *ST* I-II, q. 18, a. 7, ad 2; q. 20, a. 1, ad 2; q. 25, a. 2; q. 84, a. 2; and Kobusch, "Grace," 208.

[80] David M. Gallagher, "The Will and Its Acts (Ia IIae, Qq. 6–17)," in Pope, *The Ethics of Aquinas*, 69–89, at 80.

greater priority as foundational ends, Father Romanus Cessario describes the activity of prudence as *enacting* the legislation previously appointed to it by the natural law,[81] which is intimately related to synderesis or *intellectus*. For Thomas, "there is a certain natural habit of the first principles of doable things, which are the natural principles of the natural law, which habit pertains to synderesis."[82] Synderesis, he says, names the habit of the principles of the natural law, whereas the natural law itself names the "universal principles of law."[83]

Among the habits required for virtue, we have thus far encountered moral virtue (present in the appetites), prudence (strictly an intellectual virtue), and understanding. The task in the pages ahead is to delineate more clearly that which is distinctive to each of them and the way they exercise causality in appointing ends. Before moving into chapter 1, in which we will consider the broader context of this question by looking to the significance of the end in general, what the pertinent ends are, and what they consist of, further explanation of the terms *intellectus* and "synderesis" are in order, in addition to an explanation of what it means to appoint (*praestituere*) an end. These will be considered in turn.

The Meaning of *Intellectus* and Synderesis

Intellectus (understanding) is as ubiquitous in the Thomistic corpus as it is equivocal—as evinced by the fact that Roy DeFerrari's *Lexicon of Saint Thomas* proffers ten definitions of the word[84] and F. Petri De Bergomo's index of Saint Thomas's works dedicates twenty-four columns spanning thirteen finely printed pages to explain its different uses.[85] Nevertheless, in the realm of moral matters, it seems to come down to two basic meanings explained by Aquinas in *ST* II-II, q. 49, a. 2:

---

[81] Romanus Cessario, *Introduction to Moral Theology*, rev. ed. (Washington, DC: Catholic University of America Press, 2013), 130.

[82] *De veritate*, q. 16, a. 1: "Est quidam habitus naturalis primorum principiorum operabilium, quae sunt naturalia principia iuris naturalis; qui quidem habitus ad synderesim pertinet."

[83] *In* II *sent*., dist. 24, q. 2, a. 4, corp.: "It is clear how synderesis, natural law, and conscience differ. Natural law names the universal principles of law; synderesis names the habit of those principles (or the power with the habit); conscience names a certain application of the natural law to something that ought to be done by way of a conclusion."

[84] See Deferrari, Barry, and McGuiness, *Lexicon of Saint Thomas*, 576.

[85] See F. Petri De Bergomo, *In Opera Sancti Thomae Aquinatis Index Seu Tabula Aurea Eximii Doctoris F. Petri De Bergomo* (New York: Editiones Paulinae, n.d.), 512–25.

> The reasoning of prudence proceeds from a twofold understanding, *one of which is cognizant of universals*, which pertains to the understanding which is considered [*ponitur*] an intellectual virtue by means of which not only universal speculative principles are made known to us but also practical ones such as, "one should do evil to no one." ... *The other is the understanding which*, as is said in the sixth book of the Ethics, *is cognizant of an extreme*; that is, of some first singular or contingent principle of a practical proposition—namely, the minor, which is necessarily singular in the syllogism of prudence, as was said [in q. 47 aa. 3 and 6]. Also, this singular principle is some singular end, as was said in that same place. Accordingly, the understanding which is considered a part of prudence is a certain right estimation of some particular end.[86]

We see here that prudence proceeds from both of these kinds of understanding (namely, the one pertaining to final ends / universal principles and the other pertaining to a singular or proximate end). This latter is "a quasi-integral part" of prudence[87] which the same article clarifies to be "a right evaluation [*aestimatio*] of a particular end" that is also known as "the interior sense, by which we make a judgment about a particular."[88]

---

[86] *ST* II-II, q. 49, a. 2, ad 1: "Ratio prudentiae ex duplici intellectu procedat. Quorum unus qui est cognoscitivus universalium; quod pertinet ad intellectum, qui ponitur virtus intellectualis, qua naturaliter nobis cognita sunt non solum universalia principia speculativa, sed etiam practica; sicut: Nulli esse malefaciendum... alius autem intellectus est, qui, ut dicitur in VI Ethic. [ch. 11], est cognoscitivus extremi, idest alicujus primi singularis, seu principii contingentis operabilis propositionis, scilicet minoris, quam oportet esse singularem in syllogismo prudentiae, ut dictum est [q. 47, aa. 3, 6]: hoc autem principium singulare est aliquis singularis finis, ut dicitur ibidem; unde intellectus, qui ponitur pars prudentiae, est quaedam recta aestimatio de aliquo particulari fine" (emphasis added). As explained in *In* VI *eth.*, lec. 7, no. 21, prudence perfects the particular reason for rightly estimating about singular practical actions ("pertinet prudentia, per quam perficitur ratio particularis ad recte aestimandum de singularibus intentionibus operabilium") and adds that it is called a natural estimative power in animals.

[87] That it is a quasi-integral part is evident by looking to the title for question 49: "on the particular, quasi-integral parts of prudence."

[88] *ST* II-II, q. 49, a. 2, ad 3. As Aquinas explains elsewhere (*In* VI *eth.*, lec. 9, no. 15), "Because singulars are properly known through the senses, it is necessary for humans to have not only an exterior sense of these singulars that we said are the principles and the extremes, but also an interior sense of them that he [Aristotle] called 'prudence'—namely, the cogitative or estimative power that is known as the particular reason. Accordingly, this 'sense' is called the intellect that is about singulars. And the

If prudence had only the second kind of understanding to go on (i.e., the quasi-integral part of prudence), the standpoint of thinkers such as Simon and Keenan that, in practical actions, one can do nothing else than feel out the end would be unassailable, but the first kind of understanding should not be overlooked.

The terminology can be somewhat confusing because we now have two kinds of "understanding" that are radically different, with the first kind being identified sometimes with "natural reason" and other times with synderesis. A careful study, however, bears out the fact that it is only the second kind of understanding that, worded differently, performs the role of discriminating or judging well about singulars and contingent practical ends.[89] Interestingly, its ends "are principles in the manner of a final cause [*ad modum causae finalis*]."[90] Though its principles act as final causes, they seem to be subordinated to higher causes. Despite the fact that Aquinas clearly says the understanding pertaining to the universal principles (i.e., synderesis) is the one that provides the major premise in

---

Philosopher calls this the passive intellect (which is corruptible) in the third book of *De anima*." Lectio 1 for book 6 adds that it pertains to contingent things as opposed to *universalia speculabilia*. The estimative power is one of the five interior senses spoken of in *ST* I, q. 78, a. 4, corp. It pertains, he says, to the apprehension of intentions that have not been received through the senses and is properly called the cogitative power in man, since it discovers intentions by some kind of comparison (*collatio*). *SCG* II, ch. 60, explains: "The intellect which Aristotle calls passive . . . is the cogitative power itself that is proper to man and in place of which other animals have a certain natural estimative power. It pertains to this cogitative power to distinguish individual intentions and to compare them to each other. Just as the intellect which is separate and unmixed compares and distinguishes universal intentions." *De veritate*, q. 10, a. 5, corp., further explains that the cogitative power can be called the particular reason and that it "has a determined organ in the body, namely in the middle of the head." See also: *ST* I, q. 79, a. 2, ad 2; q. 79, a. 4, corp.

[89] *In* VI *eth.*, lec. 9, no. 19: "The intellect that discriminates well about singulars in practical affairs is not only a kind of principle (as in speculative things), but also a kind of end. For in speculative things, demonstrations proceed from principles belonging to the intellect; however, the principles are not demonstrated [Thomas is speaking here about indemonstrable first principles]. But in practical affairs, demonstrations both proceed from singulars and are given about them." As we will discuss below, practical affairs begin with a particular as providing the end, and yet, by proceeding from the understanding of universal principles, one can demonstrate that these ends are able to be ordered to universally good ends.

[90] *In* VI *eth.*, lec. 9, no. 14: "It is made clear why an extreme of this sort is called 'understanding' through the fact that 'understanding' pertains to principles. The principles which we say understanding is concerned, are principles for the sake of which; that is, they are principles in the manner of a final cause [*ad modum causae finalis*]."

practical syllogisms, whereas the other understanding provides the minor term,[91] the former is often overlooked. For this reason, I nearly entitled this book *On the Loss of Understanding*, because it seems that the loss of objectivity has largely resulted from failing to recognize the indispensably preceptive role of the principles found in the first kind of understanding. Without them, we will neither have a complete picture of the moral life nor be able, on a personal level, to ever know that what Maritain would refer to as our "knowledge by inclination" is actually only a true species of knowledge when it is conformed not only to appetite but also to the ends appointed to it by the natural habit of higher principles. For Thomas, regardless of the kinds of ends we are referring to, they must be cognized rationally because "the truth of the practical intellect is the good, which is the end of an operation" and this kind of good does not "move the appetite except inasmuch as it is apprehended."[92]

Sherwin helps us further grasp the meaning of the understanding (*intellectus*) that is "cognizant of universals" in *ST* II-II, q. 49:

> He here refers to this natural habit as *intellectus*. Elsewhere in his mature treatment of prudence he describes it as *ratio naturalis* or *synderesis*. Yet, no matter what term he employs, his meaning is clear. On the cognitive level, the foundation of the acquired human virtues is a natural virtue of the mind that contains the primary principles of practical reasoning.[93]

The natural reason or synderesis is, then, a natural virtue. In the *Scriptum*, Thomas explains "there is no acquired or infused habit about ends that

---

[91] See *ST* II-II, q. 49, a. 2, ad 1 (see note 86 above). See also *In* IV *sent.*, dist. 50, q. 1, a. 3, ad sc 3 says: "The practical intellect, as is said in the third book of *De anima*, needs the particular reason, by which means the opinion that is universal (which is in the intellect) is applied to a particular, as when a syllogism arises whose major term is a universal opinion of the practical intellect, whose minor is a singular judgment of the particular reason (which is otherwise called the cogitative [power]), and whose conclusion consists in the choice of an action." An example of a practical syllogism is given in *In* II *sent.*, dist. 24, q. 2, a. 4, corp.: "Synderesis proposes this: 'every evil ought to be avoided." The higher reason assumes this principle: 'adultery is evil because it is prohibited by the law of God' (or the lower reason assumes it is evil because it is unjust or unfitting). The conclusion, though, which is that adultery ought to be avoided, pertains to conscience—and indifferently as to whether [this principle applies] to the present or the past or the future."

[92] *De virtutibus*, q. 1, a. 6, ad 5: "Verum intellectus practici est bonum, quod et finis operationis: bonum enim non movet appetitum, nisi in quantum est apprehensum."

[93] Sherwin, *By Knowledge and By Love*, 113.

are innate principles of demonstration that are connatural to man in the practical reason." For this reason, synderesis is a natural habit.[94]

With reason, then, it is sometimes called "reason as nature" (*ratio ut natura*), "that is, inasmuch as it [reason] knows something naturally" without dialectical reasoning.[95] All of these terms are identical and refer to something that is not the subject of many questions or articles in Aquinas's corpus. There is, in fact, only one complete question dedicated to synderesis (*De veritate*, q. 16, a. 1) and a few articles (especially, *ST* I, q. 79, a. 12). It is, nevertheless, very prominent in some articles that are not exclusively dedicated to it, such as the one wherein Aquinas denies that prudence appoints the end to the moral virtues, *ST* II-II, q. 47, a. 6. In the first reply of that article, he says, "natural reason, which is called synderesis, appoints the end to the moral virtues [*virtutibus moralibus praestituit finem ratio naturalis, quae dicitur synderesis*]." The reason it is inseparably united to a consideration of practical ends is that it is so intimately connected with the natural law that Aquinas considers it to be the "law of our understanding" (*lex intellectus nostri*)[96] or, more precisely, the habit of the principles of law.[97] We proceed from the principles it contains to deliberation and choice because its principles are the beginning of choice. In explaining how this is, Aquinas draws a link between synderesis and prudence that will provide the basis for our further considerations. He says in *De veritate*:

---

[94] *In* IV *sent.*, dist. 33, q. 2, a. 4, qc 4, corp.: "Just as there are innate principles of demonstrations in the speculative intellect, so there are innate connatural ends of man in the practical reason; accordingly, there is no acquired or infused habit pertaining to it, but rather a natural habit—as synderesis is."

[95] See *De veritate*, q. 16, a. 1, corp.

[96] Although John Damascene refers to this law as conscience (see, for instance, I. q. 79, a. 13, corp.), Aquinas takes it as a reference to synderesis properly speaking. Conscience is a particular determination of the principles contained in synderesis and is an act, whereas synderesis is the habit of these principles of natural law. See: *ST* I-II, q. 94, a. 1, obj. 1 and ad 1; *De veritate*, q. 17, a. 1, sc 1 and ad sc 1; and *Quolibet* III, q. 12, a. 1, ad 1: "Particular principles have conclusive power [*virtutem concludendi*] in virtue of first universal principles. Therefore, the conclusion is principally attributed to the first principles as the effect of the first cause. And for the same reason, since the power [*virtus*] of conscience principally depends upon the principles of the natural law as from first and per se known principles, conscience is principally called the natural law or the natural judging power [*naturale iudicatorium*]." As Aquinas explains in *In* II *sent.*, dist. 24, q. 2, a. 4, ad 5, the act of conscience is especially taken from the *lex intellectus nostri*: "Conscience, when taken as a habit, is able to be called the natural law because the act of conscience is especially elicited from that habit."

[97] See *In* II *sent.*, dist. 24, q. 2, a. 4, obj. 5 and ad 5.

> The eternal law ought to be considered in God in a similar way to how the naturally known principles of activity that pertain to prudence or foresight (and from which we proceed in deliberating and choosing) are considered in us. In this way, the law of our understanding is related to prudence as an indemonstrable principle is to a demonstration, . . . just as every effect is attributed to indemonstrable principles.[98]

In other words, prudence, which "applies universal principles to particular conclusions of practical matters [*operabilium*],"[99] begins with indemonstrable principles when it syllogizes to practical conclusions. Those principles are supplied by synderesis.

Neither the person endowed with understanding (or its "practical" counterpart, synderesis) nor the prudent person is wholly dependent upon the appetites. Sometimes Saint Thomas gives this impression in regard to prudence, but since it actually presupposes the principles of the natural law, it too is able to apply them to particular contingent situations (with the help of the will[100]) in such a way that the word "appoint" (*praestituere*) can be predicated of this activity. Before turning to the first chapter as a propaedeutic to our endeavor, we should have greater familiarity with the word that stands at the center of our consideration, so we will conclude this introduction with explaining its meaning.

The Meaning of *Praestituere*

The task laid out for us in the coming pages is to determine the best way of explaining why Aquinas says prudence appoints (*praestituit*) the end/s to the moral virtues in some places and while he says elsewhere that prudence

---

[98] *De veritate*, q. 5, a. 1, ad 6: "Lex enim aeterna est consideranda in Deo, sicut accipiuntur in nobis principia operabilium naturaliter nota, ex quibus procedimus in consiliando et eligendo: quod est prudentiae, sive providentiae; unde hoc modo se habet lex intellectus nostri ad prudentiam sicut principium indemonstrabile ad demonstrationem . . . sicut et omnis effectus demonstrationis principiis indemonstrabilibus attribuitur."

[99] *ST* II-II, q. 47, a. 6, corp.

[100] *ST* II-II, q. 47, a. 1, ad 3: "The commendation of prudence does not consist only in its consideration but in the application to a work, which is the end of the practical reason. And therefore if there happens to be a defect in this, it is most of all contrary to prudence, because just as the end is most potent in any given thing, so also the defect that pertains to the end is the worst. Therefore, in the same place, the Philosopher adds that prudence is not only *with reason* as skill is because it has, as was said there, the application to a work that comes about through the will."

does *not* appoint them because it is the role of synderesis to do so. Given our ultimate calling to ends that transcend the order to the proportionate natural good, we will want to do so in reference to the ultimate and final good of the beatific vision as well. In either case, the exercise will be somewhat futile if we omit the foundational consideration of the meaning of the central term, *praestituere*. In making an effort to render this word faithfully by providing an English equivalent, William Barnstone's words come to mind: "The Italian maxim *traduttore, traditore* (translator, traitor) is in the end correct. . . . When a translation passes as original, it is a profound betrayal."[101] Any translation I provide will necessarily include some element of exegesis. At the least, I can provide some *apologia* for the way I have decided to render it (as "to appoint").

Praestituere comes up in the corpus usually in the context of some kind of end which is placed in front of the appetites either by God or by the creature and always presupposes understanding. God, of course, is understanding itself ("Deus est intellectus"[102]) and is, therefore, the one who ultimately appoints the end to all creatures. Since, moreover, "God and nature do nothing in vain, as the Philosopher says in the first book of *De coelo*,"[103] ends that have been placed in front of the creature by God[104] as ends are not able to be changed; one cannot even deliberate about them,

---

[101] Willis Barnstone, *The Poetics of Translation: History, Theory, Practice* (New Haven, CT: Yale University Press, 1993), 260, as cited by Robert G. Bratcher's review in *Critical Review of Books in Religion 1994* (Atlanta, GA: Society of Biblical Literature Press, 1994), 79.

[102] *ST* III, q. 6, a. 2, corp.

[103] *ST* III, q. 9, a. 4, corp.: "Deus, et natura nihil frustra faciunt, ut Philos. dicit in 1. de Coelo." (see *De caelo* 1.4.271a34).

[104] *SCG* I, ch. 44: "Natural things, though, tend to determined ends because natural purposes [*utilitates*] are not pursued by chance because they would not then be realized always or for the most part, but rarely, which is what happens in the case of chance. Since, then, they do not appoint [*praestituant*] the end to themselves because they do not know the *ratio* of the end, it is necessary that the end be appointed to them by another, who is the creator [*institutor*] of nature. This is the one who gives being [*esse*] to all things and is the *per se* necessary being we call God, as is clear from what was said above. He would not, though, be able to appoint the end to nature unless he understands. God, therefore, is understanding." [Naturalia autem tendunt in fines determinatos: non enim a casu naturales utilitates consequuntur: sic enim non essent semper aut in pluribus, sed raro; horum enim est casus. Cum ergo ipsa non praestituant sibi finem, quia rationem finis non cognoscunt; oportet quod eis praestituatur finis ab alio, qui sit naturae institutor. Hic autem est qui praebet omnibus esse, et est per seipsum necesse-esse, quem Deum dicimus, ut ex supra dictis patet. Non autem posset naturae finem praestituere nisi intelligeret. Deus igitur est intelligens.]

they are simply what we are ordered to. As Terrence Irwin says, mirroring Aquinas,[105] "the right ends of human life are 'fixed' or 'definite,' whereas the means to these ends are not fixed, and hence are subject to the deliberative virtue of prudence."[106]

Besides implying an intelligent being making the *praestituens* possible, then, this word also implies antecedence (hence, the *prae*). Though I will always translate the word as "appoint," some others have translated it as "set in advance." Lewis and Short render it "to determine or appoint beforehand, to prescribe," though they render the phrase *nulla praestituta die* as "without any fixed term," thus implying "fixed" as a translation as well.[107] Deferrari's Thomistic lexicon similarly has "to determine or appoint beforehand, prescribe."[108]

By rendering it "appoint," I am attempting to make provision for the necessary conclusion that, if Aquinas is able to be reconciled with himself, it must have a slightly different meaning when referring to prudence as opposed to the way it is used when referring to understanding. Essentially everyone who has tried to explain this apparent contradiction has said something similar to this, so I have chosen to consistently use a rather generic term to cover the way it is used in every situation. In so doing, I have chosen to follow the lead of Father Dominic Farrell, who consistently translates it as "to fix" in his book on the ends of the moral virtues.[109] An alternative that was quite tempting was to follow Cessario's lead and render it as "to appoint beforehand" in regard to synderesis and as "to enact" in regard to prudence.[110] Though I agree wholeheartedly with that rendering of the word in those respective circumstances,[111]

---

[105] See *ST* I-II, q. 47, a. 15, corp.

[106] Terrence Irwin, *The Development of Ethics*, vol. 1 (New York: Oxford University Press, 2011), 575.

[107] Charlton T. Lewis and Charles Short, *Harpers' Latin Dictionary* (Oxford: Clarendon, 1891), 1430.

[108] Deferrari, Barry, and McGuiness, *Lexicon of Saint Thomas Aquinas*, 878.

[109] See Farrell's rationale for doing so in *Ends of the Moral Virtues*, 59, "on the understanding that this end-setting is anterior to something else." I would not go this far, because it seems to me that prudence, in the end, really more appoints or "sets" in the sense of applying or enacting that which is prescribed in either natural inclinations or the natural law, as I hope to show.

[110] See Cessario, *Introduction to Moral Theology*, 130.

[111] There is, to be sure, a downside of the translation "enact" in regard to prudence inasmuch as it arguably implies too little about the way that prudence enjoys the superior light of the fixed principle when it makes the "fixing" here and now operative. Nevertheless, this drawback is, in my opinion, offset by the clarity the translation provides by distinguishing between the kinds of appointing that takes place.

I intend to show the wisdom behind Cessario's *modus interpretandi* before following his lead. This seems necessary because, if I were to do so from the beginning, I would be presupposing the conclusion I am trying to prove. In the context of a work an integral component of which precisely pertains to unraveling the implications involved in rendering the word one way or another, such a *modus operandi* would be *inconveniens*, to say the least.

CHAPTER 1

The Importance of the End

Given Saint Thomas's teleological worldview, the word "end" comes up very frequently in his writings. Before we specifically investigate the way the end is appointed by synderesis or prudence (or any other quality[1] such as grace or faith), an understanding of the meaning and role of the end in general is a necessary foundation. The genus of end could be divided variously, such as into created and uncreated, proximate/intermediate and remote/final, or natural and supernatural. One of the most fascinating divisions is into the "end by which" (*finis quo*) and the "end for the sake of which" (*finis gratia cuius*), which comes from Aristotle,[2] is repeated in some form by Aquinas,[3] and is adroitly applied as follows by William Wheatley, whose words were mistaken as being from Aquinas for a time:

> The end is twofold: namely, the end *by which* and the end *for the sake of which* all things come about [*fiunt*]. The latter is one; namely, God or beatitude; and this end is desired by all under one aspect [*ratione*] inasmuch as it is the good satisfying man's desire

---

[1] The difficulty in finding the common genus of these four qualities is that synderesis is a habit but not a virtue in the strict sense. Grace is described as a habit in the soul in *ST* I-II, q. 110, a. 2, corp., and in I-II, q. 109, a. 1.

[2] The *hou heneka hois* and *hou heneka hō* (*De anime* 2.4.415b20–21). Roy Deferrari quoted this passage in his entry on *finis* (with Inviolata M. Barr and Ignatius McGuiness, *A Lexicon of Saint Thomas Aquinas Based on the Summa Theologica and Selected Passages of His Other Works* [Baltimore, MD: Catholic University of America Press, 1948], 425).

[3] In *ST* I, q. 26, a. 3, ad 2, Aquinas says: "The end is twofold—namely, the end for which and the end by which as the Philosopher says (*Magna moralia* 1.3)—that is to say, the thing itself and the use of the thing. Thus, for a greedy person, the end is money and the acquisition of money. God, therefore, is certainly the last end of a rational creature, as the thing itself, while beatitude is the use—or rather enjoyment—of the thing."

[*appetitum*]. But the end *by which* is an action whereby men strive to attain the end *for the sake of which*—and such an end is not one just as all do not share the same action.[4]

This text draws attention to the fact that, whatever we say about the end in general or the end of the moral virtues in particular (and, indeed, the way they are appointed), "God or beatitude" must be included in our account.

Thomas suggests the proximate ends of the moral virtues are infinite in number and yet have one common end of happiness.[5] They are all ordered to the good, and since happiness is nothing else than the perfect good, they are all ordered to it.[6] What unites these virtues in their pursuit of the perfect good is reason because:

> The proper end of any given moral virtue precisely consists in its conformity to right reason, for temperance exerts itself lest a man be diverted from reason due to carnal desires; fortitude lest he be diverted from the right judgment of reason out of fear or presumption: and this end is appointed [*praestitutus*] to man according to the natural reason since reason dictates to each one that he should act according to reason.[7]

---

[4] Guillelmus Wheatley, *In de consolatione philosophiae* 3.3: "Duplex est finis: scilicet finis quo, et finis gratia cujus omnia fiunt. Ille enim est unus sicut Deus vel beatitudo; et iste finis appetitur ab omnibus sub una ratione, inquantum est bonum satians appetitum hominis. Finis autem quo, est operatio qua homines nituntur adipisci finem gratia cujus: et talis finis non est unus sicut non est una operatio omnium" (from corpusthomisticum.org, as this work was thought to be written by Aquinas for a time).

[5] See *ST* I-II, q. 60, a. 1, obj. 3 and ad 3: "Things pertaining to morals receive their species from the end, as was said above (I-II, q. 1, a. 3). But the common end of every moral virtue is one—namely, happiness. Now the proper and proximate ends are infinite, while the moral virtues are not infinite. It seems, therefore, that there is but one.... To the third it should be said that things pertaining to morals do not receive their species from the last end, but from proximate ends that, even if they are infinite in number, are nevertheless not infinite in species."

[6] See: *ST* I-II, q. 5, a. 8, ad 3 ("the perfect good, which is happiness") ; I-II, q. 5, a. 8, corp. ("Every man desires happiness. Now, the common notion of happiness is that it is the perfect good"); I-II, q. 10, a. 2, corp.: "Because a defect of any kind of good has the notion of the good, only that good that is perfect, and which is lacking in nothing, is the kind of good that the will is not able not to will—and this is happiness"; I-II, q. 13, a. 6, corp.: "Reason is unable to apprehend the perfect good, which is happiness, under some aspect of evil. Therefore, man wills happiness necessarily."

[7] *ST* II-II, q. 47, a. 7, corp.: "Respondeo dicendum, quod hoc ipsum quod est conformari rationi rectae, est finis proprius cujuslibet virtutis moralis: temperantia enim hoc

Although this text refers only to the moral virtues that are in the sensitive appetites, something similar can be said about the virtues in the will, because the will, too, as R. P. F. Dominici Báñez says, "is determined by its nature to the good of reason."[8] Simply put then, the natural reason directs the moral virtues and unites them in the pursuit of the perfect good of happiness. Corresponding to this, Aquinas says in a passage slightly different from the one we just saw that the first thing required for the perfection of moral virtue is the appointing of the end (*praestitutio finis*). He adds:

> The proximate end of human life is the *bonum rationi in communi*. For this reason, Dionysius says that man's evil is to be contrary to reason; it is intended in all the moral virtues, therefore, that passions and actions be reduced to the rectitude of reason. Now the rectitude of reason is natural so in this way, the appointing of the end pertains to the natural reason.[9]

We can conclude from this, as Arnaldo Milhet has, that "synderesis dictates the good of reason in common,"[10] because, again, the natural reason and synderesis are synonymous. Nevertheless, the natural reason is not

---

intendit, ne propter concupiscentias homo divertat a ratione: et similiter fortitudo, ne a recto judicio rationis divertat propter timorem, vel audaciam: et hic finis praestitutus est homini secundum naturalem rationem: naturalis enim ratio dictat unicuique, ut secundum rationem operetur." II-II, q. 141, a. 2, corp., gives a similar explanation of how temperance and fortitude pursue the good of reason: "Nam temperantia retrahit ab his quae contra rationem appetitum alliciunt, fortitudo autem impellit ad ea sustinenda vel aggredienda."

[8] R. P. F. Dominici Báñez, O.P., *Commentarii Fr. Dominici Báñez Super Secundam Secundae S. Thomae* (Venice: Minimam Societatem, 1595), q. 27 (*De iustitia*), a. 5: "Sic etiam voluntas est determinata ex natura sua ad bonum rationis in communi" (p. 25).

[9] *In III sent.*, dist. 33, q. 2, a. 3, corp.: "Respondeo dicendum, quod ad perfectionem virtutis. moralis tria sunt necessaria. Primum est praestitutio finis; secundum autem est inclinatio ad finem praestitutum; tertium est electio eorum quae sunt ad finem. Finis autem proximus humanae vitae est bonum rationis in communi; unde dicit Dionysius, quod malum hominis est contra rationem esse: et ideo est intentum in omnibus virtutibus moralibus, ut passiones et operationes ad rectitudinem rationis reducantur. Rectitudo autem rationis naturalis est; unde hoc modo praestitutio finis ad naturalem rationem pertinet."

[10] Arnaldo Milhet, *Summa Philosophiae Angelicae, Pars IV: Ethica Seu Philosophia Moralis* (Toulouse: Bernardus Dupuy, 1664), 616: "Synderesis dictates the good of reason in common. . . . The inclination of the will follows the discourse of the practical intellect proceeding in this way from the principles of synderesis. The good of reason ought to be followed both in actions and in passions, the matter of temperance, chastity, etc."

the *supreme* rule of action. Although Aquinas says synderesis is more *like* the first rule of human actions than is conscience (which he calls a ruled rule),[11] the first rule of human actions in itself is nothing other than the eternal law in which the natural law and its principles held by the habit of synderesis[12] participate. As Thomas words it, "it is from the eternal law, which is the divine reason, that the human reason is the rule of the human will, from which its goodness is measured."[13] As a consequence, "the moral virtues attain to reason as the proximate rule, but to God as the first rule."[14]

Since God or the eternal law (which are identical *in re*[15]) is more

---

[11] *De veritate*, q. 17, a. 2, ad 7: "Synderesis is more properly the first rule of human actions than conscience is. Now, conscience is, as it were, a ruled rule; accordingly, we should marvel if it is able to fall into error." In *ST*, Thomas clarifies that the natural reason/synderesis is not the measure of nature but only of thing that man ought (or ought not) to do: "Human reason is not, of itself, the rule of things, but the principles naturally implanted in it are certain general rules and measures of all of those things that ought to be done by man. Natural reason is the rule and measure of those things, although it is not the measure of things that are from nature" (I-II, q. 91, a. 3, ad 2).

[12] *In II sent.*, dist. 24, q. 2, a. 4, corp.: "It is clear how synderesis, natural law, and conscience differ, because the natural law names the universal principles of law itself, whereas synderesis names the habit pertaining to those principles (or the power with the habit) and conscience names a certain application of natural law to something that ought to be done by way of a certain conclusion."

[13] *ST* I-II, q. 19, a. 4, corp.: "Quod autem ratio humana sit regula voluntatis humanae, ex qua ejus bonitas mensuretur, habet ex lege aeterna, quae est ratio divina."

[14] *De virtutibus*, q. 5, a. 1, ad 10. He continues here: "Now, a thing is specified according to proper and proximate principles, not according to first principles." The objection, which was not rejected on this point, was: "The definition of moral virtue is taken inasmuch as it is concordant with reason, as is clear by the words of the Philosopher, who defines virtue through its being in keeping with right reason in *Ethics* II. But right reason is the rule that is ruled by the first rule that is God, from which rule it has the power of ruling. Therefore the moral virtues especially have the notion of virtue from the fact that they attain the first rule, namely God." See also: *In* III *sent.*, dist. 33, q. 1, a. 1, qc 1, corp. ("The good to which human virtues are proximately ordered is the good of reason"); *ST* I-II, q. 71, a. 6, corp. ("Now, the rule of the human will is twofold. One is proximate and of the same kind—namely, human reason itself—and the other is the first rule—namely, the eternal law, which is, so to speak, the reason of God"); II-II, q. 17, a. 1, corp.

[15] Though this is not said in these terms, *ST* I-II, q. 71, a. 6, corp., equates the eternal law with the *ratio Dei*, which is certainly not distinct from his essence. Also, *ST* I-II, q. 93, a. 4, ad 2, says Christ is not subject to the eternal law because he is the eternal law. The *index tertius* of the 1894 Editio altera Romana of *ST* thus makes this conclusion saying: "The rule of human acts is twofold—namely, human reason and the eternal law that is [*scilicet*] God."

absolute, their goodness depends more upon the eternal law than upon human reason.[16] On one level, human reason and the eternal law should not be thought of as having an untraversable chasm between them. After all, the natural law, which is known by reason, is the rational creature's participation in the eternal law. Worded differently, "man naturally participates in the eternal law according to certain common principles on the part of the practical reason"[17] and he is set apart from all the other animals precisely because of this cognitional participation he has in addition to the various kinds of natural teleological participation creatures devoid of reason enjoy.[18] At the same time, the "human reason is not able to participate in the full dictate of the divine reason," but only "in its way and imperfectly,"[19] because "the eternal law is unknown to us inasmuch as it is in the divine mind." It is known by our minds only in some measure (*aliqualiter*), either by the natural reason, which is derived from the eternal law, or "from some additional [*superadditam*] revelation."[20] What this implies is that when "human reason falls short, it must have recourse to the eternal reason."[21]

Returning to Wheatley's statement that "God or beatitude" is the end

---

[16] *ST* I-II, q. 19, a. 4, corp. ("The goodness of the human will depends much more on the eternal law than on human reason"); q. 93, a. 1, sc: ("The eternal law is the highest reason which always ought to be complied with"); q. 71, a. 6, corp. (see note 15 above).

[17] *ST* I-II, q. 91, a. 3, ad 1: "Ex parte rationis practicae naturaliter homo participat legem aeternam secundum quaedam communia principia."

[18] *ST* I-II, q. 93, a. 6, corp.: "There are two ways in which a thing is subject to the eternal law, as explained above (A. 5): first, by partaking of the eternal law by way of knowledge; secondly, by way of action and passion, i.e., by partaking of the eternal law by way of an inward motive principle: and in this second way, irrational creatures are subject to the eternal law, as stated above (*ibid.*). But since the rational nature, together with that which it has in common with all creatures, has something proper to itself inasmuch as it is rational, consequently it is subject to the eternal law in both ways; because while each rational creature has some knowledge of the eternal law, as stated above (A. 2), it also has a natural inclination to that which is in harmony with the eternal law; for *we are naturally adapted to be the recipients of virtue*" (Dominican Fathers trans.).

[19] *ST* I-II, q. 91, a. 3, ad 1: "Ratio humana non potest participare ad plenum dictamen rationis divinae, sed suo modo, et imperfecte."

[20] *ST* I-II, q. 19, a. 4, ad 3: "Although the eternal law is unknown to us inasmuch as it is in the divine mind, it nevertheless becomes known to us in some way either through natural reason (which is derived from it as its proper image) or through some additional revelation."

[21] *ST* I-II, q. 19, a. 4, corp.: "Multo magis dependet bonitas voluntatis humanae a lege aeterna, quam a ratione humana: et ubi deficit humana ratio, oportet ad rationem aeternam recurrere."

for the sake of which everyone acts, the participation in the eternal law that comes by means of reason alone is certainly not extended to the point of considering the very essence of God himself as the end for the sake of which (*finis gratia cuius*) and the "object of beatitude,"[22] because *gratia* (in another sense of the word, of course) would be necessary for this. Consider first *ST* I-II, q. 62, a. 1, ad 3:

> The reason and the will are ordered to God naturally inasmuch as He is the beginning and end of nature according to the proportion of nature. But the reason and will are not ordered sufficiently to him inasmuch as he is the object of supernatural beatitude.[23]

Then, in comparison, consider *In* II *sent.*, dist. 41, q. 1, a. 1, ad 2:

> Reason is not able to sufficiently direct one to that which exceeds natural human knowledge. Nevertheless, all of our acts must be ordered toward it as towards an ultimate end: thus is it necessary that faith direct us.[24]

The Dominican commentators of Saint Thomas, as Thomas Joseph White observes, insisted that the natural desire for God has to be elicited precisely on the basis of "the desire to know the hidden cause of manifest effects. Therefore it is properly natural in both its formal constitution

---

[22] II-II, q. 4, a. 7, corp.: "Since the last end is... in the intellect by faith, it is necessary that faith be first among all the virtues, since natural knowledge is not able to attain to God inasmuch as he is the object of beatitude."

[23] *ST* I-II, q. 62, a. 1, ad 3: "Ad tertium dicendum quod ad Deum naturaliter ratio et voluntas ordinatur prout est naturae principium et finis, secundum tamen proportionem naturae. Sed ad ipsum secundum quod est obiectum beatitudinis supernaturalis, ratio et voluntas secundum suam naturam non ordinantur sufficienter." Something analogous can be said about the love that flows from this knowledge in I-II, q. 109, a. 3, ad 1: "Charity loves God over all things in a more eminent way than nature. For nature loves God over all things inasmuch as he is the beginning and end of the natural good whereas charity loves him according as he is the object of beatitude and inasmuch as man has a certain spiritual friendship with God" ("Caritas diligit deum super omnia eminentius quam natura. Natura enim diligit deum super omnia, prout est principium et finis naturalis boni, caritas autem secundum quod est obiectum beatitudinis, et secundum quod homo habet quandam societatem spiritualem cum deo").

[24] *In* II *sent.*, dist. 41, q. 1, a. 1, ad 2: "Ad secundum dicendum, quod ratio non potest sufficienter dirigere ad hoc quod humanam cognitionem naturalem excedit; in quod tamen, sicut in finem ultimum, oportet omnes actus nostros ordinari: ideo oportet quod fides dirigat."

and its end or object, and not supernatural as such."[25] Although one might wonder, as Steven Long does, whether this elicited desire could be considered "natural" without qualification, it is nevertheless "clearly natural as opposed to being supernatural . . . that is to say that it is a desire to know the essence of the God who is *incognito*, known only through the effects of creatures."[26] This is not to deny, of course, that the graced desire for the beatific vision simply cannot be in the genus of nature, given its intrinsically supernatural end. What we are speaking about is simply the desire to know the cause of created effects even though the individual cannot possibly conceive of what "God has prepared" for those who attain to beatific knowledge.[27]

In any event, man is in some way able to use natural reason to know that the perfect good is necessarily bound up with knowing the highest cause and man's will, which is an "inclination following an understood form,"[28] is apt to be moved to desire that good as an object of happiness. The primary emphasis in this chapter will be on seeing how far man's natural reason, which is central to our consideration and which Thomas sometimes identifies with synderesis,[29] can get him in coming to see that God is the perfect good he implicitly desires, although we will turn to the role of grace once that has been sufficiently established.

Returning to the question of the end in general, James Keenan expresses how crucial the notion is for Aquinas:

> In his *Commentary on the Sentences*, Thomas declares that it is in the end, as the cause of the causes, that the meaning of good is to be found.[30] This affirmation that the end is "the cause of the causes" continues throughout his writings.[31] Similarly, he holds

---

[25] Thomas Joseph White, O.P., Review of *The Natural Desire to See God according to St. Thomas Aquinas and His Interpreters* by Lawrence Feingold, *The Thomist* 74, no. 3 (2010): 463.

[26] Steven Long, "On the Possibility of a Purely Natural End for Man," *The Thomist* 64, no. 2 (2000): 211–37, at 222.

[27] See 1 Cor 2:9.

[28] *Quolibet* II, q. 2, a. 2: "The motion of the will is an inclination following an understood form" ("motus voluntatis est inclinatio sequens formam intellectam").

[29] *ST* II-II, q. 47, a. 6, ad 1: "Natural reason, which is called synderesis, appoints the end to the moral virtues."

[30] *In I sent.*, dist. 38, q. 1, a. 1, ad 4. Cf.: *In I sent.*, dist. 45, q. 1, a. 3, corp.; *In II sent.*, dist. 9, q. 1, a. 1, ad 1.

[31] See, for instance, *De principiis naturae ad fratrem Sylvestrum*, ch. 3: "The end is the cause of the causes because it is the cause of causality in all causes."

the end as the "first of all the causes."³² These titles are used fundamentally to affirm causal primacy: without the end, the agent does not act.³³ Because the end moves the agent, all other causes derive their causality from the end, and all other causes receive from the final cause their status as causes.³⁴

Each of the four causes (the final, efficient, material, and formal) are important, but the final is paramount. Edward Feser summarizes Aquinas's position on the relationship among the causes as being that "the formal and material causes depend on final causes by way of efficient causes."³⁵ We can deduce from this that another kind of causality which stands out is the efficient cause, even though it remains subordinated to the final one. This is true in a particular way when we speak of moral activity, in which humans act as efficient causes or agents who direct their activities toward certain ends. Corresponding to this, Aquinas singles out "the agent and the reason for acting" as necessary to be "taken into account in any action."³⁶

The final cause, from which activity and motion begin, is the principle for an efficient cause (*principium ad causam agentem*)³⁷ in the sense that the "end is said to effect by moving the efficient cause," thereby giving the efficient cause its efficiency.³⁸ Whenever anything is done, the activ-

---

[32] See *ST* I-II, q. 1, a. 2, corp.: "Prima autem inter omnes causas est causa finalis." See also: *In* I *sent.*, dist. 8, q. 1, a. 3, corp; *In De divinis nominibus*, ch. 1, lec. 3; *ST* I, q. 5, a. 4, corp; q. 39, a. 8, obj. 4 and corp.; q. 44, a. 4, obj. 4; q. 82, a. 3, obj. 1.

[33] *ST* I, q. 5, a. 2, ad 1: ". . . agens non agit nisi propter finem."

[34] James Keenan, *Goodness and Rightness in Thomas Aquinas's Summa theologiae* (Washington, DC: Georgetown University Press, 1992), 27. It should be kept in mind that Keenan thinks Aquinas changed his minds on these points, but I intend to show that the contrary is, in fact, the case. On the final point, St. Thomas says: "Among the causes, the end preserves the first place, and all the other causes owe the fact that they are actually causes to it" (*SCG* III, ch. 17, no. 9). The cause known as the end has primacy among the causes throughout his writings. Keenan points to: *In* I *sent.*, dist. 38, q. 1, a. 1, ad 4; *De veritate*, q. 21, a. 3, ad 5; *ST* I, q. 5, a. 2, ad 1; *In* I *eth.*, lec. 5, no. 58; *In* II *metaphys.*, lec. 4, no. 318: "With the final cause removed, the nature and notion of the good is removed because the *ratio* of the good and of the end is the same."

[35] Edward Feser, *Scholastic Metaphysics: A Contemporary Introduction* (Lancaster, UK: Editiones Scholasticae, 2014), 91.

[36] *De veritate* q. 22, a. 12, corp.: "In qualibet actione duo considerentur: scilicet agens, et ratio agendi."

[37] *In De divinis nominibus*, ch. 1, lec. 2: "The end . . . is the first of the causes and the principle for the agent cause from which action and motion begin."

[38] *ST* I, q. 48, a. 1, ad 4: "Aliquid agere dicitur . . . per modum causae finalis, sicut finis

ity is due to a final cause.[39] John of Saint Thomas clarifies that the role (*munus*) of the end is "to terminate and conclude" whatever was done for the sake of carrying something out." He adds:

> Nothing is moved toward doing or attaining something unless the end of the action and motion be placed before it. Otherwise, if something were not specified that would terminate and put the action at rest, the action would not be susceptible to coming to an end and would be indefinite. The end, therefore, implies the goodness or perfection that causes motion to cease, ... and it thus diffuses its goodness ... by putting that thing forward [*praebendo*] in which the agent's motion terminates.[40]

Whenever we act for an end, we have some potency that has yet to be actualized or perfected by attaining that end. When that end is put forward to us, we are naturally drawn toward it to the degree it is good, and if we attain it, we rest in it.

Implicit in the way that act and potency relate to each other is the fact that, as Feser says, "efficient and final causality go hand in hand" because "efficient causation is just the actualization of a potency" and a potency, for its part, is always a potency for some end.[41] Aquinas further elaborates on the mutual causality that the causes can have upon each other in *De principiis naturae*, where we learn that the final cause, or the reason the agent acts, "is called the cause of the efficient cause" and that, inversely, the efficient or agent cause "is the cause of that which is the end."[42] He

---

dicitur efficere movendo efficientem." Similarly, in *ST* I, q. 82, a. 4, corp., the end is said to move the agent because the understood good moves the will as an end. Regarding the efficient cause receiving its efficiency from the final cause, *De principiis naturae*, ch. 4, says, "the end is the cause of the causality of the efficient cause because it makes the efficient cause to be an efficient cause [*facit efficiens esse efficiens*]."

[39] See *SCG* III, ch. 2.

[40] "Munus finis ... est ... terminare, et ultimare ea quod pertinent ad exercitium, et executionem rei fiendae: nullus enim movetur ad aliquid faciendum, vel exequendum, nisi sibi ponatur finis operationis, et motus, alias maneret infinitus, et impertransibilis, si non poneretur sibi aliquid ubi sisteret et quiesceret, et ideo finis importat bonitatem, seu perfectionem sistentem motum ... et sic diffundit suam bonitatem ... praebendo id ad quod efficientiae motus terminetur" (John of Saint Thomas, *Cursus philosophicus thomisticus* [new edition], vol. 2, *Philosophia Naturalis*, pt. 1 [*Philosophiae naturalis*], q. 13 [*De fine*], a. 1 [Paris: Ludovicus Vives, 1883], 244).

[41] Feser, *Scholastic Metaphysics*, 90.

[42] *De principiis naturae*, ch. 4: "It should be known that the same thing can be both a

explains their mutual causality (that is, the fact that "the same thing can be both a cause and caused in respect of the same thing, though in different ways") by means of an example.

He observes that walking or performing the medical art is able to be an efficient cause of health while health is able to be the final cause of either of them. The final and the efficient causes are causes of each other. Though the efficient cause does not make the end to be an end, it does make the end to act as an end (*facit finem esse finalem*) in the sense that the agent makes the end to be an end he strives to bring about. The doctor, of course, does not make health to *be* an end toward which man's nature is ordered (he does not *facit finem esse finem* and he is not the cause of the causality of the end), but he does actualize the ability his patients' bodies have for health (i.e., he *facit sanitatem esse in actu*) as a result of efficiently working toward it.[43] In all of this, the end retains primacy, and thus Saint Thomas concludes this portion of *De principiis* by pointing out that the end is the cause not only of the causality of the efficient causes, but also of that of all the causes.[44]

The end is that toward which something tends, as the name *intentio* implies.[45] Since intention is an act of the will and the proper object of the will is the universal good,[46] the end must at least be perceived in some way as good if the will is to follow after it.[47] In fact, the end and the good are so

---

cause and caused in respect of the same thing, though in diverse ways.... The efficient cause is called a cause with respect to the end, since the end is not an end in act except through the activity of the agent. But the end is called the cause of the efficient cause, since the efficient cause does not operate without the intention of the end. Hence the efficient cause is the cause of that which is the end.... It does not, however make the end to be an end."

[43] *De principiis naturae*, ch. 4: "The efficient cause is the cause of that which is the end, as health is. It does not, however, make the end to be an end and thus it is not the cause of the causality of the end; that is, it does not make the end to act as an end (or, 'to be final'): as a doctor actualizes the patients ability for health [*facit sanitatem esse in actu*]. He does not, however, make health to be an end."

[44] *De principiis naturae*, ch. 4: "The end is the cause of the causality of the efficient cause because it makes the efficient cause to be an efficient cause. Similarly, it makes the matter to be the matter and the form to be the form (since matter receives the form only for the sake of the end and the form perfects the matter only through the end. For this reason, the end is called the cause of the causes, because it is the cause of the causality in all causes."

[45] *ST* I-II, q. 12, a. 1, corp.: "Intentio, sicut ipsum nomen sonat, significat in aliquid tendere."

[46] See *De potentia*, q. 3, a. 15, ad 5.

[47] As Simon Francis Gaine says, "no one can will without aiming at something good in some respect, even if it is illusory" (*Will There Be Free Will in Heaven?: Freedom,*

connected that Aquinas sometimes says that the proper object of the will is "the end *and* the good," which two things (seen as conjoined to each other[48]) are "that by which one is moved to act."[49] They cannot be separated from each other because, "when the final cause is removed, the nature and *ratio* of the good is removed, since the *ratio* of the good is the same as the *ratio* of the end."[50] If this is so, there must be one end.

On the Necessity of Having One Final End

A central aspect of Aquinas's thought is that there must be one ultimate final cause. Thomas explains in his commentary on Aristotle's *Nicomachean Ethics* how this is so:

> If one were to proceed indefinitely [*in infinitum*] in the desire of ends, as would happen if one end were to always be desired on account of something else, one would never attain the desired ends that were being sought. But for no purpose [*frustra*] and in vain would someone seek that which he is not able to attain. Therefore, the desire of the end would be for nothing and in vain. But this desire is natural; for it was said above that the good is what all naturally desire. Therefore, it would follow that a natural desire would be inane and empty [*inane et vacuum*]. But this is impossible because a natural desire is nothing other than an inclination adhering to things from the ordinance of the first mover, which is not able to be pointless [*supervacua*]. Therefore, it is impossible that one would proceed indefinitely. And thus it is necessary that there be some last end on account of which all other things are desired and that it itself is not desired for the sake of something else.[51]

Impeccability, and Beatitude [New York: T&T Clark, 2003], 129).

[48] They are even conjoined with the singular of the verb "to be" in *De veritate*, q. 22, a. 12, sc 3 ("bonum et finis est obiectum voluntatis"), *SCG* III, ch. 151, no. 4 ("finis et bonum sit proprium obiectum appetitus") and *SCG* IV, ch. 19, no. 2 ("finis enim et bonum est voluntatis obiectum").

[49] *SCG* III, ch. 1 (emphasis added), and I, ch. 72. Also of note is that he says the proper object of the will is the "end" in *ST* I-II, q. 73, a. 6, corp., and the "good understood" in *SCG* I, ch. 72, no. 2, and III, ch. 107, no. 8. In *ST* I, q. 2, a. 4, corp., he says the object of the will is the *bonum et finis in communi*.

[50] *In II metaphys.*, lec. 4, no. 318.: "Remota autem causa finali, removetur natura et ratio boni: eadem enim ratio boni et finis est."

[51] *In I eth.*, lec. 2, nos 3–4: "[no. 3] Quod autem sit impossibile in finibus procedere in infinitum, probat tertia ratione quae est etiam ducens ad impossibile, hoc modo. Si

The question of how to exactly describe the good which all desire for its own sake is not as easy to resolve as one might expect. As Ralph McInerny succinctly puts it, "the human good, man's ultimate end, is complex."[52] What is certain is that this human good must pertain to reason in some way because reason is "the cause and root of the human good"[53] in virtue of its participation in the divine Reason itself.[54] As an animal whose specific difference—that whereby he is distinguished from the other animals—is reason, his good is necessarily connected to reason.[55] As Aquinas says in *Summa Contra Gentiles*, "since man is a man because he has reason, it is necessary that his own good, which is happiness, be according to that which is proper to reason."[56]

Accordingly, acts that are done without the deliberation of reason (such as the scratching of one's beard might be) are not even human acts properly speaking because their end is not appointed by reason (*per rationem praestitutum*).[57] Presupposing, however, that a man acts from a

---

procedatur in infinitum in desiderio finium, ut scilicet semper unus finis desideretur propter alium in infinitum, nunquam erit devenire ad hoc quod homo consequatur fines desideratos. Sed frustra et vane aliquis desiderat id quod non potest assequi; ergo desiderium finis esset frustra et vanum. Sed hoc desiderium est naturale: dictum enim est supra quod bonum est, quod naturaliter omnia desiderant; ergo sequetur quod naturale desiderium sit inane et vacuum. Sed hoc est impossibile. Quia naturale desiderium nihil aliud est quam inclinatio inhaerens rebus ex ordinatione primi moventis, quae non potest esse supervacua; ergo impossibile est quod in finibus procedatur in infinitum. [no. 4] Et sic necesse est esse aliquem ultimum finem propter quem omnia alia desiderantur et ipse non desideratur propter alia. Et ita necesse est esse aliquem optimum finem rerum humanarum." See also *SCG* III, ch. 2, nos. 3–5.

[52] Ralph McInerny, *Ethica Thomistica: The Moral Philosophy of Thomas Aquinas* (Washington, DC: Catholic University of America Press, 1997), 46.

[53] *ST* I-II, q. 66, a. 1, corp.: "Causa et radix humani boni est ratio." Similarly, in *De malo*, q. 10, a. 2, corp., reason is called the beginning of a moral act (see also *ST* I-II, q. 104, a. 1, ad 3), and *ST* I-II, q. 90, a. 1, corp., refers to it as the principle of human acts.

[54] *ST* I-II, q. 19, a. 4, corp.: "It is because of the eternal law, which is the divine reason, that the human reason is the rule of the human will and the measure of the will's goodness."

[55] For this reason, every voluntary human act that is in accordance with (*concordat*) reason and the eternal law is a good one and every one that falls back form the order of reason and the eternal law is evil (see *ST* I-II, q. 21, a. 1, corp.). Reason is the proximate rule of human acts, and the eternal law—"which is as the reason of God"—is the first or remote rule (see *ST* I-II, q. 71, a. 6, corp.).

[56] *SCG* III, ch. 34, no. 4.

[57] *ST* I-II, q. 1, a. 1, ad 3: "Actions of this sort are not properly human because they do not proceed from reason's deliberation, which is the proper principle of human acts. And, therefore, they have a certain imagined end but not the end appointed [*praestitutum*] by reason." See also I-II, q. 18, a. 9, corp.

deliberated will ("one that flows from a will under the direction of reason's consideration of the end and the means to that end"[58]), and that his action is consequently not merely an act of man (*actus humani*) but a human act (*actus humanus*),[59] it is vital that the end he appoints to himself be a fitting end (*debitum finem*)[60] and also that his appetites be habitually disposed to follow such an end if he is to be truly virtuous.[61]

The practical import of this, of course, is that, since "man is composed of a twofold nature, intellective and sensitive,"[62] he needs to both know what to do in his intellect and have appetites that are correctly ordered. Unfortunately, however, "the good in view of which someone acts is not always a true good, but sometimes a true good and sometimes an apparent one;"[63] that is, sometimes that which is not truly good can be the motivating factor in an action. Part of the reason for this is that a person's disposition can change when a passion moves his will. If he develops a vicious habit, then, he will habitually see a false good as a true good because, "as each one is, so does the end seem to him."[64] Because man is hylomorphic, both his matter (his body) and his form (his rational soul) need to work together.[65]

---

[58] Michael S. Sherwin, O.P., *By Knowledge and By Love*, 23. Cf. *ST* I-II, q. 1, a. 3, corp.: "Acts are called human inasmuch as they proceed from a deliberated will."

[59] *ST* III, q. 19, a. 2, corp.: "Because man is what he is by his reason, that action is simply speaking called human that proceeds from reason through the will, which is reason's appetite. Now, if there is an act in man that does not proceed from reason and will, it is not simply a human act." See also: *De virtutibus*, q. 1, a. 4, corp.: *ST* I, q. 1, a. 4; *In* II *sent.*, dist. 25, q. 1, a. 3, ad 3.

[60] *ST* I-II, q. 18, a. 9, corp.: "Since it pertains to reason to order, an act that proceeds from the deliberating reason is repugnant to reason and has the *ratio* of evil if it is not ordered to a fitting end [*debitum finem*]." Elsewhere, Thomas explains that "the more the will tends toward unfitting ends, the more difficult it will be for it to return to the proper and fitting end" (*SCG* III, ch. 12, no. 7). See also *SCG* III, ch. 1, no. 5.

[61] Thomas argues that "a prudent man is said to be wise inasmuch as he ordered human acts to a fitting end" in *ST* I, q. 1, a. 6, corp. Also, *In* III *eth.*, lec. 17, no. 5, he says rage can be utilized in acts of fortitude *if* it is ordered to a further *debitum finem* for which it works as a final cause (*cuius gratia operetur*).

[62] *ST* II-II, q. 165, a. 2, corp.: "Homo compositus est ex duplici natura, intellectiva scilicet, et sensitiva."

[63] *ST* I-II, q. 18, a. 4, ad 1: "Bonum, ad quod aliquis respiciens operatur, non semper est verum bonum, sed quandoque verum bonum, et quandoque apparens."

[64] *ST* I-II, q. 9, a. 2, corp.: "That which is apprehended as good and fitting moves the will by way of an object. Now, something seems good and fitting due on account of two things—namely, the condition of that which is proposed or the condition of the one to whom something is proposed.... As each one is, so does the end seem to him." See also *SCG* III, ch. 12, no. 7.

[65] *ST* I-II, q. 63, a. 1, corp.: "The form of man is the rational soul, and the matter is the body."

That this cooperation does not always take place is evident from the fact that humans pursue or appoint (*praestituant*) to themselves many different ends (such as riches or power) as if they were final ends. Aquinas elaborates:

> Just as we find a highest cause regarding those things which are truly good; namely, the greatest good which is the last end, by knowing which, man is said to be truly wise, so also in evil things one is able to find something to which all others are to be referred as to a last end, by knowing which, man is said to be wise about how to act badly. . . . Now whoever turns away from the fitting end, necessarily appoints to himself [*sibi praestituat*] some unfitting end, because every agent acts for an end. Wherefore, if he appoints to himself an end that consists in external earthly things, his wisdom is called earthly, if in bodily goods, it is called brutish wisdom, if in some excellence, it is called diabolical wisdom, because it imitates the devil's pride, concerning which it is written in Job 41 [v. 25], "He is king over all the children of pride."[66]

When a person is lacking the kind of virtuous disposition that comes from subjecting passions to reason, he may be wise in one of these senses, but he will not have the kind of wisdom that would keep him from turning away from his true end, which is the sovereign good. That kind of practical wisdom, what Aquinas calls "wisdom in human things,"[67] is known as prudence—which both presupposes and ensures right appetite. When a man happily possesses this habit, his appetites will promptly

---

[66] *ST* II-II, q. 45, a. 1, ad 1: "Sicut circa ea, quae sunt vere bona, invenitur aliqua altissima causa, quae est summum bonum, quod est ultimus finis, per cujus cognitionem dicitur homo vere sapiens: ita etiam in malis est invenire aliquid, ad quod alia referuntur, sicut ad ultimum finem, per cujus cognitionem homo dicitur esse sapiens ad male agendum, secundum illud Hierem. 4: Sapientes sunt, ut faciam mala; bene autem facere nescierunt: quicumque autem avertitur a fine debito, necesse est quod aliquem finem indebitum sibi praestituat: quia omne agens agit propter finem; unde si praestituat sibi finem in bonis exterioribus terrenis, vocatur sapientia terrena: si autem in bonis corporalibus, vocatur sapientia animalis: si autem in aliqua excellentia, vocatur sapientia diabolica, propter imitationem superbiae diaboli, de quo dicitur Job 41.: Ipse est rex super omnes filios superbiae."

[67] *ST* II-II, q. 47, a. 2, ad 1: "Prudence is wisdom in human things. It is not, however, wisdom simply speaking, because it is not about the highest cause in an unqualified sense."

and joyfully[68] follow the human good of reason, thus paving the way for true happiness.[69]

Among human appetites, the noblest one is the will (the rational appetite), the proportionate object of which is the understood good.[70] It is essential for the attainment of virtue and the pursuit of happiness, therefore, that the good be apprehended by reason, which is the "proper principle of human acts."[71] When the good that is proper to man is so apprehended, his will is enabled to pursue it.[72] We now turn to the fundamental consideration of what the good that is proper to us as humans actually is.

The End qua "Perfect Good of Happiness"

For Aquinas, the "first principle in practical matters" is happiness or beatitude (*felicitas vel beatitudo*).[73] As simple as it may sound to say we all

---

[68] *De virtutibus*, q. 5, a. 2, ad 2: "A habit as such makes someone act promptly and with pleasure."

[69] This can be said even more so about the habit of wisdom that is a gift of the Holy Spirit. Someone who is wise in any particular genus is able to judge and order everything in that particular genus, but he who is wise simply and thus has the gift of the Holy Spirit is able "to judge and order *everything* according to the divine rules" (see *ST* II-II, q. 45, a. 1, corp.). If he can do that, he necessarily has virtues that have been informed by charity and is thus able to follow the promptings of reason even better than the man for whom prudence is the form of the virtues.

[70] *ST* I-II, q. 19, a. 3, corp.; I, q. 82, a. 4, corp.; and *SCG* I, ch. 81, no. 3 say the same of the good without the qualification "proportionate." *SCG* I, ch. 95, no. 3, and *ST* I, q. 13, a. 5, ad 2, refer to its object as an "apprehended good." *SCG* I, ch. 90, no. 3, notably, says "the apprehended good and evil are the object" of the intellective appetite.

[71] *ST* II-II, q. 157, a. 2, corp.: "proprium principium humanorum actuum." See I-II, q. 1, a. 1, ad 3, and I-II, q. 100, a. 1, corp. In *De malo*, he specifies that the deliberation of reason is "the proper and principal active principle of human acts": ". . . procedit a ratione deliberante, quae est proprium et principale activum principium humanorum actuum" (*De malo*, q. 10, a. 2, ad 1).

[72] "When the will tends to an act, having been moved by the apprehension of reason presenting to it its proper good, a fitting action follows (*SCG* III, ch. 10, no. 16). "Fitting action," of course, does not always follow. One instance in which the will does not tend to its proper good, Thomas says, is when "the judgment of reason is intercepted by passion" (see *De virtutibus*, q. 1, a. 5, ad 2).

[73] *ST* I-II, q. 90, a. 2, corp.: "As reason is a principle of human actions, so also in reason itself there is something that is a principle in respect of all else. . . . Now, the first principle in practical matters, which practical reason pertains to, is the last end. Now, the last end of human life is happiness or beatitude."

desire this "kind of most perfect state"[74] which is sometimes called "the perfect good"[75] because it is the last end and object of the will,[76] we will be contemplating the implications of this fact in essentially every chapter so as to investigate the way *intellectus* and reason (and particularly *recta ratio agibilium* or prudence) relates to this desire as an end, what this perfect good consists of, and finally, the freedom that ensues from fittingly pursuing such a compelling end.

The Angelic Doctor teaches that, if something is not sought "as the perfect good which is the ultimate end, it is necessary that it be sought as tending towards the perfect good."[77] This is basically to say that anything we seek must at least be an apparent good of some sort. For this reason, a "perverse appetite" is always accompanied by "some falsity of practical knowledge."[78] The causal force of what Thomas refers to as "the perfect good of happiness"[79] can be exemplified by the way he explains Augustine's stealing of a neighbor's pears. One problem he is dealing with in this section of the *Scriptum* is that the end is, *ex suppositio*, something good that all men pursue as an end. He had quoted Augustine and Pseudo-Dionysius to argue that "all creatures, according to an impression received from the Creator, are, each according to its own mode, inclined by appetite to the good, so that a certain circular pattern is found in things: for, having gone forth from the good, they tend toward the good."[80] This being so, all things must have a desire for their own good and rational creatures in particular must have a natural desire for their own beatitude.[81] As is made clear in *De malo*, both angels and men "have the end of beatitude naturally appointed

---

[74] *In II sent.*, dist. 38, q. 1, a. 2, ad 2: "Although happiness [*beatitude*] is hidden in regard to its substance, the notion of it is known, since all understand by 'happiness' a kind of most perfect state. Nevertheless, in what that perfect state consists (whether in life or after life, whether in bodily or spiritual goods—and in which spiritual goods), it is hidden."

[75] See *ST* I-II, q. 5, a. 5, ad 1.

[76] *In IV sent.*, dist. 49, q. 1, a. 1, qc 2, corp.: "Beatitude . . . is the last end and the notion [*ratio*] of the good is from the end, which is the object of the will." See also *ST* I-II, q. 90, a. 2, corp.

[77] See *ST* I-II, q. 1, a. 6, corp.

[78] See *De malo*, q. 16, a. 6, ad 11.

[79] See *ST* I-II, q. 5, a. 5, ad 1.

[80] *In IV sent.*, dist. 49, q. 1, a. 3, qc 1, corp., in Thomas Aquinas, *On Love and Charity: Readings from the Commentary on the Sentences of Peter Lombard*, trans. Peter A. Kwasniewski, Thomas Bolin, and Joseph Bolin (Washington, DC: Catholic University of America Press, 2008).

[81] The same question is taken up in: *ST* I-II, q. 1, a. 6; I, q. 60, a. 2; *SCG* I, chs. 100–101.

[*praestitutum*] to them; accordingly, they naturally desire it."[82]

To act in a way that is evil by disregarding the natural law and stealing another's goods is, however, contrary to one's own happiness. For this reason, the pear incident is especially engaging because Augustine himself says the pears he stole were unappealing either to look at or eat; in fact, "the pleasure was in the evil act itself."[83] Aquinas explains that he must have nevertheless been doing it because he saw it as tending toward the good:

> In that thievery, as Augustine says in the same place, there was something having an appearance of good, in which a certain shadow of freedom appeared; hence he says: "What, therefore, did I love in that thievery, and how was I imitating you, my God, [though] viciously and perversely?" And he answers, saying: "Or was it not pleasing to act against the law at least by trickery, since I could not do so by power, in order that I, being a slave, might imitate freedom by doing with impunity what was unlawful, in a dark likeness of omnipotence?"[84]

Even in that evil act Augustine was seeking the good of happiness as an end. By attempting to imitate God's omnipotent nature by "trickery," he certainly turned away from the "unchangeable good" in which the *ratio of the ultimate end is truly found*," but he could not have turned away from intending the last end as an ultimate goal.[85] Aquinas establishes some principles for this fact in the body of the article:

> According to the Philosopher in *Ethics* VII, in the order of appetible items, the end holds the rank that a principle holds in the order of intelligible items.[86] Now, since that which is first and maximum in any genus is the cause of those that are after it, so knowledge of the principles in speculative matters is the cause of the knowledge of all other such matters; and likewise, appetite for the end is the cause of having appetite for all other things that are

---

[82] *De malo*, q. 16, a. 5, corp.: "Angelus et homo habent finem naturaliter praestitutum sibi beatitudinem; unde naturaliter appetunt eam, nec possunt velle miseriam."
[83] Augustine, *Confessions* 2.8.16, ed. Roy Joseph Deferrari, trans. Vernon J. Bourke, The Fathers of the Church 21 (Washington, DC: Catholic University of America Press, 1953), 46.
[84] *In* IV *sent.*, dist. 49, q. 1, a. 3, qc 4, ad 3 (*On Love and Charity*, 376).
[85] See *ST* I-II, q. 1, a. 7, ad 1 and obj. 1.
[86] See Aristotle, *Nicomachean Ethics* 7.8.1151a16–17.

toward the end. Hence, since beatitude is the end of human life, whatever the will has appetite to bring about is ordered to beatitude. This is clear also from experience; for whoever has appetite for something has appetite for it insofar as it is judged a good. But by the very fact that someone has something that he judges good, he reckons himself nearer to beatitude, since the addition of a good to a good makes one approach nearer to the perfect good, which is beatitude itself. And, therefore, any and every appetite is ordered to beatitude.[87]

In regard to the end known as beatitude or happiness, every rational creature necessarily pursues it as a good. As *SCG* says, "Whoever wills necessarily wills his last end just as man necessarily wills his happiness."[88] Whatever anyone does is necessarily ordered toward it, because it is desired "for its own sake and never for the sake of another."[89] One may certainly be defectively ordered toward it by pursuing that which has only the semblance of good (i.e., that which is merely an apparent good), but the perfect good of happiness is pursued by all even if all do not know that in which it objectively consists.

John of Saint Thomas explains there are final causes that are not the last end because they are subordinated to a further end and dependent upon it. They have the true *ratio* of an end, but since they are means in some way, they can be considered ends only in virtue of their participation in the last end. Because they are simply speaking desirable, they can be considered last ends inasmuch as they are supreme in a certain genus. They remain, however, distinct from the supreme end to which anything in any genus at all is subordinated.[90] In other words, only the ultimate end is

---

[87] *In* IV *sent.*, dist. 49, q. 1, a. 3, qc 4, corp. (*On Love and Charity*, 375).
[88] *SCG* I, ch. 80, no. 3: "Quilibet volens de necessitate vult suum ultimum finem: sicut homo de necessitate vult suam beatitudinem."
[89] *In* IV *sent.*, dist. 49, q. 1, a. 3, qc 4, corp. (*On Love and Charity*, 375).
[90] John of St. Thomas, *Cursus philosophicus thomisticus: tomus secundus philosophia naturalis*, q. 12 (*De fine*): "The end for the sake of which [a thing is done] is divided into the last end and the non-last end. The last end is that to which all things are ordered without any subordination to something else. The non-last end is that to which some things are ordered with subordination and dependency upon something else. Even a non-last end has a true *ratio* of an end, albeit a participated end, which puts on the *ratio* of a means in some way; nevertheless, it has the notion of an end simply speaking because it is simply speaking desirable, albeit in a participated way—just as a created substance is a being *per se* even though it is a being only in virtue of its participation in something uncreated . . . the last end simply (which is in every genus and which is that to which

never desired for the sake of another end, though one may desire another end (such as one of these) as if it were absolute. Final causes such as these would include ends such as knowledge, virtue, health, life, and being,[91] each of which can be seen as falling short of the perfect good in some way (e.g., one could sacrifice life for virtue or one's temporal health for eternal life).[92] Nevertheless, the truly last end is that which sets every desire at rest and leaves nothing to be desired.[93] Everything else that is desired must, therefore, have "reference to the desire for beatitude, whether mediately or immediately."[94]

What the rational creature does may be ordered toward beatitude

---

everything in any genus is subordinated) is one thing, and the last end in some genus is another" ([Paris: Ludovicus Vives, 1883], 242).

[91] *In* I *sent.*, dist. 48, q. 1, a. 4, corp., speaks of knowledge, virtue, and health: "Since there are diverse grades of appetite following diverse kinds of apprehensions, no appetite is held to tend to a good that reason does not apprehend.... There is a kind of natural will in us, by which we desire [*appetimus*] that which is good for man as man in virtue of what it is [*secundum se*] and this natural will follows the apprehension of reason considering something absolutely: as when a man wants knowledge, virtue, health, and things of this sort." Parenthetically, Aquinas suggests in the conclusion of this article that these naturally desired ends need to be ordered by reason lest one merely follow an impulse toward any one of them: "The motion of the deliberated will is corrupt in sinners, who relinquish the deliberation of reason and follow the impetus of the natural will." *In* I *de interp.*, lec. 14, no. 24, speaks of being (*esse*), living (*vivere*), and understanding (*intelligere*) and necessarily desirable goods of this sort, whereas *De malo*, q. 6, ad 1, speaks of living and understanding: "All men naturally desire to be, to live, and to understand." In his commentary on Pseudo-Dionysius *Divine Names*, Aquinas points out that, even though all desire naturally to be and live and understand, they are able through their free will to "voluntarily avert their understanding" from considering the good inasmuch as it is good because they do not want to follow it. As a consequence, they fall back from "the goods that belong to them according to the order of their nature and they are called evil inasmuch as they are not." In other words, they fall back from being even though they naturally desire it. For more on this, see, *De divinis nominibus*, ch. 4, lec. 20. See also, *ST* I-II, q. 10, a. 2, ad 3, and *De veritate*, q. 22, a. 5, corp.

[92] In *ST* I-II, q. 12, a. 1, ad 3, Aquinas says we will health absolutely, which means it pertains to something willed as opposed to something intended. However, even when we come to will something absolutely (*absolute*), this can fall short of the perfect good as the following text indicates: "The will as nature is moved toward something absolutely. Thus, if reason does not order that which the will as nature is moved toward into something else, the will as nature will accept it absolutely and it will act as an end. If, though, reason orders that which will as nature is moved toward to a [further] end, it will not accept it absolutely" (*In* III *sent.*, dist. 17, q. 1, a. 2, qc 1, corp.). On the relationship of the preservation of health or being to the last end, see *ST* I-II, q. 2, a. 5, corp.

[93] See *SCG* I, ch. 100.

[94] *In* IV *sent.*, dist. 49, q. 1, a. 3, qc 4, sc 1 (*On Love and Charity*, 375).

mediately (as a means), as when "someone wants to undertake works of virtue so that through this, he may merit beatitude," or alternatively, the action may be ordered to it inasmuch as it possesses "some likeness to beatitude," because it is not only perfect happiness that is naturally desired, "but even any likeness or participation in it."[95] In the case of Augustine, Thomas suggests, his sinful action was ordered toward beatitude in the second way; he was "striving for beatitude and toward an imitation of God" by performing an act which was merely a "dark likeness"[96] of God's omnipotence.[97] Augustine was necessarily striving for happiness in that act (indeed, the desire for happiness is not even subject to free will),[98] but he failed either to attain it or do something truly conducive to it. As Aquinas explains it in *ST*, every sin of the will necessarily falls short of the "ultimate intended end" of happiness because "no evil act of the will is able to be ordered to happiness, which is the ultimate end." Even if the sinful person attains the proximate end he had intended as an "end that is ordered to the ultimate end," he is not able to be considered truly happy,[99] both because sin itself is a falling away from reason[100] and because nothing but the perfect and universal good is able to satisfy man's appetite as an ultimate end.[101]

This brings us back yet again to the fact that, even if God so ordains human nature that all men desire happiness, that in which happiness consists is not clear to all. Saint Thomas speaks to this fact in the fifth question of the *ST* I-II. He explains that the common notion of happiness is that it

---

[95] *ST* I-II, q. 3, a. 6, ad 2: "Naturaliter desideratur non solum perfecta beatitudo, sed etiam qualiscumque similitudo, vel participatio ipsius [al. *ejus*]."

[96] See, *In IV sent.*, dist. 49, q. 1, a. 3, qc 4, ad 3 (*On Love and Charity*, 376).

[97] *In IV sent.*, dist. 49, q. 1, a. 3, qc 4, ad 2: "For the result of the will's having appetite for something is that it also desires that in which the thing's likeness is found, even if it cannot have the chief desideratum; and in this way, all who have appetite for sins are [still] striving for beatitude and toward an imitation of God" (*On Love and Charity*, 376).

[98] *ST* I, q. 83, a. 1, ad 5: "Man naturally desires the last end that is happiness, which desire, certainly, is natural and not subject to free will."

[99] *ST* I-II, q. 21, a. 1, ad 2: "The end is twofold—namely, the last end and the proximate end. . . . In the sin of the will there is always a falling away from the ultimate intended end, because no evil act of the will is able to be ordered to happiness, which is the ultimate end."

[100] In *ST* I-II, q. 73, a. 2, Thomas suggests that the gradations of sins depend on the degree to which the sinner recedes from the rectitude of reason. Of course, what makes a man human is that he has reason, so "his proper good which is happiness" must be "according to that which is proper to reason," as *SCG* III, ch. 34, says.

[101] *ST* I-II, q. 2, a. 7, corp.: "The good that is the last end is the perfect good fulfilling the appetite for good. Now, a human appetite, which is the will, is for a universal good."

is the "perfect good" that completely satisfies the will and leaves nothing to be desired. Since everyone wants this, everyone wills happiness. However, just as the young Augustine was, they are sometimes ignorant of the more proper (*specialem*) notion of happiness that pertains to that in which happiness consists: "And thus all do not know happiness because they are ignorant of that to which the common notion of happiness belongs."[102] Worded differently, although happiness itself is necessarily known and desired, one can appoint various subordinate ends to himself. Part of the mystery here is that this dynamic presupposes the dispositions of the individual. In the *De virtutibus*, Thomas clarifies:

> The will does not pertain only to the ultimate end, but also to other ends. But in regard to the appetite for the other ends, the will is able to be rightly or non-rightly ordered. After all, good people appoint to themselves [*praestituunt sibi*] good ends whereas bad people appoint bad ends. As it is said in the third book of the *Ethics*, "as each one is, so does the end appear to him."[103]

Since whatever end one prescribes for himself to follow must be seen as good, the habit one has acquired must color the various possible ends and make some stand out as the best means to the ultimate end of happiness even though they are merely apparent goods in some cases. Prescinding from subjective inclinations, though, what is the end itself actually and what things are necessarily constitutive of it? At the end of this chapter, we will focus on filling out the answer to this question from the theological standpoint, which requires the aid of revelation and grace. As Long observes, "grace orders human nature to an end that infinitely transcends the most profound philosophic contemplation of human finality."[104] Since, however, synderesis (which is also known as natural reason[105]) is one of the protagonists of this book, it seems best to first establish what the end is on the natural level before bringing in the inestimable role of grace.

---

[102] See *ST* I-II, q. 5, a. 8.

[103] *De virtutibus*, q. 1, a. 5, arg. 2: "Sed contra, voluntas non solum est finis ultimi, sed etiam finium aliorum. Sed circa appetitum aliorum finium contingit voluntatem et recte et non recte se habere. Nam boni praestituunt sibi bonos fines, mali vero malos, ut dicitur in III Ethic.: qualis unusquisque est, talis finis videtur ei."

[104] Steven Long, "On the Possibility," 235.

[105] See: *ST* II-II, q. 47, a. 6, ad 1; I-II, q. 100, a. 1, corp.

In What Does This Perfect Good Consist?

The Perfect Good, Nature, and Synderesis

Among non-angelic creatures, man's nature alone is, properly speaking, made according to (*ad*) the image of God. This results from the kind of likeness to God he has in virtue of his immaterial soul. Because he has the ability to know and understand immaterial things—the intellect being ordered to the universal true, and the will to the universal good, as object—he is capable of the highest good (*capax summi boni*).[106] The question that arises, of course, is what the highest good is exactly. Aquinas often says the perfect good is happiness,[107] but that will not get us very far if we do not know that in which it consists. Nature and the reason that is founded upon it (i.e., the natural reason, "which is called synderesis"[108]) at least provide the foundation for discerning this.

For Thomas, natural reason ensures that men assent to the good.[109] Owing to the fact that it is natural, it is necessarily a permanent principle. He explains in *De veritate*:

> Nature intends the good in all of its works in addition to the conservation of those things that come about through its works. Therefore, in all of nature's works, the principles are permanent and unchangeable and preservative of right order because it is necessary for the principles to remain. . . . In order for there to be rectitude in human actions, there must be some permanent principle which is immutably upright and that resists all evil and assents to every good so that all human works can be examined. And this is synderesis, whose duty [*officium*] it is to warn against evil and to incline to the good.[110]

---

[106] See *ST* I, q. 93, a. 2.

[107] See, for instance: *ST* I-II, q. 2, a. 2, corp.; q. 13, a. 6.

[108] *ST* II-II, q. 47, a. 6, ad 1: "ratio naturalis, quae dicitur synderesis."

[109] *De veritate*, q. 16, a. 2, corp.: "That permanent principle resists all evil and assents to every good. And this is synderesis."

[110] *De veritate*, q. 16, a. 2, corp.: "Natura in omnibus suis operibus bonum intendit, et conservationem eorum quae per operationem naturae fiunt; et ideo in omnibus naturae operibus semper principia sunt permanentia et immutabilia, et rectitudinem conservantia . . . in operibus humanis, ad hoc quod aliqua rectitudo in eis esse possit, oportet esse aliquod principium permanens, quod rectitudinem immutabilem habeat, ad quod omnia humana opera examinentur; ita quod illud principium permanens omni malo resistat, et omni bono assentiat. Et haec est synderesis, cuius officium est remurmurare malo, et inclinare ad bonum." See also *ST* I, q. 79, a. 12, corp.: "Synderesis is said to incite to good."

Thanks to the "imprint on us of the Divine light,"[111] human nature itself has been given a capacity that makes it cognizant of the perfect good that the will necessarily moves toward once the reason has presented it.[112] When referring respectively to the most natural cognitive and appetitive movements in man, Thomas sometimes employs Damascene's terms "reason as nature" (*ratio ut natura*) and "will as nature" (*voluntas ut natura* or *thelēsis*[113]). The former apprehends common goods and ensures that people will naturally perceive absolutely good things. "Reason as nature" is not used in *ST*, but as Martin Rhonheimer notes, even though it

> is seldom used (four times in *Super sent.* and three in *De veritate*) and never occurs in the *Summa theologiae*, . . . it would perfectly fit with *voluntas ut natura* in the sense of what is "naturally known" by the intellect and, therefore, becoming "naturally desired" by the will.[114]

Thomas explains that the *voluntas ut natura* follows the judgment of reason in regard to an indemonstrably known principle of practical activity that

---

[111] *ST* I-II, q. 91, a. 2, corp.: "Lumen rationis naturalis, quo discernimus quid sit bonum, et quid malum, quod pertinet ad naturalem legem, nihil aliud sit, quam impressio divini luminis in nobis" ("the light of natural reason, whereby we discern what is good and what is evil, which is the function of the natural law, is nothing else than an imprint on us of the Divine light").

[112] *ST* I-II, q. 10, a. 2, ad 3: "The last end necessarily moves the will (because it is the perfect good) and, similarly, those things that are ordered to this end as requisite for attaining it, such as 'to be' and 'to live' and things of this sort." I added the clause about reason necessarily first presenting the perfect good to the will because the will only follows that which has been apprehended intellectually. As *ST* I, q. 87, a. 4, corp. says, "an act of the will is nothing other than an inclination following an understood form."

[113] *ST* III, q. 18, a. 3, corp.: "There is one *ratio* for the act of the will inasmuch as it is carried toward something that is willed of itself, as health. This is called thelēsis (that is, 'simple will') by Damascene and 'will as nature' by the masters. There is another *ratio* for the act of the will inasmuch as it is carried toward something that is willed only due to its order toward something else, such as the taking of medicine. This act of the will Damascene calls boulēsis (that is, an advising will), but is called 'will as reason' by the masters." See, In IV sent., dist. 17, q. 1, a. 1, qc 3, ad 1. Thomas also speaks of the will as a kind of nature in *ST* I., q. 41, a. 2, ad 3: "Voluntas, inquantum est natura quaedam, aliquid naturaliter vult; sicut voluntas hominis naturaliter tendit ad beatitudinem."

[114] Martin Rhonheimer, "Nature as Reason: A Thomistic Theory of the Natural Law," *Studies in Christian Ethics* 19, no. 3 (2006): 357–78, at 363.

has the role of a final cause [*se habet per modum finis*] because in doable things, the end has the place of the beginning, as it says in the sixth book of the *Ethics*. Therefore, that which is the end of man is naturally known in the reason to be good and to be sought out [*appetendum*] and the will following this knowledge is called the will as nature.[115]

This end of man that is naturally known, therefore, is consequently naturally desired, since there is nothing about it that is imperfectly good; since the object of the will is the good defined by reason,[116] the will necessarily is drawn to an end that is good in all respects. As Thomas words it in the *ST* I-II, the will of man is "not able not to will" the perfect good precisely because it is that "which lacks nothing."[117] One might wonder how the will, which is called the "master of its own acts" and is "open to opposites,"[118] could *necessarily* be drawn toward the end that is naturally known. Thomas replies that it is only when we speak of the "will as nature" that this is the case and that the necessity that "is present in the voluntary appetite with respect to the end" does not necessitate necessity in regard to the means.[119]

It is only natural and good for us to follow our reason and let it guide us regarding the end which Thomas spoke of as the "end which has the place of the beginning" and which is sometimes explained as the "perfect and final good."[120] Because we are rational creatures, we are ordered toward

---

[115] *In II sent.*, dist. 39, q. 2, a. 2, ad 2: "Voluntas ut ... natura ... sequitur judicium rationis: quia in ratione est aliquid naturaliter cognitum quasi principium indemonstrabile in operabilibus, quod se habet per modum finis, quia in operabilibus finis habet locum principii, ut in 6 Ethic. dicitur. Unde illud quod finis est hominis, est naturaliter in ratione cognitum esse bonum et appetendum, et voluntas consequens istam cognitionem dicitur voluntas ut natura."

[116] See *ST* I-II, q. 77, a. 1, obj. 1 and ad 1.

[117] See *ST* I-II, q. 10, a. 2, corp.

[118] *De veritate*, q. 22, a. 5, ad sc 5: "The will, inasmuch as it is rational, is open [literally 'related to'] to opposites. Now, this is to consider it according to that which is proper to it, but inasmuch as it is a certain kind of nature, nothing prohibits it from being determined to one thing." See also *De veritate*, q. 22, a. 5, ad sc 7: "What is proper to the will ... is that it be the master of its own acts."

[119] See *De veritate*, q. 22, a. 6, ad 4 and the previous note (118).

[120] See *ST* I-II, q. 5, a. 8, ad 2. As is explained in that reply, everyone naturally desires the "general *ratio* of happiness," which is understood by all to be the "final and perfect good." Not everyone knows that it consists in the beatific vision, but the distinction between the beatific vision and the perfect good is not a real distinction, but only a logical one (*secundum rationis considerationem*).

happiness necessarily because our reason is unable to see the perfect and final good in a negative way. Once it is perceived as perfect and final, we want it, and it is beneficial for us that we want it precisely because it is perfective of us—and all men naturally desire perfection[121] just as "every imperfect thing" in general tends to perfection.[122]

Given that nature is that whereby this natural inclination arises, one might think the perfect good should be sought in nature. After all, Aquinas oft repeats Aristotle's adage that "nature does nothing in vain,"[123] so it would seem that, by simply lending an ear to nature and heeding its promptings, one would attain the perfect good.[124] The essence of nature itself is that it is the "intrinsic principle of motion" in things;[125] why not, then, simply allow it to tend where it wills? Is it not supremely virtuous to simply be natural, since God himself imprinted his light upon our natural reason? In support of this conclusion, one could cite the great doctor of the Church Saint John Damascene, for whom "the virtues are natural qualities, and are implanted in all by nature and in equal measure."[126] In commenting upon this quote, Thomas affirms that natural things are never eradicated,[127] and he goes on to say nature disposes man to attain a kind of happiness through his own natural powers ("ad quamdam felicitatem ... homo natus est acquirere per propria naturalia"[128]). For this reason, the option of entrusting one's happiness to the natural inclinations (at least inasmuch as God is the author of them) is worthy of consideration.

Aquinas explains man's natural aptitude to the perfection that is found in virtue by relating this aptitude to the three subjects of virtue—namely, the intellect, the will, and the lower appetite. Although the intellect can

---

[121] See: *ST* I-II, q. 84, a. 4, corp.; I, q. 5, a. 1, corp.

[122] *ST* I-II, q. 16, a. 4, corp.: "omne autem imperfectum tendit in perfectionem." *SCG* IV, ch. 79: "Imperfect things naturally strive to attain perfection."

[123] As in *SCG* III, ch. 48: "The natural desire cannot be void because *nature does nothing in vain*." Aristotle's original is: *outhen matēn hē physis poiei* (*Politics* 1.2.1253a9).

[124] As Heraclitus said, "wisdom is ... to act according to nature, giving ear thereto" (*sophiē alēthea legein kai poiein kata physin epaiontas*; from Fragmentum B 112 in *Fragmente der Vorsokratiker*, ed. Hermann Diels [Berlin: Weidmann, 1903]; translation my own).

[125] *ST* III, q. 2, a. 1, corp.: "[Nature is] the intrinsic principle of motion, as is indicated by the Philosopher in *Physics* II, where he says that 'nature is the principle of motion in that in which it is *per se* and not by accident.'"

[126] "The virtues are natural powers" is a translation of *physikai men gar eisiv hai aretai* (see John Damascene, *De fide orthodoxa* 3.14, trans. S. D. F. Salmond in *NPNF*2, 9:60). See also Cicero's *De legibus* 1.

[127] See *De virtutibus*, q. 1, a. 8, obj. 1 and ad 1.

[128] *De virtutibus*, q. 1, a. 9, ad 7.

be divided into the active and the passive intellect, it is considered one subject of virtue. The second is the rational appetite known as the will, and the third is that which is sometimes called the "lower appetite," even though, like the intellect, it can be divided into two (in this case, into the irascible and concupiscible appetites). He elaborates:

> In the intellective part, there is [1] the possible intellect, which is in ability for all understandable things (in the knowledge of which intellectual virtue consists), and [2] the agent intellect, in whose light things become understandable in act. Immediately and without any study or inquiry [*inquisitio*], such things are naturally made known to man from the beginning. The first principles are about such things—not only regarding speculative matters (such as "the whole is greater than its part" and like things), but also regarding practical [*operativus*] ones (such as "evil ought to be avoided" and such things). Now these naturally known things are the principles of all the following knowledge—whether practical or speculative—that is acquired by study.
>
> It is similarly manifest in regards to the will that there is some first natural principle that is active. For the will is naturally inclined toward the ultimate end. But the end in practical things has the notion of a natural principle. Therefore, the inclination of the will is a certain active principle in respect to every disposition that is acquired through exercise in the affective part. For it is manifest that the will itself, inasmuch as it is a power related in different ways [*utrumlibet se habens*] to the means [*quae sunt ad finem*], is susceptible of a habitual inclination into this or that.
>
> Now, the irascible and the concupiscible are naturally able to obey reason and are, therefore, naturally susceptive of virtue, which is brought to perfection in them to the degree they are disposed to follow the good of the reason.
>
> All the aforementioned beginnings of the virtues follow upon the nature of the human species and are, therefore, common to everyone.[129]

The agent intellect is the principle of the subject of natural virtue[130]—

---

[129] *De virtutibus*, q. 1, a. 8, corp.

[130] In *De veritate*, q. 16, a. 1, ad 13, Thomas says the agent intellect, which is that whereby

which kind of virtue can pertain to either speculative notions that have no immediate import for practical matters or practical ones that more directly pertain to practical activity. In either case, the first naturally known principles are the foundation of all the knowledge that results from them. Similarly, the will is necessarily ordered toward the ultimate end, but anything that is a means toward this end (and is thus anything that is a kind of application of that end to something particular) is able to vary; as a consequence, an inclination that follows upon the natural will is necessary if someone is to be habitually inclined regarding certain particular goods. There thus arises the need for virtues in the sensitive appetites as well. These appetites are apt to obey the reason, but need to be continually guided in that direction. In other words, they need to be habituated to obey reason. Aquinas, continuing his explanation of the natural seeds of virtue, elaborates:

> All of the aforementioned beginnings of the virtues follow upon the nature of the human species and are, therefore, common to all. Now there is a certain beginning of virtue, which is attendant upon the nature of the individual inasmuch as some man is inclined by either his natural disposition [*complexione*] or celestial influence [*caelesti impressione*] to an act of some virtue. And this inclination is, indeed, a kind of beginning of virtue, but it is not a perfected virtue, because a perfected virtue requires the moderation that comes from the reason. Accordingly, reason is placed in the definition of virtue because virtue is something pertaining to choice of means according to right reason.[131] For if someone would follow an inclination of this sort without discretion, he would frequently sin. And just as, if this beginning of virtue were devoid of reason's activity, it would not have the

---

the intelligible in potency becomes intelligible in act, is not the subject of habits (and thus it is not the subject of virtues) and adds that the possible intellect has this role. We must, therefore, call the agent intellect the principle/foundation of the subject of virtue and not the subject of virtue *simpliciter*.

[131] This is Aristotle's definition, which says in its complete form, "Virtue, then, is a habit [*hexis*], resulting from choice [*proairetikē*], lying in the middle [of two extremes] relative to us and determined by reason as a prudent man would determine it [*hē aretē hexis proairetikē, en mesotēti ousa tē pros hēmas, hōrisomenē logō kai hō an ho phronimos horiseien*]" (*Nicomachean Ethics* 2.6.1107a1, Greek ed. J. Bywater [Medford, MA: Perseus Digital Library, 1894]). The Latin of Thomas reads, "Quod est electiva medii secundum rationem rectam."

ratio of perfected virtue, so neither would any of the other aforementioned beginnings of virtue. For one arrives at that which is specific [by proceeding from] universal principles by means of reason's examination [*inquisitionem*]. It is also by means of reason's official duty that a man is led from the appetite of the last end toward those things that are befitting that end. By commanding the irascible and concupiscible appetites, reason also makes them subject to itself. So it is manifest that the work of reason is required for the consummation of virtue; whether the virtue be in the intellect, or in the will, or in the irascible or concupiscible appetite. It is, then, clear from this that the reason, which is superior, works for the completion of every virtue. For the operative principle which is reason is different from [*dividitur contra*] the operative principle which is nature (as is clear in the second book of the *Physics*) because the rational power relates to opposites whereas nature is ordered to one. It is obvious, then, that the perfection of virtue is not from nature, but from reason.[132]

We can see in this quote from this first question of *De virtutibus* something similar to what he says in *ST* about the importance of the examination or inquiry (*inquisitionem*) of reason. Though there is a natural inclination to virtue in man precisely because he has a natural disposition to perform acts

---

[132] *De virtutibus*, q. 1, a. 8, corp.: "Et omnes praedictae inchoationes virtutum consequuntur naturam speciei humanae unde et omnibus sunt communes. Est autem aliqua inchoatio virtutis, quae consequitur naturam individui, secundum quod aliquis homo ex naturali complexione vel caelesti impressione inclinatur ad actum alicuius virtutis. Et haec quidem inclinatio est quaedam virtutis inchoatio; non tamen est virtus perfecta; quia ad virtutem perfectam requiritur moderatio rationis: unde et in definitione virtutis ponitur, quod est electiva medii secundum rationem rectam. Si enim aliquis absque rationis discretione inclinationem huiusmodi sequeretur, frequenter peccaret. Et sicut haec virtutis inchoatio absque rationis opere, perfectae virtutis rationem non habet, ita nec aliqua praemissarum. Nam ex universalibus principiis in specialia pervenitur per inquisitionem rationis. Rationis etiam officio ex appetitu ultimi finis homo deducitur in ea quae sunt convenientia illi fini. Ipsa etiam ratio imperando irascibilem et concupiscibilem facit sibi esse subiectas. Unde manifestum est quod ad consummationem virtutis requiritur opus rationis; sive virtus sit in intellectu, sive sit in voluntate, sive in irascibili et concupiscibili . . . Unde etiam manifestum est, quod ratio, quae est superior, operatur ad completionem omnis virtutis. Dividitur autem principium operativum quod est ratio, contra principium operativum quod est natura, ut patet in II Phys.; eo quod rationalis potestas est ad opposita, natura autem ordinatur ad unum. Unde manifestum est quod perfectio virtutis non est a natura, sed a ratione."

that are consonant with his rational form, "many actions are made to come about in accordance with virtue" precisely because reason's inquiry makes them come about.[133]

The guiding influence of reason, of course, is made possible by the virtue of prudence, which is placed in the definition of moral virtue as the intellectual virtue that "directs all the [moral] virtues."[134] Without its moderating influence, the moral virtues (or, rather, the inclinations which have potencies of becoming moral virtues and which are present in the will or the lower appetites) would not be perfected[135] virtues, because "moral virtue has the *ratio* of virtue only to the degree it participates in intellectual virtue."[136] Aquinas goes so far as to suggest prudence is "in a certain measure an efficient cause" of moral virtue.[137] The importance of prudence to perform its "official duty" of leading man "from the appetite of the last end toward those things that are befitting that end"[138] is evident in another section of the first question of *De virtutibus*:

> The comment of Cicero ["virtue . . . acts in the manner of nature; "virtus . . . agit in modum naturae"] is understood in regard to the inclination of the appetite tending toward some common good, such as acting courageously or something of the sort. But unless it be directed by the judgment of reason, such an inclination would frequently be led to a precipice and all the more so to the degree it is more vehement; as the example the Philosopher gives in the sixth book of the *Ethics* about the blind person who gets injured yet more when running into a wall if he is a fast runner.[139]

---

[133] *ST* I-II, q. 94, a. 3, corp.

[134] *ST* I-II, q. 58, a. 2, ad 4.

[135] By translating "perfectae virtutis rationem non habet" (in *De virtutibus*, q. 1, a. 8) as "it would not have the *ratio* of perfect virtue," I may have made it sound as if a natural inclination would be a virtue without prudence, but in the strict sense, a moral virtue must make the one possessing it good and natural inclination does not ensure this.

[136] *ST* II-II, q. 47, a. 5, ad 1.

[137] *De virtutibus*, q. 1, a. 12, ad 16: "The 'right reason' of prudence is not placed in the definition of moral virtue as something existing from its essence. It is, rather, in a certain measure an efficient [*effectiva*] cause of it." Similarly, he says in replying to the second objection of article six: prudentia . . . non parum sed multum confert ad virtutem; immo ipsam virtutem causat."

[138] *De virtutibus*, q. 1, a. 8.

[139] *De virtutibus*, q. 1, a. 6, ad 4: "Ad quartum dicendum, quod verbum Tullii intelligitur quantum ad inclinationem appetitus tendentis in aliquod bonum commune, sicut in fortiter agere, vel aliquid huiusmodi. Sed nisi rationis iudicio dirigeretur, talis

In a sense, the "right reason about contingent things"[140] that is prudence transcends nature even prescinding from the question of whether or not it is infused prudence (which is, strictly speaking, the only true prudence[141]). This explains the notion that "the operative principle which is reason is different from the operative principle which is nature" that we saw above.[142] Prudence goes beyond the natural reason precisely because it is able to order one thing to another by a process of ratiocination in virtue of what is sometimes called "reason as reason," which is explained as follows in *De veritate*:

> "Reason as nature" is understood to refer to the reason being compared to those things one naturally knows or desires, whereas "reason as reason" is understood to refer to the reason inasmuch as it is ordered to knowing or desiring [something] since it is the proper function of the reason to make a comparison. Now there are certain things that when considered in themselves ought to be shunned and yet are desired due to the way they are ordered to something else: as hunger and thirst are to be shunned when considered in themselves and yet they are desired to the extent they are considered as useful for the health of the soul or the body. And thus "reason as reason" rejoices in them whereas "reason as nature" is saddened by them.[143]

---

inclinatio frequenter duceretur in praecipitium; et tanto magis, quanto esset vehementior; sicut ponit philosophus exemplum de caeco, in VI Ethic., qui tanto magis laeditur ad parietem impingens, quanto fortius currit." Inclinations to virtue do not become perfect or true virtues until prudence is present.

[140] *In* III *de an.*, lec. 4, no. 16; *ST* I, q. 22, a. 2, obj. 1.

[141] *ST* I-II, q. 65, a. 2, corp.: "The moral virtues, inasmuch as they pertain to good works that are ordered to an end that does not surpass the natural power of man, are able to be acquired by human works. In this way, the acquired virtues are able to be without charity as was the case for many gentiles. However, inasmuch as they pertain to good works that are ordered to the ultimate supernatural end, they perfectly and truly have the character of virtue and are not able to be acquired by human acts, but are infused by God."

[142] See *De virtutibus*, q. 1, a. 8. Of course, "nature" here is being taken in a restrictive sense (i.e., in regard to inclinations) in order to distinguish reason from nature inasmuch as reason transcends inclinations. Strictly speaking, though, reason pertains to man's nature as well. For this reason, Thomas divides them (at least to my knowledge) only when making this particular distinction.

[143] *De veritate*, q. 26, a. 9, ad 7: "Dicamus rationem ut naturam intelligi secundum quod ratio comparatur ad ea quae naturaliter cognoscit vel appetit; rationem vero ut rationem, secundum quod per quamdam collationem ordinatur ad aliquid cognoscendum vel appetendum, eo quod rationis est proprium conferre. Sunt enim quaedam quae

Because prudence is able to reason properly in the sense that it is not limited to natural impulses, it can ensure the appetites are not "led to a precipice" while rushing headlong. At the same time, when it performs the duty that is proper to it (i.e., the ordering of "contingent future things, inasmuch as they are orderable by man to the end of human life"), it does so while presupposing "certain things that are necessary on account of the end and which are subjected to divine providence" qua absolutely necessary.[144] Those things that are necessary on account of the ultimate end, though, are things pertaining to the natural law which is so close to the eternal law in which it participates that it is not "something different" from it according to Thomas.[145] For this reason, it must be said that, as important as prudence is in applying first principles and rectifying appetites, the starting point[146] of its process of reasoning "as reason" is the natural reason, which retains a kind of primacy because "all dialectical reasoning [*omnis ratiocinatio*] is derived from the principles that are naturally known."[147] According to the analysis provided by Aquinas in *ST* II-II, q. 47, prudence (which, again, is "right reason about contingent matters"[148] or "right reason about doable things"[149]) tends to the end appointed (*praestitutum*) by the natural reason, and thus is moved by it just as the habit of knowledge is moved by the understanding (i.e., the intellectual virtue pertaining to speculative principles).[150] Though we need to return to this central question, as he seemed to argue otherwise in *ST* I-II, q. 66, he says something similar in *ST* I: "Although our intellect acts on its own in regard to some things, others are appointed in advance [*praestituta*] by nature, as are the first principles to which everyone has a necessary

---

secundum se considerata sunt fugienda, appetuntur vero secundum ordinem ad aliud: sicut fames et sitis secundum se considerata sunt fugienda; prout autem considerantur ut utilia ad salutem animae vel corporis, sic appetuntur. Et sic ratio ut ratio de eis gaudet, ratio vero ut natura de eis tristatur."

[144] See *ST* II-II, q. 49, a. 6, corp.

[145] See *ST* I-II, q. 91, a. 2, ad 1.

[146] At least if God and nature itself are left out of the consideration.

[147] *ST* I-II, q. 91, a. 2, ad 2: "Omnis ratiocinatio derivatur a principiis naturaliter notis."

[148] *In* III *de an.*, lec. 4, no. 16; *ST* I, q. 22, a. 2, obj. 1.

[149] See: *ST* II-II, q. 47, a. 2, sc; q. 47, a. 8, corp.: *Quolibet* XII, q. 15, corp.

[150] *ST* II-II, q. 47, a. 6, ad 3: "The end does not pertain to the moral virtues as if they themselves appoint the end, but because they tend to the end appointed by the natural reason, to which they are helped by prudence, which prepares the way for them by disposing the means. For this reason, it follows that prudence is more noble than the moral virtues and moves them. But synderesis moves prudence, as the understanding of principles moves the virtue of knowledge [*scientia*]."

relationship [*circa quae non potest aliter se habere*] and also the last end, which one is not able not to will."[151]

We might tend to think that, if God wanted us to be truly perfect, we should have the ability to think as we wish about any given thing without being limited by nature, but for Aquinas, a kind of natural habit or virtue[152] is indispensable. Even God himself, who necessarily acts in accord with his own infinite goodness, cannot will something impossible and is able to will only things that are (or are able to be) good.[153] So we should not be surprised if rational creatures are also called to conform themselves to the good even if it excludes that which is not good. One of the ways he shows this is by observing that the natural inclination of anything at all is for its own operation. Just as something warm such as fire naturally inclines to heating something else and something heavy naturally inclines to descending, man naturally inclines to the operation that is proper to him as a man—namely to understand.[154] The act of understanding is good for man as one of those things providentially necessary for the ultimate end, so whatever the perfect good is for humans, it must at least be founded upon this connatural good. Aquinas elaborates:

> The nature of any given thing is chiefly the form from which the species of the thing is derived. Now man is established in his species through his rational soul. Therefore, whatever is contrary to the order of the reason is properly contrary to man's nature

---

[151] *ST* q. 1, a. 3, corp.: "Sed quamvis intellectus noster ad aliqua se agat, tamen aliqua sunt ei praestituta a natura; sicut sunt prima principia, circa quae non potest aliter se habere, et ultimus finis, quem non potest non velle."

[152] "Virtue" is used equivocally in Thomas. On many levels, a natural virtue would be not virtue at all. This would be the case whether it were divided against acquired or infused virtue (the three kinds of habit enumerated in *In* III *sent.*, dist. 33, q. 2, a. 4, qc 4, corp., are natural, acquired and infused). At the same time, "virtus" essentially means "power" and natural virtue is a kind of power; moreover, it adds to the notion of "disposition" that it is firm and habitual, and thus on this level, even something natural can be considered a virtue (the definition of virtue in §1803 of the *Catechism of the Catholic Church* is precisely that it is "an habitual and firm disposition to do the good").

[153] *SCG* I, ch. 84, no. 5: "As a thing is related to being, it is related to goodness. But impossible things are those which are not able to be. Therefore, they are not able to be good. Therefore they are not willed by God, who does not will anything but those things that are, or are able to be, good."

[154] *In* I *metaphys.*, lec. 1, no. 3: "Everything has a natural inclination to it proper act: as heat for heating and something heavy for going downward. But man's proper act, inasmuch as he is man, is to understand."

inasmuch as he is a man [i.e., inasmuch as he is not just an animal, but a rational one] while that which is in accord with reason is in accordance with man's nature, inasmuch as he is a man. Now, the good of man is to be in accord with reason and his evil is to place himself beyond reason's reach [*est praeter rationem esse*],[155] . . . wherefore, human virtue, which makes a man good and renders his work good, is in accordance with the nature of man insofar as it accords with his reason.[156]

It is through the operation of understanding that man differs from other animals, because his form, which is the principle of his action, is rational, and thus has an end appointed to it by God that befits its rationality.[157] As a consequence, the desire of man naturally inclines toward intellectual activity[158] and toward acting "according to reason—and this is to

---

[155] Although *praeter* could possibly be translated as "against," it usually signifies being beyond in some way. It is bad for man to act outside of reason's reach if he does so intentionally (as Thomas teaches when speaking about consequent ignorance) just as it is bad to act directly against the judgment of reason known as conscience (see, *De veritate*, q. 17, a. 1, ad 4). I have also rendered *praeter* in this way in view of the fact that man appoints to himself the end, albeit while presupposing his natural ordering to the common end, which is the perfect good. If a man were beyond reason's reach unintentionally (such as by scratching himself without deliberating about it), it would not be an evil act, as Aquinas explicitly says in *ST* I-II, q. 18, a. 9, corp. He must, therefore, be referring here to an act that is intentionally beyond reason's reach in some way.

[156] *ST* I-II, q. 71, a. 2, corp.: "Natura uniuscujusque rei potissime est forma, secundum quam res speciem sortitur: homo autem in specie constituitur per animam rationalem; et ideo id, quod est contra ordinem rationis, proprie est contra naturam hominis, inquantum est homo: quod autem est secundum rationem, est secundum naturam hominis, inquantum est homo: bonum autem hominis est secundum rationem esse, et malum hominis est praeter rationem esse, ut Dionys. dicit 4. cap. *de Div. Nom.* (pt. 4. lec. 22.); unde virtus humana, quae hominem facit bonum, et opus ipsius bonum reddit, intantum est secundum naturam hominis, inquantum convenit rationi: vitium autem intantum est contra naturam hominis, quantum est contra ordinem rationis." See Oderberg's discussion of this passage, including John Finnis's take on it, in "The Metaphysical Foundation of Natural Law," in *Natural Moral Law in Contemporary Society* (Washington, DC: Catholic University of America Press, 2010): 44–75, at 70.

[157] *ST* II-II, q. 23, a. 2, corp.

[158] *In* I *metaphys.*, lec. 1, no. 3 (see note 154 above). See also *ST* I, q. 62, a. 2, corp.: "The natural inclination of the will is for that which is fitting according to nature." The consequence of this principle is that, since that which essentially distinguishes humans from other animals within the genus of "animal" is that they are rational (in other words, since reason is the specific difference), humans have a natural volitional inclination to follow the dictates of reason.

act according to virtue."[159] This natural desire to live in accordance with reason is, for Thomas, so strong that the human will naturally inclines to ends that are possessed in the practical reason by the natural habit of synderesis:

> There is not able to be a moral virtue in the will in regard to the end [*ex parte illa qua est de fine*] because the end is the principle in practical activities [*operativis*[160]]. Therefore, just as there are innate principles of demonstrations in the speculative reason, so in the practical reason there are innate ends that are connatural to man. Thus, there is no acquired or infused habit about these ends, but only natural, as synderesis—which Aristotle posits to be the understanding of practical affairs.[161]

Aquinas goes on to say the natural desire for the end can be understood in terms of a natural agreement (*communicatio*) by which "it comes about that the appetite, naturally joined to the reason, tends to conform itself to the reason as to a rule[162]—and from this the will is naturally inclined to the end, which is naturally implanted in the reason."[163]

---

[159] *ST* I-II, q. 94, a. 3, corp.

[160] See Deferrari, Barry, and McGuiness, *Lexicon of Saint Thomas Aquinas*, 772 (s.v. *operativis*): "*belonging to* or *concerning the operative* and *the active*, the opposite of *speculativus* and *theoricus*."

[161] *In III sent.*, dist. 33, q. 2, a. 4, qc 4, corp.: "Sicut in voluntate non potest esse virtus moralis ex parte illa qua est finis, propter naturalem inclinationem, ita etiam nec in ratione ex parte illa qua est de fine, quia finis est principium in operativis. Unde sicut in ratione speculativa sunt innata principia demonstrationum, ita in ratione practica sunt innati fines connaturales homini; unde circa illa non est habitus acquisitus aut infusus, sed naturalis, sicut synderesis, loco cujus philosophus in 6 Ethic. ponit intellectum in operativis."

[162] That reason is the rule of the will is also evident from the following: *ST* I-II, q. 19, a. 4, corp. ("Human reason is the rule of the human will and that from which its goodness is measured"); q. 64, a. 1, corp. ("The measure and the rule of the appetitive motion regarding desirable things is reason itself"); q. 90, a. 1, corp. ("The rule and measure of human acts is reason, which is the first principle of human acts").

[163] *In III sent.*, dist. 33, q. 2, a. 4, qc 4, corp.: "Naturalis inclinatio ad finem aliquem est ex praestituente naturam, qui talem ordinem naturae tribuit [The natural inclination to some end is from the appointing of nature, which assigns . . . order to nature]; ideo naturalis inclinatio voluntatis ad finem non est ex ratione, nisi forte secundum naturalem communicantiam, qua fit ut appetitus rationi conjunctus naturaliter tendat ad conformandum se rationi sicut regulae; et ex hoc est quod voluntas est naturaliter inclinata ad finem, qui naturaliter rationi est inditus." This might make it seem as if justice, which

So, is it possible to locate the perfect good in nature or natural reason? There are actually many reasons why the perfect good of happiness cannot be attained by simply allowing nature to run its course and acting "naturally" on the pretext that nature does nothing in vain (and will thus surely lead to perfection). One reason is that the natural reason is not specific enough to lead a person to do what is perfectly good for him in the present moment and that a man consequently needs the ratiocination of prudence to guide him toward enacting its norms in a virtuous manner. Though Aquinas speaks of "certain natural virtues" which provide some men and women with the ability to make correct judgments in regard to particular right ends (*rectos fines*), he insists the knowledge of the means toward those ends is something that can be in no one naturally. For this reason, prudence is necessary in matters of particular, practical actions.[164]

A further reason why the perfect good cannot be found in human nature itself is provided by Thomas de Vio Cajetan, who argues that the consequence of the human person being composed of both a sensitive part and a rational part in his very nature (*in puris naturalibus*) is that it is impossible for him not at some time to turn inordinately more to one of those contraries than another.[165] Or, as Thomas himself said, "man is composed from contraries in regard to . . . the appetite of the sense [the sensitive appetites, whether irascible or concupiscible] and the appetite of the intellect [the will]."[166] Necessarily, therefore, one must always exercise vigilance and cultivate habits of true virtue while transcending, in a sense, the merely natural habit of either synderesis or some other natural "virtue." Otherwise, he will not be able to know and pursue the ends that are truly best suited to the dignity of his rational nature. Even while presupposing moral virtues, Thomas speaks of the need of prudence's guidance so that he may do so:

> Moral virtue intends to attain the mean by way of nature. But because the mean as such is not found in the same way in everyone, it follows that the inclination of nature, which always works in the same way, does not suffice for this purpose, but requires the ruling [*ratio*] of prudence.[167]

---

is in the will, is not an acquired virtue, but even in the *Scriptum*, he speaks of aquired justice as contrasted with infused justice (*In* III *sent.*, dist. 40, q. 1, a. 3; cf. *De veritate*, q. 28, a. 3, and *ST* I-II, q. 100, a. 12).

[164] See *ST* II-II, q. 47, a. 15, corp.
[165] See the Leonine edition's commentary on *ST* I-II, q. 109, a. 2 (9:292).
[166] *In* IV *sent.*, dist. 4, q. 2, a. 1, qc 3, corp.
[167] *ST* II-II, q. 47, a. 7, ad 3: "Virtus moralis per modum naturae intendit pervenire ad

At the end of the present chapter, we will see that original sin altered the moral landscape such that man needed healing grace to do even things that are connatural to his nature.[168] Even "the natural reason was beclouded by the lusts of sin."[169] Prescinding from this consideration, though, it seems there is a tension in nature itself between the reason and the appetites, for as Cajetan says, intellectual goods and bodily ones do not always align.[170] For example, someone may need to direct his attention toward procuring food even when doing so would hamper the apprehension of universal truth—or vice versa. In either case, the individual could be excessively drawn in one direction when he should be pursuing the other. Although Adam enjoyed the praeternatural gift of integrity, this is not something man enjoys in virtue of nature itself. Reason, then, must exercise some kind of rule over all the person's actions.

Though the truths made known by the *natural* reason[171] are indispensable, habits of virtue also have to be developed in man due to the deliberative reason. Such is both the burden and the dignity of humans. They partake more perfectly in divine providence (which is a *ratio* existing in the divine Mind[172]) by being providential over themselves and others thanks to their possession of reason. Because they have foresight in virtue of the faculty of reason, they are able not only to appoint for themselves (*praestituunt*) ends that are implanted in them by nature, but to rise above mere instinct and pursue ends that "they themselves appoint," and that is what sets them apart from irrational animals.[173] As Shakespeare's Hamlet says:

> What is a man
> If his chief good and market of his time

---

medium. Sed quia medium, secundum quod medium, non eodem modo invenitur in omnibus; ideo inclinatio naturae, quae semper eodem modo operatur, ad hoc non sufficit, sed requiritur ratio prudentiae."

[168] See, *ST* I-II, q. 109, a. 3, corp.

[169] See *ST* I, q. 22, a. 1, ad 1.

[170] See the Leonine edition's commentary on *ST* I-II, q. 109, a. 2 (sect. IV). This, for him, would even be the case in the state of pure nature: "In [a state of] purely natural endowments, the sensitive and the rational appetites are at odds when the sensitive appetite is not fully subjected to the rational appetite but instead is free, at times tending to its private good apart from the order of reason."

[171] In the precise sense articulated above—more widely, we speak of "natural reason" as encompassing both senses.

[172] See *ST* I, q. 22, a. 1, where providence is called a *ratio ordinandum in finem* that is *in mente divina*.

[173] See *ST* I-II, q. 18, a. 3, corp.

Be but to sleep and feed? a beast, no more.
Sure, He that hath made us with such large discourse,
Looking before and after, gave us not
That capability and godlike reason
To fust in us unus'd. (*Hamlet*, I.iv.33–39)

Reason (considered now as distinct from *intellectus* or synderesis) is discursive and not merely directed to one by a kind of simple apprehension. It pertains to an act of comparing two things (an act of composing and dividing) and to "particular doable things that are contingent," which means its judgment "has itself diversely to more than one [conclusion] and is not determined to one." It is, in a word, the very foundation of *liberum arbitrium*, the judgment that is frequently called "free will."[174] Thanks to reason, man is able to reflect upon his natural "inclinations to his proper acts and ends"[175] and the teleological order in which all creatures passively participate. In view of what he finds, he can act accordingly and attain the happiness that is proper to him as the rational animal we call "man."

The Perfect Good and Moral Virtue

As Long observes, happiness "is not merely subjective fulfillment, but the achievement of the good," by which is meant the "achievement of those ends that define a good life, and this is the work of a lifetime, a work requiring both practical and speculative virtue as authentically perfective of the person."[176] Happiness is not merely a feeling of satisfaction or joy. As the "common end of all the moral virtues,"[177] it implies, for wayfarers, the need to improve moral dispositions through repeated good actions. Though it may not be desired under this *ratio*, since the idea of expending energy is not always an attractive prospect, the perfect good in general always remains something we naturally desire.[178] Aquinas argues it can be

---

[174] For more on *liberum arbitrium* not being determined to one thing due to its relationship to reason's judgment regarding contingent matters, see *ST* I, q. 83, a. 1, corp. Note that most translations of that article render *liberum arbitrium* as "free will," although it would probably best be translated as "free judgment."

[175] See *ST* I-II, q. 91, a. 2, corp.

[176] Steven Long, *The Teleological Grammar of the Moral Act*, 2nd ed. (Naples, FL: Sapientia, 2015), 69.

[177] See *De malo*, q. 8, a. 1, ad 1.

[178] *ST* I-II, q. 5, a. 8, ad 2: "Since the will follows the apprehension of the intellect or reason; just as it happens that where there is no real distinction, there may be a distinction

demonstrated "by reason" (that is, by using philosophical arguments) that happiness is the reward of virtue, suggesting, first of all, that the idea is not an indemonstrable axiom, but also that virtue is not identical with happiness (even if it is so closely united with it that we might think it is). His argument in his letter to the King of Cyprus makes it clear he has in mind moral and not natural virtue:

> This is manifested by reason because it is implanted in the reason of everyone using it [*ratione utentium inditum*] that happiness is the reward of virtue. Now the virtue of anything whatsoever is described as that which makes the one having it good and renders his deed good.[179] Now, that which anyone strives to attain by acting well is that which is most deeply implanted in his desire. Now, this is to be happy, which no one is able to not will. That which makes man happy, then, is fittingly expected to be the reward of virtue.[180]

The desire of nature is to act well and attain virtue so as to attain complete fulfillment. Ironically, though, one in a sense has to transcend nature to do so. The primary way this is true, of course, is that supernatural grace must lead one to a supernatural end by supernatural means (which we will turn our attention to at the end of the chapter). The other way in which one must actually transcend nature in order to fulfill it is by submitting to the reason's guidance as to the means to the end(s) pointed out by the natural reason.

If the foundation of synderesis is presupposed, in other words, we must go further than that and apply those principles to particular situations,

---

according to the consideration of reason; so does it happen that one and the same thing is desired in one way, and not desired in another. So that happiness may be considered as the final and perfect good, which is the general notion of happiness: and thus the will naturally and of necessity tends thereto, as stated above. Again it can be considered under other special aspects, either on the part of the operation itself, or on the part of the operating power, or on the part of the object; and thus the will does not tend thereto of necessity" (Dominican Fathers trans.).

[179] Aquinas explains in *ST* I-II, q. 55, a. 4, that this refers to moral virtue.

[180] *De regno* I, ch. 9: "Hoc autem ratione manifestatur. Est enim mentibus omnium ratione utentium inditum, virtutis praemium beatitudinem esse. Virtus enim uniuscuiusque rei describitur, quae bonum facit habentem, et opus eius bonum reddit. Ad hoc autem quisque bene operando nititur pervenire, quod est maxime desiderio inditum; hoc autem est esse felicem, quod nullus potest non velle. Hoc igitur praemium virtutis convenienter expectatur quod hominem beatum facit."

which means its principles must be carried into individual actions. In a way, conscience does this, because conscience is a "certain application of the first law, namely of the common principles, to particular acts."[181] In the case of conscience, however, it applies those principles as if while speculating about them[182] and it arrives at conclusions based on the foundational principles of synderesis "indifferently;" in such a way that its dictate could be applicable in "the present or the past or the future."[183] Michel Therrien comments:

> An important implication presents itself in this text. Because it is speculative, the judgment of conscience acquires motive force only if we have recourse to it in our free decisions. The judgment of conscience is practical by extension, but does not have motive force, except insofar as we allow it to exercise a determinative influence on our free-decision. Right practical reasoning, therefore, always results from a decision to use and follow our conscience.[184]

In a sense, then, conscience is in potency in regard to a particular right action. When prudence engages in its act of applying the judgment of conscience to particular circumstances and commands some singular action,

---

[181] *In* II *sent.*, dist. 39, q. 3, a. 2, ad 3: "Conscience is not the first law, nor the first thing directing human actions, but is rather a certain application of the first law—namely, of common principles—to particular acts."

[182] *De veritate*, q. 17, a. 1, ad 4: "The judgment of conscience is different from that of free will because the judgment of conscience consists in knowledge alone, whereas the judgment of free will [*liberi arbitrii*] consists in the application of knowledge to desire and this judgment is the judgment of choice. And therefore it happens sometimes that the judgment of free will is perverted, but not the judgment of conscience—as when someone examines something that is incumbent upon him to do here and now and judges, still speculating through principles, that something is evil (as, for instance, to fornicate with this woman). But when he begins to apply [this judgment] to the act, many circumstances present themselves from all sides, as for instance, the pleasure of fornication. From such a consideration, the reason is bound by concupiscence so that its dictate might not break forth into choice. And thus someone errs in choosing, but not in conscience; rather, he acts against conscience and he is said to do this with an evil conscience inasmuch as the deed is not in keeping with the judgment made from knowledge."

[183] *In* II *sent.*, dist. 24, q. 2, a. 4, corp.: "The conclusion, which is that this adultery ought to be fled from, pertains to conscience—and indifferently, whether about the present or the past or the future."

[184] Michel Therrien, "Law, Liberty and Virtue: A Thomistic Defense for the Pedagogical Character of Law" (PhD diss., University of Fribourg, 2007), 54–55.

the command itself and the action that ensues as a consequence of it entail a further actualization or perfection of the potency. At this point, one would squarely be in the realm of the practical. We might then, with John Naus, consider the judgment of conscience to be *"secundum quid* speculative" or "*secundum quid* theoretical,"[185] inasmuch as it remains more remote from the actual practical act than prudence is (and especially prudence's act of commanding). It does still pertain to practical matters and it is only theoretical in a qualified way (*secundum quid*), but its judgment is not at the point of being applied in a fully distinct and practical way. Commenting on the aforementioned *De veritate* passage that spoke of conscience as speculating about principles, Naus writes:

> Reason is the specifying, directing, ordering faculty; ... prudence, it is true, will be vitiated at its roots if the will is not rectified towards the end by the moral virtues. But the will rectified by moral virtues will not move to a virtuous choice of a singular concrete action unless reason perfected by prudence applies the correct judgment of conscience to particular circumstances of persons, place and time.... The will rectified by moral virtues chooses what the practical reason prudently judges to be good for me here and now in light of what my conscience dictates.[186]

If someone is going to virtuously apply first principles that are naturally known to a tangible situation in such a way that the "perfect good" will actually begin to be approached, he or she will have to go beyond merely applying some principles to a deed in an abstract or *secundum quid* theoretical way (in the sense that it may or may not be done). In other words, the judgment of conscience will have to be chosen. As Michael Sherwin says, "the judgment of conscience . . . only concludes in knowledge, while the judgment of choice concludes in action," the action that results when "knowledge is applied to affection."[187]

If that which conscience dictates is to be chosen and enacted

---

[185] See John Naus, *The Nature of the Practical Intellect according to Saint Thomas Aquinas* (Rome: Libreria Editrice dell'Universita Gregoriana, 1959), 167, 189. He places prudence in the category of the "purely practical," and in regard to conscience, he actually leaves it open whether it is *secundum quid* speculative or *secundum quid* practical, but since he calls its judgment theoretical, it seems he would have placed it in the former category if pressed on the matter (he had it listed with a number of other faculties/acts/etc.).

[186] Naus, *Nature of the Practical Intellect*, 189.

[187] Sherwin, *By Knowledge and By Love*, 36.

virtuously, though, prudence is necessary, since "the right choice of the means pertains to prudence."[188] One could, of course, make a choice about what we might call the proximate ends proposed by the judgment of conscience without prudence, but because prudence presupposes the rightly ordered appetites of the moral virtues, it ensures the proper application of the principles of the natural reason all the way down to a particular act taking place here and now in a virtuous manner in view of the circumstances and dispositions of the acting person. Thomas says, "the praise of prudence consists not in the consideration only, but in the application to a deed [*ad opus*]."[189] Although conscience also applies principles to a deed (*ad opus*),[190] prudence seems to go even further than conscience, because it pertains to more than a kind of speculation about particular principles.[191]

The "perfection of virtue" requires being in accordance with right reason,[192] and since humans are composed of body and soul, their sensitive appetites also ought to be conformed to reason. Unlike the will, the irascible and concupiscible appetites are not in themselves rational appetites that naturally incline toward following the reason. Instead, they are merely *able* to obey (*obedibiles*) it.[193] Reason rules them only as free subjects that are not "wholly subject to command," and therefore Aquinas and Aristotle liken the sensitive appetites to free citizens living in a society under constitutional rule.[194] For this reason, virtuous habits that have been acquired by repeated acts (and are, therefore, not merely natural, since a habit is a *second* nature)

---

[188] *ST* II-II, q. 54, a. 2, corp.: "Electio autem recta eorum quae sunt ad finem, ad prudentiam pertinet."

[189] *ST* II-II, q. 47, a. 1, ad 3: "Laus prudentiae non consistit in sola consideratione, sed in applicatione ad opus, quod est finis practicae rationis."

[190] *Super Rom* 14, lec. 3: "Conscience applies that which we universally hold by faith . . . to a work that has been done or ought to be done."

[191] The example of the kind of principle that can be considered in a quasi-speculative mode by conscience given in the following pertains to not fornicating with a particular woman: "And therefore it happens sometimes that the judgment of free will is perverted but not the judgment of conscience—as when someone examines something that is incumbent upon him to do here and now and judges, still speculating through principles, that something is evil (as, for instance, to fornicate with this woman)" (*De veritate*, q. 17, a. 1, ad 4).

[192] *ST* III, q. 15, a. 2, ad 1: "The perfection of virtue . . . is according to right reason."

[193] *ST* III, q. 15, a. 2, ad 1: "The inferior powers pertaining to the sensitive appetite naturally obey reason." See also: *In* III *sent.*, dist. 33, q. 2, a. 4, qc 4, corp.: ("The inferior appetite naturally obeys reason"); *In* III *sent.*, dist. 33, q. 3, a. 1, qc 3, corp. ("It pertains to reason to command what ought to be done because the other powers obey reason in some way").

[194] See: *De malo*, q. 3, a. 9, ad 14; *ST* I-II, q. 17, a. 7; Aristotle, *Politics* 1.5.1254b.3–5.

are, in a sense, especially necessary for the attainment of the perfect good in one's practical affairs. As Aquinas goes on to say in the passage from the *Scriptum*:

> The habit perfecting the reason deliberating about the means [namely, prudence] presupposes an inclination of the appetite toward the end. This inclination [for the end] that is in the superior appetite known as the will is natural. But in the inferior appetite, it is either from custom or from a gift of God in regard to its attainment. There is, however, some beginning of it from nature, inasmuch as it is naturally able to obey the reason [*naturaliter obaudibilis rationi*]. In this, then, prudence differs from continence: the continent person has perfect reason about those things that are for the end, presupposing, however, the natural inclination for the end, whereas the prudent person's presupposed inclination is from either an acquired or an infused virtue in his lower powers. As the Philosopher says, therefore, it has its principles in the moral virtues.[195]

The continent man reasons well but only has nature to go on in the sense that he has not developed a moral virtue. He may even enjoy the possession of practical science, but even that would remain impotent in leading him to habitually perform upright acts with alacrity. In *De virtutibus*, Thomas explains this while distinguishing between practical science and prudence:

> Prudence implies more than practical science. For the universal judgment about things to be done pertains to practical science—as, for instance, the judgment that fornication is evil, one ought not to steal, and things of this sort. Even with this science existing, though, the judgment of reason is sometimes intercepted so

---

[195] *In* III *sent.*, dist. 33, q. 2, a. 4, qc 4, corp.: "Oportet quod habitus perficiens rationem negotiantem de his quae sunt ad finem, praesupponat inclinationem appetitus ad finem: quae quidem inclinatio in appetitu superiori, scilicet voluntate, est naturalis; in appetitu autem inferiori est ex assuetudine, vel ex Dei dono, quantum ad sui complementum; sed aliqua ejus inchoatio etiam est a natura, inquantum est naturaliter obaudibilis rationi. In hoc igitur differt prudens a continente; quia continens habet perfectam rationem de his quae sunt ad finem, praesupposita tamen naturali inclinatione voluntatis ad finem; prudens autem praesupposita inclinatione quae est ex virtute acquisita vel infusa in potentiis inferioribus; et ideo prudentia, ut dicit philosophus, habet sua principia in aliis virtutibus moralibus."

that one fails to adjudicate rightly, and on account of this it is said to avail little for virtue. . . . But it pertains to prudence to judge rightly about particular doable things inasmuch as they are to be done now—which judgment certainly is corrupted by any sin. And therefore, with prudence remaining, a man does not sin. It thus contributes much and not little to virtue; nay rather, it causes virtue.[196]

If one is to attain moral virtue and have hope of attaining the perfect good, he must consequently rely not only upon that which is natural to him but also upon virtue. In a text from the commentary on Aristotle's *Nicomachean Ethics* (one that is similar to *ST* II-II, q. 49, a. 2—which we encountered in the introduction to the present volume—though it makes some different observations), Thomas explains this in terms of the need for having two kinds of understanding—one pertaining to the first principles of the practical intellect (i.e., synderesis) and the other pertaining to an understanding of particulars that are already habitually ordered to the good of reason. He says:

> There are two kinds of understanding. One of them is about first and immutable principles in demonstrations, which proceed from immutable and first terms (that is from indemonstrable principles) that are first known and unchangeable because the knowledge about them is not able to be removed from man. But the understanding which pertains to practical things is from another kind of extreme, namely a singular and contingent one that has another proposition; i.e., not a universal one that is as the major premise in a practical syllogism, but the singular which is as the minor premise. As to why an extreme of this sort is called "understanding," it is evident because understanding treats of principles. Now these singulars about which this kind

---

[196] *De virtutibus*, q. 1, a. 6, ad 1 "Prudentia plus importat quam scientia practica: nam ad scientiam practicam pertinet universale iudicium de agendis; sicut fornicationem esse malam, furtum non esse faciendum, et huiusmodi. Qua quidem scientia existente, in particulari actu contingit iudicium rationis intercipi, ut non recte diiudicet; et propter hoc dicitur parum valere ad virtutem, quia ea existente contingit hominem contra virtutem peccare. Sed ad prudentiam pertinet recte iudicare de singulis agibilibus, prout sint nunc agenda: quod quidem iudicium corrumpitur per quodlibet peccatum. Et ideo prudentia manente, homo non peccat; unde ipsa non parum sed multum confert ad virtutem; immo ipsam virtutem causat."

of understanding is concerned are principles that are done for the sake of something [*cuius gratia*]; that is, they are principles in the manner of a final cause [*per modum causae finalis*].[197]

To attain the happiness that flows from having control over one's lower appetites and in such a way that they are subjected to reason while reason is subjected to higher reason, one has to be able to rely upon both kinds of understanding. When the extremes known by both of them line up with each other, the virtuous person will have very nearly attained the integrity Adam enjoyed,[198] for the appetites will be pointing affectively to the same end that is known cognitively. In other words, the end which is like the conclusion of a practical syllogism, will necessarily be the conclusion.

One can easily imagine the satisfaction an individual would have if everything he deemed worthy of pursuit in his intellect were simultaneously desired by the appetites. Since this happens for the virtuous man, we might think that virtue *simpliciter* is that in which we can find the happiness that is also known as the perfect good.[199] If we think carefully about it, however, there is at least a distinction to be made. Shakespeare seemed to have a good grasp of the Aristotelian-Thomistic view on this point as evinced by the words of Lucentio in *The Taming of the Shrew*: "Virtue, and that part of philosophy will I apply, that treats of happiness by virtue especially to be achieved" (I.i.18–20). Moral virtue leads to happiness but is not exactly coterminous with it. We can, therefore, distinguish

---

[197] *In* VI *eth.*, lec. 9, no. 13–14: "Est autem duplex intellectus. Quorum hic quidem est circa immobiles terminos et primos, qui sunt secundum demonstrationes, quae procedunt ab immobilibus et primis terminis, idest a principiis indemonstrabilibus, quae sunt prima cognita et immobilia, quia scilicet eorum cognitio ab homine removeri non potest. Sed intellectus qui est in practicis, est alterius modi extremi, scilicet singularis, et contingentis et alterius propositionis, idest non universalis quae est quasi maior, sed singularis quae est minor in syllogismo operativo. Quare autem huiusmodi extremi dicatur intellectus, patet per hoc, quod intellectus est principiorum; haec autem singularia, quorum dicimus esse intellectum huiusmodi, principia eius sunt quod est cuius gratia, id est sunt principia ad modum causae finalis." Thomas clarifies in the *Scriptum* that the second kind of *intellectus* is the cogitative power or the particular reason: "A syllogism comes about whose major term is a universal (which is an opinion of the practical intellect), whose minor term is a singular (which is a judgment of the particular reason, which is also called the cogitative power), and whose conclusion consists in a choice of an action" (*In* IV *sent.*, dist. 50 q. 1, a. 3, ad sc 3).

[198] Since humans do not now have the preternatural gifts, it seems unlikely one could perfectly attain the integrity of the first man.

[199] See *ST* I-II, q. 5, a. 8, ad 3: "The perfect good... is happiness." See also: *ST* I-II, q. 5, a. 8, corp.; q. 10, a. 2, corp.; q. 13, a. 6, corp.

THE IMPORTANCE OF THE END

between intellectual and moral virtue. The latter, which renders man's work good,[200] is more truly virtue than the intellectual kind. Intellectual virtues such as understanding, knowledge, and wisdom merely ensure that the one possessing them has the capacity (*facultas*) to use them well.[201] The moral virtues, on the other hand, also ensure that the individual actually uses that very capacity well, and thus allow him to more readily attain the good proper to man, which is to live in accordance with reason. Aquinas explains:

> Because a virtue is that which makes the one having it good and renders his action good, habits of this sort [moral virtues] are unqualifiedly [*simpliciter*] called virtues, because they render the work actually good and they make the one having them unqualifiedly good. The first kind of habits [the intellectual] are not unqualifiedly called virtues because they do not render the action good except inasmuch as they bestow a certain capacity, ... for a man possessing knowledge or a skill is not called unqualifiedly good because of his knowledge or skill. Rather, he is called good only in a qualified way [*secundum quid*].[202]

If someone is to be truly good, his appetites must be rightly ordered. As Gregory Reichenberg says, because the moral virtues are the virtues which "rectify the will and sense appetites,"[203] they are more truly virtues than are the intellectual ones.

Man's ultimate happiness, though, does not consist in the moral

---

[200] Aquinas indicates that the words about rendering a work good in Augustine's definition of virtue indicate the definition must pertain to moral virtue (*ST* I-II, q. 55, a. 4).

[201] *ST* I-II, q. 56, a. 3, corp.: "By a habit of this sort, man acquires aptitude for a good act." Here St. Thomas is discussing habits (such as the habit of grammar) that provide the capacity for doing things well (such as speaking in the case of grammar) but that do not guarantee the proper use of that habit. He says the intellectual habits fall into that category.

[202] *ST* I-II, q. 56, a. 3, corp.: "Virtus est, quae bonum facit habentem, et opus ejus bonum reddit, hujusmodi habitus simpliciter dicuntur virtutes, quia reddunt bonum opus in actu, et simpliciter faciunt bonum habentem. Primi vero habitus non simpliciter dicuntur virtutes; quia non reddunt bonum opus, nisi in quadam facultate, nec simpliciter faciunt bonum habentem; non enim dicitur simpliciter aliquis homo bonus ex hoc, quod est sciens, vel artifex, sed dicitur bonus solum secundum quid."

[203] Gregory M. Reichberg, "The Intellectual Virtues (Ia IIae, Qq. 57–58)," in *The Ethics of Aquinas*, ed. Stephen J. Pope, Moral Traditions Series (Washington, DC: Georgetown University Press, 2002), 131–50, at 140.

virtues, despite their undeniable value. Saint Thomas says this explicitly in *SCG* and implicitly in the commentary on the *Nicomachean Ethics*. In the latter, he observes that, since man's proper operation pertains to reason (because the principle of his operation, which is his form, is rational), his happiness must also pertain to reason. One way in which someone can be rational is by an act of the appetite when it participates in reason by being ruled by it, and the other is by an act of the intellect, which is rational in virtue of its very essence. Whatever is rational essentially, therefore, must be that in which happiness consists, and the human person's "principal happiness" must consequently consist in "the contemplative life more than in the active and in an act of the reason or intellect more than in an act of the appetite being ruled by reason."[204]

In *SCG*, Aquinas addresses this issue while asserting that human happiness cannot consist in act of moral virtue for six reasons, three of which are:

> [1] The moral virtues are for the sake of preserving the mean in internal passions and exterior things. But it is not possible that a modification of the passions or of exterior things be the ultimate happiness of man.... [2] Since a man is a man in virtue of his possession of reason, the good that is proper to him, which is happiness, must be in accordance with that which is proper to reason. But what reason has in itself is more proper to reason than what it brings about in something else. Since, then, the good of moral virtue is something brought about by the reason in other things, it is not able to be the best good, which is happiness; rather, it must be a good that is in the reason itself.... [3] Happiness is man's proper good. That, therefore, which is most proper to man among all the human goods in comparison with the other animals will be that in which his ultimate happiness ought to be sought. But acts of the moral virtues are not this sort of thing because the other animals partake of liberality or fortitude whereas no animal has some kind of participation in an intellectual action. Man's ultimate happiness, therefore, is not in moral acts.[205]

---

[204] *In I eth.*, lec. 10, no. 9: "... felicitas principalius consistit in vita contemplativa quam in activa; et in actu rationis vel intellectus, quam in actu appetitus ratione regulati."

[205] *SCG* III, ch. 34, nos. 3–4 and 6: "[1] Virtutes morales ad hoc sunt ut per eas conservetur medium in passionibus intrinsecis et exterioribus rebus. Non est autem possibile quod modificatio passionum vel rerum exteriorum sit ultimus finis humanae vitae: cum ipsae passiones et exteriores res sint ad aliud ordinabiles. Non est igitur possibile quod in actibus virtutum moralium sit ultima hominis felicitas.... [2] Cum homo sit

THE IMPORTANCE OF THE END

In other words, as eminent as moral virtue is, it does not directly pertain to what is highest in us. It ensures that our appetites are rectified and that inordinate attachments do not unnecessarily becloud our reason, but it does not rectify the reason itself, which pertains to the intellectual virtues.[206] The intellectual virtues, therefore, bring us closer to the perfect good than do the moral ones. Thomas does consider the possibility that the moral virtues may "perhaps" be closer to happiness, inasmuch as they are closer to it by way of preparation (inasmuch as they eliminate the impediments to happiness such as disordered passions), but in the end, he consistently insists it is that only an "act of the reason or intellect" can pertain to the essence of perfect happiness itself.[207]

The Perfect Good and Intellectual Virtue

Among the intellectual virtues, prudence and art pertain to the practical realm. Since the *SCG* passage deemed it impossible for the modification of exterior things to be man's ultimate happiness, we can rule out the virtue of art as a candidate for being a virtue in which happiness could consist. Prudence, however, is more interesting to consider in this context. It is an intellectual virtue "according to its essence," and yet since it is about moral works (which is what the *agibilia* in *recta ratio agibilium* refers to),[208] it is "sometimes enumerated with the moral virtues, existing somehow midway between the intellectual and the moral virtues."[209] It directs all the moral

---

homo ex eo quod est rationem habens, oportet quod proprium eius bonum, quod est felicitas, sit secundum id quod est proprium rationi. Magis autem est proprium rationis quod ipsa in se habet, quam quod in alio facit. Cum igitur bonum moralis virtutis sit quoddam a ratione in rebus aliis a se institutum, non poterit esse optimum hominis, quod est felicitas: sed magis bonum quod est in ipsa ratione situm. . . . [3] Felicitas est proprium hominis bonum. Illud igitur quod est maxime proprium hominis inter omnia bona humana respectu aliorum animalium, est in quo quaerenda est eius ultima felicitas. Huiusmodi autem non est virtutum moralium actus: nam aliqua animalia aliquid participant vel liberalitatis vel fortitudinis; intellectualis autem actionis nullum animal aliquid participat. Non est igitur ultima hominis felicitas in actibus moralibus."

[206] See *ST* II-II, q. 123, a. 1, corp.

[207] See: *De virtutibus*, q. 1, a. 7, ad 4; q. 1, a. 5, ad 8.

[208] *De virtutibus*, q. 5, a. 1, ad 3: "Prudence is right reason about doable things [*recta ratio agibilium*]. Now, the 'doable things' spoken of refer to moral actions, as is clear from the things that are said there [Aristotle, *Ethics* 2.6]. And therefore prudence belongs with the moral virtues because of its matter, and on account of this it is numbered among them, although in regard to its essence or subject it is an intellectual virtue."

[209] See *De virtutibus*, q. 1, a. 12, ad 14.

virtues[210] and is spoken of as "effective" of moral virtue in a way (*quodammodo*).[211] Similarly, Aquinas says it *quodammodo* "appoints [*praestituit*] the end to the moral virtues,"[212] because it determines the mean that is the end of each moral virtue.[213] It might, for example, help the virtuous person attain the mean of fortitude, which would be somewhere between cowardice and recklessness,[214] depending on the individual's natural inclinations.[215] Nevertheless, happiness cannot consist in an act of prudence precisely because it also pertains to matter that is contingent and particular, just as the moral virtues do:[216]

> Man's happiness is in the best activity of man. But the best operation of man, inasmuch as it is proper to him, is in comparison with the most perfect objects. But the activity of prudence is not about the most perfect objects of the intellect or the reason because it is not about necessary things, but contingent doable things. Its activity, therefore, is not man's ultimate happiness.[217]

---

[210] See, *ST* I-II, q. 58, a. 2, ad 4.

[211] *De virtutibus*, q. 1, a. 12, ad 16: "The 'right reason' of prudence is not placed in the definition of moral virtue as something existing from its essence. It is, rather, in a certain measure an effective [*effectiva*] cause of it."

[212] *In* III *sent.*, dist. 33, q. 2, a. 3, corp.: "Medium virtutis moralis, ut in 2 Ethic. dicitur, est secundum rationem rectam, quae est prudentia; et sic quodammodo prudentia praestituit finem virtutibus moralibus, et ejus actus in earum actibus immiscetur" ("the mean of moral virtue, as is said in the second book of the ethics, is that which is in accordance with right reason, which is prudence; and thus prudence somehow appoints the end to the moral virtues and its act is intermingled with theirs").

[213] *ST* I-II, q. 66, a. 3, ad 2: "Prudentia non solum dirigit virtutes morales in eligendo ea quae sunt ad finem, sed etiam in praestituendo finem: est autem finis uniuscujusque virtutis moralis attingere medium in proria materia; quod quidem medium determinatur secundum rectam rationem prudentiae" ("prudence directs the moral virtues not only in choosing those things that are for the end, but also in appointing the end: for the end of each moral virtue is to attain the mean in the matter proper to that virtue; which mean, to be sure, is determined in accordance with the right reason of prudence").

[214] See, Jean Porter, "The Virtue of Justice (IIa IIae, Qq. 58–122)," in Pope, *Ethics of Aquinas*, 272–89, at 274.

[215] In Aristotle's definition, virtue is said to exist in the mean *toward us* precisely because the mean varies for the individual. Someone who is disposed to temerity will need to allow fear to have more influence over him on the battlefield than someone who is inclined to pusillanimity.

[216] See: *ST* II-II, q. 49, a. 5, ad 2; II-II, q. 49, a. 8, corp.

[217] *SCG* III, ch. 35, no. 4: "Quod ordinatur ad alterum sicut ad finem, non est ultima hominis felicitas. Operatio autem prudentiae ordinatur ad alterum sicut ad finem: tum quia omnis practica cognitio, sub qua continetur prudentia, ordinatur ad operationem; tum

The Importance of the End

Prudence is like the moral virtues in that it merely enables a person to habitually perform actions that are conducive to happiness.[218] More than any of the moral virtues, it is "that by which we live rightly,"[219] and because it is an intellectual virtue, it is able to cognize the means that lead to happiness[220] and issue commands in regard to it; however, it remains subordinate to happiness in some way,[221] even if constitutive of it.[222]

As we might expect, Thomas says the act that is essentially happiness itself must ultimately be an act either of reason or of the intellect and that it must be about necessary and non-contingent things. Even more specifically, it "is nothing other than the perfect contemplation of the highest truth" to which the "will is ordered by a natural desire."[223] We might be led to guess that it consists, therefore, in an act of the speculative intellect and particularly one of understanding, since this habit is the very foundation of knowledge. Nevertheless, Aquinas argues it is not possible for "the ultimate happiness of man" to consist in "the contemplation that is according to the understanding of principles" primarily because this habit "is most imperfect." By this he seems to mean it provides only the beginning of the dialectical process which concludes in knowledge and is consequently at the opposite extreme of the conclusions that flow from its principles (i.e., it does not stand at the *finis humani studii*,[224] but at the beginning). Also, the principles contained in this natural habit come forth to us from our nature instead of resulting from the zeal for truth, and its principles are "most universal," meaning they need to be led to their conclusions.[225]

---

etiam quia prudentia facit hominem bene se habere in his quae sunt ad finem eligenda, sicut patet per Aristotelem, in VI Ethicorum. Non est igitur in operatione prudentiae ultima hominis felicitas."

[218] *ST* I-II, q. 62, a. 1, corp.: "Man is perfected . . . by virtue for those actions that direct him to happiness."

[219] See, *ST* I-II, q. 55, a. 4, corp.

[220] See *ST* I-II, q. 66, a. 5, ad 1.

[221] *SCG* III, ch. 2, says happiness is obtained through virtue, and *ST* I-II, q. 5, a. 7, says happiness is the reward of works of virtue. See also *In* IV *sent.*, dist. 49, q. 1, qc 4, ad 2, which speaks of someone undertaking works of virtue for the sake of attaining happiness.

[222] *ST* I-II, q. 5, a. 4, says happiness principally consists in an act of virtue.

[223] See *De veritate*, q. 1, a. 5, ad 8, which also says the natural desire is for "the contemplative happiness of which the philosophers spoke."

[224] See the following note (225).

[225] *SCG* III, ch. 37, no. 8: "Now, it is not possible that the ultimate happiness of man consists in the kind of contemplation that pertains to the understanding of principles, as this understanding is most imperfect as most universal. . . . It is the beginning, not the end, of human pursuits." As he says in the next chapter of the *SCG* III, ch. 38, no. 6,

The two other speculative virtues are knowledge (*scientia*) and wisdom. Although the former pertains to the end of a process of enquiry (ratiocination) and, unlike understanding, actually provides the conclusions, Thomas says knowledge is necessarily less perfect than understanding because it relies upon it for its principles.[226] By process of elimination, therefore, "it remains that the ultimate happiness of man consists in wisdom's contemplation regarding divine things."[227] Wisdom, as pertaining to the very object of happiness which is the most understandable being there is, "is a beginning of future happiness" enjoyed in this life and the closest approximation to it of all the intellectual virtues.[228] It does, however, remain a mere approximation of the future happiness. Rightly, therefore, Thomas speaks of two "things that are honored besides virtue" and even as being "more excellent than [it]: God and happiness."[229]

The Perfect Good in Relation to God

Aristotle, Augustine, and Aquinas all speak of the pursuit of the perfect good as inseparably connected with God in some way. This begs the question of whether or not it would be more proper to say that God himself is the final end (which is synonymous with the perfect good[230]), rather than happiness or beatitude.[231]

For Saint Thomas:

> In any genus of causes, the first cause is more a cause than a second cause, for a second cause is only a cause through the first cause. Therefore, that which is the first cause in the order of final causes

---

"happiness is a perfect action, and the highest good of man must be according to that which is in act and not according to that which is in potency only because a potency is perfected by an act that has the essential character of the good" ("Felicitas autem est operatio perfecta; et summum hominis bonum oportet esse secundum id quod est actu, et non secundum quod est potentia tantum; nam potentia per actum perfecta habet boni rationem)."

[226] See *ST* I-II, q. 57, a. 2, ad 2.

[227] *SCG* III, ch. 37, no. 8: "Relinquitur igitur quod in contemplatione sapientiae ultima hominis felicitas consistat, secundum divinorum considerationem."

[228] See *ST* I-II, q. 66, a. 5, ad 1.

[229] *ST* II-II, q. 145, a. 1, ad 2: "Eorum quae honorantur praeter virtutem, aliquid est virtute excellentius; scilicet: Deus et beatitudo."

[230] *ST* I-II, q. 2, a. 7, corp.: "Ultimis finis est bonum perfectum complens boni appetitum."

[231] *ST* supp., q. 75, a. 1, corp.: "The last end of man, which all people naturally desire, is happiness" (originally from *In IV sent.*, dist. 43, q. 1, a. 1, qc 1, corp.)

is necessarily more the final cause of anything than its proximate final cause is. But God is the first cause in the order of final causes, since he is the highest in the order of goods. He is, therefore, more the end of everything than some proximate end is.[232]

If God is the most final cause among the final causes, it seems manifest that he and not happiness (or an act of wisdom that is merely a beginning of happiness) is the ultimate end. However, if he is himself the end, then how is it that something other than he can be desired as the ultimate end when, *ex suppositio*, that end is naturally desired by all rational creatures? Aquinas clearly says the angels appointed (*praestituerunt*) as their end either God or something other than God and that they were consequently either happy or miserable.[233] If it is possible for angels to appoint ends to themselves other than God, then men (who are far less perfect than the angels) can certainly do so. In fact, many—even philosophers—have sought happiness in an end other than God. Aquinas speaks to this in his commentary on Psalm 32:

> Different people have thought about beatitude in different ways and according to the different opinions concerning it, there are different sects of philosophers. For some placed it in bodily goods, as did Epicurus; some, in the works of the active life, as did the Stoics; while still others, in the contemplation of truth, as did the Peripatetics. [Yet] to seek beatitude in what is beneath us is vain, because beatitude is something above us. But the one above us is God.[234]

---

[232] *SCG* III, ch. 17, no. 4. He said essentially the same thing in fewer words in *SCG* III, ch. 17, no. 2: "If nothing tends toward a thing as into an end unless the thing is good, it is therefore necessary that the good, as good, be an end. That which is the highest good, then, is most of all an end. But the highest good is only one, and this is God, as was proved in the first book. Therefore, all things are ordered as to an end toward the one good that is God." For an interesting discussion of this latter passage, see Georg Wieland, "Happiness (Ia-IIae, qq. 1–5)," trans. Grant Kaplan, in Pope, *Ethics of Aquinas*, 57–68, at 59.

[233] *CT* I, ch. 184: "The Angels, when they first willfully deliberated, appointed to themselves [*sibi finem praestituerunt*] an end that was either God or something created and from that point they were either happy or miserable."

[234] See *Super Psalmo* 32, no. 11 (trans. Peter Kwasniewsksi, in *On Love and Charity*, 131). See also, Peter A. Kwasniewski, "Divine Drunkenness: The Secret Life of Thomistic Reason," *The Modern Schoolman* 82 (2004): 1–31, esp. 3–7 and 12–15.

How is it possible for God to be the "end of each thing more even than the proximate end"[235] if he is not recognized as such by all? Would we not have to say *happiness* is the true universal end that is the perfect good if all men necessarily desire happiness while many do not desire God? Since the ultimate end is the first principle in morals,[236] the answer to this question will necessarily have significant implications. If, for instance, God is the last end, and thus the first principle in morality, one might think of even eternal happiness as a subordinated end that might have to be sacrificed. By neglecting to advert to the goodness of nature and natural desires, in other words, one could arrive at the conclusions of Père Fénelon and the Quietists that God ought to be loved for himself alone and *not* "because of the happiness to be found in loving him" or even because of the joy to be found in contemplating him. If this were the case, the Quietists would be right that the ideal is to "wish nothing for ourselves"—even virtue or salvation—and solely wish "all for God," with no consideration of self interest.[237] As it turns out, however, those sentiments were condemned by the Church. In an effort to avoid such conclusions, we might be tempted to prescind from any further consideration of how the "last end" of happiness relates to God. However, just as bracketing the issue of happiness when discussing the final end qua God could lead to the errors of Fénelon, prescinding from considering how God factors into the final end of happiness could easily lead to the errors of Pelagianism, because we might find ourselves thinking we are able to actualize our potency for beatitude on our own. Besides, for Aquinas, the "ultimate happiness of man consists" not only "in wisdom's consideration of divine things" in general, but particularly in "the contemplation of God,"[238] who is the best of divine things.

We have seen that certain philosophical schools fell far short of the true ideal of happiness. Aquinas makes a more general observation that, even if "all people grasp that happiness is some kind of perfect state," they do not agree about "that in which this perfect state consists, whether in life or something in the afterlife, whether in bodily or spiritual goods,"

---

[235] *SCG* III, ch. 17.

[236] As Aquinas says, "The principle of the whole moral order is the ultimate end, which is related to practical matters as the indemonstrable principle is related to speculative matters" (*ST* I-II, q. 72, a. 5, corp.).

[237] These and similar condemned propositions can be found in *The Sources of Catholic Dogma*, ed. Henry Denzinger and Karl Rahner, trans. Roy J. Deferrari (St. Louis, MO: B. Herder, 1954), 343'–45.

[238] See, *SCG* III, ch. 37.

because these things are hidden to them.²³⁹ At the same time, it is possible to make philosophical arguments that happiness must pertain to something above man and something that is truly found only in God. One such argument along these lines is found in the *Scriptum*:

> It should be said that the good that all long for is being [*esse*], as is evident from Boethius in *On the Consolation of Philosophy*.²⁴⁰ Hence the ultimate object of desire for all things is perfect being, to the extent that it is possible in their nature. Now, everything that has being from another has its perfection from another, since each one receives being the more perfectly, the more truly it is conjoined to the principle of its being. . . . And so the ultimate end of anything whatsoever that has being from another is twofold: one outside [itself], namely according to that which is the principle of the desired perfection; another within [itself], namely its very own perfection, which union to its principle brings about. Hence, since beatitude is man's ultimate end, beatitude will be twofold: one that is within man himself, namely that ultimate perfection of himself which it is possible for him to attain, and this is created beatitude; whereas the other is outside himself, through union with which the aforementioned beatitude is *caused* in him; and this is uncreated beatitude, which is God himself.²⁴¹

All creatures desire to be, and thus desire the very principle of being who, as the perfect being, exists in virtue of his own being (as the one who is *per se ipsum necesse-esse* and *ipsum esse subsistens*²⁴²). Since there is no way of escaping this desire, the creature is "ordained in a natural manner to God as to an end."²⁴³ However, only rational animals have as a last end the attainment of the uncreated end as their proper end. Jörn Müller explains:

---

²³⁹ See *In* II *sent.*, dist. 38, q. 1, a. 2, ad 2.
²⁴⁰ Boethius, *De consolatione philosophiae* III, prose 11 (CCSL, 94:58–59).
²⁴¹ *In* IV *sent.*, d 49, q. 1, a. 2, corp. (*On Love and Charity*, 353). *ST* I-II, q. 2, a. 7, corp., says something at least similar: "The thing itself which one has an appetite for as an end is that in which beatitude consists, and which makes happy; but the attainment of this is called happiness. Accordingly, it should be said that happiness is something of the soul but that in which happiness consists is something outside of the soul" ("Res ergo ipsa, quae appetitur ut finis, est id, in quo beatitudo consistit, et quod beatum facit: sed hujus rei adeptio vocatur beatitudo, unde dicendum est, quod beatitudo est aliquid animae; sed id, in quo consistit beatitudo, est aliquid extra animam").
²⁴² See *SCG* I, ch. 44, no. 7, and *ST* I, q. 4, a. 2, corp., respectively.
²⁴³ *ST* III, q. 1, a. 3, ad 2.

Aquinas's treatise on happiness in *ST* I-2.1–5 relies heavily on a distinction that comes to the fore when he inquires if there is one final goal (*finis ultimus*) for all beings (*ST* I-2.1.8). In some sense, there is: God as the final cause at which all creatures aim is the single end (*finis cuius*) of everything. On the other hand, all creatures have their specific *finis quo*, their proper mode of attaining their end or perfection: they participate in the similitude of God in different manners. In the case of rational creatures like human beings this specific *finis quo* is to have knowledge of God.[244] The *finis cuius* thus is the "external" end or good, while the *finis quo* is its "internal acquisition" (see *In Sent.* 4.49.I.1 qc.2 resp.).[245]

All animals concur in having the thing that *is* the end as their last end "because God is the ultimate end of man and of all other things,"[246] but only rational animals can come to know and embrace the fact that their happiness consists in God,[247] and only they have a capacity of nature that enables them to actually attain him. In other words, even though all things participate in the divine reason (also known as the eternal law),[248] the rational creature can subject itself to divine providence in a more excellent way (*excellentiori quodam modo*) by becoming a partaker of divine providence in a manner wherein it can even be providential over its *own* actions, thanks to the "light of the natural reason" present in rational creatures due to the impression made upon them by the reason of God.[249]

---

[244] See *SCG* III, ch. 40: "The knowledge of God is called the end inasmuch as it is joined to the last end of things; namely, God."

[245] Jörn Müller, "*Duplex Beatitudo*: Aristotle's Legacy and Aquinas's Conception of Human Happiness," in *Aquinas and the Nicomachean Ethics*, ed. Tobias Hoffmann, Jörn Müller, and Matthias Perkams (Cambridge: Cambridge University Press, 2013), 52–71, at 66.

[246] See *ST* I-II, q. 1, a. 8, corp.

[247] *ST* I, q. 82, a. 2, speaks of God as the one "in quo solo vera beatitudo consistit." I-II, q. 3, a. 4, sc, and *SCG* III, ch. 25, say it consists in the knowledge of God ("beatitudo hominis in cognitione Dei consistit," to quote the former), but as we have seen, the attainment of him by means of union with him and his essence itself can be considered as one qua end.

[248] *ST* I-II, q. 19, a. 4: "The eternal law, which is the divine reason." See also I-II, q. 93, a. 1: "The eternal law is the highest *ratio* existing in God." Since God has no accidents, this is, of course, really God himself, and thus the twofold rule of our actions is often referred to as the human reason and God, where "God" is synonymous with the *ratio Dei* (see: *ST* I-II, q. 23, a. 6, corp.; II-II, q. 23, a. 3, corp.; I-II, q. 63, a. 4, corp.; *De virtutibus*, q. 5, a. 2, corp.).

[249] See *ST* I-II, q. 91, a. 2, from which the Latin quotations were taken. Regarding the

Humans, therefore, need to be perceptive and let the natural desire for being lead them to the pursuit and contemplation of the source of being itself. That is to say, they need to be attentive to nature, to that which is highest in the nature specific to them in comparison with the other animals (i.e., reason), and allow the laws of nature to provide them with guidance by doing good and avoiding evil. If they do that, they will implicitly understand there is no "competitive finality" when it comes to the end that is God and the end of happiness (and especially, of eternal happiness).[250]

Aristotle is one of those who, whether wittingly or not, took to heart the words of Heraclitus, who said true wisdom is concerned with acting "according to nature, giving ear thereto."[251] As a Peripatetic, he certainly thought of happiness as consisting of performing the highest act of man's nature, the act of reasoning, as well as possible while directing that act to the highest end to which his rational nature directed him—namely, God. Thomas was struck by the fact that Aristotle connected happiness to contemplation of God, and he (Aquinas) deduced from this fact that the contemplation of God is something attainable by nature:

> According to the Philosopher, the last end of human life is the contemplation of God. If therefore, man were not able to attain

---

eternal law being equated with the divine Reason, see I-II, q. 19, a. 4 ("the eternal law, which is the divine reason"), and q. 93, a. 1 (the eternal law is the highest Reason existing in God).

[250] We have seen that the Quietists were condemned for thinking God might want them to sacrifice their eternal happiness. This condemnation does not, however, mean to suggest we will have perfect happiness here by doing God's will. In the third apparition to St. Bernadette on February 18, 1858, Mary is reported to have said, "I do not promise to make you happy in this world but only in the other" (see Johannes Jørgensen, *Lourdes*, trans. Ingeborg Lund [London: Longmans and Green, 1914], 19).

Insofar as God is, objectively, infinite happiness, being joined to God in perfect knowledge and love in the beatific vision is attaining the only ontologically perfect happiness (as opposed to a happiness perfect in its natural species, but ontologically limited). In other words, if what is desired is perfect happiness, and God *is* perfect happiness, then union with God and the subjective perfection that ensues is happiness *simpliciter* for the rational creature. Of course, the notion of the beatific vision presupposes revelation, but the contemplative approach to God in this life is limited, and so involves a participation of true happiness even though it cannot constitute perfect happiness.

[251] Heraclitus: *sophiē alēthea legein kai poiein kata physin epaiontas* ("wisdom is to speak the truth and to act according to nature, giving ear thereto"; Fragmentum B 112 in *Fragmente der Vorsokratiker*).

this, we would be constituted in vain, because what is in vain, according to the Philosopher, is that which is for the sake of some end that is not attained. But this is unfitting. As it is said in Psalm 88:48, "you did not constitute man in vain, did you?"[252]

Despite his undeniably high estimation of the Philosopher, though, Thomas argues he limited himself to speaking about the imperfect happiness humans can attain "as men:"[253]

> Aristotle [*Nicomachean Ethics* 8.10] says that man's ultimate happiness is the most perfect contemplation by which the supremely understandable being that is God is able to be contemplated in this life: but over this happiness there is another happiness which we expect in the future, by which we will see God as he is. This, certainly, is above any given created intellect at all.[254]

In other words, Saint Thomas held the happiness Aristotle was seeking was the kind that is certainly "a participation of [supernatural] beatitude," but that remains an earthly and natural happiness.[255] Such happiness must

---

[252] *In* I *sent.*, dist. 3, q. 1, a. 1, sc 2: "Ut supra dictum est, etiam secundum philosophum, ultimus finis humanae vitae est contemplatio Dei. Si igitur ad hoc homo non posset pertingere, in vanum esset constitutus; quia vanum est, secundum philosophum, quod ad aliquem finem est, quem non attingit; et hoc est inconveniens, ut dicitur in Psal. 88, 48: numquid enim vane constituisti eum?" Interestingly, the RSVCE renders this verse: "For what vanity thou hast created all the sons of men!" A similar text is found in *De malo* 5, a. 1, ad 1, in which Thomas says God ensured man had not been made in vain by making him able to attain happiness by proposing a remedy for man from the beginning of the human race, namely Christ: "Man would have been made useless and in vain if he were not able to attain happiness, as anything at all would be were it not able to attain its last end. Thus, lest man be made useless and in vain, when he was born with original sin, God put forward a remedy for man from the beginning of the human race, through which he was freed from this vanity—namely, the mediator between God and man, Jesus Christ himself, through whose faithfulness the impediment of original sin was able to be withdrawn."

[253] See, *SCG* III, ch. 48.

[254] *ST* I, q. 62, a. 1, corp.: "Unde et Arist. (*Ethics* 10.8) perfectissimam hominis contemplationem, qua optimum intelligibile, quod est Deus, contemplari potest in hac vita, dicit esse ultimam hominis felicitatem: sed super hanc felicitatem est alia felicitas, quam in futuro expectamus, qua videbimus Deum sicuti est. Quod quidem est supra cujuslibet intellectus creati naturam."

[255] *In* IV *sent.*, dist. 49, q. 1, a. 1, qc 4, corp.: "There can be a participation of [supernatural] beatitude in this life, according as man is perfect in the goods of reason.... It is about this

be imperfect because the perfect good is simply unattainable in this life.[256]

In the following text, Thomas contrasts a participated good (such as an action of contemplating God that Aristotle spoke of) with that which is participated in (and is thus is the only truly perfect good or true source of happiness). It is a worthwhile text because, even though he is answering what might seem to be a sophistical question of whether happiness is the soul, it helps clarify the difference between contemplation and the object of contemplation (God) in addition to the dependence of the former upon the latter, thus preparing the way for a more accurate delineation between what can be known naturally and that which requires divine aid. He says:

> "End" is twofold: the thing itself that we desire to attain and the use; namely, the attainment or possession of the thing. If we speak of the last end of man as regards the thing itself which we desire as a last end, it is impossible for the last end of man to be the soul itself or something pertaining to it, because the soul itself, considered in itself, exists as in potency because it is made to know in act from only knowing in potency and is made to be virtuous in act from being virtuous in potency. Now since potency is for the sake of act as for that which completes it, it is impossible that something existing in potency in itself could have the *ratio* of the last end. Accordingly, it is impossible that the soul itself is its own last end. Similarly, however, neither can something pertaining to it [*aliquid eius*], whether it be a power or a habit or an act. For the good that is the last end is the perfect good fulfilling the appetite. But the human appetite, which is the will, is for the universal good. And whatever good adheres to the soul is a participated good and is thus a particular good. It is, therefore, impossible that one of these [a power or habit or act] be the last end of man. But if

---

[earthly] happiness that the Philosopher determines in the book of *Ethics* neither asserting nor denying another [happiness] that is after this life" (*On Love and Charity*, 351).

[256] *SCG* III, ch. 48, no. 5: "All admit that happiness is a perfect good: else it would not bring rest to the appetite. Now perfect good is that which is wholly free from any admixture of evil: just as that which is perfectly white is that which is entirely free from any admixture of black. But man cannot be wholly free from evils in this state of life; not only from evils of the body, such as hunger, thirst, heat, cold and the like, but also from evils of the soul. For no one is there who at times is not disturbed by inordinate passions; who sometimes does not go beyond the mean, wherein virtue consists, either in excess or in deficiency; who is not deceived in some thing or another; or at least ignores what he would wish to know, or feels doubtful about an opinion of which he would like to be certain. Therefore no man is happy in this life" (Dominican Fathers trans.).

we speak of the last end of man as to the attainment or possession of it or as to any use of the thing itself that is desired as an end, in this way something pertaining to man's soul does belong to the last end. Therefore, the thing itself which is desired as an end is that in which happiness consists and is that which makes man happy, but the attainment of it is called happiness. Accordingly, it should be said that happiness is something pertaining to the soul but that in which beatitude consists is something outside of the soul.[257]

Applying this text to the habit of virtue, we can gather that no natural virtue can be the last end, because it is not proportioned to the object of true beatitude, which is not only outside of the soul, but infinitely transcends it. As Thomas says, "the natural inclination of the will is for that which is suitable to it according to nature. And therefore if something is above nature, the will is not able to be carried into it unless it be helped by some higher principle." But "to see God by [his] essence, in which the ultimate beatitude of the rational creature consists, is above the nature of any created intellect whatever. Therefore, no rational creature is able to have a motion of the will ordered to that beatitude unless moved by a supernatural agent: and we call this the help of grace."[258] Just as God appoints the end to all things in virtue of their nature,[259] so he must appoint to them a supernatural end if they are to know what to direct their activity toward:

---

[257] *ST* I-II, q. 2, a. 7, corp. A nearly identical text is found in the next question, in which he distinguishes between the uncreated good who is God and the created attainment of him: "End is spoken of in two ways. In one way, regarding the thing itself that we desire to attain. . . . In another way, either the attainment (or possession) or the use (or enjoyment) of a thing that is desired. . . . In the first way, the ultimate end of man is the uncreated good, namely God, who alone is able to perfectly fulfill the will by his own infinite goodness. In the second way, the ultimate end of man is something created existing within him, which is nothing other than the attainment or enjoyment of the ultimate end. The ultimate end, however, is called beatitude. If, then, man's beatitude is considered in regard to the cause or the object, it is something uncreated, but if it is considered in regard to the essence itself of beatitude, it is something created" (I-II, q. 3, a. 1, corp.).

[258] *ST* I, q. 62, a. 2, corp.: "[The natural inclination of the will is for that which is fitting according to nature. And therefore if something is above nature, the will is not able to be drawn toward it unless it be helped by some supernatural principle.] . . . Videre Deum per essentiam, in quo ultima beatitudo rationalis creaturae consistit, est supra naturam cujuslibet intellectus creati. Unde nulla creatura rationalis potest habere motum voluntatis ordinatum ad illam beatitudinem, nisi mota a supernaturali agente: et hoc dicimus auxilium gratiae."

[259] See *SCG* III, ch. 44, no. 7.

The knowledge of the ultimate end must be appointed [*praestituatur*] to us by grace so that we might voluntarily be directed toward it. But this knowledge is not able to be one of clear vision in this state of life, as was proved. Necessarily, therefore, this knowledge is through faith.[260]

Grace is thus indispensable for attaining that which is above our nature. Synderesis may appoint the natural end of living according to reason and other ends constitutive of the perfect good, but faith that has been caused by grace[261] must do so as well:

> The goodness of the human will depends much more upon the eternal law than upon human reason, and where human reason is insufficient, it is necessary to have recourse to the eternal reason.[262]

The eternal reason, which is synonymous with the eternal law,[263] "directs us in many things that surpass human reason, e.g. in matters of faith."[264] Principal among those things is the knowledge of what our ultimate perfection consists of:

> By the name of "beatitude" is understood the ultimate perfection of a rational or intellectual nature: accordingly, it is naturally desired, since everything naturally desires its perfection. Now the ultimate perfection of a rational or intellectual nature is twofold. One, certainly, which is able to be attained in virtue of one's own

---

[260] *SCG* III, ch. 152, no. 2: "Motus enim quo per gratiam in ultimum finem dirigimur, est voluntarius, non violentus, ut supra ostensum est. Voluntarius autem motus in aliquid esse non potest nisi sit cognitum. Oportet igitur quod per gratiam in nobis cognitio ultimi finis praestituatur, ad hoc quod voluntarie dirigamur in ipsum. Haec autem cognitio non potest esse secundum apertam visionem in statu isto, ut supra probatum est. Oportet igitur quod sit cognitio per fidem."

[261] *SCG* III, ch. 152, no. 1: "It is necessary that ... faith be caused by grace in us."

[262] *ST* I-II, q. 19, a. 4, corp.: "Multo magis dependet bonitas voluntatis humanae a lege aeterna, quam a ratione humana: et ubi deficit humana ratio, oportet ad rationem aeternam recurrere."

[263] *ST* I-II, q. 91, a. 2, corp. speaks of the natural inclination of a creature to its proper act and end in terms of participation both in "eternal reason" and in "eternal law." *ST* I-II, q. 71 . 6, corp., specifically says the eternal law is "as it were" [*quasi*] God's reason. See also, *ST* I-II, q. 91, a. 2, ad 3.

[264] *ST* I-II, q. 71, a. 6, ad 5: "Per legem aeternam regulemur in multis, quae excedunt rationem humanam; sicut in his, quae sunt fidei" (Dominican Fathers trans.).

nature, and this is, in a manner, called "beatitude" or "happiness." ... But over this happiness there is another happiness which we expect in the future, by which we will see God as he is. This, certainly, is above any given created intellect at all.[265]

This teaching from *ST* I, q. 62, a. 1, is repeated in the following article, which introduces the concept of a twofold happiness corresponding to man's twofold perfection. Virtue, he says, perfects man so that he can attain happiness, but to attain the happiness that surpasses what is proportionate to human nature, he needs the theological virtues because there can be no natural desire "to see God by his essence, in which the ultimate beatitude of a rational creature consists."[266]

The natural virtues, in addition to the form of the natural virtues which is prudence, stand in need of being oriented to the supernatural. Thomas explains that, without charity, which is "more excellent than the other virtues"[267] as that which "most attains God,"[268] man's will cannot be properly related to God:

> God is the end of those with upright wills—and charity and good delight and happiness; nevertheless in such a way that God is the ultimate end and happiness encompassing charity and delight, even as an end under the end, being joined together by the ultimate end, since an operation tends to the object; nor is there a right relation of the will toward God except by means of these three.[269]

Charity, which is constitutive of true happiness, unites man with the supreme end, God himself. Although it is not a natural but an accidental

---

[265] *ST* I, q. 62, a. 1, corp.: "Nomine beatitudinis intelligitur ultima perfectio rationalis, seu intellectualis naturae: et inde est, quod naturaliter desideratur; quia unumquodque naturaliter desiderat suam ultimam perfectionem. Ultima autem perfectio rationalis, seu intellectualis naturae est duplex. Una quidem, quam potest assequi virtute suae naturae; et haec quodammodo beatitudo, vel felicitas dicitur. Unde et Arist. (bk. 10. Eth. cap. 8.) perfectissimam hominis contemplationem, qua optimum intelligibile, quod est Deus, contemplari potest in hac vita, dicit esse ultimam hominis felicitatem: sed super hanc felicitatem est alia felicitas, quam in futuro expectamus, qua videbimus Deum sicuti est. Quod quidem est supra cujuslibet intellectus creati naturam."

[266] *ST* I, q. 62, a. 2, corp.

[267] *ST* II-II, q. 24, a. 4, ad 2: "... sequitur, quod ipsa sit excellentior aliis virtutibus." II-II, q. 157, a. 4, ad 2, similarly refers to charity as the *maxima virtutum*.

[268] *ST* II-II, q. 23, a. 6, corp.

[269] *In* II *sent.*, dist. 38, q. 1, a. 2, corp.

form,[270] the fact that "every agent acts by virtue of form"[271] implies that those who have it act in virtue of it. Granted that prudence is the form of the moral virtues, charity holds the place of honor as the form of *all* the virtues,[272] which means that prudence relies upon charity and faith if it is to direct someone to the supernatural happiness[273] that surpasses man's natural capacity.[274] In other words, prudence needs to be infused by charity, which for its part necessarily presupposes faith[275] since the will is able to be moved toward the last end only if that end is first in the intellect.[276]

Without charity moving prudence efficiently[277] toward the supernatural end, prudence cannot enable man to attain the truly "right realization"[278] of himself:

---

[270] See, *ST* II-II, q. 23, a. 3, ad 2.

[271] *De potentia*, q. 3, a. 9, ad 5 (trans. S. C. Selner-Wright in *On Creation*, Thomas Aquinas in Translation [Washington, DC: Catholic University of America Press, 2011], 79). Cf. Aristotle, *Physics* 3.2.202a9–12, on which Thomas commentates likewise that every agent acts by virtue of form (*In* III *phys.*, lec. 4, no. 593).

[272] *In* II *sent.*, dist. 27, q. 2, a. 4, qc 3, corp.: "Charity is the form of *all* the other virtues, as prudence is the form of the *moral* virtues" (*On Love and Charity*, 166).

[273] *ST* II-II, q. 4, a. 7, corp., says faith is *per se* first among all the virtues, and *In* II *sent.*, dist. 41, q. 1, a. 1, ad 2, elaborates on its importance in directing all of our acts to the last end. Ad 3 in this article emphasizes that natural prudence is not sufficient: "Prudence sufficiently directs to that end that is the human good, but not to the end that is the divine good, which is what is promised in heaven." *In* II *sent.*, dist. 38, q. 1, a. 2, corp., clarifies that the beatitude or happiness that is the ultimate end is the kind of happiness that "embraces charity" as an end under the end (*sicut finis sub fine*). For this reason, we might say that true prudence leads one to true happiness in virtue of charity. Finally, *In* III *sent.*, dist. 23, q. 1, a. 4, qc 3, ad 3, further elaborates on the need for each of the theological virtues: "Regarding the end that is elevated above nature, it is necessary for a gratuitous habit to precede the other habits both in the intellectual part (as faith) and in the affective part (as charity and hope), since the natural inclination does not extend to it."

[274] See, *ST* I, q. 62, a. 1, corp.

[275] *ST* II-II, q. 4, a. 7, ad 5: "Ad quintum dicendum, quod actus voluntatis praeexigitur ad fidem, non tamen actus voluntatis charitate informatus: sed talis actus praesupponit fidem; quia non potest voluntas perfecto amore in Deum tendere, nisi intellectus rectam fidem habeat circa ipsum."

[276] *ST* II-II, q. 4, a. 7, corp.

[277] *ST* II-II, q. 23, a. 8, ad 1.

[278] This is an oblique reference to Keenan. I use the phrase somewhat tongue in cheek because Keenan does not seem to fully grasp the point I am trying to make here, as he seems in the following quote to think of natural prudence as being sufficient for some: "This move allows Thomas to speak across confessional lines so as to engage all human beings to see that the quest we each have for the right realization of our own selves is accessible to each one of us. The thirteenth-century Dominican offers through prudence . . . a way that one can determine oneself according to one's own inclinations."

It is evident that the rectitude of human reason is compared to divine reason as a lower motive principle. Because it is moved to the higher one, it is also referred to it; for the eternal reason is the supreme rule of all human rectitude—and thus prudence, which implies rectitude of reason, is most of all perfected and helped inasmuch as it is ruled and moved by the Holy Spirit.[279]

Although "prudence sufficiently directs one toward that end which is the human good," it does not sufficiently direct a man toward "the divine good, which is promised in the heavenly fatherland."[280] As an intellectual virtue, it is, in a sense, especially reliant upon faith for this because:

> There cannot be a voluntary motion toward something unless that thing be known. It is necessary, therefore, that the knowledge of the ultimate end be appointed [*praestituatur*] in us by grace so that we might voluntarily be directed toward it. This knowledge, though, is not able to be according to an open vision in the present state, as was shown. Therefore, it must be known by faith.... By the help of divine grace, we are directed toward this end, which is the manifest vision of the first truth in itself. Necessarily, then, before this end is attained, man's intellect must be subjected to God by way of believing, with divine grace bringing this about.[281]

Keenan, "The Virtue of Prudence (IIa IIae, Qq. 47–56)," in Pope, *Ethics of Aquinas*, 259–74, at 264 (including note 57).

[279] *ST* II-II, q. 52, a. 2, corp.: "Manifestum est autem, quod rectitudo rationis humanae comparatur ad rationem divinam, sicut principium motivum inferius; quod movetur ad superius, et refertur in ipsum; ratio enim aeterna est suprema regula omnis humanae rectitudinis; et ideo prudentia, quae importat rationis rectitudinem, maxime perficitur, et juvatur, secundum quod regulatur, et movetur a Spiritu Sancto." See also I-II, q. 109, a. 3, ad 1: "Charity loves God over all things in a more eminent way than nature. For nature loves God over all things inasmuch as he is the beginning and end of the natural good whereas charity loves him according as he is the object of beatitude and inasmuch as man has a certain spiritual friendship with God" ("Caritas diligit deum super omnia eminentius quam natura. Natura enim diligit deum super omnia, prout est principium et finis naturalis boni, caritas autem secundum quod est obiectum beatitudinis, et secundum quod homo habet quandam societatem spiritualem cum Deo"). He is referring to the gift of counsel, but the theological virtues are the origin of the gifts (I-II, q. 69, a. 4, ad 3).

[280] *In* II *sent.*, dist. 41, q. 1, a. 1, ad 3: "Prudence sufficiently directs to that end that is the human good, but not to the end that is the divine good, which is what is promised in the heavenly fatherland."

[281] *SCG* III, ch. 152, no. 2 "Voluntarius autem motus in aliquid esse non potest nisi sit

The virtue of faith is preeminent among all the virtues inasmuch as it ensures the human intellect has the supernatural end appointed (*praestituatur*) to it.[282] Saint Thomas even says faith is *per se* first among all the virtues precisely for this reason:

> Since, in practical affairs [*agibilium*], the end is the beginning, . . . it is necessary that the theological virtues, the object of which is the ultimate end, be prior to the other virtues. It is necessary, however, that the ultimate end itself be in the intellect before it is in the will, because the will is not carried into something except to the degree that it is apprehended by the intellect.[283] Accordingly, since the ultimate end is in the will through hope and charity but in the intellect through faith, it is necessary that faith be first among all the virtues because natural knowledge is not able to attain to God inasmuch as he is the object of beatitude, according to which aspect hope and charity tend to him.[284]

Faith is the foundational virtue that makes actions that lead to the attainment of eternal beatitude possible. Although not all have it, everyone

---

cognitum. Oportet igitur quod per gratiam in nobis cognitio ultimi finis praestituatur, ad hoc quod voluntarie dirigamur in ipsum. Haec autem cognitio non potest esse secundum apertam visionem in statu isto, ut supra probatum est. Oportet igitur quod sit cognitio per fidem. . . . Auxilio divinae gratiae dirigimur in ultimum finem, qui est manifesta visio Primae Veritatis in seipsa. Ergo oportet quod, antequam ad istum finem veniatur, intellectus hominis Deo subdatur per modum credulitatis, divina gratia hoc faciente."

[282] *SCG* III, ch. 152, no. 2: "It is necessary, therefore, that knowledge of the last end be appointed [*praestituatur*] in order that we be directed toward it voluntarily." *SCG* III, ch. 118, no. 6: "This is what is said in Heb 11:6: 'without faith it is impossible to please God.' And Exod 20:2 says that, before other precepts of law were laid down, right faith about God was appointed, when it is said, 'Hear, O Israel, the Lord your God is one.'"

[283] As John of St. Thomas says: "To be apprehended is the condition of every proposed object of the will, whether it be an end or a means. 'Nothing is willed that is not known first.'" (*Cursus philosophicus thomisticus* [new edition], vol. 2, *Philosophia Naturalis*, pt. 1 [*Philosophiae naturalis*], q. 13 [*De fine*], a. 1 [p. 243]).

[284] *ST* II-II, q. 4, a. 7, corp.: "Cum enim in agibilibus finis sit principium, ut supra dictum est, necesse est virtutes theologicas, quarum obiectum est ultimus finis, esse priores ceteris virtutibus. Ipse autem ultimus finis oportet quod prius sit in intellectu quam in voluntate, quia voluntas non fertur in aliquid nisi prout est in intellectu apprehensum. Unde cum ultimus finis sit quidem in voluntate per spem et caritatem, in intellectu autem per fidem, necesse est quod fides sit prima inter omnes virtutes, quia naturalis cognitio non potest attingere ad Deum secundum quod est obiectum beatitudinis, prout tendit in ipsum spes et caritas."

at least has knowledge of the universal and perfect good, which means they all desire happiness under the common *ratio* of it which Boethius describes as "a state that has been perfected by the coming together of all good things."[285] We can conclude from this that there must be an implicit desire for some kind of "indefinite more"[286] that might be referred to as an implicit desire for God. Aquinas speaks of this kind of desire in *De veritate*, where he says, "created existence [*esse*] itself is a likeness to the divine goodness. When things desire 'to be,' they implicitly desire a likeness to God and God himself."[287] Similarly, in the *Scriptum*, he says "everyone has an appetite for God."[288] Though he refrains from using the word "implicit" in this text, it seems to suggest the term, because it is certain that all do not know God exists and that they do not have an appetite for him "as he is in his own nature." As Saint Paul aptly puts it, "no eye has seen, nor ear heard, nor the heart of man conceived, what God has prepared for those who love him."[289] Accordingly, the appetite for "him" that is explicit in all men is merely the appetite for any given thing, inasmuch as "nothing is

---

[285] *ST* I-II, q. 3, a. 3, obj. 2: "status omnium bonorum congregatione perfectus."

[286] I first heard this felicitious phrase from Steven Long, and have appropriated it because it is clearly implied in *ST* I-II, q. 3, a. 8.

[287] *De veritate*, q. 22, a. 2, ad 2.: "Ipsum esse creatum est similitudo divinae bonitatis; unde in quantum aliqua desiderant esse, desiderant Dei similitudinem et Deum implicite." He said something similar in the ad 1 in regard to implicit knowledge of God: "All knowing beings implicitly know God in anything known. For just as nothing has the *ratio* of appetibility except through a likeness to the first goodness, so nothing is knowable except through a likeness to the first truth" ("Ad primum igitur dicendum, quod etiam omnia cognoscentia cognoscunt implicite Deum in quolibet cognito. Sicut enim nihil habet rationem appetibilis nisi per similitudinem primae bonitatis, ita nihil est cognoscibile nisi per similitudinem primae veritatis"). See also, *De virtutibus*, q. 2, a. 12, ad 16.

[288] *In I sent.*, dist. 3, q. 1, a. 2, ad 1. I have not been consistent in the way I have translated this word, but in this case, I defer to Kwasniewski's way of translating it. As he notes, "have appetite for" is certainly lacking in elegance, but at the least it makes the reader wonder what Aquinas meant by using this word. As he says, "it will not do to substitute systematically 'desire' or 'seek' or some other verb that has its own solid Latin equivalent (*desiderunt, concupiscunt, quaerunt,* etc.) when there is a metaphysical issue at stake, namely the understanding of *appetitus* as such, and not merely *desiderium* or *concupiscentia*. A different formula, such as 'to desire x,' suggests false associations—for example, that we are dealing here with emotions." He observes that Aquinas asks the question "whether someone can have an appetite for misery" (*In IV sent.*, dist. 49, q. 1, a. 3 [*On Love and Charity*, 366]). He could not ask that if *appetere* ought to be translated as "feel." We are certainly speaking about what St. Francis de Sales would call our "higher natures" here, and not the sensitive appetite.

[289] 1 Cor 2:9, a verse often cited by Aquinas.

desired except to the degree it has a likeness to him."[290]

We are ordered to God and our nature makes us capable of knowing him and being directed toward him. Without the agency of God moving us, however, we do not know that of which we are capable. The potency for even the life of grace, for being conformed to the *imago Christi*, is one that only a divine agent can actualize. As Long says regarding this ability known as obediential potency:

> Obediential potency is a passive potency that when conjoined with the active agency of God is susceptible of a definite range of actuation otherwise unattainable (consider the simile of stained glass and the sun's illumination). The natural desire for God signifies the profundity of the human spirit whereby it is able to receive such aid. Yet it is not simply in itself a desire for essentially supernatural beatific vision, but arches toward God along an infravalent trajectory proportioned to the nature of the finite faculty whose perfection is indeterminately sought before being uplifted in desire for the triune God.[291]

Since this potency is passive, there is, strictly speaking, nothing man can do to get God to actualize it. As Aquinas puts it, "all knowledge, which is in accord with the mode of the created substance, falls short of the vision of the divine essence, which infinitely exceeds every created substance. For this reason, neither man nor any creature is able to attain ultimate beatitude through their own natural powers."[292] Nevertheless, Sacred Scripture

---

[290] *In* I *sent.*, dist. 3, q. 1, a. 2, ad 1.

[291] Steven A. Long, "Obediential Potency, Human Knowledge and the Natural Desire for God," *International Philosophical Quarterly* 37, no. 1 (March 1997): 45–63, at 58. As he words it elsewhere: "The 'necessary desire for the perfect good or happiness that structures the will' is the desire for the intelligible-good-in-general. Under the active agency of God this desire is susceptible of becoming a true desire for divine beatitude. But in and of itself this natural desire is not the desire for supernatural beatitude, for the-good-in-general is neither naturally identical with, nor does it naturally 'include,' the divine good. The full perfection of the good subsists uniquely and super-eminently in God, and hence under God's active agency we may be brought to graced desire for the divine good" ("On the Possibility," 225). See also: *De veritate*, q. 8, a. 4, ad 13; a. 12, ad 4; q. 29, a. 3; *De virtutibus*, q. 1, a. 10, ad 13; Long, "Obediential Potency"; Peter A. Pagan-Aguiar, "St. Thomas Aquinas and Human Finality: Paradox or *Mysterium Fidei?*" *The Thomist* 64 (2000): 375–99.

[292] *ST* I-II, q. 5, a. 5, corp.: "Omnis autem cognitio, quae est secundum modum substantiae creatae, deficit a visione divinae essentiae, quae in infinitum excedit omnem

is clear that God "desires all to be saved and come to a knowledge of the truth,"[293] so no one need despair that God will abandon him or her. With this in mind, Saint Thomas says man is instructed to do what is within himself to turn (*convertat*) himself to God, which comes about by free will (*per liberum arbitrium*).[294] Although "man is not able to prepare himself to receive the light of grace except through the gratuitous help of God moving him interiorly,"[295] and although man's *nature* itself cannot "give him some principle by which he is able to attain [supernatural] beatitude," he is nevertheless exhorted to do "that which is within himself,"[296] because his nature does at least provide him with the faculty of "free will by which he can turn himself to God, who can make him attain beatitude."[297] In other words, despite the fact that it is impossible for man "to be turned towards his ultimate beatitude"[298] on his own, it *is* possible in the qualified sense that "what we can do with the divine aid is not *altogether* impossible for us," since "what we can do through our friends, we can in some way do by ourselves."[299]

In the *De veritate*, this capacity to turn to God (which must presuppose some initial help of God[300]) is referred to as the ability of man to appoint (*praestituere*) to himself as an end the supreme end which is God himself:

> If someone does what is within himself when he enters adulthood [i.e., when he reaches the age of reason], the grace through which he will be exempt from original sin will be given to him, and if he

---

substantiam creatam; unde nec homo, nec aliqua creatura potest consequi beatitudinem ultimam per sua naturalia."

[293] 1 Tim 2:4: *hos pantas anthrōpous thelei sōthēnai kai eis epignōsin alētheias elthein* (*Novum Testamentum Graece*, ed. Kurt Aland et al., 28th ed. [Stuttgart: Deutsche Bibelgesellschaft, 2012]).

[294] See: *ST* I-II, q. 109, a. 6, ad 1; q. 112, a. 3, sc.

[295] *ST* I-II, q. 109, a. 6, corp.: "Homo non potest se praeparare ad lumen gratiae suscipiendum, nisi per auxilium gratuitum Dei interius moventis." See also, *De veritate*, q. 24, a. 1, ad 2.

[296] *ST* II-II, q. 33, a. 2, ad 1.

[297] *ST* I-II, q. 5, a. 5, ad 1, explains that nature does not give man the desire for happiness in vain.

[298] See *ST* I, q. 62, a. 2, ad 2, which says it is impossible, inasmuch as it is beyond his nature.

[299] *ST* I-II, q. 109, a. 4, ad 2: "Possumus cum auxilio divino, non est nobis omnino impossibile."

[300] As the body of *ST* I-II, q. 112, a. 3, says, God's help is necessary even for the preparation for grace: "Man's preparation for grace is from God, as from the one moving, and from free will, as from that which is moved."

does not do what is within himself, there will be guilt due to the sin of omission. Now, since any given man is held to avoid sin, and this cannot be done unless he has appointed a fitting end for himself, everyone is held, when he first attains control over his mind, to turn himself to God and to establish the end in him—and by this, he is disposed for grace.[301]

In the case of the angels, who never lack the possession of reason, "some of them immediately appointed / placed [*praestitisset*] an impediment to their happiness."[302] Humans can do the same when they reach the age of reason. They are charged, however, to instead place the *ratio* of perfect happiness before themselves, which would at least implicitly be placing God before themselves as their end. Thomas explains the relationship between happiness and God:

> Happiness is the perfect good which totally sets the appetite at rest; otherwise, it would not be the ultimate end if there remained an appetite for something further. But the object of the will (which is the human appetite) is the universal good just as the object of the intellect is the universal true. And from this it is clear that nothing is able to set the will of man at rest but the universal good; which is not found in anything created, but only in God.[303]

The natural desire of man is for the universal good which alone can make him truly happy.[304] If he places this end before himself as a goal to pur-

---

[301] *De veritate*, q. 28, a. 3, ad 4: "Cum enim adultus esse incipit, si quod in se est, faciat, gratia ei dabitur, per quam a peccato originali erit immunis; quod si non faciat, reus erit peccato omissionis. Cum enim quilibet teneatur peccatum vitare, et hoc fieri non possit nisi praestituto sibi debito fine; tenetur quilibet, cum primo suae mentis est compos, ad Deum se convertere, et in eo finem constituere; et per hoc ad gratiam disponitur." *ST* I-II, q. 89, a. 6, corp., is practically identical.

[302] *ST* I, q. 63, a. 6, ad 3.

[303] *ST* I-II, q. 2, a. 8, corp.: "Beatitudo enim est bonum perfectum, quod totaliter quietat appetitum: alioquin non esset ultimus finis, si adhuc restaret aliquid appetendum: objectum autem voluntatis, quae est appetitus humanus, est universale bonum: sicut obiectum intellectus est universale verum: ex quo patet, quod nihil potest quietare voluntatem hominis, nisi bonum universale; quod non invenitur in aliquo creato, sed solum in Deo."

[304] *De regno*, ch. 9, no. 63: "Now, since the desire of an intellectual nature is for the universal good, this good is the only one that is able to make someone truly happy. Indeed,

sue,³⁰⁵ divine grace may make him cognizant of the fact that Providence has ordered him toward the vision of God, considered in his own nature and not simply under the *ratio* of being the cause of certain created effects.³⁰⁶

In this chapter, we have seen that, even if all do not come to see that the "end for the sake of which" is God, there is at least the possibility of coming to realize that in virtue of man's intellectual nature and the desire to know ultimate causes. The mere aptitude man has for knowing and loving God neither suffices for perceiving him as the perfectly good object of supernatural beatitude nor for loving him habitually; nevertheless, it does provide an indispensable foundation for doing so and is an indication of how significant it is to be made *ad imaginem Dei*.³⁰⁷

Synderesis, which is only possible because man was made in the image of God, unites unites all of man's activities in the pursuit of the perfect

---

once this good is secured, no other good is able to be desired. Accordingly, happiness is called the 'perfect good' as embracing all other desirable things in itself. Now, such a good is not able to be some earthly good."

[305] I speak this way to make clear that man has a role to play in disposing himself for grace. We should always keep in mind, however, that "man is able to do nothing, unless he be moved by God—as is stated in John 15, 'without me you can do nothing'—and therefore when man is said to do that which is within himself, this is said to be in man's power insofar as he is moved by God" (I-II, q. 109, a. 6, ad 2).

[306] *ST* I-II, q. 3, a. 8, corp.: "If, then, the human intellect knows something of the created effects but does not know anything about God other than that he is, the perfection of that intellect does not yet attain, simply speaking, to the first cause. Instead, there remains for it some natural desire to seek the cause and it is not yet perfectly happy. Consequently, it is required for perfect happiness that the intellect reach to the essence itself of the first cause." See Jacques Maritain, *Approaches to God*, trans. Peter O'Reilly (New York: Harper, 1954), 109–10: "But this desire to know the *First Cause through its essence* is a desire which does not know what it asks, like the sons of Zebedee when they asked to sit on the right and on the left of the Son of Man. *Ye know not what ye ask*, Jesus replied to them. For to know the First Cause in its essence, or without the intermediary of any other thing, is to know the First cause otherwise than as First Cause" (quoted in Long, "Obediential Potency," 60n49).

[307] See Gen 1:26. In *ST* I, q. 93, a. 1, Thomas observes that Christ alone is the image of God whereas intellectual creatures are made ad *imaginem Dei* (see also a. 2). In *ST* I-II, q. 113, a. 10, corp., we learn that the soul is "naturally capable of grace," because to be made *ad imaginem Dei* implies having "a natural aptitude for knowing and loving God" even though grace is necessary to "actually and habitually" love him (see I, q. 93, a. 4, corp.). In other words, man has a capacity of nature that is not a natural capacity because grace needs to perfect nature in order for the created good of which man is capable to be raised to the good he is capable of "as an object, which is infinite" (see, I-II, q. 2 a. 8, corp.).

good, and dialectical reasoning enables him to apply principles held in virtue of natural reason to particular actions. Happiness is, therefore, not found in synderesis, because one has to apply those most basic principles, such as that "one ought to act according to reason"[308] and that "evil should be done to no one,"[309] to particular practical actions. However, by pointing toward ends such as the need to act in accordance with reason, synderesis does direct man toward the attainment of happiness. I have already made many arguments to the effect that synderesis is primary as that which appoints the end that the appetites follow after in the pursuit of the perfect good. According to this model, synderesis would direct prudence to the end that it pursues even though prudence also relies upon upright appetites to help direct a person to happiness. For many, however, Aquinas had a significant change of thought over the course of his lifetime and came to think that reason (even the natural reason) does not have the possibility of appointing ends to the will in any meaningful sense because that would indicate a kind of intellectual determinism. We will consider those arguments in the coming chapter and then attempt to explain as clearly and definitively as possible in chapter 3 how synderesis and prudence can respectively be said to appoint the end to the moral virtues—albeit under the guidance of the supernatural virtue of faith.

---

[308] *ST* II-II, q. 47, a. 7, corp. *ST* II-II, q. 141, a. 2, corp., gives a similar explanation of how temperance and fortitude pursue the good of reason.
[309] *ST* II-II, q. 49, a. 2, ad 1.

CHAPTER 2

On the Causality of the Intellect

WITH GOOD REASON, Daniel Westberg asserts that "one of the most fundamental and challenging problems in the interpretation of Saint Thomas is the proper relationship of intellect and will, on which so much of moral theology (and thus of the *Summa Theologiae*) hinges."[1] One's theology is radically dependent upon such fundamental philosophical principles, and thus Saint Thomas says the theologian must be concerned with all of the effects of God, even on the level of nature.[2] Because being is God's proper effect,[3] the relationship between being and the good (and, by extension, between the intellect and the will[4]) is a foundational consideration even for the theologian.

In a chapter of Kevin Flannery's extraordinary work *Acts Amid Precepts,* which is dedicated to the relationship of the intellect and the will, he says, as if by way of an *apologia*, that the question of this relationship "is not an abstract, 'metaphysical' issue; nor is it of merely historical interest, although the approach I take in this chapter is historical."[5] For my

---

[1] Daniel Westberg: "Did Aquinas Change His Mind about the Will?," *The Thomist* 58, no. 1 (1994): 41–60, at 41.
[2] *ST* I, q. 1, a. 7, ad 1: "Although we are not able to know what God is, we nevertheless make use of his effects in theology, whether those pertaining to nature or to grace."
[3] See *ST* I, q. 8, a. 1, corp. ("Since God is being itself through his own essence, it is necessary that created being be his proper effect"; q. 45, a. 5, corp. ("Now among effects, the most universal is being itself. It is therefore necessary that it be the proper effect of the first and most universal cause, which is God.... Now the proper effect of God creating is that which is presupposed by all the others; namely, absolute being").
[4] Being is the "proper object of the intellect" (*ST* I, q. 5, a. 2, corp.), whereas "good is the proper object of the will" (*De potentia*, q. 3, a. 15, ad 5).
[5] Kevin Flannery, S.J., *Acts Amid Precepts: The Aristotelian Logical Structure of Thomas Aquinas's Moral Theory* (Washington, DC: Catholic University of America Press, 2001), 111.

part, I would say the question of the relationship between cognition and volition is, in fact, metaphysical to some extent, even while insisting that metaphysics enjoys a "privileged instrumentality" within the science of theology.[6] Moreover, since this foundational question has such far-reaching implications (and particularly in regard to whether the intellect can be said to appoint ends at all), it seems imperative to spend a few pages exploring the relationship in combination with historical considerations that are frequently raised alongside of the philosophical question in contemporary scholarship. This is, in a sense, the condition for entering into the modern debate about the significance of the intellect's role in the moral life because, as Denis Bradley notes:

> Contemporary discussions of free choice/decision often begin by affirming or denying Odon Lottin's claim (publicized first in 1928 and, thereafter, reasserted with various nuances until the mid-1950s) that Aquinas moved away (around 1270, with the publication of the *De Malo*, specifically in question 6 thereof) from an Aristotelian intellectual determinism towards a more radically voluntaristic notion of freedom.[7]

Evaluating this claim—which coincides with a more particular claim of Lottin that this supposed voluntaristic move coincided with a move away from referring to the intellect as acting in the manner of a final cause[8]—is

---

[6] See Steven Long, "Pruning the Vine of *La Nouvelle Theologie* in the Garden of Thomism: Regarding the Thomistic Corrective to 'La Nouvelle Theologie,'" *Angelicum* 93 (2016): 135–56, at 139: "*Esse* as the act of being posits and implies substantial nature with its powers and connatural ends. Thus arises the privileged instrumentality of metaphysics, and of ontology of nature, within *sacra doctrina*."

[7] Denis J. M. Bradley, "Reason and the Natural Law: Flannery's Reconstruction of Aquinas's Moral Theory," *The Thomist* 67, no. 1 (2003): 119–31, at 123–124.

[8] See Odon Lottin, "La preuve de la liberté humaine chez Thomas d'Aquin," *Recherches de théologie ancienne et médiévale* 23 (1956): 325: "At no point before *De malo* was reason, the formal cause of human nature, presented as a formal cause of human action" (cited from James Keenan, *Goodness and Rightness in Thomas Aquinas's Summa theologiae* [Washington, DC: Georgetown University Press, 1992], 38n1). Lottin further suggests Thomas came to think final causality and efficient causality could not be separated and that, as a result, they would have to be attributed to the will, whereas formal causality would have to be attributed to the reason. He comes to this conclusion after asking this rhetorical question: "Can one separate, as Thomas had done up until then, final causality and efficient causality on account of the fact that the efficient cause does not move to act except in view of an end and since the will, which is the efficient cause of the free act, cannot act except in view of the good (of the end), which is its proper

actually a vital means to a right evaluation of our metanarrative about the appointing of the end. That is, if Aquinas gradually became more voluntaristic in his approach, perhaps the right way of reconciling his apparently conflicting comments regarding synderesis and prudence vis-à-vis the end of the moral virtues would be to argue that the "mature" Thomas would say they both appoint the end in a quasi-passive fashion. Each of them, after all, is referred to as a kind of reason, and if reason is ultimately subjected to will, the sentiment of the earlier Thomas that a human agent is not able to determine to do anything unless his determination arises "from some knowledge appointing [*praestituente*] the end to that action" would certainly be called into question.[9] Were this to occur, one could defensibly maintain that the mature Thomas would say synderesis and prudence (regardless of which has a more fundamental role in the task of appointing ends) appoint only ends that can be judged in terms of their moral goodness thanks to one's subjective appetites. Were this the case, a kind of visceral perceptivity would appear to be the final arbiter of moral goodness.

James Keenan is one of the theologians who arrives at a conclusion very similar to this. His teaching, which he attributes to post-1270 Thomas, is that the first exercise of the will is always prior to any intellectual specification[10] and that the will is autonomous.[11] Because he is one of the few[12] modern authors who have taken time to attempt a careful

---

object?" In answer to this, he argues that, later in *De malo*, Thomas will argue that it is "the will that simultaneously plays the roles of efficient and of final cause, and the role of formal cause thus falls to reason (see Lottin, *Psychologie et morale aux XIIe et XIIIe siecles*, 1:254, 256; cited from Rosemary Zita Lauer, "St. Thomas's Theory of Intellectual Causality in Election," *The New Scholasticism* 28, no. 3 (1954): 299–319, at 301).

[9] *In II sent.*, dist. 25, q. 1, a. 1, corp.: "Now it is necessary that the determination of an agent to perform some act proceed from some knowledge appointing [*praestituente*] the end to that action."

[10] See Keenan, *Goodness and Rightness*, 47: "As first mover, the will's movement is independent of and prior to reason's presentation of the object." Keenan elsewhere speaks of exercise as preceding specification (e.g., 148). This is because he believes that "formal interior acts" are "antecedent to questions concerning specification" (142).

[11] Keenan, *Goodness and Rightness*, 44 (where he explains this realization came about for Thomas when he switched from speaking of the intellect's influence in terms of final causality to speaking of it in terms of formal causality). Keenan explains this autonomy in virtue of the will's ability to move itself from potency to act (33, 46).

[12] One may also point, above all else, to Dominic Farrell, *The Ends of the Moral Virtues and the First Principles of Practical Reason in Thomas Aquinas* (Rome: Gregorian and Biblical Press, 2012). Others have also taken the issue seriously, though, such as: John Finnis, *Reason in Action* (Oxford University Press, 2011), 26–29; Terrence Irwin, *The*

explanation of the differing statements made in regard to prudence in *ST* I-II, q. 66, and II-II, q. 47, his ideas are certainly worthy of consideration. We will address his understanding of those texts in particular in the next chapter. More germane to our present consideration is his view of the roles of the intellect and the will, according to which "Lottin and his contemporaries" were correct in positing "a reversal of Thomas's earlier position on the will."[13] If it becomes evident that, *pace* Keenan, there was no "significant shift,"[14] the stage will be set for better addressing his explanation regarding that manner in which ends are appointed to the moral virtues in chapter 3 of the present book.

Keenan is not alone in arguing Aquinas became less and less focused on the causal power of the intellect and its ability to propose anything to the will. Aquinas wrote in a later work that "the end moves the desire of the agent,"[15] and in the present chapter, I will argue that he never altered his position that desire must always follow some intellectual apprehension which inseparably links the intellect to the end. In other words, every agent possessed of free will must "act through an *understood* form"[16] because knowledge proposing the end comes first. Saint Thomas's terminology did shift in view of circumstances and audience, but his teaching is remarkably consistent. Accordingly, when Thomas de Vio Cajetan argues that, for Aquinas, the intellect has primacy among the powers of the soul and is even a cause of the other powers (and moves them all)[17] and when

---

Development of Ethics, vol. 1 (New York: Oxford University Press, 2011), 521–22, 550, 562, 582; Denis J. M. Bradley, *Aquinas on the Twofold Good: Reason and Human Happiness in Aquinas's Moral Science* (Washington, DC: Catholic University of America Press, 1997), 207, 247, 237–56; Scott MacDonald, "Foundations in Aquinas's Ethics," in *Objectivism, Subjectivism and Relativism in Ethics*, ed. Ellen Frankel Paul, Fred D. Miller Jr., and Jeffrey Paul (Cambridge: Cambridge University Press, 2008), 350–68.

[13] Keenan, *Goodness and Rightness*, 41.

[14] Keenan, *Goodness and Rightness*, 41.

[15] *In I eth.*, lec. 9, no. 6: "Finis movet desiderium agentis." This work is dated to 1271–1272.

[16] *ST* I, q. 47, a. 1, ad 1: "Agens autem voluntarium . . . agit per formam intellectam" (emphasis added).

[17] Cajetan commentary on *ST* I-II, q. 9, a. 2: "In keeping with the maxim 'the first in any genus is the cause of all the things that are after it,' the intellect moves the other powers" (Leonine ed., 6:76). According to *SCG* I, ch.47, the powers of the soul (and the intellect is a power of the soul, as is clear from *SCG* II, ch 61) are distinguished according to their objects. In view of this and the fact that the true is absolutely speaking prior to the good as to the *suppositum* (see *ST* I, q. 16, a. 4, corp.), one could arrive at the same conclusion as Cajetan regarding the primacy of the intellect over the other powers. Also, Aquinas says the powers of the soul that precede the other powers in the order of perfection and

Francesco Silvestri (whose annotations have been added to the Leonine edition of the *Summa contra gentiles*) says Thomas teaches the intellect is the *superior mover* in man[18] that is "simply prior to the will,"[19] they represent the consistent views of the Angelic Doctor, even if many modern scholars differ with them on this point.[20]

The intellect's importance in general is particularly evident from the way Saint Thomas speaks throughout the corpus of the way it appoints the end. *De potentia* (1265–1266[21]) refers to a gradation among beings that is contingent upon their ability (or lack thereof) to determine their own practical ends for themselves.[22] This determination, though, can

---

nature are the principle of the others by way of an end and active principle (*ST* I, q. 77, a. 7, corp.). Perhaps he is referring to the intellect moving as a final cause and the will as an effiicient cause.

[18] Commenting on *SCG* III, ch. 25, no. 7 (Leonine ed., 14:69). He goes on: "By taking mover in the common sense, as to extend oneself to moving by way of an end . . . the intellect is the first mover in man, because it moves the will by way of an end, which Saint Thomas signifies when he teaches that it moves the appetite 'by proposing its object to it'; for the good and the end is the object of the will." He is also known as Silvester of Ferrara or Sylvestris.

[19] Francesco Silvestri, commentary on *SCG* III, ch. 26: "The intellect is simply prior to the will while the will is prior to the intellect only in a qualified way. Now, in the first part, . . . he compares these powers according to their proper notions and he shows the intellect, even according to its proper understanding (rationem), to be unqualifiedly more noble than the will and the will to be more noble in a qualified way" (Leonine ed., 14:78).

[20] See Westberg: "Did Aquinas Change His Mind?," 51, where he takes a position on this that "is definitely not the standard, 'received' view of traditional scholastic commentators," even though he also argues for greater continuity than do most scholars who have considered the question of development on this point.

[21] See Jean-Pierre Torrell, *Saint Thomas Aquinas*, vol. 1, *The Person and His Work*, rev. ed., trans. Robert Royal (Washington, DC: Catholic University of America Press, 2005), 328.

[22] *De potentia*, q. 1, a. 5, corp.: "Every agent acts on account of an end, because all things want the good. Now, if the action of an agent is to be appropriate for the end, it is necessary that it be adapted and proportionate to it, which is able to be done only by some intellect that knows the notion [*ratio*] of the end and the proper relationship of the end to the means. Otherwise, the suitability of the action to the end would be by chance. But the intellect ordering toward the end in advance is sometimes joined to the agent or the mover (as a man in his own action), and sometimes it is separated (as happens when a bow tends toward a determined end, not by an intellect that it has itself but by the intellect of the man directing it). Now it is impossible for that which acts from a necessity of nature to determine the end for itself because whatever does so acts from itself—and because it is acting or moved from itself, the principle of acting or not acting and moving or being moved is from itself (as is said in the eighth book of the *Physics*).

occur only in intellectual creatures. Although rational beings rely upon nature in regard to certain general ends, those ends must be cognized and appropriated in the individual.[23] Aquinas cites Cicero in the *Scriptum* (1255–1266[24]) when he says that virtue acts in accordance with a certain natural and affective inclination, but he insists that humans, unlike irrational animals, must use their reason to appoint (*praestituere*) both the common and particular end to the virtues.[25] In question 18 of *ST* I (ca.

But this is not able to be the case for that which is moved from necessity since it is determined to one."

[23] *In* II *sent.*, dist. 25, q. 1, a. 1, corp., similarly divides creatures basically into two—namely, those who are able to determine their own actions and others who have it determined to them by another since they do not have rational natures and thus cannot appoint it to themselves: "Now it is necessary that the determination of an agent to perform some act proceed from some knowledge appointing [*praestituente*] the end to that act. But the knowledge determining an action and appointing [*praestituens*] the end is joined to some (as a man who appoints [*praestituit*] the end of his action himself), whereas in others it is separated (as in those things which act by nature)." Because this determination pertains to knowledge, Thomas says in *De veritate*, q. 3, a. 1, that this self-determination is brought about through the intellect: "The agent himself determines the end for himself, as is the case in all agents acting in virtue of intellect." *ST* I-II, q. 6, a. 2, corp., speaks of this intellectual apprehension as a perfect kind of knowledge that rational creatures alone enjoy: "Now there is a twofold knowledge of the end—namely, a perfect and an imperfect one. Now, knowledge of the end is perfect when not only the thing [*res*] that is the end is apprehended, but also the notion [*ratio*] of the end and the way the means is ordered to the end itself—and such knowledge belongs to the rational nature alone. Knowledge of the end is imperfect when it consists solely in the apprehension of the end and when neither the notion of the end is known nor the way the act relates to the end—and such knowledge of the end is found in brute animals through their senses and their natural valuation [*aestimationem*]. Therefore, the perfect notion of the voluntary follows upon perfect knowledge of the end. The end being apprehended, then, someone is able to deliberate about the end, and of those things that are for the end [the means], and also able to be moved toward the end, or not to be moved." See also: *ST* I, q. 6, a. 2, corp.; q. 11, a. 2, corp.; q. 18, a. 3; and an interesting variation of the theme in *In* I *eth.*, lec. 9, no. 6. These texts indicate John Capreolus was correct to divide creatures into those who have some knowledge conjoined to them in virtue of their rational nature (such as man, who is able to appoint/*praestituit* the end for himself) and those who do not; see *Defensiones Theologiae Divi Thomae Aquinatis*, vol. 4, dist. 24 (Turin: Cattier, 1903), 228.

[24] Torrell, *Saint Thomas Aquinas*, 1:328.

[25] *In* III *sent.*, dist. 33, q. 2, a. 5, corp.: "For Virtue, as Tully [Cicero] says, moves in the manner of nature—namely, by a certain inclination of the inclination [*affectus*]. . . . It is necessary that through reason . . . the end be appointed [*praestituatur*] to the other virtues, not only the common ones but also the proximate. This is to attain the mean in one's own nature. Now the mean is determined in keeping with right reason."

1270), he adds that those who are not able to do so (*non tamen per seipsa praestituunt sibi finem suae operationis*) are on an entirely inferior level to rational creatures because, even though rational creatures are dependent upon God, apropos of the way they are ordered toward their ultimate ends,[26] they are in a certain way able to have dominion over the way they react to that natural ordination. As such, they

> move themselves even in respect to an end they appoint to themselves [*movent seipsa, etiam habito respectu ad finem, quem sibi praestituunt*], which only comes about through reason and understanding since it pertains to these to know the proportion between the end and that which is for the end and to move the one towards the other.[27]

The intellect, therefore, is the power that enables a man to appoint an end to himself even though this must, of course, be seen in tandem with the fact that "all motions, whether bodily or spiritual, are reduced to the first mover, who is God."[28] Indeed, the intellect's subordinated causality is evident from what Aquinas goes on to say in question 18 to the effect that, even though our reason or intellect[29] moves itself (*se agat*) in regard

---

[26] *ST* I, q. 18, a. 3, corp.: "Although our intellect moves itself toward some things, other things are appointed [*praestituata*] by nature, as are the first principles, which cannot be doubted, and the last end, which one cannot not will. Thus although the intellect moves itself toward one thing [*ad aliquid*], it is moved by another toward other things [*ad aliqua*]. Therefore, that whose own nature is to understand—and which naturally possesses that which is not determined by another—is that which has life in the highest degree; now such a thing is God."

[27] *ST* I, q. 18, a. 3, corp.: "Unde supra talia animalia sunt illa, quae movent seipsa, etiam habito respectu ad finem, quem sibi praestituunt. Quod quidem non fit, nisi per rationem, et intellectum, cujus est cognoscere proportionem finis, et ejus, quod est ad finem, et unum ordinare in alterum."

[28] *ST* I-II, q. 109, a. 1, corp.: "Omnes motus tam corporales quam spirituales reducuntur in primum movens simpliciter, quod est Deus." For a discussion of the implications of this important text, see Steven Long, "Perfect Storm: Loss of Nature as Normative Principle," in *What Happened in and to Moral Philosophy in the Twentieth Century? Philosophical Essays in Honor of Alasdair Macintyre*, ed. Fran O'Rourke (Notre Dame, IN: University of Notre Dame Press, 2013), 273–305, at 284–85.

[29] Although these two are distinguished because the intellect pertains to simple apprehension and the reason to a dialectical process of ratiocination, they are often spoken of as synonymous. Aquinas does so by saying, "reason or intellect" in many places (e.g., *ST* I, q. 21, a. 2, ad 1; I-II, q. 13, a. 1, corp.); in *ST* I-II, q. 62, a. 3, corp., he even speaks of the "reason or intellect" as containing the first universal principles, even though those

to some things, other things (such as the first principles one cannot doubt[30]) are appointed (*praestituta*) by nature.[31] That is, even if the intellect can move itself, it is naturally ordered toward first principles that God implants in man by means of nature. Consequently, Thomas insists the natural and universal judgment of synderesis is distinct from *liberum arbitrium*: "Judgment does not relate to free will [*liberum arbitrium*] and to synderesis in the same way. A judgment that is *universal* pertains to synderesis according to universal principles of law, since we always make judgments about conclusions through principles, ... whereas a *particular* judgment about a certain doable thing, which is the judgment of choice, pertains to free will [*liberum arbitrium*]. Therefore, synderesis is not the same as free will [*liberum arbitrium*]."[32]

Since nature is subordinated to the God of nature, man's reason or intellect is a rule that is ruled by the first rule, which is God.[33] In God, the act of understanding itself is identical to his nature ("sua natura est ipsum ejus intelligere"), and thus he not only has a nature that cannot be determined by another,[34] but he also appoints the end to every being.[35] Presupposing the end he appoints through nature or grace, one is able to make those ends one's own if one is endowed with reason, and this fact is indicative of the

---

principles are simply apprehended.

[30] Literally, "one cannot be related to otherwise," but this relation is one of apprehending the truth immediately and thus such principles are not able to be doubted.

[31] *ST* I, q. 18, a. 3, corp. (see trans. in note 26 above).

[32] *In II sent.*, dist. 24, q. 2, a. 3, ad 4: "Judicium non eodem modo libero arbitrio et synderesi convenit: quia ad synderesim pertinet universale judicium, secundum universalia juris principia: semper enim de conclusionibus per principia judicatur ... sed ad liberum arbitrium pertinet judicium particulare de hoc operabili, quod est judicium electionis. Unde synderesis non est idem quod liberum arbitrium." Regarding the link between the *liberum arbitrium* and the judgment of choice, Thomas also says the *liberum arbitrium* is the same as the will though it names the will's order to its act, which is to choose, in *De veritate*, q. 24, a. 6, corp. In ad 1 of the same article, he explains it somewhat differently by saying it does not name the will absolutely, but only in relation to the order to reason.

[33] *De virtutibus*, q. 5, a. 1, arg. 10: "Moreover, the definition of moral virtue is understood in the way it pertains to reason, as the Philosopher makes clear in the second book of the *Ethics*, which defines virtue through the fact that it is in keeping with right reason. But right reason is a measured measure from the first measure, who is God. It has the power of ruling from him." De virtutibus, q. 5, a. 1, ad 10: "The moral virtues pertain to reason as their proximate rule and to God as their first rule."

[34] *ST* I, q. 18, a. 3, corp.: "That, therefore, whose own nature is to understand—and which naturally possesses that which is not determined by another—is that which has life in the highest degree; now such a thing is God."

[35] For passages explicitly stating this fact, see *SCG* I, 1, ch. 44, no. 7, and *De veritate*, q. 3, a. 1.

intellect's dignity. But what kind of causality does the intellect exercise when it makes a natural or free judgment? We have seen that faith and synderesis both pertain to knowledge that one must further apply to particular acts; but how does the reason or the intellect in general do that?

For Thomas, "intention presupposes an act of the reason or of the intellect"[36] because it "presupposes knowledge through which the end toward which it moves is proposed to the will."[37] Before anyone intends to do anything as a means, the intellect has to have first apprehended some truth that it proposes to the will as an object of pursuit. When someone has intellectual knowledge about a thing as good (i.e., when he has knowledge of it *sub ratione boni*), his will necessarily is drawn toward it to the degree it is perceived as good and fitting.[38] If he judges that it is attainable, he may then intend it as an end[39] that would terminate the

---

[36] *ST* I-II, q. 12, a. 3, obj. 3. The reply does not refute the premise. In fact, it is affirmed a few times in question twelve.

[37] *ST* I-II, q. 12, a. 1, ad 1: "Intentio nominatur oculus metaphorice; non quia ad cognitionem pertinet; sed quia cognitionem praesupponit, per quam proponitur voluntati finis, ad quem movet."

[38] This is at least so inasmuch as it is apprehended as good "according to all the particulars that can be considered" (*De malo*, q. 6, corp.: "Si ergo apprehendatur aliquid ut bonum conveniens secundum omnia particularia quae considerari possunt, ex necessitate movebit voluntatem"). Note that the qualification "*to the degree* it is perceived as good" is essential. In regard to things that are necessarily willed by nature, see *ST* I-II, q. 10, a. 1, corp., which speaks of man naturally willing the knowledge of the truth, being, living and other such things that pertain to natural well-being. Also, *De veritate*, q. 22, a. 5, corp., mentions the ultimate end in addition to "those things that are included in it, as being, the knowledge of the truth, and other things of this sort" as things which the will naturally wills (since nature is the *volunatis fundamentum*). Finally, in *De malo*, q. 3, a. 3, corp., Thomas speaks of the will being moved necessarily to *whatever* has a necessary connection with happiness, "which is naturally willed." In regard to fittingness, see *De malo*, q. 6, and *ST* I-II, q. 9, a. 2, corp. The thing that moves the will as an object is "that which is apprehended under the notion of the good and the fitting." Although Thomas sometimes omits mentioning the need for that object to be apprehended as fitting (*conveniens*), the notion seems implied by earlier texts such as that of *In III sent.*, dist. 27, q. 1, a. 1, ad 3 ("the root of love, per se speaking, is the likeness of the loved to the one loving; because in this way it is good and befitting to it") and sc 4 of the same article, which makes an argument for the *bonum conveniens* being the object of the concupiscible appetite that could be applied to the rational appetite. The perfectly fitting good that is man's happiness itself (*ST* I-II, q. 2, a. 6, corp.), of course, is the only good that necessarily moves the will because it alone "is apprehended as a good according to all the particulars that can be considered" (see *De malo*, q. 6).

[39] On these acts concerning the end of human actions, see: J. A. Oesterle, *Ethics: The Introduction to Moral Science* (Englewood Cliffs, NJ: Pretnice-Hall, 1957), 85;

motion of his will once attained.[40] For the will to go after it in that way, however, the intellect must point to it. The question, again, is *how* it points to (one might say *appoints*) it exactly.

The final cause, of course, takes precedence over the other causes, and the will does whatever it does for the sake of the final cause. Nevertheless, if the soul's potencies are to be moved toward actualization on the level of exercise, the will must act as a principle of that motion.[41] In other words, "the will must act as the efficient or agent cause of the act"[42] for there to be motion toward the end, because it is the "first mover among the powers of the soul vis-à-vis the exercise of the act."[43] If, at least in Aquinas's earlier writings, this activity of the will is ultimately reduced to the causality of the intellect (which, in turn, acts in the manner of a final cause), would this essentially lead to the elimination of free will? In other words, would linking the intellect to final causality essentially make the intellect to be an efficient cause as well? That is, was Lottin correct to suggest that the early Thomas should not have attempted to separate final and efficient causality and should have attributed both to the will instead?[44]

The end does, in fact, act in such a way that Thomas sometimes speaks of its causality in a way that is reminiscent of efficient causality. As Aquinas says in *ST* I:

> Something is said to act in a threefold way. In one way, formally, in the way of speaking whereby whiteness makes white. ... In another way, something is said to act effectively, as when a painter is said to make a wall white. In the third way, by way of a final

---

Francis L. B. Cunningham, O.P., *The Christian Life* (Eugene, OR: Wipf and Stock, n.d.; originally Priory Press, 1959), 51–55. Michael S. Sherwin, O.P, similarly speaks of apprehension, *simplex voluntas*, and *ordinatio*, in which "the practical reason apprehends the good as an end attainable by us" in regard to the end (*By Knowledge and By Love: Charity and Knowledge in the Moral Theology of Thomas Aquinas* [Washington, DC: Catholic University of America Press, 2005], 85).

[40] *ST* I-II, q. 12, a. 2, corp.: "Intentio respicit finem, secundum quod est terminus motus voluntatis."

[41] *De malo*, q. 6, corp.: "If we consider the motion of the powers of the soul on the part of the exercise of the act, the principle of motion is from the will."

[42] Sherwin, *By Knowledge and By Love*, 51.

[43] *ST* I-II, q. 17, a. 1, corp.: "Primum autem movens in viribus animae ad exercitium actus est voluntas."

[44] See Lottin, *Psychologie et morale*, 1:254, 256, as cited by Lauer, "St. Thomas's Theory of Intellectual Causality in Election," 301 (see note 8 above for English trans.).

cause [*per modum causae finalis*], as an end is said to effect [*efficere*] by moving the efficient cause [*efficientem*].[45]

One might observe that Thomas is merely asserting here that the intellect is effective in moving an efficient cause in virtue of its presentation of the object, but it remains effective—even if in a qualified sense. If the intellect acts in this manner when it acts as a kind of final cause, is there room for free will? The first thing to establish is that Saint Thomas does speak of the causality of the intellect in terms of final causality (at times, at least). Since he does so most frequently in his earlier writings, we will begin there.

The Intellect as a Final Cause in the Earlier Works

The subject of the intellect's final causality—or more precisely, the subject of whether the intellect acts *in the manner of* a final cause—is indispensable for us as we attempt to determine the way the intellectual habits of synderesis and prudence can be said to appoint or present the end to the moral virtues. In fact, the more general question of how the cognitive and appetitive "parts" of man interact is even more foundational and far reaching in its consequences because the moral virtues, which pertain to the appetitive part, have the good of reason as their end.[46] As such, the intellect or reason must propose (i.e., appoint[47]) the common end of human life

---

[45] *ST* I, q. 48, a. 1, ad 4: "Aliquid agere dicitur tripliciter. Uno modo formaliter, eo modo loquendi, quo dicitur albedo facere album. Et sic malum etiam ratione ipsius privationis dicitur corrumpere bonum; quia est ipsa corruptio, vel privatio boni. Alio modo dicitur aliquid agere effective: sicut pictor dicitur facere album parietem. Tertio modo per modum causae finalis, sicut finis dicitur efficere movendo efficientem."

[46] *In III sent.*, dist. 33, q. 1, a. 1, qc 1, corp. ("Now, the good to which the human virtues are proximately ordered is the good of reason"); *De virtutibus*, q. 2, a. 2, corp. ("The proper good of man inasmuch as he is man is the good of reason because to be man is to be rational"); see also, *ST* II-II, q. 141, a. 6, corp.

[47] It seems likely that the word *praestituere* ("to appoint") was originally used to refer to the way that God arranged nature by setting it up in an orderly fashion by means of certain laws. That meaning then was carried over and applied to the agent intellect in particular, since it was a kind of participation in the *ratio Dei* and thus also able to set up in advance or appoint the end to man. This meaning then was applied further to any way the intellect or the reason in general puts something forward to the will. In this sense, it is synonymous with *proponit*; and thus, when the intellect is said to propose the end to the will when it acts in the manner of a final cause, it is doing nothing other than appointing the end.

(which is, again, the *bonum rationis*[48]) to the appetitive part because they are the two indispensable moving principles in the human person and must act in unison if the final end is to be attained.[49] Daniel De Haan appropriately refers to this dynamic as an "inextricable confluence of cognitional operations specifying appetitive operations by final causality, and the efficient causality of appetitive operations drawing the person to the object known and sought."[50] Without this confluence, man simply will not attain the last end.

One of the works in which Saint Thomas refers to the intellect moving the will "not according to the manner of an efficient or agent cause, but according to the manner of a final cause . . . by proposing its object to it"[51] is the *Summa contra gentiles*. Interestingly, this way of speaking essentially says *intellectus* appoints (*praestituit*) the end to the will, because *proponere* ("to place before") and *praestituere* ("to set up before / appoint") are practically synonymous. They are also very close to *praebere* ("to proffer, supply") in meaning, which is significant, as John of St. Thomas explains final causality in terms of antecedently supplying—*praebendo*—that in which the agent's motion terminates.[52] No matter which exact word is used, therefore, final causality seems to be inseparably connected with the intellectual activity of putting some object forward that has been apprehended as good in some way. As a consequence, Aquinas is saying the intellect or reason (they

---

[48] *In III sent.*, dist. 33, q. 2, a. 3, corp.: "The proximate end of human life is the good of reason in general."

[49] *In I eth.*, lec. 1, no. 8 ("There are two principles of human acts—namely, the intellect or reason and the appetite"); *ST* I-II, q. 58, a. 3, corp. ("Human virtue is a certain habit perfecting man for acting well. But the beginning of human acts in man is nothing if not twofold—namely, the intellect or reason and the appetite—for these are the two moving powers in man")

[50] Daniel D. De Haan, "Moral Perception and the Function of the *Vis Cogitativa* in Thomas Aquinas's Doctrine of Antecedent and Consequent Passions," *Documenti e studi sulla tradizione filosofica medievale* 25 (2014): 289–330, at 303.

[51] *SCG* III, ch. 72, no. 7: "Intellectus, non secundum modum causae efficientis et moventis, sed secundum modum causae finalis, moveat voluntatem, proponendo sibi suum obiectum, quod est finis."

[52] John of St. Thomas, *Cursus philosophicus thomisticus* (new edition), vol. 2, *Philosophia Naturalis*, pt. 1 [*Philosophiae naturalis*], q. 13 [*De fine*], a. 1: "The end carries in the notion of goodness . . . by supplying that in which the movement of the efficient cause terminates ([Paris: Ludovicus Vives, 1883], 244).

are one power,[53] though it is important to distinguish them at times[54]) places or appoints the end as a final cause, which is the way, as we will see, the *intellectus* that is translated as "understanding" (and that is often analogous to *synderesis* or natural reason) appoints or proposes the end.

In one of the places in *SCG* that speaks of the intellect acting in this way, Aquinas is proving it to be "manifestly false" to say the will is higher than the intellect on the pretext that the will "moves the intellect to its act since the intellect only actually considers something that it holds habitually whenever someone wills it."[55] In response to this idea, he says:

> First and *per se*, the intellect moves the will because the will, as such, is moved by its object, which is the apprehended good. For the will moves the intellect *per accidens* inasmuch as the act of understanding is apprehended as a good and is thus desired by the will, from which it follows that the intellect understands in act. And in this [act of understanding] itself, the intellect precedes the will: for the will would never desire to understand unless the intellect first apprehended understanding itself as a good. And again, the will moves the intellect for doing things in act in the way an agent is said to move. The intellect, however, moves the will in the way an end moves because the good understood is the end of the will; the agent, however, comes later in moving than the end because the agent does not move except on account of the end. For this reason, it is apparent that the intellect is simply higher than the will.[56]

---

[53] *ST* I, q. 79, a. 8, corp.: "We understand and reason discursively [*ratiocinamur*] through the same power. It is clear, then, that the reason and the intellect are the same power in man." For this reason, Thomas himself often speaks of them as synonyms; see *In I eth.*, lec. 1, no. 8, and *ST* I-II, q. 58, a. 3, corp.

[54] See, for instance, *ST* I, q. 82, a. 1, ad 2.

[55] *SCG* III, ch. 26, no. 22: "Voluntas movet intellectum ad suum actum; intellectus enim actu considerat quae habitu tenet, cum aliquis voluerit."

[56] *SCG* III, ch. 26, no. 22: "Primo et per se intellectus movet voluntatem: voluntas enim, inquantum huiusmodi, movetur a suo obiecto, quod est bonum apprehensum. Voluntas autem movet intellectum quasi per accidens, inquantum scilicet intelligere ipsum apprehenditur ut bonum, et sic desideratur a voluntate, ex quo sequitur quod intellectus actu intelligit. Et in hoc ipso intellectus voluntatem praecedit: nunquam enim voluntas desideraret intelligere nisi prius intellectus ipsum intelligere apprehenderet ut bonum. Et iterum, voluntas movet intellectum ad operandum in actu per modum quo agens movere dicitur; intellectus autem voluntatem per modum quo finis movet, nam bonum intellectum est finis voluntatis; agens autem est posterior in movendo quam finis, nam agens non movet nisi propter finem. Unde apparet intellectum simpliciter esse altiorem voluntate."

Aquinas could hardly be more clear when he says the intellect is higher *simpliciter* than the will. Likewise unequivocal is the notion that, even when the will moves the intellect to understand in act, it is dependent upon the preceding activity of the intellect. Even so, Cajetan's explanation of this doctrine helps unpack the reasons for Aquinas's teaching on this point. He explains that the intellect is more noble than the will because the object of the intellect is, in a sense, more universal. Indeed, the very notion of the good is particularized, inasmuch as it implies an order to something else (and thus the will implies a going out), whereas the notion of the true, which the intellect is concerned with,[57] is more abstract[58] (in the sense, I take it, that one can rest in the truth[59] and it is considered for its own sake without reference to something else).

For Cajetan, the object of the intellect is a thing inasmuch as it is "that which is" (*res ut quod quid est*), whereas the object of the will, though referred to as an apprehended or understood good[60] (or even *bonum simpliciter*[61] in many places), is really a *particular* being in the sense that it is understood as being good only because it is first a being. Lawrence Dewan, who finds this teaching in both *ST* I, q. 82, a. 4 (pre-1270), and I-II, q. 9, a. 1 (written around 1270 and the locus of the purported voluntarist shift in Aquinas's thought) explains:

> The intellect moves the will because "the good itself" (*ipsum bonum*), the very object of the will as will, is apprehended in function of a special notion (*secundum quandam specialem rationem*) included under the universal notion of "the true" (*sub universali ratione veri*). The special notion here is . . . an object of intellect inasmuch as it falls within the proper domain of intellect as itself a particular notion. It is particular as compared to "that which is" (*ens*) and "the true" (*verum*). If goodness is not seen *as a being*, it will not be seen at all.[62]

---

[57] Although in *ST* I, q. 105 a 4, corp., universal being is said to be the object of the intellect, the true is said to be its object in II-II, q. 4, a. 1. In I-II, q. 9, a. 1, corp., the "formal principle of the intellect" is *ens et verum universale*.

[58] Cajetan commentary on *ST* I, q. 82, a. 3, no. 21: "Boni ratio magis dicitur ad alterum, ratio vero veri dicitur magis absolute.

[59] *ST* II-II, q. 180, a. 3, corp.: "The ultimate crowning act is the contemplation of the truth."

[60] In *SCG* III, ch. 85, the object of the will is the apprehended good, and in *SCG* I, ch. 72, it is the *bonum intellectum*. Interestingly, in *SCG* III, ch. 148, it is the "good and the end."

[61] *ST* I, 48, a. 5.

[62] Lawrence Dewan, *Wisdom, Law, and Virtue: Essays in Thomistic Ethics* (New York:

The good itself is necessarily something that *is*. In other words, it is a *being* which thus has the *ratio* of the good inasmuch as it exists. For this reason, the causality on the side of the object of the intellect is more absolute and causal.[63] He argues, moreover, that the motion of the will is necessarily subordinated to that of the intellect because the "motion of the intellect as intellect" goes before the will, which is the reason "intellectual activity [*intellectio*] is first simply."[64] In the later Thomas, this is even the case in regard to "the ultimate end itself," because this last end "must be in the intellect previously to its being in the will, because the will is not borne toward anything save inasmuch as it is apprehended by the intellect."[65]

Returning to Thomas's earlier assertions, *ST* I speaks of the intellect's causality as follows:

> That which is first simply and according to the order of nature is more perfect. For this reason, act is prior to potency. In this way, the intellect is prior to the will as the mover is prior to the movable and as the active is prior to the passive; for the understood good moves the will.[66]

Fordham University Press, 2007), 167. See also *ST* I, q. 82, a. 4, ad 1, according to which "the intellect is simply higher and more noble than the will" and "the good is contained under the true inasmuch as it is a certain understood true thing [*quoddam verum intellectum*]." The ad 4 of the same article is also most noteworthy, as it places the beginning of the mutual causality of the intellect and will in the intellect ("It is not necessary to proceed infinitely, but one must stop at the intellect as that which is first. For, apprehension must precede every motion of the will, but a motion of the will need not precede every apprehension").

[63] Cajetan's commentary on *ST* I, q. 82, a. 3, nos. 14–17, argues that the object of the intellect, which is some given thing considered *qua* existing, is more abstract *simpliciter* than the object of the will, which is an object having being (*obiectum habens esse*). He also says the "boni ratio magis dicitur ad alterum, ratio vero veri dicitur magis absolute and objectum intellectus est res ut quod quid est; voluntatis autem ut habens esse."

[64] Cajetan's commentary on *ST* I, q. 82, a. 4, no. 10: "Since our intellectual motions are ordered, the will's motions are reduced [to act] by means of an intellective motion, whereas the intellect's motion [is so reduced] by itself. And because the motion of the intellect as intellect is not one commanded by the will, but one that comes before the will, intellectual activity is first simply [*simpliciter*]; therefore, as is the case in primary intellection simply, primary intellectual activity is traced back to God as the universal and first principle of that which is intellectual."

[65] *ST* II-II, q. 4, a. 7, corp.: "Ultimus finis oportet quod prius sit in intellectu, quam in voluntate: quia voluntas non fertur in aliquid, nisi prout est in intellectu apprehensum" (trans. from Dewan, *Wisdom, Law and Virtue*, 173).

[66] *ST* I, q. 82, a. 3, ad 2: "Illud, quod est prius simpliciter, et secundum naturae ordinem, est perfectius: sic enim actus est prior potentia. Et hoc modo intellectus est prior voluntate,

This passage is somewhat striking in its profound simplicity. Aquinas suggests that *act* is to *potency* (1) as the *intellect* is to the *will*, (2) as a *mover* is to something *movable*,[67] (3) as something *active* is to something *passive*, and finally (4) as the *understood good* is to the *will*.[68] The intellect essentially functions something like the understood good does while acting as some kind of mover. In view of I, q. 82, a. 4 (the very next article after that just quoted) stating, "the intellect moves the will because the understood good is the object of the will and moves it as an *end*,"[69] the intellect seems to be most closely associated with final causality at this point in the writings of the Angelic Doctor. Given that "the first mover in man is the intellect," since "the intellect by its intelligible object moves the will,"[70] and that the end is that which is first in intention, it seems natural to say the way the intellect moves or brings things about is as a final cause. In moral matters, that which comes first is something that is inseparably connected with finality—namely, the end. The intellect makes it possible for the end to be intended, because intention itself indicates an act of the will with special emphasis on the "order to reason."[71] Whenever we intend something, our will presupposes an intellectual apprehension of an end.[72] If that end were

---

sicut motivum mobili, et activum passivo: bonum enim intellectum movet voluntatem."

[67] *ST* I, q. 83, a. 4, ad 3: "Intellectus comparatur ad voluntatem ut movens."

[68] Namely, as a proximate mover: "The proximate motive of the will is the understood good, which is its object and is moved by it as sight is by color" (*SCG* III, ch. 88, no. 2). It is necessarily willed (*SCG* I, ch.72, no. 2: "Since the understood good is the proper object of the will, it is necessary that the understood good, inasmuch as it is such, is willed"), though something bad is sometimes joined to the good that is understood (*De malo* q. 3, a, 12, ad 2: "The will is always principally carried into something good; and from a vehement motion into something good, it happens that an evil that is joined to that good is endured").

[69] *ST* I, q. 82, a. 4, corp.: "Intellectus movet voluntatem, quia bonum intellectum . . . movet ipsam ut finis." See also *De veritate*, q. 22, a. 12, ad 3: "The intellect moves in the manner of an end; for it is in this way that the apprehended good is related to the will."

[70] *SCG* II, ch. 60, no. 4: "Primum autem movens in homine est intellectus: nam intellectus suo intelligibili movet voluntatem."

[71] *De veritate*, q. 22, a. 13, corp.: "Since, then, the object of this act of intention is the good which is the end (which is also the object of the will), it is necessary for intention to be an act of the will. It is not, however, an act of the will absolutely, but only in regard to its order to reason."

[72] On the link between intention and the end, see the previous footnote. On the presupposed intellectual apprehension, *ST* I, q. 79, a. 10, ad 3 says that the intellectual power known as intelligence precedes intention, which directs that which it apprehended to something else. The later *ST* I-II, q. 12, a. 1, ad 3 expresses the idea by saying that intention "names an act of the will, presupposing the decree of reason ordering something to the end." Of course, the will itself follows the reason, as *Quolibet* VI, q. 2, a. 2,

not cognized intellectually, it would simply never be willed.[73]

Nevertheless, many commentators posit an outright reversal of this position. Since all of the pertinent[74] quotes in this section thus far are considered to be pre-1270, further consideration is called for lest we be accused of disregarding George Klubertanz's complaint that too many read Aquinas in an "ahistorical" fashion and "continue to discuss the relationship between the will and reason without consideration for any historical development within Thomas's writings."[75] If it turns out that he did, in fact, alter his position and that he came to think the intellect is not able to act in the manner of a final cause by proposing the end to the will, it will be impossible for *any* habit of the intellect (whether synderesis, faith, or prudence) to appoint the end to the moral virtues in any significant sense of the word "appoint."

Shift in Aquinas's Teaching?

In Westberg's article "Did Aquinas Change His Mind about the Will?," he relates the development that led many authors, including Bernard Lonergan,[76] to follow Lottin's 1928 thesis[77] that one should look to the ninth question of *ST* I-II and the sixth question of *De malo* for a turning point in Aquinas's thought.[78] He explains that the position they put for-

---

demonstrates ("the motion of the will is an inclination following an understood form"), but intention is, in a sense, more intimately bound up with it.

[73] At this point, we can again call to mind *Quolibet* VI, q. 2, a. 2 ("The motion of the will is an inclination following an understood form") and the first book of the first chapter of *CT*: "The appetite following the intellect is the will."

[74] The commentary on the *Ethics*, *ST* I-II, q. 58, and II-II, q. 180, are exceptions, but they address indirectly related ideas.

[75] Cited in Keenan, *Goodness and Rightness*, 82.

[76] Bernard Lonergan, *Collected Works of Bernard Lonergan. Grace and Freedom*, vol. 1, *Operative Grace in the Thought of Thomas Aquinas* (Buffalo, NY: University of Toronto Press, 2013), 96n: "In these latter works, St. Thomas conceived the distinction between the specification and the exercise of the act of the will" (he cites both passages in this note. See also: Lonergan, *Collected Works*, 1:370; Lonergan, "St. Thomas's Thought on *Gratia Operans*," *Theological Studies* 3 (1942): 69–88, 375–402, 533–78, at 534; Westberg, "Did Aquinas Change His Mind?," 42.

[77] See Odon Lottin, "La date de la Question Disputée *De malo* de Saint Thomas d'Aquin," *Revue d'histoire ecclésiastique* 24 (1928): 373–88, and Westberg, "Did Aquinas Change His Mind?," 42.

[78] As David Gallagher says, such scholars see the supposed "introduction" of this distinction "as a response to the condemnation of certain propositions in Paris in 1270, maintaining that Thomas wished to emphasize the will's freedom and self-motion,"

ward is that Aquinas went from a kind of "intellectualist" account that "pictures the will having to follow what the intellect concludes" to one that de-emphasizes the causality of the intellect and might even be called a quasi-voluntarist account according to which "the will is free to decide on an action no matter what the intellect comes up with."[79] No doubt this fascinating theory has some modicum of truth to it. Although Flannery adeptly demonstrates that "Lottin's various disclaimers ensure that his position itself will always defy falsification, with the natural consequence that it also lacks a clear sense,"[80] so many scholars would not have gone along with his general attitude toward the question if there were not at least the possibility of coherently arguing Aquinas undertook some sort of significant shift. At the same time, it will serve us well to have in the back of our minds a question Dewan urges us to consider in regard to this very issue: whether any change in terminology or emphasis we happen upon should be considered "a development in Thomas's conception of the very things being discussed" or, rather, a somewhat insignificant "revision in the interests of pedagogy."[81]

Placing the question in its context, Saint Thomas was "in the middle of his second full academic year in Paris" when Steven Tempier, the bishop of that city, condemned thirteen propositions pertaining to Latin Averroism.[82] As a proponent of Augustinianism who tended not to sympathize

---

while others think "Thomas's response to the condemnations accentuated a movement to be found throughout his career toward a more 'voluntaristic' understanding of choice" ("The Will and Its Acts (Ia IIae, Qq. 6–17)," in *The Ethics of Aquinas*, ed. Stephen J. Pope, Moral Traditions Series [Washington, DC: Georgetown University Press, 2002], 69–89, at 75n19). Gallagher cites: Lottin, *Psychologie et morale*, 1:207–16, 225–43; O.-H. Pesch, "Philosophie und Theologie der Freiheit bei Thomas von Aquin in quaest. disp. 6 De malo," *Münchener theologische Zeitschrift* 13 (1962): 1–25; H. M. Manteau-Bonamy, "La liberté de l'homme selon Thomas d'Aquin (la datation de la Q. Disp. De malo)," *Archives d'histoire doctrinale et littéraire du moyen age* 46 (1979): 7–34. Keenan notes there has been some pushback to this thesis of development, citing: Lauer, "St. Thomas's Theory of Intellectual Causality in Election," and Tibor Horváth, *Caritas est in ratione* (Münster: Aschendoffsche, 1966), 56–57 (*Goodness and Rightness*, 41 and note 15).

[79] Westberg, "Did Aquinas Change His Mind?," 51.
[80] See Flannery, *Acts Amid Precepts*, 115. He demonstrates that either Lottin was rather unconvinced of the veracity of his own position or it was at least frequently in a state of flux.
[81] See Dewan, *Wisdom, Law, and Virtue*, 153.
[82] On these condemnations, see James A. Weisheipl, O.P, *Friar Thomas D'Aquino: His Life, Thought and Works* (New York: Doubleday, 1974), 276.

with the attempt to incorporate the thought of Aristotle into theology,[83] the bishop took issue with two propositions of the Averroists that must have especially influenced Aquinas to either rethink or reformulate (at least for expediency's sake) his teachings. One condemned proposition was "the will of man wills or chooses necessarily," and another was "liberum arbitrium est potentia passiva, non activa; et quod necessitate movetur ab appetibili [free judgment is a passive power, not an active one, and that it is necessarily moved by the desired object]."[84] In this quote, *liberum arbitrium* is often translated as "free will."[85] Although "free will" is a conventional way of rendering *liberum arbitrium*, it is important to note that *arbitrium* (judgment) is strictly speaking different from *voluntas* (will).

With this distinction in mind, Sherwin argues that, even though Thomas did, in fact, affirm that the *will* is a passive potency, the thesis that was condemned was affirming that free *judgment* is a passive potency, "something Thomas never held."[86] That he at least did not hold it to be an entirely passive power in his earlier thought is indicated by question *ST* I, q. 83, in which he says free judgment (*liberum arbitrium*) is "the cause of its own motion because man moves himself to acting by means of free judgment," adding that it is "indifferently related to choosing well or badly."[87] This being the case, it seems unlikely he ever considered it to be entirely passive.[88]

---

[83] See Weisheipl, *Friar Thomas D'Aquino*, 285: "[that] free judgment is a passive power, not active, and that it is necessarily moved by the desirable object."

[84] *Chartularium Universitatis Parisiensis*, ed. H. Denifle, vol. 1 (Paris, 1899), 48.

[85] Weisheipl, *Friar Thomas D'Aquino*, 276.

[86] Sherwin, *By Knowledge and By Love*, 96n126. That the earlier Thomas considered the will to be passive is evident from *ST* I, q. 82, a. 3, ad 2 ("The intellect is prior to the will as . . . the active is prior to the passive") and that the later Thomas did so is evident from I-II, q. 51, aa. 2–3, I-II, q. 18, a. 2, and *De malo*, q. 6, ad 7 (where the will is said to be in potency). Other indications that Thomas did not consider free judgment to be a passive potency can be found in questions 19 (a. 8, sc) and 83 (a. 2, corp.) of the *ST* I. In q. 19, he denies that the will necessarily wills whatever it wills on the grounds that *liberum arbitrium* would then perish, and in q. 86, he says "free judgment [*liberum arbitrium*] is indifferently related to choosing well or badly."

[87] In *ST* I, q. 83, a. 1, ad 3, he says: "Free judgment is the cause of its own motion because man moves himself by free judgment to acting by means of free judgment." In the body of the next article, we read: "Free judgment is indifferently related to choosing well or badly."

[88] It may be worth noting that Sherwin's analysis needs to be qualified. It seems undeniable that, since *liberum arbitrium* is an active power that needs to be applied, the doctrine of physical premotion would require that it be passive on some level. Sherwin's point remains helpful, however, because Thomas certainly would have made a distinction

The reality, however, is that some would not have made the distinction between the will and what is often translated as "free will" (*liberum arbitrium*) because the two are so closely connected. Thomas spoke of how closely allied they are while insisting upon their distinction in the *Scriptum*:

> The will which is of the end and the free judgment are not diverse powers, . . . but *boulesis* [which pertains to choosing means] and *thelesis* [which pertains to the end itself [89]] differ because it pertains to free judgment to choose something in relation to the end while the will is of the end absolutely.[90]

Just as the speculative and the practical intellects have different ends despite the fact that they are not strictly distinct powers,[91] something similar can be said about the will (i.e., *thelēsis*, which regards the end) and the free judgment of choice (i.e., *boulēsis*, which regards the means).[92] One can

---

between the way the will is passive and the way *liberum arbitrium* is.

[89] *ST* I, q. 83, a. 4, obj. 1: "*Thelēsis* and *boulēsis* are different. *Thelēsis* is the will, but *boulēsis* seems to be free judgment because *boulesis* according to him [Damascene] is the will regarding an object pertaining to a comparison of two things." See also *ST* III, q. 18, a. 3, obj. 1: "There is twofold will in man; namely, the natural will which is called *thelēsis*, and the rational will which is called *boulēsis*."

[90] *In* III *sent.*, dist. 17, q. 1, a. 1, qc 3, ad 5: "Voluntas quae est finis, et liberum arbitrium, non sunt diversae potentiae, sicut in 2 Lib., dist. 24, quaest. 1, art. 3, dictum est; sed differunt bulesis et thelesis, quia ad liberum arbitrium pertinet eligere aliquid in ordine ad finem, voluntas autem est de fine absolute."

[91] See *ST* I, q. 79, a. 11.

[92] By referring to *boulēsis* as the "free judgment of choice," I am trying to emphasize that there is a distinction between the judgments of the intellect alone (the natural one, the judgment of conscience and the theoretical judgment) and the judgment that pertains to the will (since choice is materially of the will even if formally of the intellect). *ST* I, q. 83, a. 4, suggests *thelēsis* "est voluntas" while *boulēsis* seems to be *arbitrium liberum* (see obj., 1, and the reply to it). The judgment of the will is distinguished from the judgment of the reason as follows in *De veritate*, q. 24, a. 6, ad 1: "The power by which we freely judge is not understood to be that by which we judge simply, which pertains to reason, but that which makes one free in judging, which is the will. Therefore free judgment is the will itself. For it does not name it absolutely, but in the order toward one of its acts, which is to choose." It is distinguished from the judgment of conscience in *De veritate*, q. 17, a. 1, ad 4: "The judgment of conscience is different from that of free will [*liberi arbitrii*] because the judgment of conscience consists in knowledge alone, whereas the judgment of free will consists in the application of knowledge to desire and this judgment is the judgment of choice." It is distinguished from the judgment of synderesis in *De veritate*, q. 16, a. 1, ad 15 ("Judgment is twofold—namely, in the universal

speak of each of them individually even though the difference between them is accidental:

> The act of the will, inasmuch as it is drawn to anything desired of itself, as health, which act is called by Damascene *thelēsis*—that is, simple will—and by the masters "will as nature," is different from the act of the will as it is drawn to anything which is desired only in order to something else, as to take medicine; and this act of the will Damascene calls *boulēsis*—that is, conciliative will; and by the masters is called "will as reason." But this diversity of acts does not diversify the power, since both acts regard the one common *ratio* of the object, which is goodness.[93]

The will, inasmuch as it is naturally inclined to one thing (such as happiness), is "not subject to free judgment,"[94] but that does not mean it is not free to choose otherwise. Regardless, many would easily fail to make these distinctions, and Thomas may have been careful to avoid language that could be brought under censure by the Parisian scholars who advised Tempier and who tended to view Aquinas's Aristotelian categories with suspicion. What seems most remarkable, though, is how consistent

---

(and this pertains to synderesis) and in a particular doable (and this is the judgment of choice and this pertains to free will [*arbitrium*]). For this reason, it does not follow that they are the same"), and *In* II *sent.*, dist. 24, q. 2, a. 3, ad 4 ("Judgment does not pertain to free will [arbitrio] and to synderesis in the same way because universal judgment pertains to synderesis according to universal principles of law, since conclusions are always judged through principles . . . but a particular judgment about this doable thing pertains to free will [*iudicium*], which is a judgment of choice. Thus, synderesis is not the same as free will [*arbitrium*]"). It is distinguished from the theoretical judgment pertaining to "conclusions in speculative sciences" in *De veritate*, q. 24, a. 1, ad 17: "The judgment to which freedom is attributed is the judgment of choice. Now it is not the judgment by which man opines something about conclusions in the speculative sciences, because choice itself is, as it were, a kind of knowledge about things one has taken counsel about." On these various judgments, see David Gallagher, "Thomas Aquinas on the Causes of Human Choice" (PhD diss., Catholic University of America, 1988), 62–64. Sherwin takes his explanation of the same from this dissertation. See Reginald G. Doherty, *The Judgments of Conscience and Prudence* (River Forest, IL: Aquinas Library, 1961), and Ralph McInerny, *Aquinas on Human Action: A Theory of Practice* (Washington, DC: Catholic University of America Press, 2012, 228).

[93] *ST* III, q. 18, a. 3, corp.

[94] *ST* I, q. 83, a. 2, corp.: "Those things to which we are naturally inclined are not subject to free judgment, as was said about the desire for happiness. For this reason, it is contrary to the notion of free will [*liberi arbitrii*] that it be a natural habit."

Aquinas was over the years regardless of any efforts he may have made to avoid unjust accusations of heterodoxy.

Westberg points out that one of the difficulties with the thesis that Aquinas had a radical change around the time he is supposed to have written both *ST* I-II, q. 9, and *De malo*, q. 6,[95] regards pinpointing when such a radical transition in Aquinas's thought would have come about. Despite the fact that this thesis is becoming more and more widely accepted,[96] Westberg observes:

> There is ... quite a problem in dating implied by this revisionist program, especially by the enthusiasts for *De Malo* 6. There is little disagreement with Glorieux's or Lottin's date of late 1270, in Paris, for this disputed question; but this of course causes trouble for our treatment of the *secunda pars* of the *Summa Theologiae* which was being composed also during this period. If Thomas had had the breakthrough in his view of the freedom of the will which is alleged, then this should have shown up in the remainder of his work; but the evidence for the unity of treatment in the *ST* is far stronger than the evidence for a change in doctrine.[97]

---

[95] Torrell says: "The date of the disputation of the Questions *De malo* remains difficult to establish ... As to Q. 6, it must be put a little before or after the condemnation of 1270"; *ST* I-II "was put together in Paris" in 1271 (*Saint Thomas Aquinas*, 1:336). Both of these refrain from speaking of the intellect acting in the manner of a final cause and explicitly say the will moves itself. Weisheipl says *ST* I was completed "towards the end of 1270" and that *"De libero arbitrio,* inserted into *De malo* as question 6) ... seems to have been disputed in Paris in 1270" (*Friar Thomas D'Aquino*, 361, 366).

[96] Keenan says the "reversal" Aquinas made regarding his earlier position now "enjoys considerable acceptance and has prompted further investigations citing Giuseppe Abbà, *Lex et Virtus* (Romas: LAS, 1983), 165–73 and 215–217; Mario Gigante, *Genesi e struttura dell'atto libero in S. Tommaso* (Naples: Giannini, 1980), 72–119; Karl-Wilhelm Merks, *Theologische Grundlegung der sittlichen Autonomie* (Düsseldorf: Patmos, 1978); Dorothée Welp, *Willensfreiheit bei Thomas von Aquin* (Freibourg: Universitätsverlag, 1979) (*Goodness and Rightness*, 41n15). On page 40 (n. 11), he says: "Otto Pesch in his article "Philosophie und Theologie der Freiheit bei Thomas von Aquin in quaest. disp. 6 *De malo*" (*Münchener Theologische Zeitschrift* 13 (1962): 1–25), argues against Odon Lottin's claim that *De malo* is the first work (*Psychologie et morale aux XIIe et XIIIe siècles* [Gembloux: Duculot, 1942–1954], vol. 1 p. 260)." Klaus Riesenhuber sides with Lottin and argues that *De malo* "seems to show the still fresh traces of a controversy," whereas *ST* I-II, q. 9, appears in its wording "more settled and academic" ("The Basis and Meaning of Freedom in Thomas Aquinas," *American Catholic Philosophical Association* 48 [1974]: 109).

[97] Westberg, "Did Aquinas Change His Mind?," 48–49.

There are, moreover, indications that many of the supposedly changed elements resurfaced even after the purported change[98] and that many of the "innovations" were, in fact, present in Aquinas's earliest writings. Actually, Flannery was so unconvinced by what we might call the "majority opinion" (arguing there was a development in Aquinas in *De malo*, q. 6, and *ST* I-II, q. 9, that consisted of a reversal of the *De veritate* doctrine) that he argues that at least some of *De veritate* was written after *De malo* and that question 24 of the later work is actually "a rewrite" of question 6 of the earlier work, representing the "more finished version" of it.[99]

Be that as it may, a section of Keenan's book is focused on the purported transition in Aquinas's thought, and is thus entitled "Making the Shift."[100] Many others likewise follow Lottin's thesis, so it ought to be taken seriously. For Keenan in particular, Aquinas went from attributing "final causality to reason and not the will"[101] to "designating reason's presentation of the object as the *formal* cause of the specific act of the will" (emphasis added). He argues that, if Aquinas were correct when he spoke of the intellect as moving in the manner of a final cause while maintaining that "[the] final cause is the cause of the causes, and [that] all movement is derived from this cause," all movement would necessarily be "attributed to reason" as "the source of all movement."[102] In view of the fact that, well into *ST* II-II, Thomas argues reason is the "proper beginning of human acts," one might not think such a teaching would be a problem, but for Keenan, the truth

---

[98] Joseph Lebacqz, *Libre arbitre et jugement* (Paris: Desclée, 1960), 35, noticed that supposedly deterministic ideas surface in *ST* I-II, q. 13, a. 1 (in which article, the will, which is called an inferior power to the reason, is said to tend to its object according to the order of reason). Also: in I-II, q. 13, a. 5, ad 1, the intellect is said to be a principle of the will's motion because it proposes the will's object to it; in I-II, q. 46, a. 2, a *motus appetitivae virtutis* is said to follow an *actum virtutis apprehensivae*; and in I-II, q. 100, a. 1, corp., the reason (and not "the reason and the appetite" as is sometimes said) is said to be the principle of human acts: "Human morals are spoken of in regard to the order to reason, which is the proper principle of human acts." Westberg notices some other passages: "In *ST* I-II, q. 76 ... the relation of sin to ignorance is given an intellectualist base, using the practical syllogism as the basis for decision, and not giving the will the weight that one would expect if he had made the "shift" by this point. When we come to *ST* III, q. 18, a. 4, in the question whether there was *liberum arbitrium* in Christ, the discussion picks up the framework used in *ST* I, q. 83 without any indication that Thomas had a new way of looking at the will's role in decision" ("Did Aquinas Change His Mind?," 48).

[99] See Flannery, *Acts Amid Precepts*, 117, 248.

[100] See Keenan, *Goodness and Rightness*, 43–45.

[101] Keenan, *Goodness and Rightness*, 29.

[102] Keenan, *Goodness and Rightness*, 31.

of the matter is that the will must be the proper beginning if it is to enjoy what Josef Fuchs had referred to as "basic freedom."[103] Moreover, because in earlier texts Thomas thought that "since reason presents the object, which, in turn, acts as final cause," he was led to what Keenan considers a deterministic outlook according to which "bad action can only result from erroneous thinking."[104] If "reason . . . and not the will is the final cause in an act of the will," Thomas would not be able to explain on "what grounds" the will is able to deny the object that reason presents.[105] Thomas, then, essentially had no choice but to definitively decide on "the form over the final end"[106] and to argue, "the object gives the form of specification; it no longer [as of 1270] gives the end."[107] Had he not done so, Keenan thinks the results "would be startling:" sin would come from error whereas the will would be passive and "reason alone" could explain freedom.[108]

Keenan would, perhaps, agree with Kevin White that, by speaking of the intellect as moving in the *manner* of a final cause instead of saying it *is* a final cause, he is speaking in a sort of "exploratory and tentative way,"[109] but he insists that the younger Thomas "refers to no other causality. Final causality alone is Thomas's best description of reason's presentation of the

---

[103] See Keenan, *Goodness and Rightness*, 47. His teaching relies heavily upon his mentor, Josef Fuchs. See Fuchs, "Basic Freedom and Morality," in *Human Values and Christian Morality* (Dublin: Gill and Macmillan, 1970), 92–111.

[104] See Keenan, *Goodness and Rightness*, 30, regarding the determination charge, and *De veritate*, q. 22, a. 6, corp.: "Where there is not a defect in apprehending and judging, there is not able to be a will for something evil even in those things that are for the end [i.e., means], as is clear in the blessed. And for this reason it is said that to will evil is neither freedom nor a part of freedom, although it is a certain sign of freedom."

[105] Keenan, *Goodness and Rightness*, 40.

[106] Keenan, *Goodness and Rightness*, 73.

[107] Keenan, *Goodness and Rightness*, 79.

[108] Keenan, *Goodness and Rightness*, 29. I should point out that it is, in fact, the *rational* character of the will that explains freedom, because the will is ultimately ordained to the good inasmuch as it is intellectually apprehended. Keenan seems to think this would necessarily imply determinism. We will discuss this more below. For now, we might observe that all finite goods are able to be known in some way as *not* good, which means there must, in fact, be knowledge of pertinent goodness if one is to be free (in a perfective sense as distinguished from a merely non-coercive sense)—though there must also be inclinations that neither originatively occlude or impede this knowledge nor cause some kind of undue and rationally unjustified aversion from the already achieved consideration.

[109] See Kevin White, "Pleasure, a Supervenient End," in *Aquinas and the Nicomachean Ethics*, ed. Tobias Hoffmann, Jorn Muller, and Matthias Perkams (Cambridge: Cambridge University Press, 2013), 220–238, at 235.

object to the will. By this presentation, the will is moved to act. Without this presentation of the (known) good, the will remains a passive power."[110] For Keenan, in other words, if the intellect were to act in the manner of a final cause, the will would be entirely unable to act in the manner of an efficient cause.

This view seems to envision the will's causality and the intellect's causality as mutually exclusive. In every act, Keenan seems to think either the intellect or the will has to have supreme priority. It is my contention, however, that, even though the intellect does in fact have priority *simpliciter*, this does not rule out the possibility that, in contingent matters pertaining to the means that lead toward ultimate ends, the will has priority in one way and the intellect in another. In other words, the intellect has priority both because it gives the end (and without cognition of the end, there is no volition whatsoever) and also because it is as act to potency (or mover to moved), for absent specification with respect to the good, the will cannot act or move. At the same time, the will has a kind of priority, for if one wills to avert his will from the consideration of something proposed to it as good by the intellect, the intellect's appointing will be feckless. This failure to act upon that which is presented by the intellect is attributed to the will by Saint Thomas, who points out that the will, which is able to hinder not-acting, is sometimes responsible for the failure to act upon that which is proposed to it.[111] Both the intellect and the will, therefore, have a kind of priority. Keenan seems to preclude this possibility, while there are others besides myself who refuse to think of the intellect and the will as somehow in competition with each other.

De Haan goes so far as to argue that, since both are so important, the effort that has been spent determining whether Aquinas's teaching is intellectualist or voluntarist has been unnecessary:[112]

---

[110] Keenan, *Goodness and Rightness*, 28: "Thomas's affirmation that reason moves the will in the way an end moves something is always stated in careful analogical language. Thomas does not state that reason is the final cause but that reason moves the will as an end or as a final cause moves something. By the same token, however, Thomas refers to no other causality. Final causality alone is Thomas's best description of reason's presentation of the object to the will. By this presentation, the will is moved to act. Without this presentation of the (known) good, the will remains a passive power. 'The intellect precedes the will, as the motive power precedes the thing movable, and as the active precedes the passive; for good which is understood moves the will.'"

[111] *ST* I-II, q. 6, a. 3, corp.: "Because the will, when willing and acting, is able (and sometimes ought) to impede non-willing and non-acting, this non-willing and non-acting is attributed to it as proceeding from itself."

[112] See Daniel De Haan, "Perception and the *Vis Cogitativa*: A Thomistic Analysis of

In nearly every question in the *Prima Secundae* on the distinctive cognitive and appetitive moments of human action, Aquinas has an article on whether *fruitio, intentio, electio, consilium, consensus, usus,* or *imperium* are cognitive or appetitive.[113] Aquinas's answer always clearly concludes in favor of one or the other, but not without first explaining that the two are inextricable from each other, and that to indicate one involves the intelligibility of the other. The cognitive specifies by final causality what the appetitive exercises by efficient causality; they mutually interlock as act and potency within irreducibly diverse, yet inseparably reciprocal, orders of causality.[114]

This seems especially true in regard to individual matters of choice, although it also should be incontrovertible that, for Thomas, the reason does in fact remain the "first principle of human acts."[115] In other words, even if Saint Thomas is, in fact, ultimately "intellectualist," once we have entered the deliberative activity of any individual action, it may well be unnecessary to attempt to explain whether Saint Thomas is emphasizing the intellect or the will because any given practical action necessarily involves the reciprocal causality of both. The final (or indeed formal) causality made possible by the intellect—since the end is specified when the intellect or reason presents it to the will—is compatible with the efficient causality of the will, and these causes can be considered mutually enriching at every stage of the moral act pertaining to intentional action.[116]

Just after stating that the will is able to move itself in *ST* I-II, q. 9, a. 3,

---

Aspectual, Actional, and Affectional Percepts," *American Catholic Philosophical Quarterly* 88, no. 3 (2014): 397–437, at 409: "A great deal of effort has been wasted and confusions have been generated over the question of whether Aquinas's doctrine of human action is intellectualist or voluntarist. It is neither."

[113] See *ST* I, q. 83, a. 3; I-II, q. 6, a. 6; q. 9, a. 1; q. 11, a. 1; q. 12, a. 1; q. 13, a. 1; q. 14, a. 1, ad 2; q. 15, a. 1; q. 16, a. 1; q. 17, a. 1.

[114] De Haan, "Perception and the *Vis Cogitativa*," 409–10.

[115] *ST* I-II, q. 90, a. 1, corp.: "The rule and measure of human acts is the reason, which is the first principle of human acts." See also I-II, q. 18, a. 8, corp.: "the principle of human acts, which is the reason."

[116] The qualifications "moral" and "pertaining to intentional action" are essential because I agree with De Haan inasmuch as we are presupposing intention of the end. The end/s are appointed naturally and need not be influenced by the efficient causality of the will. For this reason, Aquinas distinguishes between the judgments of synderesis, conscience, and theoretical judgment, on the one hand, and that of free judgment, on the other. See: *De veritate*, q. 16, a. 1, ad 15; q. 17, a. 1, ad 4; q. 24, a. 1, ad 17; q. 24, a. 6, ad 1.

Aquinas taught that, if God moves the will, it is not possible for it not to be moved.[117] If God is a final cause not only of the will but of all things and yet man retains free will when God moves the will,[118] why would the intellect not be able to move the will (and, in its case, by merely presenting its object to it) without the will losing its freedom? Just as God moves the will while respecting its contingency,[119] it seems that the intellect can present any finite object to the will without moving it in an absolutely necessary fashion.[120] As Thomas says in *ST* I, q. 83, a. 1, ad 3, God moves natural causes in such a way that he does not prevent their acts from being natural. He can, then, move the will without depriving it of its voluntariness and he can even do so through the mediation of the intellect without denuding either faculty of the properties concomitant with their natural character. This, parenthetically, could account for why Aquinas occasionally says without qualification that God is the first mover of the will but at other times that the intellect is.[121] Actually, because "all motions, whether bodily or spiritual" are, simply speaking, "reduced to

---

[117] See *ST* I-II, q. 10, a. 4, ad 3: "If God moves the will toward something, it is impossible to posit that the will is not moved toward it. Nevertheless, it is not impossible simply speaking. Accordingly, it does not follow that the will is moved necessarily by God."

[118] As *De malo*, q. 3, a. 2, ad 4, observes, when something is said to be a mover, it is not necessarily the first mover. Actually, it may simultaneously be moved and moving. In the case of God's causality, the will is moved by him, "from whom it has this that it moves itself." That cannot be the case with the way the intellect moves the will, but when Aquinas demonstrates that God or humans have free will, he often begins with rationality because it is the source of free will. See *De veritate*, q. 24, a. 1: "To be sure, man is able to pronounce sentence [*iudicare*] about his own judgment [*arbitrio*] by the power of reason judging about things to be done. He is able to do this inasmuch as he knows the meaning of an end and of the means to the end in addition to the relationship and order of the one to the other. And, therefore, he is not his own cause only in moving, but also in judging. And therefore, he has free will [*arbitrio*]; that is, he is endowed with a free judgment about acting or not acting." This being the case, *mutatis mutandis*, something analogous may be said of the intellect vis-à-vis the will.

[119] *ST* I-II, q. 10, a. 4, corp.: "Because the will is an active principle that is not determined to one thing but is indifferently related to many things, God so moves it that it is not determined to one thing necessarily. Instead, its movement remains contingent and not necessary (except in regard to those things it moves toward necessarily)."

[120] *ST* I-II, q. 10, a. 2, ad 3, says the last end which is the perfect good necessarily moves the will, and the body of the article referred to that perfect good that lacks nothing as happiness, which cannot not be willed.

[121] See, e.g., *ST* I-II, q. 9, a. 6 ("God moves the will of man as the universal mover and the universal object of the will, . . . and without this universal motion, man is not able to will anything"), and *SCG* II, ch. 60: ("The first mover in man is the intellect, since the intellect moves the will by its own intelligible object").

the first mover, which is God,"[122] he must be the *primum movens*[123] even of the intellect. This is so despite the fact that the intellect, in turn, also moves the will by presenting its end to it (and, needless to say, without violating its nature).[124] In a chapter of *SCG* dedicated to showing that God alone can directly move the will as an agent cause, he says it is a "law of providence itself" that "everything is moved immediately by its proximate cause." This proximate causality holds even though "the actions of all creatures are subordinated to the ordering of divine providence such that they are unable to act beyond its laws." The consequence of this for our consideration is that since "the proximate moving cause of the will is the understood good, which is its proper object, and it is moved by it as sight is moved by color,"[125] it is essential in every case that the good in fact be understood by means of the intellect, which is the *sine qua non* for something to be understood. God is, of course, the remote cause whose providence is responsible for the intellect's activity, but the proximate cause remains a cause—and one that is able to exert its causality without any kind of coercion.

On this point, John Capreolus insists—against John Duns Scotus, whose understanding of the will was remarkably close to that of the theologians of moral motivation—that, even though the intellect moves the will as an end moves an efficient cause, the intellect is not the complete mover of the will as if it alone were sufficient to move it.[126] In other words,

---

[122] *ST* I-II, q. 109, a. 1, corp.: "In an unqualified way, all movements—whether bodily or spiritual—are reduced to the First Mover, which is God. And therefore, no matter how perfect some corporeal or spiritual nature is posited to be, it cannot proceed to its own act unless it be moved by God."

[123] See *ST* I, q. 2, a. 3, corp.

[124] The intellect, of course, may for its part be applied to its act by the will (though only as specified by a prior act of the intellect).

[125] SCG III, ch. 88, no. 2: "Omnium enim creaturorum actiones sub ordine divinae providentiae continentur: unde praeter leges ipsius agere non possunt. . . . Proximum autem motivum voluntatis est bonum intellectum, quod est suum obiectum, et movetur ab ipso sicut visus a colore."

[126] Regarding Scotus, Albert Stöckl rightly says: "The freedom of the will is steadfastly maintained by Duns Scotus, and this in the sense of absolute indifferentism. The will determines itself according to its own choice; to it alone is to be ascribed the determination to any action: it is the entire cause of its volition" (*Handbook of the History of Philosophy*, trans. T. A. Finlay, 2nd ed., vol. 1, *Pre-Scholastic and Scholastic Philosophy* [London: Longmans and Green, 1914], 418). This is, of course, similar to the notion that the strivings of the will precede intention and choice. Capreolus argues in his *Defensiones Theologiae Divi Thomae Aquinatis*, Positio, dist. 7, q. 1: "The position of Saint Thomas does not suppose that the intellect is the complete mover of the will or

the will still has the ability to make a free judgment (*liberum arbitrium*) despite the fact the intellect can necessarily move it when it offers an unmitigated good to the will as an end.

Keenan argues Thomas originally held that the source of all movement was "found in the object that reason presented to the will,"[127] but sometime around 1270 not only clearly distinguished between the levels of specification and exercise but also came to think of the will as having an activity of its own enabling it to be completely autonomous.[128] For Keenan, this meant Thomas "discovered" that the will is actually completely autonomous on the level of exercise. This supposed autonomy being presupposed, moreover, one may distinguish between the orders of rightness and goodness (which need not be compatible) while maintaining that this distinction is a development of the mature thought of Thomas. This latter teaching is thus a practically implicit teaching of Aquinas in his later years[129] made possible by "a deep shift in his thought: while in his earlier works Thomas described all of the will's acts as subsequent to and dependent on reason, in his later works he recognizes an act of will that is antecedent to and independent of reason."[130]

---

that it is alone sufficient to move the will.... He shows how the intellect moves the will in the manner that an end moves an efficient cause, whereas the will moves the intellect and the other powers in the manner of an agent." ([Turin: Alfred Cattier, 1902], 449).

[127] Keenan, *Goodness and Rightness*, 180. Ironically, even in *ST* I-II, q. 9, a 1, corp., Thomas says, "the motion of the subject itself is from some agent: and since every agent acts for an end, as was shown above, the principle [one might say, "source"] of this motion [one might say, "movement"] is from the end" ("Motio autem ipsius subjecti est ex agente aliquo: et cum omne agens agat propter finem, ut supra ostensum est [q. 1, a. 2], principium hujus motionis est ex fine").

[128] Keenan, *Goodness and Rightness*, 180: "Before 1270 Thomas held that the source of all movement was found in the object that reason presented to the will. Later, however, he presented two sources and distinguished the will's formal movement from its specification informed by objects." Keenan does grant Aquinas spoke of the distinction between the levels of specification and exercise in a text of the *In* III *sent.*, dist. 36, q. 1, a. 5, ad 4) that was of course written before 1270 (41), but he downplays its significance because Thomas does not address "the freedom of the will vis-á-vis reason" there (31).

[129] Keenan, *Goodness and Rightness*: "Thomas, distinguishes charity from reason and, therefore, implicitly goodness from rightness." As Keenan says later on in the same work, "Had Thomas used both the primary and the secondary *exercitium*, he may have discovered the notion of goodness as distinct from rightness. I state this because by explaining reason's presentation of the object as formal and not final causality, Thomas establishes a unique concept: a primary *exercitium*. Had he used his own concept of the primary *exercitium* (rather than Aristotle's or Avicenna's secondary *exercitium*, an *exercitium* of right judgment), he may have arrived at moral goodness" (page 56).

[130] This is an excellent summary of Keenan's position in Sherwin, *By Knowledge and By Love*, 14 (see 12 for more on the antecedent motion).

Is this, in fact, the case, though?

Sherwin is one of those who agrees Thomas had a significant shift, but he explains the relevance of the shift in significantly different terms. He says:

> St. Thomas in his later works more clearly delineates the types of causality exercised by the intellect and will in the genesis of human action. The intellect functions as the formal cause of the act, while the will functions as the efficient cause. In order to illustrate this difference, Thomas introduces his celebrated distinction between specification and exercise.[131]

In other words, for Sherwin, the shift from emphasizing the intellect's final causality (inasmuch as it presents the cognized good) to emphasizing its formal causality provided Thomas with the ability to speak of the intellect as having priority of specification and the will as having priority of exercise. He does not concur with Keenan, then, that there was a major development (or even contradiction) according to which Thomas went from seeing the intellect as imposing blind servitude upon the will to seeing the will as radically autonomous. Sherwin's position is manifestly more tenable, inasmuch as there is no evidence Thomas ever came to refute his earlier central claims about the intellect's indispensable role, as will be most manifest by turning to the texts before and after the Parisian condemnations.

Texts prior to 1270

General Observations

Among the relevant texts prior to 1270, *De veritate* is frequently cited as pertaining to a time when Aquinas overemphasized the intellect's causal force. Before turning to some particular articles, it may profit us to have the opinions of Sherwin and Keenan before us. For Father Sherwin,

> Aquinas' analysis of intellect and will in the *De veritate* has two principal limitations: he fails to grasp the true nature of reason's causal influence upon the will, and he fails to explain how the will shapes reason's practical judgments.[132]

---

[131] Sherwin, *By Knowledge and By Love*, 64.
[132] Sherwin, *By Knowledge and By Love*, 50.

Elsewhere he says, "the difficulty the reader confronts in *De Veritate* is that Aquinas . . . never explains how in the judgment of choice, the will is simultaneously dependent on reason and free to choose."[133] For Sherwin, this omission is not necessarily very problematic because Aquinas arrives at the same conclusion as elsewhere—namely, that the will

> "does not necessarily follow reason," because even after reason has "put one thing ahead of another"—in other words even after reason has considered one thing to be the better means to the end—the agent has not yet accepted this consideration as a principle of action until the will accepts it in the act of choice.[134]

However, what Thomas lacks in this earlier text is the ability to persuade (he "seems to stumble at this point"[135]) even if his conclusion is correct. What leads to Thomas's lack of persuasiveness for Sherwin is his (a) failure to distinguish between the levels of exercise and specification (with the will having priority in regard to the former and the intellect in regard to the latter) and (b) his "error" that the intellect acts in the manner of a final cause.[136]

Keenan's criticisms are more pronounced than Sherwin's. The former says:

> In *De veritate*, when asking whether humanity is endowed with free choice, Thomas argues that freedom comes from reason. His argument is clear: we act because we are moved, we are moved by a judgment, the judgment comes from reason. Thus, as freedom is derived from movement, so freedom comes from reason.[137]

---

[133] Sherwin, *By Knowledge and By Love*, 37.

[134] Sherwin, *By Knowledge and By Love*, 35.

[135] Sherwin, *By Knowledge and by Love*, 29.

[136] Regarding (a), Sherwin describes the later clarity by explaining that in *De malo*, q. 6: "Aquinas underlines that deliberation (*consilium*) and choice (*electio*) are about particular things. This emphasis enables Aquinas to explain more fully the will's freedom on the level of exercise. It enables him to explain how happiness necessarily moves the will on the level of specification but not on the level of exercise" (*By Knowledge and By Love*; see also page 43). Regarding (b), Sherwin says on page 30 of the same work that "Aquinas fails to see [in *De veritate*, q. 22, a.11, ad 5] that the act of showing the end is not an act of final causality, but of formal causality. As we shall see, Aquinas later rectifies this mistake." For his explanation of this "rectification" see pages 40–41 and 50–51.

[137] Keenan here cites *De veritate*, q. 24, a. 1, corp. He could have cited *ST* I-II, q. 17, a. 1,

... Thomas decisively identifies reason and not the will as the source of freedom. To judge about one's judgment belongs only to reason, which reflects upon its own act and knows the relationship of things about which it judges and of those by which it judges. Hence the first beginning of all freedom is located in reason. Consequently, a being is related to free choice in the same way as it is related to reason.[138] Thomas adds to this puzzling remark: "Though judgment is a function of reason, the freedom of judging belongs immediately to the will."[139] ... Thomas expressly points out that the will has no autonomy: "Free choice does not refer to the will absolutely but in subordination to reason."[140] Furthermore, Thomas establishes freedom in the will solely through the power of reason. Reason alone is the ultimate ground of freedom.[141]

Whereas for Sherwin (who unequivocally critiqued Keenan's voluntaristic reading of Thomas), the early Thomas merely failed to delineate the lines of causality in human action,[142] for Keenan, Aquinas's understanding of the intellect's primacy "expressly" argues "the will has no autonomy."

---

ad 2, which calls reason the *causa libertatis* and says: "The will is able to be freely carried to diverse things because reason is able to have diverse conceptions of the good." Citing this text, Martin Rhonheimer says: "Human persons act on the basis of reason and thus with freedom, since reason is 'open to many things' and can have 'various notions of good'—false ones as well as true" ("The Cognitive Structure of the Natural Law and the Truth of Subjectivity," *The Thomist* 67, no. 1 [2003]: 1–44, at 5–6).

[138] Keenan cites *De veritate*, q. 24, a. 2, corp.: "To make a judgment about one's own judgment pertains only to reason, which reflects upon its own act and knows the relationships of those things it judges and of those things through which it judges. Hence the first beginning of all freedom is located in reason. As a consequence, a thing is related to reason in the same way it is related to free will [*arbitrium*]."

[139] *De veritate*, q. 24, a. 6, ad 3: "Quamvis iudicium sit rationis, tamen libertas iudicandi est voluntatis immediate."

[140] *De veritate*, q. 26, a. 6, ad 1: "Quia liberum arbitrium non nominat voluntatem absolute, sed in ordine ad rationem..."

[141] Keenan, *Goodness and Rightness*, 31–32.

[142] Sherwin refers to Keenan's understanding of the will on p. 66 of *Goodness and Rightness* as a "voluntarist reading of the will" on p. 211 of *By Knowledge and By Love*. Regarding Sherwin's understanding of the way Thomas corrected his perceived lack of precision in his later years, he says the following: "Aquinas underlines that deliberation (*consilium*) and choice (*electio*) are about particular things. This emphasis enables Aquinas to explain more fully the will's freedom on the level of exercise. It enables him to explain how happiness necessarily moves the will on the level of specification but not on the level of exercise. Happiness defined as 'a state made perfect by the gathering together of all good things,' is the only object of thought apprehended as fitting according to all its

On the Causality of the Intellect

Keenan elsewhere explains the "autonomy" he has in mind is that wherein the will would be independent of reason and precede it.[143] For him, Thomas does not "clearly establish" this kind of autonomy "until the time he writes the *Prima secundae* of the *Summa theologiae*." He explains:

> In earlier writings, Thomas maintains that the will is a moved mover, first moved by reason. He describes this movement by reason as exerting a causality similar to final causality. This description, in effect, precludes any autonomous movement of the will, because any movement is ultimately derived not from what is moved, but from the mover. Insofar as Thomas describes reason and not the will itself as the will's mover, any achievement or any fault in the will must, therefore, originate in reason.[144]

The notion that Aquinas ever came to believe the will had that kind of autonomy is one of the least viable of Keenan's claims. Although this section is dedicated to Thomas's earlier years, it seems worth disproving so that we can move on to assertions that are at least more *prima facie* tenable. We will do so by adverting our attention to two texts from *ST* III, which was indisputably written after 1270. In the first, Thomas grants that "motion certainly pertains to the appetitive power" (the will, of course, is such a power) and even that it pertains to it as to a moving principle (*principium movens*). Nevertheless, even there he insists that an appetitive power moves only "according to the command and direction of reason"[145] which is a concept that admits of no hint of any radically autonomous volitional activity. In the second text, Thomas says:

> The motion or act of this power that is called the will is sometimes natural and necessary (e.g., with respect to happiness) and

---

particulars" (*By Knowledge and By Love*, 45; see also 43). Interestingly, these ideas seem implicit in many texts prior to 1270 even if not the exact words.

[143] See Keenan, *Goodness and Rightness*, 55, and Sherwin, *By Knowledge and By Love*, 11.

[144] Keenan, *Goodness and Rightness*, 23. In regard to this last comment, we should note it does not follow that, because there is a fault with an origin in reason, it originates solely in the reason; for example, a vicious habit affects one's willingness to reason, and that unwillingness to reason about certain things is itself "unreasonable." It also includes a prior defect with respect to reason, but there is also causality here on the part of the defective appetite.

[145] *ST* II-II, q. 47, a. 9, ad 1: "Motion pertains to the appetitive power, as to the principle moving power; nevertheless, according to the command and direction of reason."

sometimes goes forth from the free judgment of the reason and is neither necessary nor natural as is clear from what was said in the first part [cf. *ST* I, q. 82, a. 2]. And yet even reason itself, which is the principle of this motion, is natural.[146]

These texts from *ST* III are significant because they evince the fact that the later Thomas maintained that when the appetitive power of the will is not moved necessarily, it is moved by the reason. Also of note is that Thomas expressly reasserts something he had said in *ST* I, thereby affirming the continuity between his earlier and later views. The will, then, is clearly not autonomous even though it remains distinct from the judgment of reason.[147] Reason, whether "natural" or deliberative, is the principle of the motion of the will.

It is worth noting that Sherwin pointed to a metaphysical difficulty that might make Keenan's pensive endeavor to find at least some realm of the will that is not dependent upon the reason more understandable. Actually, it is very similar to Keenan's concerns. He wonders how one could say the will is free if Aquinas was correct to say in the text we have seen from *De veritate* that "when there is no failure in apprehending and comparing, there can be no willing of evil."[148] For him, this simply "does not explain

---

[146] *ST* III, q. 18, a. 1, ad 3: "Motus, vel actus hujus potentiae, qui etiam voluntas dicitur, quandoque quidem est naturalis, et necessarius; puta respectu felicitatis: quandoque autem ex libero arbitrio rationis proveniens, et non necessarius, neque naturalis, sicut patet ex his quae in prima parte dicta sunt; et tamen etiam ipsa ratio, quae est principium hujus motus, est naturalis."

[147] For the ways Thomas distinguishes the judgment of the will from the judgment of the reason (in *De veritate*, q. 24), from that of conscience (in *De veritate*, q. 17, a. 1, ad 4), from the judgment of synderesis (in *De veritate*, q. 16, a. 1, ad 15), and, finally from the theoretical judgment pertaining to "conclusions in speculative sciences" (in *De veritate*, q. 24, a. 1, ad 17: "The judgment to which freedom is attributed is the judgment of choice. Now it is not the judgment by which man opines something about conclusions in the speculative sciences, because choice itself is, as it were, a kind of knowledge about things one has taken counsel about").

[148] See Sherwin, *By Knowledge and By Love*, 29, and *De veritate*, q. 22, a. 6. This is the point at which Sherwin thinks "Aquinas seems to stumble." This quote from *De veritate* is very similar to that of *ST* I-II, q. 77, a. 2, which also says the will would not tend to evil without error or ignorance in the reason. See *In* II *sent.*, dist. 5, q 1, a. 1, which says: "Where there is no failure in apprehending and comparing, there can be no willing of evil even in those things that are for the end [i.e., means], as is clear in the blessed. And for this reason it is said that to will evil is neither freedom nor a part of freedom, although it is a certain sign of freedom."

how the will is free."[149] Can it ever do anything contrary to what the reason indicates as good? If not, can it be free?

The answer, for Aquinas, is that the will would remain free (at least in some sense) even if it were unable to act contrary to reason. He says in *SCG*, for instance, that the immobility of the wills of separated just souls (i.e., of the saints in heaven) is "not repugnant to free judgment, the act of which is to choose," even though these just souls are unable to reject the apprehended good.[150] Seeing how such immobility is compatible with freedom, however, takes some explaining, and we will thus need to revisit the question in the pages that follow. For now, it can simply be observed that the will manifestly cannot reject the perfect good once it has been apprehended by the intellect and proposed to the will. In fact, in both *De virtutibus* (1271–1272[151]) and *De veritate*, the will is said not even to need a habit to be directed toward it because the power itself suffices.

The will is immediately inclined toward the "understood good" made known to it by the natural habit of the intellect (synderesis) which principally (*praecipue*) moves the will.[152] Dewan explains this in terms of the

---

[149] Sherwin, *By Knowledge and By Love*, 29.

[150] *SCG* IV, ch. 95 nos. 6–7: "The will of the separated soul is not changeable from good to evil.... Such immobility of the will is not in conflict with free judgment, the act of which is to choose. For choice pertains to the means and not to the last end. Therefore, just as there is now no contradiction of free judgment simply because we desire happiness with an immutable will and flee misery in general, so there will then be nothing contrary to free judgment on account of the will being unchangeably carried toward something determined as towards a final end." Note that "free judgment" could just as readily be translated "free will" here.

[151] See Torrell, *Saint Thomas Aquinas*, 1:329.

[152] *De virtutibus*, q. 1, a. 8, ad 13: "The will does not proceed to its own act by means of certain species informing it as the possible intellect does. Therefore, some natural habit is not required in the will for there to be a natural desire, and especially since the will is moved by the natural habit of the intellect [i.e., synderesis], inasmuch as the understood good is the object of the will." In view of *ST* I-II, q. 9, a. 1, ad 2, which says it is the *practical* intellect that moves the will and not the speculative, we must gather that synderesis is the natural habit of the intellect referred to here. *De veritate*, q. 24, a. 4, ad 9: "The higher affective part does not need some habit in this way because it naturally tends to the good that is connatural to it as to its proper object. For this reason, nothing other is required for it to will the good but that it be shown to it through the cognitive power." It should be noted that, even though the higher affective part also known as the will does not need a natural or acquired habit in order to tend to the good in any particular instance (as the irascible and concupiscible appetites do), both the lower and higher affective parts of the soul need a habit in order for a supernatural action that is meritorious to be educed from the power, as stated in the beginning of this ninth reply. We should also note that the habit of the virtue of justice would certainly be necessary in

will's "readiness" for the "universal being and goodness" that is "identical with the nature of the power" of the will itself.[153] Because this power stands in constant readiness to embrace an unmitigated good, Thomas precludes the will's ability to reject it when it is presented to it as such.

A good Thomist might think Aquinas's doctrine that it comes so naturally to the will to be drawn toward the good that is "shown to it by the cognitive power"[154] is a liberating one. If true, man is naturally apt to attain the excellence that comes from imitating the Incarnate Word's habit of always acting reasonably.[155] Nevertheless, one might sympathize with thinkers such as Keenan who wonder where liberty would be if the will were so readily drawn toward the good. Is the will at least able to diverge from the reason in regard to goods that fall short of being unmitigated? Is it able to be good on the level of basic freedom or moral motivation irrespective of the data provided it by the reason?

The Texts (Especially *De veritate*)

To grapple with these possibilities, we need to begin reflecting upon *De veritate* in more detail. We will start with question 22, which speaks of the intellect acting as a final cause. Doing so will make it possible to assess the implications for free will. Although the explicit reference to final causality is in the third reply of article 12, we will begin with the body:

> The reason for acting [*ratio agendi*] is the form of the agent by which the agent acts; it is necessary, therefore, for it to be in the agent for the agent to act. It is not in it, however, according to the perfection of its nature[156] because, if it were present in this way,

---

the higher affective part of the will even to attain the natural mean on a consistent basis.
[153] See Dewan, *Wisdom, Law, and Virtue*, 158.
[154] *De veritate*, q. 24, a. 4, ad 9 (trans. in note 152).
[155] In *ST* I, q. 83, a. 2, ad 3, Thomas speaks of the freedom that comes from being without fault. The fact that the will is naturally drawn to the good proposed to it would help an individual attain that kind of freedom. The reality is that true freedom is freedom for excellence and not freedom of indifference, as Pinckaers is rightly praised for making so clear. See the section "Freedom for Excellence" below in this chapter. Also, note that the "habit" of the Incarnate Word refers to the human nature.
[156] "Non autem inest secundum esse naturae perfectum." James McGlynn, S.J., *The Disputed Questions on Truth*, vol. 1 (Chicago: Henry Regnery, 1953), translates this: "It is not there, however, according to its perfect act of being." Roy Deferrari has "perfect according to its nature or essence" for *perfectum secundum naturam seu speciem*, which he considers synonymous in this clause (Roy J. Deferrari, Inviolata M. Barry, and Ignatius McGuiness, *A Lexicon of Saint Thomas Aquinas Based on the Summa Theologica and*

the motion would cease. Instead, it is in the agent via his intention, because the end comes earlier in intention and later in being. The end, therefore, properly preexists in the mover according to the intellect, to which it pertains to receive something intentionally [*per modum intentionis*] and not according to the being of the nature. Accordingly, the intellect moves the will in the manner by which an end is said to move, namely, inasmuch as it preconceives the *ratio* of the end and proposes it to the will. But to move in the manner of an efficient cause [*causae agentis*] pertains to the will and not the intellect.[157]

We can see from this that, at this time, Thomas thought of the intellect as moving the will, at least in a sense, in the manner of a final cause, and as doing so in virtue of the reason for acting (the *ratio agendi*). He also thought of the will as moving in the manner of an efficient cause, which is something that undeniably remains consistent throughout his life. Aquinas's intention in saying the *ratio agendi* is the "form of the agent" is not entirely clear, and the phrase is seldom used. Nevertheless, the context provided by an earlier article gives some clarity regarding the good that is desired thanks to the preexisting reason for acting (i.e., the "form of the agent by which the agent acts") that exists antecedent to action in the intellect. He says:

> Any given thing is said to desire something inasmuch as it is similar to it. If, then, something desires the good, it must necessarily be like the good. Now since similar things are those which have one quality or form, the form of the good must be in the one desiring the good. But it is not able to be there according to the being of nature, because it would then not desire any further

---

Selected Passages of His Other Works [Baltimore, MD: Catholic University of America Press, 1948], 824).

[157] *De veritate*, q. 22, a. 12, corp.: "In qualibet actione duo considerentur: scilicet agens, et ratio agenda.... Ratio autem agendi est forma agentis per quam agit; unde oportet quod insit agenti ad hoc quod agat. Non autem inest secundum esse naturae perfectum, quia hoc habito quiescit motus; sed inest agenti per modum intentionis; nam finis est prior in intentione, sed posterior in esse. Et ideo finis praeexistit in movente proprie secundum intellectum, cuius est recipere aliquid per modum intentionis, et non secundum esse naturae. Unde intellectus movet voluntatem per modum quo finis movere dicitur, in quantum scilicet praeconcipit rationem finis, et eam voluntati proponit. Sed movere per modum causae agentis est voluntatis, et non intellectus."

good; he who has something no longer desires it. Therefore, the form of the good necessarily preexists by way of intention in the one desiring the good. But the only being that acts in this way is one with knowledge.[158]

Once again, we see that whatever is received intentionally by the mind is present in the mind in a way that is not according to the "being of nature." Apparently, this means that the actual shape that any act takes will never be identical to the *ratio* of the good that moves one to act in the first place.[159]

On the one hand, E. Peter Royal appears correct in asserting that "prior knowledge serves as a 'ratio agendi,' directing the operation of the power to a definite term." Nevertheless, the texts seem to imply that the abstract norm needs to be particularized and that the way it will be present in a tangible act will necessarily be different from the way it preexists in the mind. That is, there is always more in the particular action than in the intention, because intention regards the good according to its nature and certain generalized circumstantial aspects and cannot reach to all the particularity of an act save in an abstract way. For this reason, Royal's further assertion that the definite term "will emanate in a predetermined way from existing knowledge" and that "the outcome of such operation is to a large extent settled in advance"[160] may need to be qualified signifi-

---

[158] *De veritate*, q. 22, a. 1, obj. 3: "Praeterea, secundum Boetium in libro de hebdomadibus, unumquodque dicitur appetere aliquid in quantum est sibi simile. Si igitur res aliqua appetit bonum, oportet quod sit similis bono. Cum autem similia sint quorum est qualitas vel forma una, oportet formam boni esse in appetente bonum. Sed non potest esse quod sit ibi secundum esse naturae, quia iam ulterius bonum non appeteret; quod enim habet quis, iam non appetit. Ergo oportet quod in appetente bonum forma boni praeexistat per modum intentionis. Sed in quocumque est aliquid per hunc modum, illud est cognoscens. Ergo appetitus boni non potest esse nisi in cognoscentibus; et sic idem quod prius." Although this is an objection, all that is denied in the response is that this means irrational creatures cannot desire the good. He points out there that, in irrational creatures, the form of the good thing that is desired is there in potency even if not by means of a rational apprehension of the essence of the thing desired. The meaning of *De veritate*, q. 22, a. 12, is also clarified by *Quolibet* VIII, q. 2, a. 2, corp.: "The intelligible species is a likeness of the essence itself of a thing and is, in a sense, the what-it-is and nature itself of a thing inasmuch as it is intelligible—not according as it is natural but inasmuch as it is in things. And therefore all things that do not fall under the sense and imagination but only under the intellect are known in virtue of the fact that their essences or quiddities are in some way in the intellect."

[159] In other words, the act will never be identical in its mode of being, even if there is intentional union.

[160] E. Peter Royal, "Concerning the Coercion of the Intellect," *Laval théologique et*

cantly. That is, even if the reason for acting is, in fact, "largely settled," the abstract action that is intended will be too general to determine the way the particular action will take shape. That which we are here glimpsing on the horizon, of course, is prudence and its inestimable role in specifying the final form any given intention takes on in view of the endless variety of circumstances that may present themselves at an individual moment. This is not to say Yves Simon was correct to argue prudence's "last practical judgment (about particulars) . . . results from the affective and non-logical character of the act that determines its judgment,"[161] but it is to say that the certitude attained in practical syllogisms is not the same as that attained in speculative ones.

Returning to the question of what it means for something to be received intentionally, one must already have some inclination toward the end that is preconceived of in the mind or else there will be no action; that is, if "something desires the good, it must necessarily be like the good" that is apprehended.[162] Aquinas makes a related point in *SCG* when he explains a voluntary agent acts according to the likeness of the action that is conceived of in the intellect. In other words, he is like the good he desires inasmuch as there is a likeness of the intended act in his mind and inasmuch as he acts in accordance with that conception:

> Every agent produces its like. Hence it follows that every agent works by that according to which it bears a likeness to its effect: thus fire heats in keeping with the mode of its heat. Now in every voluntary agent, as such, the likeness to his effect is in respect of the apprehension of his intellect. . . . Therefore every voluntary agent produces an effect according to the reason of his intellect.[163]

Relating this back to the notion that, for something good to be desired, the agent must be good,[164] there must be an inclination toward the good that is conceived of in the intellect if there is to be good action—and thus, even if intellectual apprehension comes first, the action that follows remains voluntary because like is attracted to like.[165]

---

philosophique 13, no. 1 (1957): 97–111, at 103.
[161] Yves Simon, *Practical Knowledge*, ed. Vukan Kuic (New York, Fordham University Press, 1986), 24.
[162] *De veritate*, q. 22, a. 1.
[163] *SCG* II, ch. 24 (Dominican Fathers trans., 2:42).
[164] See *De veritate*, q. 22, a. 1
[165] The notion that "like tends to like" is described by Thomas as "so patent" that it is

In a text we have already seen, the intellect was said to move "the will in the way an end moves because the good understood is the end of the will."[166] In *De veritate*, q. 22, a. 12, he says essentially the same thing in replying to the following objection:

> Every passive power is moved by its object. But the will is a passive power because it is that kind of appetite that is a "moved mover" as is said in *De anima* III. Therefore, it is moved by its object. But its object is the good understood or apprehended, as is said in the same place. Therefore the intellect or another apprehensive power moves the will and not the other way around.[167]

The reply is a simple one:

> That argument shows that the intellect moves in the manner of an end; for the apprehended good is related to the will in this way.[168]

Keenan comments:

> Citing Aristotle's *De anima* III, 10, Thomas argues in *De veritate* that the apprehended good moves the appetite and that the will, therefore, is a passive power.[169] Thus, only knowledge of an end

---

considered an axiom; see Thomas Aquinas, *An Exposition of the "On the Hebdomads" of Boethius*, trans. Janice L. Schultz and Edward A. Synan (Washington, DC: Catholic University of America Press, 2001), xxxii.

[166] *SCG* III, ch. 26, no. 22: "Intellectus autem voluntatem per modum quo finis movet, nam bonum intellectum est finis voluntatis." Aquinas goes on here: "Now, in the process of moving, the agent comes later than the end does because the agent moves only for the sake of the end. Hence, it is apparent that the intellect is unqualifiedly higher than the will."

[167] *De veritate*, q. 22, a. 12, obj. 3: "Praeterea, omnis potentia passiva movetur a suo obiecto. Sed voluntas est potentia passiva; est enim appetitus movens motum, ut dicitur in III de anima. Ergo movetur a suo obiecto. Sed obiectum eius est bonum intellectum vel apprehensum, ut dicitur in III de anima. Ergo intellectus, aut alia vis apprehensiva, movet voluntatem, et non e converso."

[168] *De veritate* q. 22, a. 12, ad 3: "Intellectus movet per modum finis; hoc enim se habet bonum apprehensum ad voluntatem."

[169] This is true, but it is passive because it is a moved *mover*. In other words, it is both passive and active. *De veritate*, q. 22, a. 12, obj. 3: "Every passive power is moved by its own object. But the will is a passive power because it is the appetite that moves the will." In replying to this, Thomas evidently accepts that the will is passive, but he says this fact merely shows that "the intellect moves in the manner of an end," because "in this way the apprehended good is related to the will."

moves the will and an end, therefore, is an object, presented by the reason, moving the will. Thomas concludes that the reason moves in the manner of an end. If then the end is the cause of the efficient cause, then the will only moves at the command of reason.[170]

Keenan's position rests, as Thomas Hibbs says, on the "thesis that Thomas develops in the *Summa theologiae* a doctrine of the autonomy of the will, based on the distinction between the orders of specification and exercise."[171] Although Aquinas does not explicitly make this distinction in *De veritate*, he comes close to doing so, and even in the text referring to *De anima*, he speaks of the will acting in one way and the intellect in another (just as he says in other places that the intellect has priority on the level of specification and the will on the level of exercise). We read in *De veritate*, q. 14:

> The will and the intellect precede each other in different ways. The intellect precedes the will by way of receptivity, because if something is to move the will, it is necessary that it first be received in the intellect, as is clear in *De anima* III. But in moving or acting, the will is prior because every action or motion is from the intention one has for the good.[172]

If the will is prior in moving or acting, it seems the will must at least be able to move the intellect when one is in the realm of the practical (which begins with intention even if intention is not a fully practical act).[173] As

---

[170] Keenan, *Goodness and Rightness*, 26. He cites here *De veritate* q. 14, a. 5, ad 5; q. 22, a. 3, corp.; q. 12, obj. 3 and ad 3; q. 6, a. 2, ad3; q. 25, a. 4, corp.

[171] Thomas S. Hibbs, "Interpretations of Aquinas's Ethics Since Vatican II," in Pope, *Ethics of Aquinas*, 412–25, at 420.

[172] *De veritate*, q. 14, a. 5, ad 5: "Ad quintum dicendum, quod voluntas et intellectus diversimode invicem se praecedunt. Intellectus enim praecedit voluntatem in via receptionis: ad hoc enim quod aliquid voluntatem moveat oportet quod prius in intellectu recipiatur, ut patet in III de anima. Sed in movendo sive agendo voluntas est prior: quia omnis actio vel motus est ex intentione boni."

[173] John Naus says: "St. Thomas does not say that knowledge becomes actually practical *when* or *as soon as* the agent intends to act. Certainly it will not become so *unless* or *before* the agent intends to act. Intention is a necessary condition: he must have willed the end. . . . Arguing from common experience, a man may want the end and consequently deliberate about the means and even judge that this is the best means. Certainly these acts are placed under the original and continued impetus of intention. However, at the last moment, some passion or distraction may interpose so that the man does

Thomas explains in *ST* I-II, q. 58, although reason apprehending the end precedes the appetite for the end, "the appetite for the end precedes discursive reasoning [*rationem ratiocinantem*] in regard to the choosing of means, which pertains to prudence."[174]

Thomas does not stop there, though. He goes on to insist that the "will moves *all* the powers of the soul."[175] As a power, it is even able to move itself. In the sixth article of the same question, Aquinas had spoken of the will as "flexible" in that it could be directed toward evil. The reason he gave is not that it is moved by the intellect to do evil, but rather that it is made *de nihilo* and is thus able to return to nothingness by turning away from God.[176] Aquinas's intention is not, presumably, to repudiate the teaching that the intellect acts *per modum finis*,[177] or that one must apprehend the goodness of any given action intellectually (even if the goodness is only apparent) for the will qua rational appetite to go after it, but he does seem to grant some latitude to the will by speaking of its ability to "flex" itself in some way. Finally, he even rules out the possibility that the will is able to move only the *practical* intellect (and not the speculative one) by saying:

> When the will moves the other powers toward their acts, it does so in respect not only of those acts which pertain to the practical

---

not order this knowledge to a concrete operable. He does not choose to do this particular act here and now. The judgment which terminated his deliberation, although made because he desired the end, remains not completely practical, therefore in some sense speculative" (*The Nature of the Practical Intellect* [Rome: Libreria Editrice Dell' Universita Gregoriana, 1959], 175).

[174] *ST* I-II, q. 58, a. 5, ad 1: "Reason, inasmuch as it apprehends the end, precedes the appetite for the end, but the appetite for the end precedes discursive reasoning in regard to the choosing of means, which pertains to prudence. Similarly, the understanding of principles is the beginning of reason syllogizing in speculative things."

[175] *De veritate*, q. 22, a. 12, sc 1: "Anselmus dicit in Lib. de similitudinis, cap. II, quod voluntas movet omnes animae vires."

[176] *De veritate*, q. 22, a. 6, ad 3: "In God there is not a passive or material potency that is divided against act as the objection supposes. There is, however, an active potency that is act itself, because any given being is able to act to the degree it is in act. And nevertheless, the fact that the will is able to turn toward evil is not due to its being from God but to its being made from nothing."

[177] *De veritate*, q. 22, a. 12, ad 3 ("The intellect moves in the manner of an end, for this is the way the apprehended good is related to the will"); SCG III, ch. 26, no. 22: "Now, the intellect moves the will in the manner of an end because the understood good is the end of the will. Now, the agent comes later in moving than the end since the agent moves only for the sake of the end").

intellect but even of those which pertain to the speculative intellect. For, just as a man wills to walk or do something of that sort, he also wills to consider some question and find out the answer to it.[178]

The will, then, moves even the speculative intellect to do things such as deliberating about theoretical truths without reference to practical activity. Does this mean it is strictly autonomous from the intellect even in the *De veritate*? One might think so given that he later says, "however much the reason prefers one thing to another, preference is not given to one thing to be done over another thing to be done until the moment that the will is inclined more toward one [of them] than the other: for the will does not necessarily follow the reason."[179] Even at this early date, therefore, the will is given a robust kind of activity. Nevertheless, the very next sentence clarifies that it is "proper to the reason" either to "compare one thing to another, or to prefer [one thing to another]," while adding that such a thing is "found in an act of the will from the impression of reason."[180] At least at this time, then, the will is unequivocally not autonomous.

These texts do, however, make it clear that, even in the early Thomas, the will was far from being considered feckless, and this remains the case even presupposing its status as a moved mover and the intellect's status as a potent causality that enjoys a kind of primacy. We must say, then, that, even though Saint Thomas attributed the ultimate foundation of freedom to the intellect,[181] he seemed just as solicitous to defend the freedom of the will as Keenan does (though the latter does so in a much different

---

[178] *In II sent.*, dist. 38, q. 1, a. 3, ad 4: "Cum voluntas moveat omnes potentias in actus suos, non solum est respectu eorum quae ad practicum intellectum pertinent, sed etiam eorum quae ad speculativum: sicut enim homo vult ambulare, vel aliquid hujusmodi facere; ita etiam vult considerare, et veritatem quaestionis alicujus invenire."

[179] *De veritate*, q. 22, a. 15, corp.: "Nam quantumcumque ratio unum alteri praefert, nondum est unum alteri praeacceptatum ad operandum, quousque [until the moment] voluntas inclinetur in unum magis quam in aliud: non enim voluntas de necessitate sequitur rationem."

[180] *De veritate*, q. 22, a. 15, corp: "In electione apparet id quod est proprium rationis, scilicet conferre unum alteri, vel praeferre: quod quidem in actu voluntatis invenitur ex impressione rationis, in quantum scilicet ipsa ratio proponit voluntati aliquid non ut utile simpliciter, sed ut utilius ad finem."

[181] This is clear even in later years by the fact that "freedom from sin is true freedom" (*ST* II-II, q. 183, a. 4, corp.) and that sin itself is something contrary to either "human reason" or the "reason of God" (see I-II, q. 71, a. 6, corp. and ad 4). See I-II, q. 17, a. 1, ad 2, which says reason is the "root of freedom" as the cause while adding that the will is only able to be freely carried to diverse things because of diverse rational concepts.

way, since the ideal for him is something like freedom of indifference). An indication of this is his belief that the more a creature was able to leave behind mere instinct by directing itself in some way, the more perfect that creature would be. What I am describing is certainly not freedom of indifference (in the sense that it would be liberating to act independently from reason), because one must always follow nature and God's laws and thereby attain true freedom. However, neither reason nor the rational appetite are merely constrained by natural impulse, and the creatures that possess these rational powers are more perfect than others.

In *De veritate*, q. 22, a. 3, Thomas lays out the gradation among beings in terms of whether they are "unmoved movers," "moved movers," or "solely moved." Animals, which have a sense appetite (*appetitus sensibilis*) that transcends mere inclination (such as the inclination a rock has to heed the laws of gravity) are more perfect than inanimate creatures such as rocks, because it pertains in a special way to them to be "moved of themselves" (*moventur ex se*) and to desire things in virtue of their own powers.[182] As a consequence, they can be said to move themselves in a real sense even if they do so only imperfectly.

In the *De veritate*, q. 22, a. 4, he explains that the creature with a rational nature is closest to God, and thus

> does not have an inclination toward something in the way inanimate things do. Nor does it merely have a mover of the inclination determined as it were extrinsically. Beyond this, it has its own inclination in its power. This means it does not necessarily incline to an apprehended desirable object and that it is able to be either inclined towards it or not. This ability belongs to it inasmuch as it does not make us of a bodily organ. As a consequence, it is further removed from the nature of what is moved and approaches the nature of what moves and acts. Something cannot determine the way it is inclined toward the end, though, unless it knows the end and the bearing of the end upon the things that are for the end, which belongs only to the reason. Thus such an

---

[182] *De veritate*, q. 22, a. 3, corp.: "'To tend' [*appetere*], which is somehow common to all things, is somewhat special in the case of animals, since both appetite and the mover of the appetite are found in them. For the apprehended good is that which moves the appetite, as the Philosopher says in *De anima* III. Hence, just as what distinguishes animals is that they are moved of themselves, they likewise tend of themselves. Due to this fact, the tending power [*vis appetitiva*] is a special power in the soul just as the motive power is."

appetite, which is not determined necessarily by something else, follows the apprehension of the reason. Consequently, the rational appetite, which is called the will, is a power distinct from the sense appetite.[183]

Because rational animals have more than the estimative power of brutes and are able to transcend sheer natural inclinations, they are to some extent able to determine their inclinations for themselves. We see here that the will follows the apprehension of the reason. Nevertheless, this would merely imply that the will has a kind of subordinated autonomy for Thomas. It would certainly not have occurred to him that his view would suggest that the intellect is oppressive in some way. This is clearly indicated by something he said in the *Prima Pars* (also pre-1270). That the intellect is practically oppressive would not have entered his mind:

> Man acts from judgment, because he judges by the knowing power that something should be avoided or sought. But because this judgment is not from a natural instinct in regard to a particular doable but from a kind of comparison in the reason, he acts from a free judgment and is able to be inclined toward various things. For reason in contingent matters is open to opposites as is clear in dialectical syllogisms and rhetorical arguments. Now particular doable things are contingent and the judgment of reason is consequently open to diverse [conclusions] and is not determined to one. And for this to be, man must possess the free judgment that comes from being rational.[184]

---

[183] *De veritate*, q. 22, a. 4, corp.: "Sed natura rationalis, quae est Deo vicinissima, non solum habet inclinationem in aliquid sicut habent inanimata, nec solum movens hanc inclinationem quasi aliunde eis determinatam, sicut natura sensibilis; sed ultra hoc habet in potestate ipsam inclinationem, ut non sit ei necessarium inclinari ad appetibile apprehensum, sed possit inclinari vel non inclinari. Et sic ipsa inclinatio non determinatur ei ab alio, sed a seipsa. Et hoc quidem competit ei in quantum non utitur organo corporali: et sic recedens a natura mobilis, accedit ad naturam moventis et agentis. Quod autem aliquid determinet sibi inclinationem in finem, non potest contingere nisi cognoscat finem, et habitudinem finis in ea quae sunt ad finem: quod est tantum rationis. Et ideo talis appetitus non determinatus ex aliquo alio de necessitate, sequitur apprehensionem rationis; unde appetitus rationalis, qui voluntas dicitur, est alia potentia ab appetitu sensibili."

[184] *ST* I, q. 83, a. 1, corp.: "Homo agit judicio: quia per vim cognoscitivam judicat, aliquid esse fugiendum, vel prosequendum. Sed quia judicium istud non est ex naturali instinctu in particulari operabili, sed ex collatione quadam rationis, ideo agit libero

Because of the link between rationality and the free judgment that is pursuant to it, Thomas goes on to say that, when irrational animals are sometimes said to have some kind of voluntariness, what is meant is merely that nature does not violently force them to act as they do. However, because they do not have reason, even when they act spontaneously, they lack "the use of free choice [*liberae electionis*]."[185] In the case of humans, who do have the fortune of possessing reason, there may be times when the reason is clouded by appetite or even hindered by some kind of unfortunate accident, but qua rational, they retain the freedom to choose. Choice, which is "essentially an act of the will,"[186] pertains to that rational power[187] and is, therefore, "open to opposites, and thus is not determined to something from necessity."[188] Even the ability to choose something contrary to reason, in fact, flows from the power of reason, because *liberum arbitrium* is a free judgment only because of the reason[189] in which "the first beginning of all freedom is established."[190]

Simon provides a compelling description of what it looks like when deliberation about any finite good takes place:

> By reason of its being a living relation to the comprehensive good, the will invalidates the claim of any particular good to

---

judicio, potens in diversa ferri: ratio enim circa contingens [alt.: contingentia] habet viam ad opposita, ut patet in Dialecticis syllogismis, et Rhetoricis persuasionibus: particularia autem operabilia sunt quaedam contingentia et ideo circa ea judicium rationis ad diversa se habet, et non est determinatum ad unum. Et pro tanto necesse est, quod homo sit liberi arbitrii ex hoc ipso, quod rationalis est."

[185] *De veritate*, q. 24, a. 2, ad 1: "'Something voluntary' is posited of brutes by the Philosopher . . . inasmuch as something voluntary is opposed to something violent. Thus the voluntary is said to be in brute animals and boys because they act of their own accord [*sua sponte*] but not on account of the use of free choice."

[186] *ST* I-II, q. 13, a. 1, corp.: "Choice is essentially [*substantialiter*] not an act of reason, but of the will."

[187] *ST* I, q. 83, a. 4, ad 2: "Choice and will . . . pertain to one power."

[188] *De veritate*, q. 22, a. 5, sc 5: "Moreover, rational powers are open to opposites according to the Philosopher. But the will is a rational power, since it is in the reason, as it is said in *De anima* III. The will, therefore, is open to opposites and is not determined to something from necessity."

[189] See *SCG* II, ch. 48; here, after speaking of the fact that the will results from intellectual judgments, Thomas suggests it is only *free* will because it is the "free judgment of reason": "Therefore all intellectual things have free will [*liberam voluntatem*] due to the intellect's judgment. This is to have free judgment [*liberum arbitrium*], which is defined as the free judgment of reason."

[190] *De veritate*, q. 24, a. 2, corp.: "totius libertatis radix est in ratione constituta."

bring about a determinate judgment of desirability. At the instant when the attraction of a thing good in some respect inclines the mind to utter the proposition "this is good for me," the infinite ambition of the will reverses the perspective. The thing which is good only in a certain respect discloses uncongenial aspects, and the proposition "this is not good for me" fights with its contradictory for the assent of the mind.[191]

Men are not moved solely by instinct. They retain an ability to act in accordance with their inclinations and appetites and may even refrain from acting upon that which is presented by the reason as a finite good, but even if we call the free choice or free judgment that rational creatures enjoy a kind of autonomy, we must at least recognize that the "autonomy" is not absolute, since it always relies upon the reason in one way or another. Aquinas explains in *De veritate*, q. 22, a. 13:

> When the will is moved to its object proposed to it by the reason, it is moved diversely inasmuch as the object is diversely proposed to it. Accordingly, when the reason proposes something to it absolutely, the will is moved into it absolutely, and this is to will. When, however, something is proposed to it under the aspect of the good [*sub ratione boni*] toward which other things are ordered as to an end, then the will tends toward it with a certain kind of order, which is found in an act of the will, not according to its own nature, but according to the exigence of the reason. Therefore, the act of intending is an act of the will in relation to reason.[192]

In a sense, this text manifests that the will enjoys a kind of freedom because, if something is not proposed to it as absolute, it is not absolutely carried into it. That which is proposed to it falls under the *ratio* of the good to the degree

---

[191] Yves Simon, *Freedom of Choice*, 102–3, as quoted in Clifford G. Kossel, "Thomistic Moral Philosophy in the Twentieth Century," in Pope, *Ethics of Aquinas*, 169–93, at 393n75.

[192] *De veritate*, q. 22, a. 13, ad 1: "Cum enim voluntas moveatur in suum obiectum sibi propositum a ratione, diversimode movetur, secundum quod diversimode sibi proponitur. Unde, cum ratio proponit sibi aliquid ut absolute bonum, voluntas movetur in illud absolute; et hoc est velle. Cum autem proponit sibi aliquid sub ratione boni, ad quod alia ordinentur ut ad finem, tunc tendit in illud cum quodam ordine, qui invenitur in actu voluntatis, non secundum propriam naturam, sed secundum exigentiam rationis. Et ita intendere est actus voluntatis in ordine ad rationem."

that it is a certain kind of good thing, and this is the case even if it is not the perfect good itself (which alone necessarily draws the will into it along with anything that is constitutive of the good). The phrase *sub ratione boni* is telling in this regard. The only thing that necessarily moves the will is the good—or, more specifically, the perfect good. If something falls *under* that *ratio*, it is merely ordered to that good "as to an end." In other words, the end comes first (at least structurally if not temporally) and when it is appointed by the intellect, "the will is moved into it absolutely," whereas if a means is appointed (and "the proper object of choice is the means to an end"[193]), by the intellect, the will is free to choose it or not choose it.[194]

In article six of *De veritate*, q. 22, Aquinas explains this kind of freedom (or "lack of fixity") by comparing the way various practical means relate to the end to the way principles lead to conclusions in demonstrative sciences:

> In the demonstrative sciences, the conclusions are related to the principles in such a way that, if the conclusion is removed, the principle is removed; and so from this fixity [*determinationem*] of the conclusions in respect to the principles, the intellect is compelled by the principles themselves to assent to the conclusions. But those things that are for the end [*the means*] do not have such a fixity in respect of the end that if one of them were removed, the end would [also] be removed because it is possible to attain the last end in varied ways—either in truth or in appearance. Therefore, from the necessity that is present in the voluntary appetite in regard to the end, a necessity in regard to those things that are for the end is not imposed.[195]

---

[193] *De veritate*, q. 22, a. 15, corp.: "Proprium obiectum electionis est id quod est ad finem, quod pertinet ad rationem boni."

[194] If the means is essentially connected with the end as the only way of attaining the end, one might necessarily be moved towards the means as well, but it would seem better in such a case to call such a "means" a *bonum honestum* that is actually constitutive of the end and inseparable from it.

[195] *De veritate*, q. 22, a. 6, ad 4: "In scientiis demonstrativis conclusiones hoc modo se habent ad principia, quod remota conclusione removetur principium; et sic propter hanc determinationem conclusionum respectu principiorum, ex ipsis principiis intellectus cogitur ad consentiendum conclusionibus. Sed ea quae sunt ad finem, non habent hanc determinationem respectu finis, ut remoto aliquo eorum, removeatur finis; cum per diversas vias possit perveniri ad finem ultimum vel secundum veritatem vel secundum apparentiam. Et ideo ex necessitate quae inest appetitui voluntario respectu finis, non inducitur necessitas ei respectu eorum quae sunt ad finem." Similarly, Thomas says in *ST* I-II, q. 10, a. 2, ad 3: "The last end moves the will necessarily because it is the

Even if the will is necessarily ordered to certain primary ends, then, it remains free in regard to secondary ones.

In another article of the same question of *De veritate*, Aquinas insists that "we are the lords of that which is within us" and that we are consequently able either "to will or not to will."[196] For Dewan, this "freedom to act or not to act" is the "only 'autonomy' of the will one ever has in Saint Thomas," because "it is impossible, in the doctrine of Saint Thomas, to posit an act of the will that is not formed by natural intellectual knowledge of the good."[197] This analysis coincides with Aquinas's assertion in the *Scriptum* that even the "will as nature" follows the reason's natural knowledge about that which is good.[198] Presupposing Thomas never rejected this teaching, it remains striking that he adds in *De veritate*, q. 22, that the will is able to will certain things in virtue of its "own [*propria*] disposition without any necessity"[199] and that it is not "coerced by the good" due to the "very nature of willing."[200] We must, it seems, understand this in terms of particular goods presented by the intellect.

If the will can exercise its act of willing in accordance with its proper disposition in regard to these goods (and, indeed, can turn away from them), one might think it could act contrary to the reason in its choice of something other than these goods.[201] However, Thomas refrains from

---

perfect good. And similarly, those things that are ordered to this end, without which the end is not able to be attained—as to be, and to live, and things of this sort. However, someone who wills the end does not necessarily will those things that one does not need to attain the end."

[196] *De veritate*, q. 22, a. 5, sc 7.

[197] Dewan, *Wisdom, Law, and Virtue*, 169, 170.

[198] *In II sent.*, dist. 39, q. 2, a. 2, ad 2: "The will as ... nature ... follows the judgment of the reason, because something that is naturally known in the reason as an indemonstrable principle in doable things acts [*se habet*] in the manner of an end, since the end holds the place of the beginning in doable things, as it is said in *Ethics* VI. Thus, that which is the end of man is naturally known in the reason to be good and desired, and the will following this knowledge is called the will as nature."

[199] *De veritate*, q. 22, a. 5, corp.: "The end is the foundation and the beginning of the means when it comes to desirable things. This is because the means are not desired except by reason of the end [*ratione finis*]. And therefore, that which the will necessarily wills as by a determined and natural inclination is the last end, happiness—and those things that are included in happiness, as being, the knowledge of the truth, and other such things. However, in regard to other things, there is no question of the will being determined necessarily by some natural inclination. Instead, [it is drawn to them] by its own disposition without any necessity."

[200] *De veritate*, q. 22, a. 5, ad 8: "Voluntas non cogitur a bono ... ex ipsa ratione voluntatis."

[201] This can, in fact, be done regarding some particular judgment about a finite good, but

attributing *absolute* autonomy to the will at this stage in his intellectual development. He points out, in fact, that there are times when "the operation of the intellect is able to be against the inclination of man, which is the will: as when a certain opinion pleases someone but he is led to assent to the contrary through the intellect on account of the force (*efficaciam*) of arguments."[202] If there are times that it is altered "through the intellect" it is certainly not wholly independent of it since, as Thomas says in *ST* I, "an action of the will is nothing other than a certain inclination following an *understood* form."[203] Nevertheless, it retains freedom. Steven Long explains:

> The very nature of the will as inclination following the form of reason is such that its object—the universal good or good in general—is irreducible to any finite good, wherefore no finite good can compel the will.[204]

Ultimately, the question seems to be whether Keenan is correct to suggest that the will has some positive contact with the end that is not itself specified by the intellect. We have seen that Thomas precludes that possibility regarding the *voluntas ut natura*, which follows the judgment of reason,[205] but what about the will's activity in the process of deliberating about particular goods or proximate ends? Simply put, even in regard to these goods, there is no evidence Aquinas would grant the will a strict kind of independence. If it turns from that which is presented by the intellect, it seems clear it can do so only in respect to some other judgment, such as "this is bad to consider, because it impedes a clear good." Even in this instance (when the "good" is identified erroneously and under the impetus of unrectified appetite), the will would be specified by reason. Indeed, even the will *not to know* something that it would be good or even morally obligatory to know is itself influenced by a defective reason brought about

---

even then, the will must either be in accord with some other judgment or refuse to continue considering the goodness of that good (which refusal itself would be due to some other inclination being judged more important).

[202] *De veritate*, q. 22, a. 5, ad 3: "Operatio intellectus potest esse contra inclinationem hominis, quae est voluntas; ut cum alicui placet aliqua opinio, sed propter efficaciam rationum deducitur ad assentiendum contrario per intellectum."

[203] *ST* I, q. 87, a. 4, corp.: "Actus voluntatis nihil aliud est, quam inclinatio quaedam consequens formam intellectam." See also *Quolibet* VI, q. 2, a. 2 ("The motion of the will is an inclination following an understood form"), and the *CT* I, ch. 1 ("The appetite following the intellect is the will").

[204] Steven Long, "Perfect Storm," 295n5.

[205] See *In* II *sent*., dist. 39, q. 2, a. 2, ad 2 (trans. in note 198 above).

by inordinate inclination and some measure of ignorance. One might, for instance, will *not to know* the truth—as when a person dating someone *does not wish to know whether that person is already married*—and this would surely be a voluntary act because the will would be acting in virtue of its "own [*propria*] disposition without any necessity."[206] However, the will to turn away from knowing and following the reason would be specified by reason insofar as the intellect would have to consider some other good as more worthy of consideration and pursuit, thereby enabling the will to choose to act in view of this other *cognized* good. The aspects of knowledge that could move one otherwise would thereby be minimized, but the will would remain specified by reason—albeit erroneous reason. In other words, even when the will applies the power of the intellect in such a way that it moves it to consider some other good, it is precisely under some *ratio* that it does so. This conclusion seems necessary given what Thomas says in *SCG*:

> All intellectual beings have free will [*liberam voluntatem*] from the presence [*venientem*] of the judgment of the intellect. That is to have free will [*liberum arbitrium*], which is defined as the free judgment of reason.[207]

It seems that Keenan and others who think of *De veritate* as expressive of a more "intellectualist" mindset (one Aquinas is said to have abandoned) think that, if the intellect acts as a final cause, it must act as a kind of efficient cause. Lottin himself, for instance, argued that the early Thomas had wrongly attempted to separate final causality and efficient causality (since "the efficient cause moves to the act only for the purpose of an end") and he suggests the later Thomas necessarily maintained that the will must "play both the role of efficient cause and that of final cause" while ascribing to reason merely formal causality.[208] As Dewan points out, however, even when Thomas "affirms the natural priority and nobility of the intellect over the will" on the grounds that what moves the will is the understood good, the movement implied is by no means efficient

---

[206] *De veritate*, q. 22, a. 5, corp. (trans. in note 199 above).
[207] *SCG* II, ch. 48: "Omnia igitur intellectualia liberam voluntatem habent ex iudicio intellectus venientem. Quod est liberum arbitrium habere, quod definitur esse liberum de ratione iudicium."
[208] See Lottin, *Psychologie et morale*, 1:254, 256, as cited by Lauer, "St. Thomas's Theory of Intellectual Causality in Election," 301 (see note 8 above).

causality.[209] Moreover, since the will is free to will or not to will (*velle vel non velle*),[210] as Thomas repeatedly says in this work, it must have a kind of primacy in regard to things that are not necessarily willed. The later Thomas would imply this is a kind of primacy on the level of exercise. In *ST* I-II, q. 9, a. 1, ad 3, for instance, he says, "the will moves the intellect in regard to the exercise of the act [Voluntas movet intellectum quantum ad exercitium actus]." As already suggested, though, this doctrine seems to be present in seminal form even in *De veritate*. Consider the ninth article of question 22:

> The will has a twofold object. One, to which the natural inclination is determined necessarily. And this object, certainly, is implanted in and proposed to the will by the Creator who gives to it the natural inclination.... The other, indeed, is the object of the will which is apt to incline the will inasmuch as there is some likeness or order in respect of the ultimate end that is naturally desired. The will, however, is not necessarily immutable on the side of this object, ... because there is not found in it a singular order to the naturally desired ultimate end. And by means of this object, some creature is able to incline the will to some extent although it cannot necessarily alter it; as is clear when someone persuades another that something ought to be done by proposing to him its utility or decency [*honestatem*]. Nevertheless, it is in the power of the will that it either accept what has been proposed or not because it is not naturally determined to it.[211]

---

[209] See Dewan, *Wisdom, Law, and Virtue*, 160.

[210] In *De veritate*, q. 22, a. 6, he says: "The freedom of the will is considered in regard to three things. Namely, in regard to its act (inasmuch as it is able to either will or not will), in regard to its object (inasmuch as it is able to will this or that or even its opposite), and in regard to its ordering to the end (inasmuch as it is able to will good or evil)." He sometimes says, *velle et non velle*, which he does three times in this question, but the sentiment is the same. This is essentially identical to saying the will is free on the level of exercise. In fact, combining this text with *In* IV *sent.*, dist. 49, q. 3, a. 5, sol. 3, ad 2 (which also adverts to the distinction between specification and exercise) might provide an antidote to Keenan's notion of charity unmoored from reason, because, Hibbs says, "Keenan's position rests on the controversial thesis that Thomas develops in the *Summa theologiae* a doctrine of the autonomy of the will, based on the distinction between the orders of specification and exercise" ("Interpretations of Aquinas's Ethics Since Vatican II," 420).

[211] *De veritate*, q. 22, a. 9: "Sed si consideretur actus voluntatis ex parte obiecti, sic voluntatis invenitur duplex obiectum. Unum, ad quod de necessitate naturalis inclinatio

If the will is *not* "necessarily immutable" on the side of an object that merely has a likeness to the ultimate end, it can accept or not accept such an object. That is, a good presented as such *hic et nunc* does not necessarily move the will. In the reply to the first objection of article 12, we are told that, even if "the intellect is prior to the will *simpliciter*, it is nevertheless made posterior to the will [*efficitur voluntate posterior*] by a kind of reflection."[212] In other words, on the level of exercise, the will is able to have a kind of primacy. In view of this primacy, apparently, Thomas is even open to qualifying the intellect's superiority in view of the will's nobility:

> Although the intellect is simply nobler than the will, *at least in regard to some things*, nevertheless, in regard to the aspect of moving, which belongs to the will from the distinctive character of its object, the will is found to be nobler.[213]

The will's motion is responsible for a variety of actions including those that make certain objects appear choice-worthy even if they are not actually so. This, too, implies the will's ability to be a kind of primary source of movement on the level of exercise. As Thomas says in question twenty-four, the inclination of a habit can cause someone to think a certain thing to be worth pursuing as an end that is not actually a good thing because "as each one is, so does the end seem to him." A habit "inclines

---

determinatur. Et hoc quidem obiectum est voluntati inditum et propositum a creatore, qui ei naturalem inclinationem dedit in illud. Unde nullus potest necessario per tale obiectum immutare voluntatem nisi solus Deus. Aliud vero est obiectum voluntatis, quod quidem natum est inclinare voluntatem, in quantum est in eo aliqua similitudo vel ordo respectu ultimi finis naturaliter desiderati; non tamen ex hoc obiecto voluntas de necessitate immutatur, ut prius dictum est, quia non in eo singulariter invenitur ordo ad ultimum finem naturaliter desideratum. Et mediante hoc obiecto potest aliqua creatura inclinare aliquatenus voluntatem, non tamen necessario immutare; sicut patet cum aliquis persuadet alicui aliquid faciendum proponendo ei eius utilitatem vel honestatem; tamen in potestate voluntatis est ut illud acceptet vel non acceptet, eo quod non est naturaliter determinata ad illud."

[212] *De veritate*, q. 22, a. 12, ad 1: "Since there is a certain similarity between reflection and circular motion (in which that which is the last motion is the same as that which was the beginning), it is necessary to say about reflection that that which is at first prior becomes posterior. And, therefore, although the intellect is prior to the will *simpliciter*, it is nevertheless made posterior to the will [*efficitur voluntate posterior*] by a kind of reflection—and it is in this way that the will is able to move the intellect."

[213] *De veritate*, q. 22, a. 12, ad 5: "Quamvis intellectus simpliciter sit nobilior voluntate, ad minus respectu aliquarum rerum; tamen secundum rationem movendi, quae competit voluntati ex ratione propria obiecti, voluntas nobilior invenitur" (emphasis added).

toward that which is suitable to it. It happens, therefore, that the good of the one who has a habit of voluptuousness seems to be that which corresponds to voluptuousness as to that which is connatural to him."[214] When Thomas made the same point in the *Scriptum*, he explicitly attributed that habit to the power of the one who acquired it.[215] How would such a habit be developed if not by turning against reason's presentation of some particular good and refusing to allow that object to compel it? If that is the case, there must be some movement that is not found in the reason *qua* appointing that particular object—although it must, I would suggest, be found in the reason *qua* appointing some other object since the "motion of the will is an inclination following an understood form."[216]

In question 17 of *De veritate*, Thomas speaks of the instance in which the judgment of someone's conscience tells him he should not fornicate even though he goes on to err "in choosing and not in conscience" by acting "against conscience: and this is called acting with a bad conscience inasmuch as the deed is not concordant with the judgment of knowledge."[217] As mentioned above, it seems the will would even then have to be

---

[214] *De veritate*, q. 24, a. 10, corp.: "Vitii habitus quasi natura quaedam inclinat in id quod est sibi conveniens; unde fit ut habenti habitum luxuriae bonum videatur id quod luxuriae convenit, quasi connaturale. Et hoc est quod philosophus dicit in III Ethicorum, quod qualis intus unusquisque est, talis et finis videtur ei."

[215] *In II sent.*, dist. 25, q. 1, a. 1, ad 5: "The quality of a thing is twofold, because it can be considered from the side of the habit or from the natural composition. Inasmuch as it is from a habit, the end seems to a given individual to be such as he himself is; for example, for someone who has the habit of voluptuousness, sexual delight seems best, which is in keeping with the likeness of his own habit. In regard to these, then, a quality (such as having a virtuous or vicious habit) is in our power."

[216] *Quolibet* VI, q. 2, a. 2: "motus voluntatis est inclinatio sequens formam intellectam." See also *CT* I, ch. 1: "The will is the appetite following the intellect."

[217] *De veritate*, q. 17, a. 1, ad 4. The context of this fascinating reply is as follows: "The judgment of conscience is different from that of free will because the judgment of conscience consists in knowledge alone, whereas the judgment of free will [*liberi arbitrii*] consists in the application of knowledge to desire, and this judgment is the judgment of choice. And therefore it happens sometimes that the judgment of free will is perverted but not the judgment of conscience—as when someone examines something that is incumbent upon him to do here and now and judges, still speculating through principles, that something is evil (as, for instance, to fornicate with this woman). But when he begins to apply [this judgment] to the act, many circumstances present themselves from all sides as, for instance, the pleasure of fornication. From such a consideration, the reason is bound by concupiscence so that its dictate might not break forth into choice And thus someone errs in choosing, but not in conscience; rather, he acts against conscience: this is called acting with a bad conscience inasmuch as the deed is not concordant with the judgment of knowledge."

specified by the intellect, inasmuch as it would apply the intellect only to know the objects that accent the apparent good of something contrary to the true good. In other words, the sinful man would retain natural reason despite his having turned against his conscience by adverting his attention to some good aspect of an evil act. In question 25, Thomas touches upon the will's ability to turn away from that which would truly be conducive to happiness:

> The will naturally has an appetite for the good that is the end—namely, happiness in general, and similarly the good that is for the end—for each one naturally desires what is useful to it. But in desiring this or that or in choosing this or that, the sin of the will is able to occur.[218]

When the power (*virtus*) of natural reason (i.e., synderesis) remains in one's conscience in such a way that its principles are "preserved in the conclusions," conscience is practically synonymous with synderesis,[219] and is thus in a special way related to the end—or at least, "the good that is for the end." In these cases, one can reject the proximate end proposed by choosing something other than what conscience tells him to do. Once again, therefore, we have evidence that the will, for even the younger Thomas,

---

[218] *De veritate*, q. 25, a. 8, corp.: "Voluntas naturaliter appetit bonum quod est finis, scilicet felicitatem in generali, et similiter bonum quod est ad finem; unusquisque enim naturaliter appetit utilitatem suam; sed in hoc vel illo fine appetendo, aut hoc vel illo utili eligendo, incidit peccatum voluntatis." *De veritate* q. 24, a. 8, corp., says something nearly identical: "The will naturally desires the good that is the end: namely, happiness in general and, similarly, the good that is for the sake of the end (for everyone naturally desires that which is useful for him). Nevertheless, in desiring this or that end, or in choosing this or that useful thing, sin occurs on the part of the will."

[219] *In* II *sent.*, dist. 39, q. 3, a. 2, ad 2: "Conscience is called the natural judging power [synderesis] not *per se*, but inasmuch as the power of synderesis remains in it, since the power of the principles is preserved in the conclusions and it does not err in regard to that part [i.e., the 'part' in which the power of synderesis remains]." The body of *De veritate*, q. 17, a. 2, speaks of times when the judgments of synderesis and conscience are identical (in which case, the two seem to elide): "It should be known that, in certain things, conscience is not able to make a mistake. Namely, when that particular act to which conscience is applied has a universal judgment about it in synderesis, . . . no conscience can err in making a judgment 'God should not be loved by me' or 'some evil should be done.' For, in either the speculative or the practical syllogism, the major term is *per se* known inasmuch as it exists in the universal judgment and the minor is a particular identification made, as when one says: 'Every whole is greater than its part. This whole is a whole. Therefore, it is greater than its part.'" Cf. *ST* I-II, q. 79, a. 13, ad 3.

can freely move itself away from some particular object presented by the intellect.[220]

In question 12 of *De veritate*, Thomas discusses the different ways in which the will is free. It does not, he says, necessarily will whatever it wills and is free "as regards (a) the act, inasmuch as it is able to will or not to will, (b) as regards the object, inasmuch as it is able to will this or that or even its opposite and (c) as regards the way it is ordered to the end, inasmuch as it is able to will good or evil."[221] It has freedom, therefore, "in respect of certain things that are for the end and not of the end itself."[222] This freedom includes the ability not only to be moved by itself but also to move the acts of any of the other powers:

> All the acts of the diverse powers are referred to free judgment by means of one act, which is to choose. We are moved in accordance with it by the free judgment because we choose to be moved by the free judgment; and so it is with the other acts. Accordingly, from this it . . . is shown that the free judgment . . . is one power moving the diverse powers [*potentias*] by its power [*virtute*].[223]

The free judgment truly is free, then, even though it cannot choose the last end. As we have seen, the natural judging power known as synderesis or natural reason, however, is not free in the same way. The difference between these two kinds of judgments is further clarified in question 16, where we learn that "judgment is twofold; of universals, which pertains to synderesis and [secondly] of particular doable things—and this is the judgment of choice and pertains to free will [*liberum arbitrium*]."[224] He

---

[220] When this is done, however, the intellect must be involved in some way if there is to be a human act. That is, given that it is a human act, some understanding or judgment that is contrary to that which a sufficient consideration of the implications of conscience would allow could prevail, but it would remain some kind of intellectual judgment.

[221] *De veritate*, q. 22, a. 6, corp.: ". . . scilicet quantum ad actum, in quantum potest velle vel non velle; et quantum ad obiectum, in quantum potest velle hoc vel illud, etiam eius oppositum; et quantum ad ordinem finis, in quantum potest velle bonum vel malum."

[222] *De veritate*, q. 22, a. 6, corp.: "Inest libertas voluntati . . . respectu quorumdam obiectorum, scilicet respectu eorum quae sunt ad finem et non ipsius finis."

[223] *De veritate*, q. 24, a. 5, corp.: "Omnes enim actus diversarum potentiarum non referuntur ad liberum arbitrium nisi mediante uno actu, qui est eligere: secundum hoc enim libero arbitrio movemur, quod libero arbitrio moveri eligimus; et sic de aliis actibus. Unde ex hoc non ostenditur liberum arbitrium esse plures potentias, sed esse unam potentiam moventem sua virtute potentias diversas."

[224] *De veritate*, q. 16, a. 1, ad 15: "Iudicium est duplex, scilicet in universali, et hoc pertinet

considers the latter kind of judgment, the free judgment, to be nothing other than the will itself, even though it does not "name it not absolutely" (i.e., not qua simple will or "will as nature"), but only "in relation to one of its acts, which is to choose."[225] As he worded it in the *Scriptum*, just as the act of understanding is to understand, "so that act which is to choose is attributed [*assignatur*] to free judgment."[226] In other words, the act of understanding or synderesis is known as "understanding" and the act of free judgment (*liberum arbitrium*) is known as "choosing." He indicates later in the same work that this latter judgment enjoys liberty due to the free motion of the will:

> The appetite which has the good and the end for an object[227] moves itself and the cognitive power to act. For from the desire for an act or an end, someone proceeds to exercise [*exerceat*] some act, as long as it is not from a necessity of nature.[228]

Thus, the will considered as free judgment (and not the natural one of the *voluntas ut natura*) is able to choose freely. Since the "will as nature" follows the natural reason,[229] it cannot do so in regard to the final end, but it is certainly able to do so in regard to some proximate end that is a finite good.[230] As a *rational* appetite, it is even able to command the acts

---

ad synderesim; et in particulari operabili, et est hoc iudicium electionis, et hoc pertinet ad liberum arbitrium."

[225] *De veritate*, q. 24, a. 6, corp.: "Liberum arbitrium est ipsa voluntas. Nominat autem eam non absolute, sed in ordine ad aliquem actum eius, qui est eligere."

[226] *In II sent.*, dist. 24, q. 1, a. 2, ad 3: "He says there that an act can be attributed to a power in two ways. One way is that 'it elicits it as its own, as sight elicits the act of seeing or the intellect elicits the act of understanding,' and so that act that is to choose is attributed to free judgment."

[227] This, of course, is the will. See *SCG* III, chs. 1 and 148, and *ST* II-II, q. 4, a. 1, corp.

[228] *In IV sent.*, dist. 49, q. 3, a. 5, qc 3, ad 2: "Appetitus qui habet bonum et finem pro objecto, movet seipsum et vim cognitivam in actum: ex desiderio enim actus vel finis provenit quod aliquis aliquem actum exerceat, dummodo non sit ex necessitate naturae."

[229] *In II sent.*, dist. 39, q. 2, a. 2, ad 2: "That which is the end of man is naturally known in the reason to be good and desired, the will following this knowledge is called the will as nature."

[230] *De veritate*, q. 22, a. 6, corp.: "In respect to the object, the will is indeterminate as regards the means, not, however, as regards the end itself" ("Respectu obiecti quidem est indeterminata voluntas quantum ad ea quae sunt ad finem, non quantum ad ipsum finem ultimum"). See also *De potentia*, q. 2, a. 3, ad 6: "Although the will follows the inclination of nature in being determined to that one thing that is the last end tended to by nature, it nevertheless remains undetermined in respect of other things, as is clear

of any of the "powers that are able to obey the reason," and when those powers are moved, their movement can be attributed to it because it is the "mover of all the powers."[231] We must conclude, then, that at this time, Thomas already held the will to be profoundly free despite the intellect's primacy.[232]

"Freedom" of Indifference and the Ability to Sin

The notion of indetermination is rather strong in the early Thomas[233] despite the intellect's property of acting in the manner of an end.[234] Clearly, then, he would not have agreed that "self-movement is only possible if final causality is derived from some source other than reason."[235] As Thomas asserts in *ST* I and other pre-1270 works, the free will is "related indifferently to choosing well or badly."[236] This is so because the

---

in man, who naturally wills beatitude necessarily but not other things."

[231] See, *In* II *sent.*, dist. 24, q. 1, a. 2, ad 3.

[232] This primacy is evinced by two succinct pre-1270 texts asserting, respectively, that the will's nature is to follow an *understood* form (*ST* I, q. 87, a. 4, corp.) and that the intellect is the first mover in man precisely because it moves the will (*SCG* II, ch. 60, no. 4: "The first moving [power] in man is the intellect, since the intellect moves the will by its own understandable object."

[233] Volitional "indifference" is even spoken of in *De veritate*, q. 24, a. 14, corp.: "But the will of man is not determined to some one activity, but is indifferently related to many."

[234] *De veritate* q. 22, a. 12, ad 3 ("The intellect moves in the manner of an end, for this is the way the apprehended good is related to the will"); *SCG* III, ch. 72, no. 7 ("The intellect moves the will, not in the manner of an efficient or moving cause, but in the manner of a final cause, by proposing it's own object to it, which is the end"); *In* VI *eth.*, lec. 9, no. 14 ("The singulars, which we say understanding pertains to, are principles of that for the sake of which something is done; that is, they are principles in the manner of a final cause"); *SCG* III, ch. 26, no. 22 ("Now, the intellect moves the will in the manner by which an end moves, since the understood good is the end of the will. The agent, though, is later in moving than the end is, since the agent does not move except for the sake of the end").

[235] Keenan, *Goodness and Rightness*, 31.

[236] *ST* I, q. 83, a. 2, corp.: "Free will [*liberum arbitrium*] is related indifferently to choosing well or badly. Accordingly, it is impossible that free will be a habit." I have decided to follow the convention here and translate *liberum arbitrium* as "free will." For Thomas, *liberum arbitrium* is "the will itself," though it names the will in relation to its act of choosing. (*De veritate*, q. 24, a. 6, corp.: "Free will is the will itself, though it names it not absolutely, but in the order to one of its acts, which is to choose.") The following texts affirm the indifference of the will, though without specifying that *liberum arbitrium* is intended. See: *De veritate*, q. 24, a. 14, corp. ("But the will of man is not determined to some one operation, but is related indifferently to many"); *ST* I-II, q. 10, a. 4, corp. ("The will is not determined to one, but is related indifferently to many) *De*

means toward the ultimate end are able to be chosen freely. As we have seen, part of that choosing involves moving the reason to deliberate or to focus on one particular (and perhaps only apparent) good over another. So long as the object is seen as "orderable to happiness,"[237] choosing it is possible and the will can guide the deliberation to see good in it:

> He who wills to fornicate, although he knows in general [*in universali*] that fornication is evil, nevertheless judges that an act of fornication is good for him now and he chooses it under the species of good because no one acts intending to do evil, as Dionysius says.[238]

In this light, we can understand how it is that "[even if] judgment is of the reason, nevertheless the freedom of judging is immediately of the will."[239] David Gallagher's explanation of how this can be even if the will is dependent upon the reason is insightful:

> Since the will's act depends upon the intellect's presentation of the object, and because the will can command the act of the intellect, it is possible, for any given proposed act, simply to will to cease thinking about the object and so to obviate all acts in its regard.[240]

The will is responsible for the act of thinking or the absence of that act. Even when the will obviates all acts in regard to what is proposed to it, there must be some *reason* why it does so, but it remains responsible for this obviation. The right ordering of the will is thus a *sine qua non* for the

---

malo, q. 6, ad 3 ("Necessity is not imposed [*inducitur*] upon the nature of the moved will, which is related indifferently to diverse things. Instead, freedom remains").

[237] *De veritate*, q. 22, a. 6, corp.: "The person who naturally desires happiness with a correct appetite would never be led to desire fornication except inasmuch as he apprehends it as a kind of good for man inasmuch as it is something pleasurable and as thus orderable to happiness as a certain likeness [*imaginem*] of it."

[238] *De veritate*, q. 22, a. 2, corp.: "Qui enim vult fornicari, quamvis sciat in universali fornicationem malum esse, tamen iudicat sibi ut nunc bonum esse fornicationis actum, et sub specie boni ipsum eligit. Nullus enim intendens ad malum operatur, ut Dionysius dicit."

[239] *De veritate*, q. 24, a. 6, ad 3: "Quamvis iudicium sit rationis, tamen libertas iudicandi est voluntatis immediate."

[240] Gallagher, "The Will and Its Acts," 76. Of course, even this obviation would have rational specification; we can refuse to consider something *because* we apprehend that doing so would be irritating or less enjoyable than considering something else.

very being of prudence even though the opposite is true as well. Without an upright will directing prudence to a good end,[241] sound deliberation about means would be of no avail, because the object would be unfitting and the only wisdom one would have would be "earthy wisdom"[242] (as opposed to the practical wisdom known as prudence).[243] The will's role is, therefore, not only crucial but also that to which Thomas primarily attributes sin.[244] Sin is always a possibility in regard to finite goods because, in any case involving something other than the perfect good of happiness itself, the "indetermination of the will, which is able to have an appetite for good or evil" remains.[245]

Although this indeterminacy is not objectively ideal since "the creature would be better if it were to adhere to God immovably, nevertheless, that being is good which is able to adhere or not adhere to God."[246] Man can even turn away from God and treat a creature as if it were his last end

---

[241] In *De virtutibus*, q. 1, a. 7, corp., Thomas says the end of prudence is determined by the will more than once.

[242] *ST* II-II, q. 45, a. 1, ad 1: "They are wise in order to do evil deeds, but they do not know how to do well [Jer 4:22]. Now, whoever turns away from the due end, necessarily appoints to himself [*praestituat sibi*] an undue end, since every agent acts on account of an end. For this reason, if he appoints to himself an end consisting in external earthly things, his wisdom is called earthly wisdom."

[243] *In* II *eth.*, lec. 7, no. 5: "'Wise man' here names . . . the prudent man who is wise in regard to human things." Prudence, then, is a kind of wisdom pertaining to human things. Also, *ST* II-II, q. 47, a. 2 tells us that prudence is in the practical intellect. Interestingly, St. Thomas never uses the phrase "practical wisdom" in the Latin (*sapientia practica*), but the common translation of prudence as "practical wisdom" coheres with his thought.

[244] *In* II *sent.*, dist. 44, q. 2, a. 3, expos.: "Sin occurs by the actions of many powers. But it should be said that no power elicits an act of sin unless the will or that which is moved by the will does so. Therefore, there is one power according to which sin is first present—namely, the will or free will [*liberum arbitrium*]." He also says acts are only considered moral because of the will, which is the "principle of meriting and demeriting" in *In* II *sent.*, dist. 42, q. 1, a. 1, corp. See also *In* IV *sent.*, dist. 17, q. 1, a. 1, qc 1, ad 1) and *ST* I-II, q. 71, a. 6, ad 2 (which says the first cause of sin is in the will).

[245] *De veritate*, q. 22, a. 6, corp.: "He who naturally desires [*appetit*] happiness with an upright appetite is never led to desiring fornication unless he apprehends it as a kind of good of man inasmuch as it is delightful and thus able to be ordered to happiness as a kind of image of happiness. And from this, the indetermination of the will, which is able to have an appetite for good or evil, follows."

[246] *De veritate*, q. 24, a. 1, ad 16: "Quamvis creatura esset melior si immobiliter Deo adhaereret, tamen illa est bona quae potest Deo adhaerere et non adhaerere; et ita melius est universum ubi utraque creatura invenitur."

instead of him,[247] but this ability itself remains a sign of man's dignity. In virtue of his very nature, he is "free" either to place God before him as an end by turning himself toward him as his fitting end (at least inasmuch as God is the beginning and end of created effects) or to refrain from doing so.[248] Since he is "bound to avoid sin, and this is not done without appointing to himself a fitting end," it would be better for him to "turn himself to God" (*ad Deum se convertere*), thereby disposing himself for the appointing of the end that comes by grace.[249] Nevertheless, as we have already established, he is certainly free to instead "appoint to himself an unfitting end" by putting worldly goods ahead of God,[250] in whom his true happiness lies.[251]

The good, for Thomas, is "named from the *ratio* of the end," which "is especially found in those who appoint the end to themselves."[252] The

---

[247] *ST* I-II, q. 72, a. 5, corp., speaks of the soul turning away from God, its last end, by sin. See also: I-II, q. 89, a. 1, ad 2.; II-II, q. 9, a. 4, corp.; q. 55, a. 1, sc.

[248] We must, of course, keep in mind that the "first motion of the will proceeds from the instinct" of God, the exterior moving principle, but the doctrine of physical premotion does not negate the causality of secondary causes (see *ST* I-II, q. 9, a. 4: "It is necessary to posit that, in the first motion of the will, the will goes forth from an instinct of some exterior mover, as Aristotle concludes in some chapter of the *Eudemian Ethics*"). As Thomas says in the *ad primum*, although it pertains to the notion of the voluntary that its principle is internal, this does not mean that the first instrinsic principle does not have its first principle from outside of it (*ab extra*) because the first natural motion that is *ab extra* moves nature.

[249] *De veritate*, q. 28, a. 3, ad 4: "If, when someone begins to be an adult, he does what is in himself, grace (through which he will be immune from original sin) is given to him. If he does not do so, he will be guilty of the sin of omission. For, since everyone is held to avoid sin, and this is not done without appointing to himself a fitting end, everyone is held to convert himself to God ... from the first moment he has possession of his mind; and through this, he is disposed for grace." Regarding the appointing of the ultimate end, Thomas says, "the knowledge of the ultimate end is appointed [*praestituatur*] in us by grace in order that we may be directed towards it voluntarily" (*SCG* III, ch. 152, no. 2). As *ST* I-II, q. 112, a. 3, corp., makes pellucidly clear, God's help is necessary even for this preparation: "The preparation of man for grace is from God, as from the mover and from free will as from that which is moved." See also I-II, q. 9, a. 6. Regarding the appointing of the ultimate end, Thomas says, "the knowledge of the ultimate end is appointed [*praestituatur*] in us by grace in order that we may be directed towards it voluntarily."

[250] *ST* II-II, q. 45, a. 1, ad 1 (trans. in note 242 above).

[251] *ST* I-II, q. 2, a. 8, corp.: "Nothing is able to set the will of man at rest besides the universal good, which is not found in anything created, but only in God."

[252] *In II sent.*, dist. 27, q. 1, a. 2, ad 2: "Although good is convertible with being, it is nevertheless found in a special way in animated things and in those having choice, as is said

fact that man has free will is therefore good even if this means he can appoint evil ends.[253] If he does so, he does so by freely moving his reason to justify some evil act under the *ratio* of good. Reason is not devoid of influence even in regard to an evil act because even the disordered will remains subject to the natural reason. That said, though, a kind of subordinated "self-movement" could be predicated of the will inasmuch as it would have a kind of primacy over the deliberating power known as "reason as reason."[254] As Aquinas explains in the *Scriptum*, "if it is from a desire for an act or an end that someone exercises [*exerceat*] some act, as long as it is not from a necessity of nature," he is not constrained by any object appointed by the reason as a pursuable proximate end.[255] In other words, when his reason proposes some finite good, he always retains freedom on the level of exercise, and in this way, the desiring power known as the will has primacy and a kind of self-movement.

Unrectified inclination can either lead someone not to deliberate about pursuing a worthy good in the first place or to an aversion from a particular good that has been proposed by the deliberative reason. One kind of particular good pertains to things that can be known and thus the will's exercise can lead even to a defect in knowledge (which defect could preclude the possibility of making properly informed decisions). For these reasons, freedom of the will must be intentionally placed at the service of the universal good, which leads us the consideration of true freedom.

---

in *Metaphysics* V. The reason for this is that the good is named from the account [*ratio*] of the end. Therefore, although it is found in all things in which the end is, it is nevertheless especially found in those [creatures] who appoint the end to themselves and are cognizant of the intention of the end."

[253] *In II sent.*, dist. 41, q. 1, a. 2, ad 5: "Infidels . . . appoint themselves an end from the error of faithlessness."

[254] The "reason as reason" is not ordered to one. As such, it requires the influence of the will since the will is free on the side of the object to choose "this or that or its opposite" (*De veritate*, q. 22, a. 6, corp.). *De veritate*, q. 26, a. 9, ad 7, explains that, whereas "reason as reason" is understood to "refer to the reason inasmuch as it is ordered to knowing or desiring [something] because it is the proper function of the reason to make a comparison," "reason as nature" is understood to "refer to the reason being compared to those things one naturally knows or desires."

[255] *In IV sent.*, dist. 49, q. 3, a. 5, qc 3, ad 2: "An appetite that has a good and an end for an object moves itself and the cognitive power to an act, for it is from a desire for an act or an end that someone exercises [*exerceat*] some act, as long as it is not from a necessity of nature."

Freedom for Excellence

In question 24 of *De veritate*, Thomas refers to free will (*liberum arbitrium*) as the kind of judgment that "causes [*facit*] liberty in judging."[256] Since, however, men are able to choose a variety of means of attaining the naturally desired good of happiness,[257] a question arises regarding what is requisite for attaining the goal. We should be careful to keep in mind that the freedom to choose the good is truly free (i.e., in the sense of being perfective)[258] only when it chooses in accord with natural reason and whatever one's conscience judges to be good. If, instead, man uses the act of *liberum arbitrium* (which is to choose[259]) in such a way that he wills something evil, that is not true freedom, because "to will evil is neither freedom, nor a part of freedom, although it is a certain sign of freedom."[260]

In book III of the *Scriptum*, Thomas speaks to the inclinations that come from nature and the inclinations that come from the free will of the acting person, in addition to the indispensable and liberating role of the intellect. His teaching on these points is important for understanding his approach to authentic liberty:

---

[256] *De veritate*, q. 24, a. 6, corp.: "The power by which we freely judge is not understood as that by which we simply judge, which pertains to reason, but as that which causes liberty in judging, which pertains to the will. For this reason, free will [*liberum arbitrium*] is the will itself. It names it, however, not absolutely, but in the order to its act of choice." Of course, even though this free judgment "pertains to the will," it is specified by reason in some way because the will cannot act in any other way. Even the will not to will is rationally specified. When the will applies powers to act, it is precisely under some *ratio* that it does so.

[257] *In II sent.*, dist. 7, q. 1, a. 1, ad 1: "The will ... always pertains to the good and happiness. However, people are able to choose various ways of attaining it inasmuch as they judge these ways are better suited to attaining happiness. Accordingly, there is able to be error in the choice of those things that are for the end itself."

[258] This kind of freedom can be distinguished from the freedom of indifference, which is a kind of freedom from compulsion. The latter kind of freedom, of course, pertains to the will inasmuch as it cannot be compelled by any finite object.

[259] *In II sent.*, dist. 24, q. 1, a. 2, ad 3: "Some act is attributed to some power in two ways." The first way Aquinas describes is when the power elicits the act as its own ("as the faculty of vision elicits sight and the faculty of understanding elicits understanding"). It is in this way, he says, that "that act which is to choose is attributed to free will [*libero arbitrio*]."

[260] *De veritate*, q. 22, a. 6, corp.: "Et pro tanto dicitur, quod velle malum nec est libertas, nec pars libertatis, quamvis sit quoddam libertatis signum." Interestingly, in *ST* II-II, q. 164, a. 4, ad 4, this false freedom is not qualified as such: "The eleventh grade of humility is that a man not be delighted in doing his own will, which is contrasted with the freedom by which a man is delighted to freely do what he wants."

The one knowing the end and the means ... directs himself not only to the end but also to other things just as an archer shoots his arrow toward a target. Thus someone tends to the end in two ways. In one way, he is directed by himself, which occurs only in the case of someone knowing the end and the *ratio* of the end. In another way, he is directed by another, and in this way all things tend in accordance with nature to their proper and natural ends, having been directed thereto by the wise one who is establishing nature as it is [*a sapientia instituente naturam*][261] and, in accordance with this, we find two appetites: (1) the natural appetite which is nothing other than the inclination of a thing into its natural end which is from the direction of the one establishing nature as it is and, again, (2) the voluntary appetite, which is an inclination of someone who knows the end and the order to that end....

Thus it is evident that the natural and voluntary appetite differ, inasmuch as the natural appetite is from an extrinsic principle (and therefore does not have freedom because a free thing is that which is its own cause) whereas the inclination of the voluntary appetite is in the willing individual himself (and therefore the will has freedom)....

The will, then, has in addition to [*praeter*] the natural inclination another inclination, and the one willing it causes it himself.[262]

---

[261] One might be tempted to translate *instituente* as "established," but as it is in the present tense, Aquinas surely had in mind that God is continuing, as it were, to ensure that nature acts in accordance with the eternal law which all creatures passively participate in by being directed to their proper acts and ends. See *ST* I, q. 22, a. 1, and I-II, q. 91, a. 2.

[262] *In* III *sent.*, dist. 27, q. 1, a. 2, corp.: "Cognoscens autem finem et ea quae sunt ad finem, non solum seipsum in finem dirigit, sed etiam alia, sicut sagittator emittit sagittam ad signum. Sic ergo dupliciter aliquid tendit in finem. Uno modo directum in finem a seipso, quod est tantum in cognoscente finem et rationem finis. Alio modo directum ab alio; et hoc modo omnia secundum suam naturam tendunt in fines proprios et naturales, directa a sapientia instituente naturam. Et secundum hoc invenimus duos appetitus: scilicet appetitum naturalem, qui nihil aliud est quam inclinatio rei in finem suum naturalem qui est ex directione instituentis naturam, et iterum appetitum voluntarium, qui est inclinatio cognoscentis finem, et ordinem in finem illum.... Sic ergo patet quod in hoc differt appetitus naturalis et voluntarius, quod inclinatio naturalis appetitus est ex principio extrinseco; et ideo non habet libertatem, quia liberum est quod est sui causa: inclinatio autem voluntarii appetitus est in ipso volente; et ideo habet voluntas libertatem ... voluntas autem habet praeter inclinationem naturalem, aliam, cujus est ipse volens causa."

The natural inclination here is distinguished from the inclination of the rational animal whose ability to reason and know ends (and *not* despite this ability) enables him to be authentically free. In a sense, the will is indifferent even in regard to certain means and particular goods (i.e., it enjoys the liberty attendant upon the nature of choice as rooted in the intellect[263]). However, the only liberating way to use free will is by striving for excellence and acting in accordance with nature, faith, and reason (not to mention grace). For this reason, Thomas explains elsewhere in the *Scriptum* that *liberum arbitrium* is *per se* ordered to the good and that it therefore does not tend toward evil except on account of some defect. As a consequence, *liberum arbitrium* is perfectly found only when it is, in fact, not able to tend toward evil.[264] He does not deny that freedom to choose evil is a kind of freedom, but he insists that "freedom regarding the good [*ad bonum*] is more [truly] freedom than freedom regarding evil [*ad malum*]."[265] Since choosing the good would be the more perfect form of freedom and since both *liberum arbitrium* and its act of choice involve the intellect and the will,[266] we can apply what Servais Pinckaers says even to the early writings:

> In Aquinas we find a freedom rooted in the intellect and will according to their natural inclinations to the true and the good, and this is what we call a freedom of excellence or perfection.[267]

---

[263] On the indifference of the will, see *ST* I, q. 83, a. 2, corp., and *De veritate*, q. 24, a. 14, corp. Since it is "nothing other than to choose something instead of another" (*In* II *sent.*, dist. 24, q. 1, a. 2, obj. 4), it is no surprise that it is free. Regarding the relationship of choice to the intellect, we read the following: "choice is an act of the will in subordination to reason comparing the means to an end to each other" (*De veritate*, q. 22, a. 13, ad 16); "choice is not absolutely an act of the will, but is ordered to the commanding intellect" (*In* I *sent.*, dist. 41, q. 1, a. 2, ad 1). See also *ST* I-II, q. 13, a. 3, corp.

[264] *In* II *sent.*, dist. 25, q. 1, a. 1, ad 2: "Because free will [*liberum arbitrium*] is *per se* ordered to the good (which is the object of the will), it tends toward something evil only on account of some defect whereby evil is apprehended as good. Will or choice exist only on account of a good or an apparent good. Therefore when free will [*liberum arbitrium*] is most perfect, it is not able to tend toward evil."

[265] *In* II *sent.*, dist. 25, q. 1, a. 5: "There is no freedom for evil except in a qualified way, and that which is in an unqualified way is better than that which is in a qualified way. And it should be said that this comparison is not taken into account on account of what is proper to freedom, because freedom regarding the good is more [truly] freedom than freedom regarding evil."

[266] *Liberum arbitrium*, according to the first article of *ST* I-II, is a *facultas voluntatis et rationis*. For choice being the act of *liberum arbitrium*, see *In* II *sent.*, dist. 24, q. 1, a. 2, ad 3, and *De veritate*, q. 24, a. 5, corp.

[267] Servais Pinckaers, "Dominican Moral Theology in the 20th Century," in *The Pinckaers*

This freedom is linked to the intellect as regards the inclination to the true and to the will as regards the inclination to the good. By acting virtuously for the sake of these naturally desired ends, freedom of excellence is attained.

Concluding the Section

We are now in a position to better evaluate Keenan's criticism of *De veritate* and the other earlier works. For him, the earlier Thomas's belief that "the first beginning of all freedom is located in reason"[268] necessarily implies that he "decisively identifies reason and not the will as the source of freedom."[269] If it is true, however, that the one willing is himself the cause of his inclination, and if a man's will is free in regard to its act and object and the order of the object to the end,[270] the will must necessarily at least be some kind of root of freedom[271] even if it is subordinate to the intellectual power regarding the last end and whatever is constitutive of it.[272] The intellect or reason,[273] in other words, may be responsible for presenting the last end[274] and other necessarily desired ends such as knowledge, virtue,

---

Reader: Renewing Moral Theology, ed. John Berkman and Craig Titus (Washington, DC: Catholic University of America Press, 2005), 73–91, at 81. Again, this sense of freedom is a consequence of habitually living in accordance with reason (i.e., it is a consequence of virtue) whereas freedom of choice is a natural consequence of possessing a rational appetite.

[268] *De veritate*, q. 24, a. 2, corp.: "Totius libertatis radix est in ratione constituta."

[269] Keenan, *Goodness and Rightness*, 31–32.

[270] *De veritate*, q. 22, a. 6, corp., speaks of the will's freedom in regard to the act of willing or not willing, the object of willing "this or that," and the way it is ordered to the end "inasmuch as it is able to will good or evil."

[271] As we will see, this is what Thomas says in *De veritate*, q. 23, a. 1, sc 4: "Voluntas est radix libertatis."

[272] *In II sent.*, dist. 38, q. 1, a. 2, corp., speaks of God as the last end of those with upright wills and of "happiness embracing charity and delight" as an "end under the end, joining [the individual] to the last end." Objectively, there is no "right relation of the will toward God except by means of these three." This, of course, pertains to the supernatural level. Nevertheless, there are other things necessarily connected with happiness as constitutive of it. *In I de interp.*, lec. 14, no. 24, suggests that such necessarily desirable goods of this sort are being (*esse*), living (*vivere*), and understanding (*intelligere*); see also *ST* I-II, q. 10, a. 2, ad 3, and *De veritate*, q. 22, a. 5, corp. It is in this sense, perhaps, that Thomas says understanding is an end of every intellectual substance in *SCG* III, ch. 25 ("Intelligere autem est propria operatio substantiae intellectuali. Ipsa igitur est finis ejus"); i.e., it is a *finis sub fine*.

[273] They are, again, one power (*ST* I, q. 79, a. 8, corp.: "We understand and reason by the same power. It is thus clear that reason and understanding are the same power in man).

[274] *ST* I-II, q. 62, a. 3, corp., speaks of the natural inclination ordering man to his connatural

health, life, and being,[275] but freedom remains in regard to subordinate ends. It seems one could only be concerned if he were to conflate the false freedom to choose sin with freedom for excellence and if he were to fail to see that neither nature nor grace hinders true freedom.

No doubt, reason must be the ultimate root of liberty, because the will's very nature is to follow the apprehension of the reason.[276] Keenan overlooks, however, that Thomas says in the following question that the *will* is also a root of freedom.[277] There is no need to posit competitive causality between them as Keenan does when he says "the reason and *not* the will." They are both roots of freedom, but one of the roots needs to be rooted in the other one for there to be anything other than a mere aping of true freedom. What seems implied in all this is the later teaching of *ST* I according to which "the will is the root of freedom as its subject, but reason is the root as a cause."[278] In other words, freedom for excellence would be precluded were the will to be separated from the reason because it is prerequisite to this perfective kind of freedom that the will's object (the universal good) be intellectually apprehended. If the will, moreover, were to cut itself off from the root of freedom (the *radix libertatis*) and ignorance were to ensue, any act committed in virtue of that ignorance would be sinful, as both the *Scriptum* and the *ST* say.[279]

Keenan supposes that "if the final cause is derived from reason," there would be no ground for "the will to deny the object that reason

---

end. The first way ordering occurs is "according to reason or intellect inasmuch as it contains the first universal principles known to us by the natural light of the intellect, from which the reason proceeds as much as in speculative things as in practical ones."

[275] *In I sent.*, dist. 48, q. 1, a. 4, corp., speaks of knowledge, virtue and health, and *De malo*, q. 6, ad 1, speaks of living and understanding as ends of this sort. See note 91 in ch. 1 of the present volume.

[276] In reference to "rational appetite, which is called the will," Thomas says: "An appetite of this sort, which is not determined by something else necessarily, follows the apprehension of reason" (*De veritate*, q. 22, a. 4). The will is said to "follow the apprehension of reason" in *ST* I-II, q. 19, a. 19, corp., and the "natural will" also known as the "will as nature" is said to follow reason in *In I sent.*, dist. 48, q. 1, a. 4, corp.

[277] *De veritate*, q. 23, a. 1, sc 4: "Voluntas est radix libertatis."

[278] *ST* I-II, q. 17, a. 1, ad 2: "Radix libertatis est voluntas sicut subiectum, sed sicut causa, est ratio."

[279] In the body of *In II sent.*, dist. 22, q. 2, a. 2, Thomas speaks about a kind of ignorance that follows upon sin. He gives an example of "when the will does not exercise restraint due to the desire for sin" and the "judgment of reason" is overcome (*absorbetur*) by desires that cloud the judgment of prudence. Since this kind of ignorance is due to choice, he concludes that it "does not excuse or diminish sin unless it causes involuntariness." See also: *ST* I-II, q. 76, a. 2, corp.; q. 74, a. 1, ad 2; q. 19, a. 6, ad 3.

presents,"[280] and he seems to highly value that possibility, as if reason were not that which distinguishes us from the beasts. It is true that for Aquinas the will has no unconditional autonomy, but the very desire for such autonomy would seem akin to a kind of Nietzschean "will to power" and would be quite antithetical to the spirit of Christianity.

One reason the will cannot be uncoupled from the intellect is that it is not able to be the cause of everything it knows. For Thomas, one cannot *not* know principles such as "the whole is greater than its part"[281] on the side of the speculative intellect and "one ought to live according to reason"[282] on the side of the practical intellect. Such knowledge, therefore, does not depend upon the will.[283] Keenan finds it "puzzling" that this could be the case given another dictum of Aquinas that "the freedom of judging belongs immediately to the will."[284] The reality, however, is that, even though there is no choosing when it comes to ultimate ends, when it comes to the free judgment that presupposes that universal and natural judgment, there *is* freedom and the will is responsible for it. In fact, since the causality of *intellectus* and/or synderesis is at least ontologically prior, it can be said to have dominion over lesser judgments without mediation. As *De veritate* said, the will need not follow the reason,[285] and thus presupposing *intellectus* or synderesis, it can move the judgment regarding particular contingents immediately.

We must therefore conclude that, even though the intellect was said to appoint ends in the manner of a final cause during this period, Thomas

---

[280] Keenan, *Goodness and Rightness*, 30.

[281] *De virtutibus*, q. 1, a. 8, corp.: "Some things are immediately from the beginning naturally known to man without any study and inquiry. The first principles not only in speculative things (as 'every whole is greater than its part' and similar things) are of this sort. But the first principles in practical things (as 'evil is to be avoided' and similar things) are also of this sort. These naturally known things are the principles of the whole following body of knowledge that is acquired through study, whether in practical things or in speculative."

[282] *ST* I-II, q. 94, a. 3, corp., says that every man has a "natural inclination to act according to reason" because the activity that is proper to a rational animal is to do just that. Perhaps with this in mind, Thomas argues that synderesis pertains to the unchangeably true maxim that "one ought to live according to reason" in *De veritate*, q. 17, a. 1, ad 9. See also *ST* I-II, q. 47, a. 7, corp. Synderesis or natural reason, of course, is the natural habit through which we have natural inclinations of the practical order (see *ST* I, q. 79, a. 12, corp.).

[283] Thomas argues that there is no choice or judgment in regard to first principles in *De veritate*, q. 24, a. 1, ad 20.

[284] See Keenan, *Goodness and Rightness*, 32, and *De veritate*, q. 24, a. 6, ad 3: "Although judgment pertains to reason, the freedom of judging pertains immediately to the will."

[285] *De veritate*, q. 22, a. 15, corp.: "One thing is not preferred to another in the practical

conceived of the will as retaining some kind of ability to move itself in regard to particular means. Aquinas even referred to this ability in terms of indifference.[286] If we refrain from resorting to Keenan's understanding of "autonomy" (autonomy from reason[287] wherein the will would be independent of reason and precede it[288]), the will's ability could perhaps even be labeled autonomous in a sense. After all, the will is certainly able to turn from reason's judgment about some finite good toward a merely apparent good. One example Thomas gives is when someone makes a rational judgment that something is not worthy of pursuit and the will nevertheless tends toward it voluntarily.[289] This kind of receding from the order of reason is, notably, the foundation of vice.[290] In *ST* I-II, Aquinas comes closer yet to supporting some notion of autonomy in the will by raising the possibility of "the will itself being moved to evil from itself" and not "from a defect of the reason."[291] Even in an instance such as this, however, reason would presumably have to judge the apparent good to be good in some way because the will is, by definition, a *rational* appetite that "tends toward that which is judged by reason."[292] Nevertheless, if someone were to describe the ability to choose evil in virtue of "the will itself" in terms of some kind of volitional autonomy, this would be at least defensible.

In the earlier Thomas, this kind of indifference was certainly not

---

realm until the will inclines toward one more than another, because the will does not necessarily follow reason."

[286] *ST* I, q. 83, a. 2, corp.: "Free will is indifferently related to choosing well or badly." See also: *De veritate*, q. 24, a. 14, corp. ("The will of man ... is related indifferently toward many things"), *ST* I-II, q. 10, a. 4, corp., and *De malo*, q. 6, ad 3.

[287] Keenan, *Goodness and Rightness*, 27

[288] See Keenan, *Goodness and Rightness*, 47 and 55, and Sherwin, *By Knowledge and By Love*, 11.

[289] In the Scriptum, Aquinas speaks of someone who makes a "judgment of reason" that "no fornication ought to be committed," but chooses to focus on the fact that "every [act of] fornication is delightful" and makes the depraved choice (prava electio) to commit fornication (see In II sent., dist. 24, q. 3, a. 3, corp.). Similarly, De veritate, q. 17 a. 1 ad 4 speaks of a man who chooses to do an action that does not align with the judgment of knowledge (factum iudicio scientiae non concordat).

[290] *De malo*, q. 8, a. 1, ad 3: "Vice arises from the appetitive motion receding from the order of reason."

[291] See *ST* I-II, q. 78, a. 3, corp.

[292] *ST* I-II, q. 74, a. 7, ad 1: "Voluntas tendit in id quod est ratione iudicatum." Actually, a few articles earlier in the same question, Aquinas explicitly says: "The will would never be moved toward evil unless that which is not good did not appear good to the reason in some way; so the will never would tend toward evil unless some ignorance were present or there were an error of reason."

absolute, because he said in *SCG* that the intellect "first and *per se* moves the will ... in the manner in which an end moves, for the understood good is the end of the will."[293] Despite the robust causality of the intellect, though, he insisted that the will retains the ability to bring about a "lack of order to reason" by tending "to a good that is pleasurable to sense" not only because the will is able to will or not to will but also because "it is in the will's power that the reason actually consider" something "or cease from considering it; or that it consider this matter, or that."[294]

During this same period, remarkably, Thomas even spoke of the will's role in terms of "exercise"[295] and suggested that the will is able to divert from the norm of reason or act contrary to conscience[296] (the person thereby sinning by preferring a sensible good to the norm of reason).[297] In regard to

---

[293] *SCG* III, ch. 26, no. 22.

[294] *SCG* III, ch. 10, nos. 16–17: "Consequently, the sin of action in the will is preceded by lack of order to reason, and to its proper end: to reason, as when the will, on the sudden apprehension of a sense, tends to a good that is pleasurable to sense—to its due end, as when by deliberating the reason arrives at some good which is not good now, or in some particular way; and yet the will tends to that good as though it were its proper good. Now this lack of order is voluntary: for it is in the will's power to will or not to will. Again it is in the will's power that the reason actually consider the matter, or cease from considering it; or that it consider this matter, or that. Nor is this lack of order a moral evil: for if the reason were to consider nothing, or to consider any good whatever, as yet there is no sin, until the will tends to an undue end: and this itself is an act of the will" (Dominican Fathers trans., 3:25–26).

[295] *In* IV *sent.*, dist. 49, q. 3, a. 5, qc 3, ad 2: "An appetite, which has the good and the end for an object, moves itself and the cognitive power to act; for, an act or end breaks forth because someone exercises some act unless the act arises from a necessity of nature."

[296] See *De veritate*, q. 17, a. 1, ad 4.

[297] A sin is something contrary to reason, as is evident in *ST* I-II, q. 71, a. 6, and in *De malo*, q. 2, a. 1, sc 3, the latter of which says: "In moralibus peccatum est contra rationem esse." See *SCG* III, ch. 10 (trans. in note 294 above). Similarly, *ST* I-II, q. 54, a. 3, distinguishes vice from virtue inasmuch as the former is in accordance with reason whereas the latter is contrary to it. Also, I-II, q. 78, a. 3, corp., tells us that "if a will be inclined, by its choice, to some evil, this must be occasioned by something else. Sometimes, in fact, this is occasioned through some defect in the reason, as when anyone sins through ignorance, and sometimes this arises through the impulse of the sensitive appetite, as when anyone sins through passion." At the same time, it is noteworthy that the preference to choose a sensible good "over" that of reason (thereby acting contrary to reason on one level) can be a sin only because it is a *rational* preference. As I-II, q. 21, a. 1, corp., says, a sin is that which consists in an act that is done for some end and lacks the fitting order to that end. The end, however, has to be cognized. Due to an inordinate attachment, the will can indeed divert one's consideration to something other than those universal principles whose consideration would midwife conclusions that upbraid disordered inclinations. As Thomas says in I-II, q. 75, a. 1, ad 3, the cause of sin

good acts, as well, he affirmed the will's ability to choose one particular good or another. As we have seen, his teaching about the will's freedom even allowed him to argue that the will is more noble than the intellect *secundum quid*—namely, "in moving."[298] Though Aquinas apparently did not explicitly make what Sherwin referred to as the "celebrated distinction between specification and exercise"[299] prior to 1270, the doctrine is nevertheless implied.[300] As a consequence, Keenan's contention that "if reason acts as the ultimate cause of all presentations, not only would we be unable to refuse an object; we would also be unable to look for another"[301] seems untenable. At the least, the essential elements of Thomas's teaching regarding volitional liberty were very consistent throughout his life, regardless of any supposed emphasis—or lack thereof—on cognitional causality. It would, therefore, be reasonable to wonder whether he had any significant change at all on this topic over the years. It is this consideration that leads us to the next section.

Texts after 1270

Keenan's reading of *ST* I-II, q. 9, a. 4 (which speaks of the will's self-exercise) is that it signals a radical shift in Thomas such that the will could suddenly be liberated from the intellect.[302] He says, therefore, that

---

is the will's failure to apply the rule of reason or of the divine law. However, reason has to be involved, because there must at least be an apparently good reason to act or else there will be no act.

[298] *De veritate*, q. 22, a. 11, ad sc 2: "Ad secundum dicendum, quod libertas voluntatis non ostendit eam esse nobiliorem simpliciter, sed nobiliorem in movendo: quod ex sequentibus patebit."

[299] Sherwin, *By Knowledge and by Love*, 40. Lonergan also argued that Thomas did not conceive of the distinction between the specification and the exercise of the act of the will until after the *De veritate* (see *Collected Works*, 1:96).

[300] Sherwin himself argues that "we should avoid the common tendency to exaggerate the significance of this development" (By Knowledge and By Love, 64) which may be similar to the my own proposal that the later distinction–which gave the will a distinct kind of primacy–was implied in earlier works. In any event, the early Thomas certainly granted that the intellect specifies the object of the will as is clear from the specification involved in practical syllogisms (e.g., In II sent., dist. 24, q. 3, a. 3, corp.). He also granted the will a kind of primacy (see *ST*, I, q. 82 a. 4; SCG, III, ch. 16, no. 22; De veritate, q. 14, a. 5, ad 5) pertaining to exercise (see In IV sent., bk. 4 dist. 49 q. 3 a. 5 qc. 3 ad 2, translated on p. 155). The will's freedom of exercise, finally, is hinted at in De veritate, q. 22 a. 11 ad s.c. 2 (which attributes its nobility to the fact that it is not forced).

[301] Keenan, *Goodness and Rightness*, 34.

[302] See *Goodness and Rightness*, 43. Dewan provides an incisive critique of this view in

he is "hard pressed to find clear evidence for the will's autonomy from reason in any of his works before the *Prima secundae*,"[303] which is dated to 1270–1271.[304] We would have to agree that such a teaching is not found in those works: even if the earlier writings make it possible to speak of the will as autonomous in some way, they do not permit us to speak of it as autonomous *from reason*. It is certainly true that the earlier Thomas would not have said the will has this kind of autonomy in regard to reason (and especially in regard to the natural reason or synderesis), because any kind of "autonomy" would ultimately have to be subordinated to the cognitive power. However, the later Thomas, who considered the rational specification of every act of the will to be essential for the freedom of choice (since reason is the "proper principle of human acts"[305]) would not have said so either. In Keenan's contention, then, we encounter a concept of competitive causality that appears to be foreign to the actual teaching of Aquinas.

One wonders where, exactly, Keenan would locate the radical change. He mentioned the *ST* I-II, but even there, the priority of the intellect is unequivocal:

> Every act of the will proceeds from some act of the intellect although some act of the will is prior to some act of the intellect; for the will tends to the final act of the intellect, which is happiness.[306]

Wisdom, Law, and Virtue, 156–157. I would add to Dewan's analysis that even when the will is said to "move itself" in question nine, it only does so in as much as "it wills the end." For an end to be intended, though, it must be proposed through knowledge (see I-II, q. 12 a. 1 ad 1) since the will is not able to "desire a good that is not apprehended beforehand by reason" (I-II, q. 19, a. 3, ad 1).

[303] Keenan, *Goodness and Rightness*, 27.

[304] Torrell clearly says that *De malo* 6 was written "a little before or after the condemnation of December 1270" and he links *De malo* 6 to questions 9 and 10 of the *Prima secundae* because he accepts Lottin's thesis. To be precise, then, we should say that Torrell thought at least question nine and following could be dated to 1270–1271.

[305] *ST* I-II, q. 100, a. 1, corp.: "Cum autem humani mores dicantur in ordine ad rationem, quae est proprium principium humanorum actuum." See also II-II, q. 157, a. 2, corp.

[306] *ST* I-II, q. 4, a. 4, ad 2: "Omnis actus voluntatis procedit ab aliquo actu intellectus: aliquis tamen actus voluntatis est prior, quam aliquis actus intellectus: voluntas enim tendit in finalem actum intellectus, qui est beatitudo." One could possibly argue regarding *ST,* I-II, q. 4, that it is prior to question 9, where the supposed shift takes place. After all, Keenan argues that a few of the first questions of I-II were written in 1268 (*Goodness and Rightness*, 184). There are, however, texts subsequent to question 9 (such as I-II, q. 19, a. 10 corp.) which argue that the will necessarily *follows* the apprehension of reason). Moreover, the body of I-II, q. 100 a.1 calls reason the proper principle of human actions (see also, I-II, q. 19 a. 3 ad 1, I-II, q. 74 a. 7 ad 1).

The intellect *always* precedes the will on some level, even if "some act" of the will is prior to some particular act of the intellect. That does not mean the appetite is not also a principle of action,[307] but it does indicate that the foundational principle is reason. Accordingly, Aquinas approvingly cites Augustine's aphorism that "nothing is loved unless it is known" to make it clear that love (the "first act of the appetitive power") is preceded by knowledge and that knowledge leads the way in attaining the understandable end.[308] The intellect, in other words, "apprehends the end before the will does,"[309] and the will, as a rational appetite, "follows the apprehension of the reason or the intellect,"[310] because the desirable object "first pertains to the reason under the *ratio* of true before it pertains to the will under the *ratio* of desirable."[311] Actually, the will never acts without a preceding act of the intellect because, "in order that something come about for the sake of an end, some knowledge of the thing is required."[312] Even though man is able to move himself to willing "this or that," he does so specifically "through the reason."[313] Finally, the "appetite for the fitting end presupposes the right apprehension of the end" and that end also comes through reason.[314]

Clearly, there is no radical move toward voluntarism. Moreover, we saw above that the following doctrine from *ST* I-II, q. 9, a. 1, was at least implied in earlier texts:

> The will moves the intellect in regard to the exercise of the act, because the true itself, which is a perfection of the intellect, is

---

[307] *ST* I-II, q. 58, a. 3, corp.: "The beginning of human acts is nothing other than twofold in man, namely, the intellect or reason, and appetite." That both appetite (including the rational appetite of the will) and reason are principles of action is also clear from *In I eth.*, lec. 1, no. 8: "Duo sunt principia humanorum actuum, scilicet intellectus seu ratio, et appetitus."

[308] *ST* I-II, q. 3, a. 4, ad 4: "Cognitio praevia est delictioni in attingendo. Non enim diligitur nisi cognitum." *ST* II-II q. 47 a. 1 ad 1: "Primus autem actus appetitivae virtutis est amor."

[309] *ST* I-II, q. 3, a. 4, ad 3: "Finem primo apprehendit intellectus, quam voluntas."

[310] *ST* I-II, q. 19, a. 10, corp.: "The will follows the apprehension of the reason or intellect; the more universal the notion of the apprehended good is, the more universal is the good that the will is drawn toward."

[311] *ST* I-II, q. 19, a. 3, ad 1: "Appetibilis . . . per prius pertinet ad rationem sub ratione veri, quam ad voluntatem sub ratione appetibilis: quia appetitus voluntatis non potest esse de bono, nisi prius a ratione apprehendatur."

[312] *ST* I-II, q. 6, a. 1, corp.

[313] *ST* I-II, q. 9, a. 6, ad 3. For a discussion of this text in view of the intellectualist controversy, see Gallagher, "The Will and Its Acts," 76.

[314] *ST* I-II, q. 19, a. 3, ad 2.

contained under the universal good as a certain particular good.[315]

For Keenan, Saint Thomas's goal in this article is to "prove that the will is the mover of all powers including itself and the intellect, and that its self-movement takes precedence to all other movements."[316] This would certainly seem to be a departure from previous teaching; however, as Dewan handily proves:

> Keenan's interpretation is incorrect. The meaning of 1-2.9.1 is not that first there is exercise by the will and then it accepts or does not accept some specification proposed by the intellect.[317]

Thomas's goal seems to be simply to acknowledge that the intellect and will move each other in different orders or on different levels. Accordingly, even if the will has precedence in the order of exercise, the "intellect moves the will as presenting its object to it," which is to specify the act. The principle of the will's motion, moreover, is from the end (*ex fine*), since "every agent acts for an end." Additionally, the notion or *ratio* of the end, which is the object of the will, relies upon the intellect's activity. As Dewan rightly observes, "as soon as 'object' is mentioned (and it must come into play to provide the will with its own peculiar dominance), the *intellect* has already come into play insofar as it is the source of all objectification."[318] Presuming the intellect's presentation of the object, "[the] object moves by determining the act" inasmuch as the "good itself is apprehended according to a special notion [*rationem*] comprehended under the universal notion of the true," and in this way, "the intellect moves the will."[319]

Looking to other texts in the later Thomas also leads to the conclusion that there was no significant shift in Thomas's thought despite Keenan's claim that he uses "even more significant forms of expression to highlight the independence of the will's efficiency."[320] He presents two texts in particular to defend this claim. The first is that the will is the

---

[315] *ST* I-II, q. 9, a. 1, ad 3: "Voluntas movet intellectum quantum ad exercitium actus: quia et ipsum verum, quod est perfectio intellectus, continetur sub universali bono, ut quoddam bonum particular."
[316] Keenan, *Goodness and Rightness*, 45.
[317] Dewan, *Wisdom, Law, and Virtue*, 157.
[318] Dewan, *Wisdom, Law, and Virtue*, 157.
[319] See *ST* I-II, q. 9, a. 1, corp. and ad 3.
[320] Keenan, *Goodness and Rightness*, 45.

"principle of movement." Interestingly, Keenan neglects to mention the words that immediately follow: "*nevertheless* according to the command and direction of the reason."[321] The other text is "movere absolute pertinet ad voluntatem," which the Dominican Fathers render as "simply to move belongs to the will" and Keenan renders as "to move pertains absolutely to the will."[322] The context demands the former translation because the contrast being made is between motion considered on its own and motion together with an act of ordering, which pertains to command. The more important point, though, is that the reply is presuming what was said in the objection: when the will moves, it moves inasmuch as it "has the end for its object." Since we learn elsewhere in the later part of *ST* that this end that is the object of the will is the "understood good," since the "will cannot be rightly directed to the good, unless there already be some knowledge of the truth,"[323] the will's movement is certainly not "independent of and prior to reason," as Keenan would have us think.[324]

Time and again, the later Thomas says things to the effect that the intellect "absolutely and of itself [*secundum se*] precedes the will as moving it"[325] or that "every act of the will proceeds from some act of the intellect,"[326] since the will's nature is to tend "toward that which is judged by the reason"[327] and the "intellect apprehends the end before the will does."[328] As the proper interior moving principle of human acts[329] that is also their "rule and measure,"[330] the intellect permeates all human activity from the time of its inception. Even the very freedom which the *liberum arbitrium* enjoys arises precisely because of reason,[331] which he calls the cause of freedom

---

[321] *ST* II-II, q. 47, a. 9, ad 1: "Motus quidem pertinet ad vim appetitivam, sicut ad principium movens tamen secundum directionem et praeceptum rationis..." (emphasis added).

[322] *ST* II-II, q. 47, a. 8, ad 3. See also, Keenan, *Goodness and Rightness*, 47.

[323] *ST* II-II, q. 8, a. 4, corp.: "Voluntas autem non potest recte ordinari in bonum, nisi praeexistente aliqua cognitione veritatis, quia objectum voluntatis est bonum intellectum."

[324] Keenan, *Goodness and Rightness*, 47.

[325] *De virtutibus*, q. 1, a. 7, corp.

[326] *ST* I-II, q. 4, a. 4, ad 2: "Omnis actus voluntatis procedit ab aliquo actu intellectus."

[327] *ST* I-II, q. 74, a. 7, ad 1: "Voluntas tendit in id quod est ratione iudicatum."

[328] *ST* I-II, q. 3, a. 4, ad 3: "Finem primo apprehendit intellectus, quam voluntas."

[329] *ST* I-II, q. 100, a. 1, corp. Similarly, I-II, q. 68, a. 1, corp., says: "In man there is a twofold moving principle. One is reason, which is interior and the other is exterior—namely, God." See also II-II, q. 157, a. 2, corp., and *De malo*, q. 10, a. 2, corp.

[330] *ST* I-II, q. 90, a. 1, corp.

[331] *ST* I-II, q. 6, a. 2, ad 2: "Since the deliberating reason is open to opposites [se habeat ad opposita], the will can be inclined to either." See also *SCG* II, ch. 48: "All intellectual beings have free will [*liberam voluntatem*] from the judgment of the intellect... free

(*causa libertatis*)."³³² There is, therefore, no compelling reason to posit a sweeping revision in Thomas's thought that would, in effect, denude the intellect of its role vis-à-vis volition.

THE INTELLECT'S CAUSALITY AND FREEDOM

If the will is not independent of reason, what does it mean to say free will is "related indifferently to choosing well or badly" because it is "related indifferently to many things"?³³³ If the "root of the whole of liberty is placed in the reason,"³³⁴ is the will able to be indifferent even to reason, since, according to *ST* I-II, q. 17, it is the "first mover among the powers of the soul in regard to the exercise of the act" and is responsible for the very fact that "reason moves by commanding"?³³⁵

The import of volitional activity in practical actions is especially evinced in *De virtutibus* (dated to 1271–1272³³⁶), where the will is said to determine even the end of prudence, which is an intellectual habit that "depends upon the will as upon that from which it receives its beginning: for in practical matters, the end is the beginning."³³⁷ We have already seen

---

will [*liberum arbitrium*] . . . is defined as a free judgment of reason." Perhaps even more strikingly, he says in *ST* III, q. 21, a. 4, corp., that "the will, simply speaking, is the will of reason because we will something absolutely speaking according to reason's deliberation; . . . we do not, simply speaking, will that which we will according to a motion of sensuality or even according to a motion of the will."

³³² *ST* I-II, q. 17, a. 1, corp. See also *In* II *sent.*, dist. 25, q. 1, a. 4, ad 3, which refers to the intellectual nature as the "cause of liberty."

³³³ *ST* I, q. 83, a. 2, corp.: "Liberum autem arbitrium indifferenter se habet ad bene eligendum vel male." See also: *De veritate*, q. 24, a. 14, corp. ("But the will of man is not determined to some one activity, but is related indifferently to many things"); *ST* I-II, q. 10, a. 4, corp. ("The will is an active principle that is not determined to one thing but indifferently related to many"); *De malo*, q. 6, ad 3 ("On account of the nature of the moved will, which is indifferently related to diverse things, necessity is not brought in, but liberty remains").

³³⁴ *De veritate*, q. 24, a. 2, corp.

³³⁵ *ST* I-II, q. 17, a. 1, corp. The act of commanding, which is the third act of the practical reason and the chief act of prudence (see II-II, q. 47, a. 8, corp.) takes place only in virtue of a presupposed act of the will, whose influence is also highlighted, inasmuch as it is said to move the reason itself in its act of deliberating about a particular good.

³³⁶ See Torrell, *Saint Thomas Aquinas*, 1:336.

³³⁷ *De virtutibus*, q. 1, a. 7, corp.: "Prudence is in the intellect or in the practical reason, as was said. It is not the object of prudence that is determined by the will, but only the end. For with the end of the good presupposed by the will, prudence searches the ways through which this good is both attained and preserved. . . . To be sure, some habit of the intellect depends upon the will as upon that from which it receives its beginning,

many instances of the reason being labeled "the proper principle of human acts,"[338] so it seems there must be two ends that are beginnings—one that is rational and one that is volitional. In fact, that is what Thomas says: "There are two principles of human acts; namely, the intellect or reason, and the appetite."[339]

If the appetite (whether rational or sensitive) is disordered, problems arise, because there is then no harmony between the perfect good appointed by nature/synderesis and the end appointed by the reason that has been influenced by inordinate appetites. When this happens, the will itself is moved in part by reason (on the side of the universal reason) and in part by the lower appetites.[340] Thomas explains in *De malo*:

> The will is not moved by the good except inasmuch as it is apprehended; accordingly, it cannot withdraw [*deficere*] from the appetite for the good unless some defect in the apprehension is present—not, certainly, as regards universal principles, about which synderesis is, but in regard to particular chooseable things.[341]

This is the only time there is a kind of dichotomy between the end that is appointed by the natural reason / synderesis / understanding on the one hand and the cogitative power / particular reason[342] on the other.

---

for in practical matters, the end is the beginning."

[338] *ST* I-II, q. 100, a. 1, corp. See also, e.g.: I-II, q. 68, a. 1, corp.; *De malo*, q. 10, a. 2, corp.

[339] *In I eth.*, lec. 1, no. 8: "Duo sunt principia humanorum actuum, scilicet intellectus seu ratio, et appetitus." See also *ST* I-II, q. 58, a. 3, corp.

[340] *ST* I-II, q. 9, a. 2, ad 3: "The irascible and concupiscible are able to move contrary to the will and thus nothing stands in the way of the will being moved by them at times."

[341] *De malo*, q. 16, a. 6, ad sc 6: "Ad sextum dicendum, quod voluntas non movetur a bono nisi in quantum est apprehensum: unde non potest deficere ab appetitu boni, nisi etiam subsit defectus aliquis circa apprehensionem; non quidem quantum ad universalia."

[342] In the following text, the practical syllogism is discussed in terms of applying universals to particular actions by means of the cogitative power, which Aquinas equates with the cogitative power: "The practical intellect . . . needs the particular reason, by which means the intellectual supposition that is a universal is applied to a particular work. A syllogism thus arises in which a universal (a supposition of the practical intellect) is the major term, a singular (a judgment of the particular reason that is also known as the cogitative power) is the minor term, and the choice of an action is the conclusion (*In* IV *sent.*, dist. 50, q. 1, a. 3, ad sc 3).

Twofold Understanding

When a "defect in the apprehension is present,"[343] we have defective reasoning appointing a merely apparent good that is a false application of universal principles instead of the right reasoning of prudence. Thomas accepts Aristotle's principle that "the intellect does not move except through the will"[344] and concludes that, when the will is not upright, the result is frequently an invalid practical syllogism.[345] He explains that, in order to act rightly, a "twofold knowledge" is necessary for acting well—namely, a universal and a particular kind. When the will is disordered and someone is moved by passion, he fails to "consider in particular that which he knows in the universal, inasmuch as passion impedes such a consideration," thereby impeding the reason.[346] In cases like this, "the judgment of free will is perverted" in virtue of an error "in choosing," despite the fact that the judgment of conscience or of the natural judging power is not.[347] As Thomas explains in the commentary on the *Nicomachean Ethics*, prudence perfects the particular reason for rightly estimating about singular practical actions.[348] But without the lower appetites having already been habitually moved toward their fitting ends, the particular reason will appoint unfitting ends, thus precluding the possibility of prudence, as Thomas says in question fifty-seven of the *ST* I-II, q. 55:

> For prudence, which is right reason about doable things, it is required that a man be well disposed about ends, which is certainly through right appetite. And therefore prudence requires

---

[343] See *De malo*, q. 16, a. 6, ad sc 6.

[344] *De unitate intellectus*, ch. 3 ("The intellect does not act except through the will"); *Quodlibet* VI, q. 2, a. 1, sc ("The intellect is only the beginning of activity through the will"). *De potentia*, q. 6, a. 9, obj. 8. See also *De 108 articulis*, q. 22.

[345] Prudence ensures a proper application (*ST* II-II, q. 47, a. 6, corp.: "Prudentia, applicans universalia principia ad particulares conclusiones operabilium"), whereas passion can hinder such an application in an incontinent or vicious man (I-II, q. 94, a. 6, corp.: "Reason can be impeded from applying a general principle to something doable on account of concupiscence or some other passion").

[346] See *ST* I-II, q. 77, a. 2, corp.

[347] *De veritate*, q. 17, a. 1, ad 4: "Sometimes the judgment of free will [*liberi arbitrii*] is perverted but the judgment of conscience is not, . . . and thus someone errs in choosing and not in conscience." In the previous question of *De veritate* (q. 16, a. 1, sc 5), St. Thomas argued that "Synderesis never errs," and an objection of another article suggests that the "natural judging power never errs" (*De veritate*, q. 17, a. 2, obj. 1).

[348] *In* VI *eth.*, lec. 7, no. 21: "Prudentia, per quam perficitur ratio particularis ad recte aestimandum de singularibus intentionibus operabilium . . ."

the moral virtues through which right appetite comes about.[349]

This, of course, points back to the vicious circle, on the one hand, but also to something more germane to our present purposes: the two texts speaking about the need for both the universal reason and the particular reason to be correct.

In the text we encountered in the introduction from *ST* II-II, we saw that universal reason or understanding (the intellectual virtue) is cognizant of universals such as "one should do evil to no one," whereas the second kind of understanding (which is considered a quasi-integral part of prudence[350]) is cognizant of contingent principles.[351] When there is no prudence, there is no second kind of understanding (that which is "a quasi-integral part" of prudence[352]), even though the first kind of understanding (the one equated with synderesis) remains.

In the last chapter of the present volume, we saw the other text speaking of the two kinds of understanding. It asserts that the particular ends act in the manner of a final cause once they are cognized, and it seems to suggest the other ends (or extremes) also act in that manner:

> There are two kinds of understanding. One of them is about first and immutable principles in demonstrations, which proceed from immutable and first terms (that is from indemonstrable principles) that are first known and unchangeable because the knowledge about them is not able to be removed from man. But the understanding which pertains to practical things is from another kind of extreme, namely a singular and contingent one that has another proposition—that is, not a universal one that is as the major premise in a practical syllogism, but the singular

---

[349] *ST* I-II, q. 57, a. 4, corp.: "Et ideo ad prudentiam, quae est recta ratio agibilium, requiritur quod homo sit bene dispositus circa fines: quod quidem est per appetitum rectum. Et ideo ad prudentiam requiritur moralis virtus, per quam fit appetitus rectus."

[350] That this kind of understanding—which pertains to a right judgment about a final principle—is a quasi-integral part of prudence, is made manifest by considering the second article of *ST* I-II, q. 49 and the title of question 49 itself.

[351] *ST* II-II, q. 49, a. 2, ad 1. *In* VI *eth.*, lec. 7, no. 21, explains that prudence perfects the particular reason for rightly estimating about singular practical actions ("pertinet prudentia, per quam perficitur ratio particularis ad recte aestimandum de singularibus intentionibus operabilium") and adds that it is called a natural estimative power in animals.

[352] That it is a quasi-integral part is evident by looking to the title for question 49: "The judgment of the particular reason, which is also called the cogitative power..."

which is as the minor premise. As to why an extreme of this sort is called "understanding," it is evident because understanding treats of principles. Now these singulars about which this kind of understanding is concerned are principles that are done for the sake of something [*cuius gratia*]; that is, they are principles in the manner of a final cause [*per modum causae finalis*].[353]

This text, which is from the commentary on the *Ethics* (1271–1272[354]), seems to link the understanding (*intellectus*) of either kind of extreme with final causality.[355] The reason, presumably, is that these extremes are moral *principia* (i.e., beginnings) and, in practical affairs, that which comes first is the end. In any event, the understanding that is cognizant of a particular and contingent extreme merely provides the minor premise in a practical syllogism and is necessarily less final than the universal premise.

The Intellect's Causality

Why, then, does Thomas not explicitly say in the later part of *ST* that the intellect acts in the manner of a final cause? First, he comes very close to doing so in response to the following objection in *ST* II-II, q. 47, a. 1:

> Man exceeds irrational things in virtue of his reason, whereas he has other things in common with them. As, then, the other parts of man are related to his reason, so are other creatures related to man. But man is the end of irrational creatures, as is said in the

---

[353] *In* VI *eth.*, lect. 9, no. 13–14: "Est autem duplex intellectus. Quorum hic quidem est circa immobiles terminos et primos, qui sunt secundum demonstrationes, quae procedunt ab immobilibus et primis terminis, idest a principiis indemonstrabilibus, quae sunt prima cognita et immobilia, quia scilicet eorum cognitio ab homine removeri non potest. Sed intellectus qui est in practicis, est alterius modi extremi, scilicet singularis, et contingentis et alterius propositionis, idest non universalis quae est quasi maior, sed singularis quae est minor in syllogismo operativo. Quare autem huiusmodi extremi dicatur intellectus, patet per hoc, quod intellectus est principiorum; haec autem singularia, quorum dicimus esse intellectum huiusmodi, principia eius sunt quod est cuius gratia, id est sunt principia ad modum causae finalis." Thomas clarifies in the *Scriptum* that the second kind of *intellectus* is the cogitative power or the particular reason (*In* IV *sent.*, dist. 50, q. 1, a. 3, ad sc 3; trans. in note 342 above).

[354] Torrell, *Saint Thomas Aquinas*, 1:329.

[355] Which, of course, Thomas did earlier regarding the intellect in general in the following two texts: "The intellect moves in the manner of an end; for this is the way the apprehended good is related to the will" (*De veritate* q. 22, a. 12, ad 3); "The intellect moves

Politics. Therefore, all doable things are ordered to prudence as to an end. It must, therefore, appoint the end to the moral virtues.[356]

He responds to this objection by succinctly saying, "the natural reason, which is called synderesis, appoints the end to the moral virtues."[357] Given that the argument suggested prudence is the end of practical actions and thus must appoint the end to moral virtues, the implication is that, since synderesis is that which appoints the end, synderesis must either be the end of practical actions or act in the manner of an end when it appoints their end to them. Thomas said something similar in *SCG* when he said, "understanding is the proper operation of the intellectual substance: and it is its end as a consequence."[358]

The fact remains that he apparently never explicitly said the intellect acts in the manner of a final cause in his later works, however. One response to this fact could be to simply observe there is no need to deny that the intellect also can be said to act in the manner of a formal cause even if the intellect or reason also acts in the manner of an end in some sense. The intellect specifies, and specifies with respect to the nature of the end and gives the end in this manner. We might simply grant, in fact, that the later Thomas was more precise because, strictly speaking, it is the end itself that moves owing to the presentation of the end through knowledge (in other words, the intellect is that *whereby* the final cause may specify the will), and due to this close connection, the shorthand of speaking of the final causality of the intellect is intelligible. So it is not the intellect *simpliciter* that takes on a "final" role, but the good present by way of the intellect, because of the nature of that which is apprehended (the cognized

---

the will in the manner by which an end moves because the understood good is the end of the will. Now, the agent is later in moving than the end is because the agent moves only on account of the end" (*SCG* III, ch. 26, no. 22).

[356] *ST* II-II, q. 47, a. 1: "Praeterea. Homo excedit res irrationales secundum rationem: sed secundum alia cum eis communicat; sic ergo se habent aliae partes hominis ad rationem, sicut se habet homo ad creaturas irrationales: sed homo est finis creaturarum irrationalium, ut dicitur in *Politics* I. (cap. 5; *Physics* II, tex. 24); ergo omnes aliae partes hominis ordinantur ad rationem sicut ad finem: sed prudentia est recta ratio agibilium, ut dictum est (art. 2. huj. q.); ergo omnia agibilia ordinantur ad prudentiam sicut ad finem; ipsa ergo praestituit finem omnibus virtutibus moralibus."

[357] In *ST* II-II, q. 47, a. 6, ad 1, he said the reply to the first objection was a sufficient reply to the second: "The natural reason, which is called synderesis, . . . appoints the end to the moral virtues; however, prudence does not."

[358] *SCG* III, ch. 25: "Intelligere autem est propria operatio substantiae intellectualis. Ipsa igitur est finis eius."

good that acts as an end) in relation to the nature of the human person. Accordingly, whatever is put forward intellectually as a good is inseparable from final causality, but not everything that is put forward intellectually is put forward as an end (because not everything put forward is a good). Without intellective specification making it clear to the will what is—or appears to be—a good, there can be no final causality. It is thus strictly the good preexisting in the mind as specifying the will which exerts final causality. My endeavor has simply been to argue there was no radical transition in Aquinas on this point and that any shift in terminology that took place is no indication of a shift toward de-emphasizing the causal fecundity of the intellect. For Dewan, this "issue is subtle enough,"[359] and this is evinced by the fact that there are places in *SCG* where the intellect's causality is described in terms of formal causality[360] and places in *De malo* where it is described in terms of final causality (as Flannery observes).[361] Be that as it may, Dewan seems correct to affirm that the presentation of the object by the intellect is, in fact, a presenting of the end that necessarily implies it has "a final causal role," even though speaking of the intellect's causality as "formal" actually emphasizes that which is "peculiar to the intellect's contribution" even more incisively, inasmuch as the intellect thereby has "its own universal formal character stressed, and thus one can see its *omnipresent* determination."[362] Given that "voluntariness requires an act of knowledge,"[363] it is not the case that the intellect merely appoints the end and then leaves the will to its own devices—which the notion of final causality might suggest. Instead, the intellect informs the rational appetite not only by presenting first principles to it but also by formally specifying it during any particular act it engages in. The implication, therefore, is that Thomas did not turn

---

[359] Dewan, *Wisdom, Law, and Virtue*, 160.

[360] One example might be *SCG* I, ch. 72, no. 6: "The form that is considered by the intellect does not move or cause something except by means of the will, whose object is the end and the good from which someone is moved to do something." In this text, the form that is apprehended by the intellect is affirmed to be that which moves, though it does not do so without the influence of the will. If Thomas refers to the intellect in terms of final causality in virtue of the end that is apprehended, this text may lead us to affirm that the intellect moves in the manner of a formal cause in virtue of the form that is apprehended. Perhaps both manners of causality can be attributed to the intellect if we say that, in the fully practical realm, the intellect moves as a formal cause, whereas in a quasi-speculative realm, it acts in the manner of an end or final cause when it puts an end forward.

[361] See Flannery, *Acts Amid Precepts*, 115.

[362] Dewan, *Wisdom, Law, and Virtue*, 170.

[363] *ST* I-II, q. 6, a. 3, ad 3: "Requiritur ad voluntarium actus cognitionis."

to speaking more of the intellect's formal causality in order to distance himself from an intellectualist mindset, but rather to highlight more accurately the intellect's robust "omnipresent" causality. The insight of Denis Bradley is helpful on this point:

> The views of Lottin and others notwithstanding, there is no radical spontaneity of will apart from intellect: in regard to its object, the will is always formally determined by the intellect. Even in the case of choosing whether or not to consider thinking about (and, consequently, necessarily desiring) the perfect good (happiness or some necessary constituent thereof), the will's freedom is grounded upon the intellectual judgment that "Now is *not* the time to think about happiness!"[364]

We have seen in this chapter that, regardless of how the causality of the intellect is explained (whether in terms of final or formal causality), its causality remains paramount. The intellect is the ultimate root of freedom—whether we speak of the liberty of the will in choice (i.e., the impossibility that the will could be compelled by finite good) or the perfective sense of freedom Pinckaers so adeptly spoke of in terms of *liberté de qualité*.[365] In either case, the intellect is the *radix libertatis*. The question we are now ready to investigate, then, is how the intellect's causality plays out in regard to the ends of the moral virtues. Synderesis, prudence, and conscience all pertain to the intellect. How do we explain them in terms of the appointing of ends? We turn now to the final chapter to consider this question in detail.

---

[364] Bradley "Reason and the Natural Law," 124.
[365] See Servais Pinckaers, O.P., *Sources of Christian Ethics*, trans. Sr. Mary Thomas Noble, O.P., from the 3rd ed. (Washington, DC: Catholic University of America Press, 1995), 329 [originally *Les sources de la morale chrétienne* (Fribourg: University Press, 1993); cited in Simon Francis Gaine, *Will There Be Free Will in Heaven?: Freedom, Impeccability, and Beatitude* (London; New York: T&T Clark, 2003), 88].

CHAPTER 3

What Appoints the End?

Cajetan on Two Texts in the *Summa*

In the introduction, we saw that Thomas de Vio Cajetan (1469–1534) suggested the two texts respectively saying prudence does and does not appoint the end to the moral virtues—*ST* I-II, q. 66, a. 3, obj. and ad 3 and *ST* II-II, q. 47, a. 6, ad 3—appear to be "repugnant" to each other, adding that a serious challenge arises when one attempts to reconcile them.[1] We will introduce the respective texts in turn.

First Text: ST I-II, Q. 66, A. 3, Obj. and Ad 3
ST I-II, q. 66, a. 3, obj. 3:

> The end is more noble than those things which are for the end: but, as it is said in *Ethics* VI, moral virtue makes the intention of the end right whereas prudence makes the choice of those things that are for the end right. Moral virtue, therefore, is more noble than prudence, which is the intellectual virtue pertaining to moral matters.[2]

---

[1] Cajetan argues in the commentary on *ST* I-II, q. 66, a. 3, that "a difficult question [*dubium arduum*] arises... namely, how it is true to say that prudence directs the moral virtues even in appointing [*praestituendo*] the end" (no. 11). The reason the question is difficult to answer, he says, is due to the fact that *ST* I-II, q. 66, a. 3, "seems incompatible" with the text found in *ST* II-II, q. 47, a. 6, ad 3 (Leonine ed., 6:433).

[2] *ST* I-II, q. 66, a. 3, obj. 3: "Praeterea. Finis est nobilior his, quae sunt ad finem: sed, sicut dicitur in *Ethics* VI (cap. 12, in med.), virtus moralis facit rectam intentionem finis, prudentia autem facit rectam electionem eorum quae sunt ad finem ergo virtus moralis est nobilior prudentia, quae est virtus intellectualis circa moralia."

183

ST I-II, q. 66, a. 3, ad 3:

> To the third it should be said that prudence directs the moral virtues not only in choosing those things that are for the end, but also in appointing [*praestituendo*] the end: for the end of any given moral virtue is to attain the mean in its proper matter; which mean is certainly determined according to the right reason of prudence.[3]

In what appears to be an effort to defend the nobility of prudence, Thomas says here that prudence is not completely passive in regard to the end. Indeed, even if the objection is correct in stating that "moral virtue makes the intention of the end right" (which he affirms later in *ST*[4]), and even though prudence does have jurisdiction over the means, it also appoints the end. Interestingly, the "end" being discussed is that of attaining the mean, so this response may not appear all that convincing. If the end prudence appoints is merely a mean between two extremes in the appetitive part and it relies upon the end having been rectified by moral virtue in the first place, is not the nobility of prudence lacking somewhat in comparison with that habit that appoints moral principles, insofar as prudence is so closely tied up with the appetites? In commenting on the *Ethics*, Thomas suggests moral virtue brings about the right intention of the end:

> There are two things necessary in the act of any virtue. One of which is that a man must have a right intention of the end which, indeed, moral virtue brings about inasmuch as it inclines the appetite toward the fitting end. The other is that a man is well disposed [*bene se habeat*] about the means—and prudence, which deliberates well and judges and commands about the means brings this about. Therefore prudence (which is perfective of the reason essentially) joins together with moral virtue (which is perfective

---

[3] *ST* I-II, q. 66, a. 3, ad 3: "Ad tertium dicendum, quod prudentia non solum dirigit virtutes morales in eligendo ea quae sunt ad finem, sed etiam in praestituendo finem: est autem finis uniuscujusque virtutis moralis attingere medium in propria materia; quod quidem medium determinatur secundum rectam rationem prudentiae, ut dicitur in *Ethics* II (cap. 6.) et VI (cap. ult.)."

[4] *ST* II-II, q. 47, a. 6, sc: "Moral virtue makes the intention of the end right, while prudence makes those things that are for the end right. Therefore, it does not pertain to prudence to appoint the end to the moral virtues, but only to regulate the means."

of the appetitive part which is rational by participation) in bringing about a work of virtue.[5]

Prudence, no doubt, remains indispensable, because one must deliberate well about means if he is to attain the end, but given the indisputable axiom that the end precedes the means in moral matters, how is this congruous with the notion that prudence appoints the *end*? It almost appears to be an affront to the meaning of the word "end" to say the virtue that directs the *means* toward an end appoints that end simply because it makes it possible for the individual to attain it.

Nevertheless, one way we can understand this is in view of what we saw about the nobility of man partially consisting in the ability to appoint ends himself thanks to the power of deliberative reason. At the very least, if a prudent man were to act in accordance with the inclinations of appetites, he would be making the ends founded in the appetites to be his own. We have seen this concept in Thomas already, but here is a text we have not yet encountered, from book II of the *Scriptum*:

> Nothing acts except inasmuch as it is in act, and for this reason, it is necessary that every agent be determined to one thing [instead of another] because whatever has itself equally disposed to both is somehow in potency with respect to both. Accordingly, as the Commentator[6] says in regard to *Physics* II, nothing follows from that which is equally disposed to either of two things unless it be determined [to one]. But for an agent to be determined to do

---

[5] *In* VI *eth.*, lec. 10, no. 13: "Duo enim sunt necessaria in opere virtutis, (scilicet) quorum unum est ut homo habeat rectam intentionem de fine; quod quidem facit virtus moralis, inquantum inclinat appetitum in debitum finem. Aliud autem est quod homo bene se habeat circa ea quae sunt ad finem: et hoc facit prudentia quae est bene consiliativa et iudicativa et praeceptiva eorum quae sunt ad finem. Et sic ad opus virtutis concurrit et prudentia quae est perfectiva rationalis per essentiam, et virtus moralis quae est perfectiva appetitivae quae est rationalis per participationem."

[6] The "Commentator" here is apparently Avicenna. See *In* II *phys.*, lec. 2, no. 3, where he mentions Avicenna and says: "As the moving power, which is indeterminate [literally, toward one of two things], goes forth into an act only through an appetitive power determined to one thing, so also, nothing that is indeterminate goes forth into an act unless it is determined to one thing. For that which is indeterminate is, as it were, being in potency. However, potency is not a principle of acting. Only an act is. For this reason, from that which is indeterminate, nothing happens except through something that is determined to one thing (either always or frequently). And because of this, he omitted those things that are indeterminate when discussing those things that come to be."

some action, the determination must arise from some knowledge appointing [*praestituente*] the end of that action. But the knowledge determining the action and appointing the end is connected to some agents as is the case with man, who appoints the end of his action to himself. Such knowledge is separate from others, however. Take, for instance, those things that act by nature. Due to the fact that the actions of natural things are not in vain (as is proved in the second book of the *Physics*), but are arranged by the intellect instituting nature, the whole work of nature is, in a certain way, a work of intelligence, as the Philosopher says. It is, therefore, clear that the difference among agents is that some determine both the end and the act for themselves and some do not. Nor is a given agent able to appoint the end unless it knows the end and the order of that which is for the end itself, which cannot occur except in those having understanding. For this reason, the judgment of one's own action is only in those having understanding, since their power has been established in such a way that they may choose this or that action. Accordingly, they are said to have dominion over their acts, and due to this, free will is found only in those having understanding, and not in those whose actions are not determined by the agents themselves but by certain other prior causes.[7]

From this point of view, the prudent man can be said to appoint an end for himself in the sense of making that end to be his own and deliberating about how to attain it. The last sentence of the quote mentions not being

---

[7] *In* II *sent.*, dist. 25, q. 1, a. 1, corp.: "Nihil agit nisi secundum quod est in actu; et inde est quod oportet omne agens esse determinatum ad alteram partem: quod enim ad utrumlibet est aequaliter se habens, est quodammodo potentia respectu utriusque: et inde est, quod, ut dicit Commentator in 2 Phys. ab eo quod est ad utrumlibet, nihil sequitur, nisi determinetur. Determinatio autem agentis ad aliquam actionem, oportet quod sit ab aliqua cognitione praestituente finem illi actioni. Sed cognitio determinans actionem et praestituens finem, in quibusdam quidem conjuncta est, sicut homo finem suae actionis sibi praestituit; in quibusdam vero separata est, sicut in his quae agunt per naturam: rerum enim naturalium actiones non sunt frustra, ut in 2 Physic. probatur, sed ad certos fines ordinatae ab intellectu naturam instituente, ut sic totum opus naturae sit quodammodo opus intelligentiae, ut philosophus dicit. Sic ergo patet quod haec est differentia in agentibus quia quaedam determinant sibi finem et actum in finem illum, quaedam vero non: nec aliquod agens finem sibi praestituere potest nisi rationem finis cognoscat et ordinem ejus quod est ad finem ipsum, quod solum in habentibus intellectum est: et inde est quod judicium de actione propria est solum in

determined by certain other prior causes. Aquinas certainly does not mean to say man is not constrained by the eternal or natural law. Just as he sometimes speaks of "will as will" to distinguish it from "will as nature," even though he usually is referring to the former without saying so explicitly, here too, he seems to be presupposing that man is subject to prior causes on one level even if, in the realm of deliberating about means, he is free.

The other way it makes some sense to speak of prudence appointing the end to the moral virtues is simply because the end *is* the mean. As strange as it might sound to equate the mean with the end prudence appoints (as would especially occur if we think of ends in terms of objective principles rather than a mean between two passions),[8] it is nearly an indemonstrable principle that virtue is a habit enabling someone to do exactly what he sets out to do as an end without being swayed toward one extreme or another. And this is exactly what prudence is responsible for bringing about. Moreover, since prudence is a rational habit and it is the reason that appoints things, it is fitting on some level to say it appoints this end.[9] This appointing is certainly a subordinated kind of appointing, since it is properly an enacting of what was fixed in the reason by synderesis and since the latter (which is also said to appoint) is said to be that which "moves prudence."[10] Nevertheless, it is intelligible to speak of prudential activity in terms of "appointing" so long as this appointing retains its secondary status in virtue of the fact that the "reasoning of prudence" proceeds from the *intellectus principiorum* (the understanding of principles).[11]

---

habentibus intellectum, quasi in potestate eorum constitutum sit eligere hanc actionem vel illam; unde et dominium sui actus habere dicuntur: et propter hoc in solis intellectum habentibus liberum arbitrium invenitur, non autem in illis quorum actiones non determinantur ab ipsis agentibus, sed a quibusdam aliis causis prioribus."

[8] The mean of justice would not be this sort of mean, but often times the mean is between two inordinate passions.

[9] In *ST* I, q. 18, a. 3, St. Thomas contrasts animals that act by instinct to superior animals that move themselves to an end that they appoint to themselves [*praestituunt sibi*] in virtue of reason and intellect. He clarifies that it pertains to reason and intellect to "know the proportion of the end and the means to the end, and to order one to the other."

[10] *ST* II-II, q. 47, a. 6, ad 2: "Synderesis movet prudentiam."

[11] *ST* II-II, q. 49, a. 2, ad 1: "The 'reason' of prudence proceeds from a twofold understanding, one of which is cognizant of universals. This kind of understanding is considered an intellectual virtue. By means of it, we naturally know not only universal speculative principles, but also practical ones, such as 'we ought to do harm to no one' as is clear from what has been said [q. 47, aa. 2–3]."

In the *Scriptum*, Thomas clarifies that, when prudence is said to appoint the end to the moral virtues, it is specifically the *proximate* end of each virtue which is appointed. In other words, ultimate ends are not properly appointed by prudence. The mean that is sometimes spoken of as an end, moreover, is the mean proper to the given virtue,[12] and is thus different for different virtues.[13] This mean is so closely related to reason that, in the preceding question of the *Scriptum*, he said the proximate end—the one appointed by prudence—is simply "the good of reason."[14]

The existence of any virtue (and of actual adequated motion to the end) is predicated upon some kind of participation in prudence, as is manifest by the definition of it found in Aristotle and frequently referred to by Aquinas: "a habit, resulting from choice, lying in the middle relative to us and determined by reason as the prudent man would determine it."[15] Without sharing in *recta ratio agibilium* (i.e., prudence), the mean would not be attained and there would be no virtue. Prudence is consequently "somehow an efficient cause" of moral virtue, because "moral virtue is nothing other than a certain participation in right reason in the appetitive part."[16]

---

[12] *In III sent.*, dist. 33, q. 2, a. 5, corp.: "Through reason, the end—not only the end in general, but also the proximate end, which is to attain the mean in the proper nature [of a given virtue]—is appointed to the other virtues." It is clear in view of the rest of the *Scriptum* that he must be saying the *natural* reason appoints the common end.

[13] *De virtutibus*, q. 1, a. 6, corp.: "It is necessary that practical reason be perfected by some habit in order for it to rightly judge about the human good in regard to singular acts. And this virtue is called prudence, which is in the practical reason. Prudence perfects all of the moral virtues that are in the appetitive part. Each of the moral virtues inclines the appetite toward some sort of human good: as justice makes the inclination toward the good that is an equality of whatever pertains to living in common; as temperance makes the inclination toward the good that is to refrain from the good of the concupiscible appetite; and so it is with other particular virtues. Each of these come to be in a variety of ways, and not in an identical way. For this reason, prudence of judgment is required in order for the right mode to be determined."

[14] *In III sent.*, dist. 33, q. 1, a. 1, qc 1, corp.: "The good to which human virtues are proximately ordered is the good of reason, and that which is bad for man is that which is contrary to this, as Dionysius says in the book on the Divine Names. And because it is clear that the good of reason is not found in the same way in all moral matters, it is necessary that different moral virtues be different in species."

[15] Hē aretē hexis proairetikē, en mesotēti ousa tē pros hēmas, hōrismenē logō kai hō an ho phronimos horiseiev (Aristotle, *Nicomachean Ethics* 2.6.1107a1, ed. J. Bywater [Medford, MA: Perseus Digital Library, 1894]).

[16] *De virtutibus*, q. 1, a. 12, ad 16: "The 'right reason' of prudence is not placed in the definition of moral virtue as something existing outside of the essence of the definition, but as being somehow an efficient cause of it or a participation of it. Now, moral virtue is nothing other than a certain participation in right reason in the appetitive part."

Thomas speaks to the close relationship between the mean and right reason in *ST* II-II, q. 47, a. 7:

> To be conformed to right reason is the proper end of every moral virtue, for temperance intends this lest man be diverted from reason by carnal desires, and similarly, fortitude [intends this] lest he be diverted from the right judgment of reason due to fear or temerity. And thus the end is appointed [*praestitutus*] to man in accordance with natural reason, for natural reason dictates to each one that he act in accordance with reason. But how a man attains the mean of reason according to natural reason, and through which things, pertains to the disposition of prudence. For although to attain the mean is the end of moral virtue, the mean is found through the right disposition of the means.[17]

One could conclude from this that the "common end" appointed by reason qua natural reason is no more nor less than the principle that each one act in accordance with reason. Since synderesis undeniably also "always inclines to good"[18] one would have to link this in some way to the good in order to be faithful to Thomas, but one would still be left on this account with a natural intellectual habit consisting of little else than empty space. Jean Porter's analysis is along these lines. She argues that the principle that one ought to act in accordance with reason and the first principle of the practical reason found in the second article of *ST* I-II, q. 94 ("the good is to be done and pursued and evil to be avoided"[19]) are practically identical, and also that there is no substantial content to this principle:

---

[17] *ST* II-II, q. 47, a. 7, corp.: "Hoc ipsum quod est conformari rationi rectae, est finis proprius cujuslibet virtutis moralis: temperantia enim hoc intendit, ne propter concupiscentias homo divertat a ratione: et similiter fortitudo, ne a recto judicio rationis divertat propter timorem, vel audaciam: et hic finis praestitutus est homini secundum naturalem rationem: naturalis enim ratio dictat unicuique, ut secundum rationem operetur: sed qualiter, et per quae homo in operando attingat medium rationis, pertinet ad rationem [alt. *dispositionem*] prudentiae: licet enim attingere medium sit finis virtutis moralis: tamen per rectam dispositionem eorum quae sunt ad finem, medium invenitur."

[18] *ST* I, 79, a. 12, sc: "Synderesis autem non se habet ad opposita, sed ad bonum tantum inclinat."

[19] *ST* I-II, q. 94, a. 2, corp.: "Primum praeceptum legis, quod bonum est faciendum, et prosequendum, et malum vitandum."

> From Aquinas's claim that synderesis includes the principle that the human good consists in acting in accordance with reason, we should not conclude that Aquinas holds that all persons naturally know the substance of his anthropology. This principle is universally known in the same sense as the first principle of practical reason is universally known. Not everyone could formulate it (that would indeed presuppose theoretical knowledge that not everyone shares), but everyone necessarily acts upon it. . . . The first principle of practical reason and the dictum that the good of the human soul is to be in accordance with reason, are really two ways of expressing the same principle from different perspectives. . . .
>
> While Aquinas holds that it is self-evidently true that the good is to be pursued, and evil is to be avoided, this principle does not take on substantive content apart from an account of what the concrete specific good of the human creature is. And that account is not self-evident to us, because it presupposes a particular theory of goodness in general.[20]

She concludes that all substantive content is due to prudence:

> Natural reason, functioning as synderesis, generates the principle that the good of the human person is to be in accordance with reason. Prudence, which takes account of the specifics of an individual's own character and circumstances, determines what, concretely, it means for this individual to be in accordance with reason; . . . that is to say prudence determines what amounts to a substantive theory of the human good.[21]

On this account, there appear to be no general precepts with substantive content, because the onus of determining the content is on prudence. Since Thomas often describes prudence in terms of *applying* "universal principles" to particular works,[22] Porter's description of prudence in terms of determin-

---

[20] Jean Porter, *The Recovery of Virtue: The Relevance of Aquinas for Christian Ethics* (Louisville, KY: Westminster/ John Knox, 1990), 161–62.

[21] Porter, *Recovery of Virtue*, 162.

[22] *ST* II-II, q. 47, a. 6, corp. ("Prudence, applying universal principles to particular conclusions of practical matters"); II-II, q. 47, a. 16, ad 3 ("Prudence, applying universal principles to particular conclusions of practical matters"); I-II, q. 76, a. 1, corp. ("The reason of prudence is terminated, as in a kind of conclusion, in a particular practical

ing what it means to be in accordance with reason (which *ST* II-II, q. 47, a. 7, made clear is the *end* of moral virtue) raises some questions. Does prudence determine the end as if heuristically inventing it *de novo*? Or does it merely determine it *qua applicatio*, similar to the way an act might be said to determine a potency (and in accordance with the nature of the potency)?

If prudence determines the end that is a mean,[23] it seems we have to distinguish between the end qua mean that needs to be felt out, as in Yves Simon's estimation,[24] or heuristically pursued, according to James Keenan's,[25] and the end qua universal principles to be applied. Porter yokes the precept to do good and avoid evil to the precept to act according to reason. Since Thomas says, "synderesis is said to instigate toward the good and to murmur about evil inasmuch as we proceed by first *principles* to discovering and judging what we have discovered,"[26] one might wonder whether there is, in fact, some preceptively significant content contained by "the habit of the first *principles* of doable things naturally implanted in us."[27] We will revisit this issue below.[28]

Keenan has a similar approach to Porter's. He does not explicitly unite the two principles, and thus occasionally speaks of the inclination to act according to reason as the end of the moral virtues[29] and sometimes

---

matter, to which it applies universal knowledge)." See also: II-II, q. 49, a. 5, ad 2; q. 49, a. 2, ad 1.

[23] *ST* I-II, q. 66, a. 3, ad 3: "Prudence directs the moral virtues not only in choosing the means, but also in appointing [*praestituendo*] the end. For the end of each moral virtue is to attain the mean in the proper matter, which mean is determined according to the right reason of prudence."

[24] See Yves Simon, *The Definition of Moral Virtue*, ed. Vukan Kuic (New York: Fordham University Press, 1986), 108–9.

[25] See James Keenan, "The Virtue of Prudence (IIa IIae, Qq. 47—56)," in *The Ethics of Aquinas*, ed. Stephen J. Pope, Moral Traditions Series (Washington, DC: Georgetown University Press, 2002), 259-71, at 261: "The ends of the moral virtues appointed naturally by *synderesis* are thus the principles that prudence heuristically pursues." See also 264: "Prudence as directive expresses the overarching way through which it perceives the end, provides the heuristic means to the self-disposed moral virtues, and directs them in their operations as they express those means to that end."

[26] *ST* I, q. 79, a. 12, corp.: "Synderesis dicitur instigare ad bonum, et murmurare de malo, inquantum per prima principia procedimus ad inveniendum, et judicamus inventa" (emphasis added).

[27] *ST* I, q. 79, a. 12, corp.: "Principia operabilium nobis naturaliter indita non pertinent ad specialem potentiam, sed, ad specialem habitum naturalem, quem dicimus synderesim."

[28] See the section below titled "The Content of Synderesis."

[29] Keenan argues that, in *ST* II-II, q. 47, a. 7, "synderesis appoints the end of each moral virtue, which ends are still the same: to act according to reason," and that "the 'good' is

as the precept to do good and avoid evil.[30] In either case, though, there is not much content:

> Furthermore, the end appointed by *synderesis* is not the proximate end that specifies a moral virtue, but the first principle, to do good and avoid evil. Thus, though *synderesis* appoints the general end of moral virtue, yet the moral virtues cannot tend to that end abstractly. Rather, they still need specific objects toward which to tend. They need prudence to "prepare the way," to present the right objects to the moral virtues.[31]

For him, too, then, the end provided by synderesis seems to be a somewhat nebulous inclination practically devoid of content.

Thomas speaks of an order of natural law that is "according to the order of natural inclinations," and Keenan rightly argues that "all of the inclinations of human nature" are reduced to the one first precept ("do good, etc.") inasmuch as they are ruled by reason.[32] Since he seems to equate "reason" with prudence and *not* natural reason, though, and since synderesis has no substantive content without prudence on his account, everything seems to come down to prudence. In other words, there is no accounting for the preceptive character of *natural* law because prudence is not natural but acquired (or infused). It is as if that law is practically invented by *ratio ut ratio* and as if there are no universally applicable norms known in virtue of *ratio ut natura*.

Moreover, while Keenan attributes a great deal to prudence, it is actually stripped of its ability to be truly reasonable, since universal precepts do not factor into its ratiocination about means. It has to pursue the good "heuristically," as if by trial and error, and even when it is said to direct and to appoint the end to the moral virtues, this means it "provides the

---

what reason appoints as a mean" ("Virtue of Prudence," 260).

[30] James Keenan, *Goodness and Rightness in Thomas Aquinas's Summa theologiae* (Washington, DC: Georgetown University Press, 1992), 103: "The last end of the moral virtues, which is to do good and avoid evil."

[31] Keenan, *Goodness and Rightness*, 102.

[32] See Keenan, "Virtue of Prudence," 261. The text he refers to is *ST* I-II, q. 94, a. 2, ad 2, in which Thomas responds to an objection saying that, if human nature is one, natural law should have one precept, saying the sensitive appetites are, in fact, made subject to the principle "do good and avoid evil," inasmuch as they are ruled by reason. What Keenan overlooks, of course, is that the body of the article spoke of more than that first principle. There is a whole order of precepts based upon the order of natural inclinations.

heuristic means to the *self-disposed* moral virtues, and directs them in their operations as they express those means to that end."[33] The consequence is that the end which is the mean in addition to the means to that end are both heuristically sought out. Keenan does say at one point that "any end *other than* the last end is unformed, that is, it has no particular object and therefore no determinative form,"[34] thereby apparently imputing some formed content to synderesis, but since he thinks the mature Thomas came to see "the will's movement is independent of and prior to reason's presentation of its object,"[35] even the natural inclination to the good cannot be attributed to the intellect.[36] On this account, then, Thomas is essentially a proto-Humean when it comes to the principles of human action.[37]

Second Text: ST II-II, Q. 47, A. 6, Ad 3

Possibly in an effort to exclude the possibility that he could be read as subordinating all cognition to appetite, Thomas says in *ST* II-II, q. 47, a. 6:

> The end does not pertain to the moral virtues, as if they appoint the end, but because they tend to the end appointed by the natural reason, to which they are helped by prudence, which prepares the way for them by disposing of the means. Thus it remains that prudence is more noble than the moral virtues and moves them:

---

[33] Keenan, "The Virtue of Prudence," 264 (emphasis added).

[34] Emphasis added. The full quote is: "In terms of the distinction between formal and final causality, the object gives the form of specification; it no longer gives the end. The end is no longer in the object, but in the will. Yet for Thomas any end other than the last end is unformed, that is, it has no particular object and therefore no determinative form" (Keenan, *Goodness and Rightness*, 79).

[35] Keenan, *Goodness and Rightness*, 47.

[36] This, though, would be contrary to Thomas's assertion that even the *voluntas ut natura* follows the judgment of reason: "[The will as nature] follows the judgment of reason because there is something naturally known in the reason that acts as an indemonstrable principle in practical matters, which is related in the manner of an end (because, in practical matters, the end holds the place of a principle, as is said in *Ethics VI*)." For this reason, that which is the end of man is naturally known in the reason to be a good that should be desired—and the will following this knowledge is called 'will as nature'" (*In II sent.*, dist. 39, q. 2, a. 2, ad 2).

[37] For Hume, as John Cahalan observed, "reason cannot dictate to desires about values since desires determine what things are values and what are not. When reason makes value judgments, it is a 'slave' of desire; it only reports what desires do." See John C. Cahalan, "Natural Obligation," 101.

but synderesis moves prudence as the understanding of principles moves [the virtue of] knowledge.[38]

According to Keenan, Thomas went from saying, "the end was the mean that prudence appointed," in *ST* I-II, q. 66, to saying, "the end is now something different than the mean," in II-II, q. 47.[39] My own reading of Thomas coincides exactly with Keenan's on this specific point, although the meaning and import of what he says remains questionable. Keenan actually says something similar to Cajetan, though the latter adds essential clarification. For the renowned commentator, when Thomas "expressly says prudence directs the moral virtues even in appointing the end," the meaning is that "the end of moral virtue is to attain the mean which is determined by prudence." His way of reconciling the two texts provides helpful nuance because he insists that "[prudence] does not dictate what the end is; in truth, natural reason sufficiently dictates the end and prudence dictates what the means to the end are."[40] It does not, then, "prescribe [the end to] moral virtue simply, but only by disposing of the means."[41] This coincides with Keenan's reading inasmuch as it implies

---

[38] *ST* II-II, q. 47, a. 6, ad 3: "Finis non pertinet ad virtutes morales, tamquam ipsae praestituant finem; sed quia tendunt in finem a ratione naturali praestitutum: ad quod juvantur per prudentiam, quae eis viam parat, disponendo ea quae sunt ad finem; unde relinquitur, quod prudentia sit nobilior virtutibus moralibus, et moveat eas: sed synderesis movet prudentiam, sicut intellectus principiorum scientiam."

[39] Keenan, "Virtue of Prudence," 260.

[40] Cajetan commentary on *ST* II-II, q. 47, a. 6: "He expressly said that prudence directs the moral virtues even in appointing the end. And he proves that the end of a moral virtue is to attain the mean, which is determined by prudence.... However, prudence does not dictate what the end is; in truth, natural reason sufficiently dictates the end and prudence dictates what the means to the end are" (Leonine ed., 8:354 [nos. 2 and 4]).

[41] Cajetan commentary on *ST* II-II, q. 47, a. 6: "Indeed, prudence uses the end by applying it to the means.... Although prudence naturally precedes moral virtue, prudence does not dictate about the end. Rather, the natural reason suffices for this and prudence [merely] dictates about the mean" (Leonine ed., 8:354 [nos. 3–4]). Commenting on the sixth article of the same question, Cajetan adds further clarification: "Prudence finds the mean in moral matters ... by determining the action or passion in which the *ratio* of the mean is preserved and by commanding that that operation be chosen.... Prudence disposes the means and thus prepares the way for moral virtue so that it might attain the end by choosing the means. Because of this, in the *prima secundae* [II-II, q. 47, a. 6], it is said that it directs by ascertaining in regard to the appointing of the end—and that it does not do so simply speaking" (Cajetan commentary on *ST* II-II, q. 47, a. 8 [Leonine ed., 8:356; no. 1]).

that the end prudence appoints—as opposed to the end discussed in II-II, q. 47—must only equivocally be an end. For Cajetan, though, such an end is not subject to deliberation, because it is only prudence that determines the end qua the mean (and "we do not deliberate about ends, but about means"[42]). Because it does not determine the end *de novo*, it "directs moral virtue by appointing the end to it, not first and absolutely, but by applying it to some particular matter."[43] His reading (and mine) accordingly departs from Keenan's, inasmuch as Cajetan says synderesis *sufficiently* dictates the end, whereas Keenan thinks the end must be discovered by prudence. One wonders what knowledge of the end would be based on if prudence were to rely upon the moral virtues for its ends and if the appetitive part of the soul were independent from the rational part and acted antecedently to it. Moreover, if prudence discovers the end (as Keenan says) or establishes its substantive content (as Porter does), one would be hard pressed to explain the reason that, in the first reply of II-II, q. 47, a. 6, prudence is eliminated as a candidate for appointing ends:

> The natural reason, which is called synderesis (as was related in the *prima pars*) appoints the end to the moral virtues. Prudence, however, does not.[44]

There is obviously an important role for prudence in the later Thomas, but it does not strictly appoint the ends that stand as premises in a practical syllogism. As we have seen, he explains in *ST* II-II, q. 49, that the reasoning of prudence proceeds from a twofold understanding, one of which pertains to universals such as "one should do evil to no one" and the other of which pertains to some "singular and contingent minor premise." Although it proceeds from both of them, the latter kind is "a part of prudence" because it is a right estimate of a particular end.[45] The other kind of understanding that the ratiocination of prudence proceeds from, however, seems to be directive of it in the sense of being distinct from it and

---

[42] *In* III *eth.*, lec. 8: "We do not deliberate about ends, but about means [literally, "those things that are for the ends"], just as in speculative things we do not inquire about principles but about conclusions."

[43] Cajetan commentary on *ST* I-II, q. 66, a. 3: "prudentia dirigit virtutem moralem praestituendo illi finem, non primo et absolute, sed applicando illum ad specialem materialem" (Leonine ed., 6:433 [no. 13]).

[44] *ST* II-II, q. 49, a. 6, ad 1: "Virtutibus moralibus praestituit finem ratio naturalis, quae dicitur synderesis, ut in 1. habitum est [q. 79, a. 12], non autem prudentia."

[45] *ST* II-II, q. 49, a. 2, ad 1 (see note 11).

appointing the end to it in a cognitive mode. By providing universal practical principles such as "one should do evil to no one," this *intellectus* (or natural reason/synderesis) allows prudence to be on a solid footing when performing one of its primary roles—that of deliberating about means.

Although we will consider what principles synderesis contains in further detail in the third main section of this chapter below ("The Content of Synderesis"), we can note for now that Thomas certainly thinks it dictates a significant variety of substantive precepts which do not seem to require the presence of prudence in order to be apprehended. Among them are the precepts that man ought to do nothing against a divine precept and do no injustice to anyone (*nulli injuriam faciat*)[46] and the first two precepts of the natural law (namely, the precepts to love God and to love one's neighbor), and even the Ten Commandments, which are *"per se nota* to human reason" and conclusions of the first two precepts.[47] As he explains in *ST* I-II, q. 100, the commandments are said to "pertain to the natural law" in such a way that "the natural reason of any man whatever *per se* and without mediation judges" them to be done or not to be done. Precepts such as these are "absolutely from the law of nature"[48] and do not seem to be dependent upon prudence. This is most evident from a text wherein the Angelic Doctor explains why it is that there is no commandment pertaining to prudence. He says that the "commandments of the Decalogue . . . fall into the judgment [*in existimatione*] of everyone, as pertaining to the natural reason" and adds:

---

[46] *ST* I-II, q. 100, a. 5, ad 4: "Immediately, the natural reason of man dictates that no harm should be done to anyone" [also found in *Quolibet* III, q. 12, a. 1, corp., which also mentions that "nothing ought to be done against a divine precept"]. See also I-II, q. 100, a. 3, corp.: "Man ought to do evil to no one."

[47] In *ST* I-II, q. 100, a. 3, ad 1, he speaks about the precepts *Diliges Dominum Deum tuum* and *Diliges proximum tuum* as mentioned in the first objection: "Those two precepts are the first and common precepts of the law of nature, which are *per se* known to human reason, either by nature or through faith. Therefore, all the precepts of the decalogue are referred to those two as conclusions are referred to common principles." It is certainly noteworthy that he mentions faith in this context (presumably due to the clouding of the intellect that took place after the fall of Adam). Nevertheless, the fact remains that nature is able to make these principles/precepts known and that he calls them *per se nota*.

[48] *ST* I-II, q. 100, a. 1, corp.: "All the moral precepts pertain to the natural law, although in diverse ways. For there are some that the natural reason immediately *per se* judges as things that ought to be done or that ought not to be done, such as 'honor your father and mother' and 'do not kill' and 'do not steal.' And precepts such as this are absolutely from the law of nature."

> The ends of human life especially pertain to the dictate of the natural reason, and in [practical] things to be done, they are like the principles that are naturally known in the speculative order, as was said above [q. 47, a. 6]. Prudence, though, is not about the end, but about the means, as stated above [again q. 47, a. 6]. It was not fitting, therefore, that a commandment pertaining to prudence be placed among the commandments of the Decalogue.[49]

In view of these texts, the habit of the principles of the natural law known as synderesis certainly has substantive content for Aquinas. Since, moreover, prudence presupposes the ends provided by the natural reason, substantial precepts are evidently available to man's understanding even without the presence of prudence.

Keenan comments that, in *ST* II-II, q. 47, "*synderesis* appoints the end of each moral virtue, which ends are still the same: to act according to reason."[50] Cajetan would likely agree on some level. However, whereas Keenan says, "the end appointed by *synderesis* is not the proximate end that specifies a moral virtue, but the first principle, to do good and avoid evil,"[51] Cajetan argues it goes beyond that. Although the latter does not, to my knowledge, get into great detail about the precepts enumerated in the last paragraph as related to synderesis, he at least maintains that synderesis judges and proposes "not only the ultimate end, but the proper ends of the moral virtues while it judges how one should live in accordance with reason in regard to passions and actions."[52] Because it does so, prudence, for him, is able to exist because it supplies the foundation of a right deliberation about means:

> With the appetite inchoatively inclined to these ends—namely, the good of reason in actions, the good of reason in times of fear

---

[49] *ST* II-II, q. 56, a. 1, corp.: "Praecipue autem sunt de dictamine rationis naturalis fines humanae vitae, qui se habent in agendis sicut principia naturaliter cognita in speculativis, ut ex supradictis patet. Prudentia autem non est circa finem, sed circa ea quae sunt ad finem, ut supra dictum est. Et ideo non fuit conveniens ut inter praecepta Decalogi aliquod praeceptum poneretur ad prudentiam directe pertinens."

[50] Keenan, "The Virtue of Prudence," 260.

[51] Keenan, *Goodness and Rightness*, 102.

[52] Cajetan commentary on *ST* I-II, q. 66, a. 3: "Synderesi igitur in intellectu iudicante et proponente non solum finem ultimum, sed fines proprios virtutum moralium, dum in passionibus et operationibus secundum rationem vivendum iudicat" (Leonine ed., 6:433 [no. 12]).

or boldness, the good of reason amidst delights—one discourses from firm principles of this sort that are fixed in the intellect and inchoative in the appetite, by subsuming some less universal (such as to abstain from venereal delights for the sake of defending the republic). . . . Now, this discourse is that which generates prudence.[53]

For Cajetan, then, there are firm natural beginnings in both the intellect and the appetite. Since prudence needs both universal and particular knowledge and "is not only in the reason, since it is in the reason as moved by the appetite, . . . right reason about doable things depends upon both kinds of rectitude about ends; namely, the rectitude on the side of the apprehensive part and on the side of the appetitive part."[54] This, of course, reconciles perfectly with the notion that "there are two principles of human actions, the intellect or the reason and the appetite." We turn now to considering how Cajetan explains the "difficult question," the *dubium arduum*, in view of this principle.

Cajetan's Resolution to the Dubium Arduum

Although Cajetan addresses this issue in his exposition of *ST* II-II, q. 47, the most substantial treatment is in his commentary on I-II, q. 66, a. 3. He dedicates many pages to the matter, but a key selection reads as follows:

In response to the third objection of this article, a challenging

---

[53] Cajetan commentary on *ST* I-II, q. 66, a. 3: "Appetitu inchoative inclinato ad hos fines, scilicet bonum rationis in operationibus, bonum rationis in timoribus et audaciis, bonum rationis in delectationibus, etc.: et discurritur ex huiusmodi principiis firmatis in intellectu et inchoatis in appetitu, subsumendo aliquiod minus universale, puta abstinere a delectationibus venereis, republicam defendendam; et concluditur modus in delectationibus, et sic de aliis. Hic autem discursus prudentiae generativus est" (Leonine ed., 6:433 [no. 12]). For an alternate translation and further discussion, see Dominic Farrell, *The Ends of the Moral Virtues and the First Principles of Practical Reason in Thomas Aquinas* (Rome: Gregorian and Biblical Press, 2012), 105.

[54] See *In* VI *eth.*, lec. 7, no. 7: "Prudence is not only in the reason, but has something in the appetite." Referring to Aristotle himself, Cajetan says here (commentary on *ST* I-II, q. 65, a. 1, no. 10): "Prudence is not only in the reason, as is said in *Ethics* 6. This is because it is in the reason as moved by the appetite." He goes on: "Right reason about doable things depends upon both kinds of rectitude about ends—namely, the rectitude from the apprehensive part and from the appetitive part" (Leonine ed., 6:421).

What Appoints the End?

question arises, . . . which is simply: how is it true that prudence directs the moral virtues even in appointing the end? This will be discussed in a cursory manner in the commentary on II-II. 47. . . . [This position] seems to be in tension with what was said above [in I-II, q. 58, a. 5[55]] and also to what is said below in II-II in the place brought forward [q. 47, a. 6]. After all, it was said above [in I-II, q. 58, a. 5] that the principle which is the end is had from moral virtue because, as each one is, so does the end seem to him. And the idea that prudence appoints the end to the moral virtues will be expressly denied below [in II-II, q. 47, a. 6]. . . . In order to make the difficulty of this question more clear, we should keep our reasoning process before our eyes so that we might be able to evaluate the rationale for the things said and so that we might be able to judge what is said simply and what is said in a qualified manner. The first thing in our mind is synderesis, by which we naturally judge not only that every good ought to be done and every evil fled from and that happiness ought to be desired and misery avoided, but also that the good of reason ought to be pursued and the evil that is opposed to it ought to be fled from. And from this source there is also in the appetite not only an inclination for pursuing good and avoiding bad, for desiring happiness and fleeing misery, but also a certain imperfect inclination for living according to right reason. And although synderesis is a virtue[56] because it is the understanding of principles, this incli-

---

[55] *ST* I-II, q. 58, a. 5, corp.: "In order for him [man] to be rightly disposed in regard to the particular principles of actions (which principles are ends), it is necessary that he be perfected by certain habits. In virtue of these habits, it becomes somehow connatural to man to rightly judge about the end, and this comes about through moral virtue. For the virtuous man rightly judges about the end of virtue—because as each one is, so does the end seem to him as is said in *Ethics* III. . . . And therefore it is required for right reason about doable things, which is prudence, that man has moral virtue." See also ad 1: "Reason, inasmuch as it apprehends the end, precedes the appetite of the end. But the appetite of the end precedes reason reasoning for the sake of choosing the means (which pertains to prudence) just as in speculative matters, the understanding of principles is the beginning [*principium*] of syllogizing reason."

[56] It is striking that he calls it a "virtue," because it is clearly a natural habit that is neither acquired nor infused. Nevertheless, in *ST* II-II, q. 49, a. 2, ad 1, Thomas says that "the understanding which is an intellectual virtue" is that whereby we know "practical universal principles such as 'one should do evil to no man,' as shown above," and he is thus clearly referring back to II-II, q. 47, a. 6, which speaks about synderesis. Synderesis, therefore, can be called a virtue even if it is a natural virtue.

nation of the appetite is, nevertheless, not a virtue because it is imperfect.[57]

Cajetan goes on to explain that prudence is generated by the virtue of synderesis, which enables one to "frequently discourse about the end," just as moral virtue is generated thanks to prudence, since it is in virtue of prudence that one is able to frequently choose the right mean.[58] For him, this is the reason Thomas says, "prudence is more noble than the moral virtues and moves them: but synderesis moves prudence as the understanding of principles moves [the virtue of] knowledge."[59] Accordingly, Cajetan says, "the absolutely first end of moral virtue is not from prudence, but from synderesis."[60] The natural reason is "the first of all the things in our mind," and through it (Cajetan says), "we naturally judge not only that every good ought to be pursued and every evil fled from and that happiness ought to be desired and misery avoided, but also that the good of reason ought to be pursued and the evil opposed to it ought to be shunned."[61] Through

---

[57] Cajetan commentary on *ST* I-II, q. 66, a. 3: "Responsione ad tertium eiusdem articuli, dubium arduum occurrit in via Auctoris, et simpliciter: quomodo scilicet sit verum prudentiam dirigere morales virtutes etiam in praestituendo finem. Et simpliciter quidem in II-II, loco allegato. Superioribus quidem, pro quanto dictum fuit, quod prudentia principium, quod est finis, habet a virtute morali, quia qualis unusquisque est, talis ei finis videtur. Inferioribus autem, quia expresse negabitur ex proposito, prudentiam praestituere finem moralibus virtutibus.... Ad huius difficultatis evidentiam, ponendus ante oculos est progressus nostrae mentis in istis, ut ex eo rationem dictorum sumere et reddere valeamus: et quid simpliciter, et quid secundum quid intelligatur, discernamus. ... In mente nostra primo omnium est synderesis, qua non solum omne bonum prosequendum et malum fugiendum, felicitatem appetendam et miseriam fugiendam; sed bonum rationis prosequendum, et malum oppositum vitandum, iudicamus naturaliter. Et hinc in appetitu etiam naturaliter inest non solum inclinatio ad bonum prosequendum et malum vitandum, ad beatitudinem appetendam et miseriam fugiendam; sed imperfecta quaedam inclinatio ad vivendum secundum rectam rationem. Et licet synderesis sit virtus, quia est intellectus principorum; inclinatio tamen haec appetitus non est virtus, quia imperfecta est" (Leonine ed., 6:433 [no. 12–13]).

[58] Cajetan commentary on *ST* I-II, q. 66, a. 3: "Just as prudence is generated by frequent repetition of deliberation of the already-extant end that yields the means, so also moral virtue is generated by frequent repetition of the choice that follows" (Leonine ed., 6:433 [no. 12]). The "already-extant end," of course, is presented by synderesis.

[59] *ST* II-II, q. 47, a. 6, ad 3: "Prudentia sit nobilior virtutibus moralibus, et moveat eas: sed synderesis movet prudentiam, sicut intellectus principiorum scientiam."

[60] Cajetan commentary on *ST* II, q. 66, a. 3: "finis virtutis moralis absolute praestituitur primo, non a prudentia, sed a synderesi" (Leonine ed., 6:433 [no. 12]).

[61] Cajetan commentary on *ST* I-II, q. 66, a. 3: "In mente nostra primo omnium est synderesis, qua non solum omne bonum prosequendum et malum fugiendum, felicitatem

synderesis, moreover, we also know "not only the ultimate end but also the proper ends of the moral virtues in both things we undergo and in things we do."[62] Cajetan adds that we reason "discursively from principles of this sort that have been made firm in the intellect."[63] Examples he gives of such principles are that "the good of reason ought to be followed in matters pertaining to fears, and similarly in matters of bodily desires and those pertaining to anger and operations." Synderesis, for him, appoints these ends, whereas "one looks to prudence to make use of these principles."[64]

All of this is remarkably consonant with Thomas's own view. The naturally known beginnings (*principia*) that are the ends of the moral virtues preexist, Aquinas says, in the reason.[65] Moreover, the natural reason appoints the end to man that he ought not to divert from reason on account of the appetites.[66] Prudence remains essential as a *sine qua non* for attaining the mean of reason in practical matters,[67] but the impetus to attain the mean of reason in the first place is due to the dictate of synderesis / natural reason. For this reason, Cajetan says that "prudence directs

---

appetendam et miseriam fugiendam; sed bonum rationis prosequendum et malum oppositum vitandum, iudicamus naturaliter" (Leonine ed., 6:433 [no. 12]).

[62] Cajetan commentary on *ST* I-II, q. 66, a. 3: "Synderesis, then, is in the adjudicating intellect proposing not only the ultimate end, but also the proper ends of the moral virtues (whether in the passions or actions). It judges how one should live according to reason" (Leonine ed., 6:433 [no. 12]).

[63] Cajetan commentary on *ST* I-II, q. 66, a. 3: "Synderesi igitur in intellectu iudicante et proponente non solum finem ultimum, sed fines proprios virtutum moralium" (Leonine ed., 6:433 [no. 12]).

[64] Cajetan commentary on *ST* II-II, q. 47, a. 6: "The end is appointed to moral virtue by synderesis because the natural reason dictates that in fears and delights—and, similarly, in fearful things and actions—the good of reason ought to be followed" (Leonine ed., 8:354 [no. 3]). Commenting on article 8 of the same question, Cajetan says it is necessary to look to prudence to apply principles of action because "it is attributed to prudence to discover the mean, but to synderesis to appoint the end" (Leonine ed., 8:356 [no.1]). For a discussion of this text, see Farrell, *The Ends of the Moral Virtues*, 105.

[65] *ST* II-II, q. 47, a. 6, corp.

[66] *ST* II-II, q. 47, a. 7, corp.: "The proper end of any given moral virtue is to be conformed to right reason. For temperance intends this lest a man strays from reason on account of his sensual desires, and fortitude similarly intends this lest it stray from the right judgment of the reason on account of fear or temerity. And this end is appointed [*praestitutus*] to man in accordance with the natural reason."

[67] *ST* II-II, q. 47, a. 7, corp.: "But how a man attains the mean of reason according to natural reason, and through which things, pertains to the disposition of prudence. For although to attain the mean is the end of moral virtue, the mean is found through the right disposition of the means."

moral virtue" by applying the end made known by synderesis to some particular matter."[68] Dominic Farrell accordingly observes that Cajetan can be understood to be saying synderesis sets the ends for the cardinal virtues by dictating what it means for the appetites to follow the good of reason.[69]

It is, in a sense, more accurate to say synderesis appoints the end because it appoints the ultimate ends and makes possible the "discourse ... which generates prudence."[70] Since this discourse requires "principles fixed in the intellect" and not only "inchoate in the appetite" due to the natural ordering toward reason, the prudent man is not reliant solely upon appetite. At the same time, presupposing the appetites being moved in the appropriate way thanks to their natural inclination to follow reason, prudence appoints the mean that is the end of the moral virtues, and thus appoints the end in this qualified sense.

Cajetan's perceptive reading of the *Summa* led him to understand Thomas as maintaining that there must be an antecedent apprehension of natural reason that stands as a foundation of the moral life. We now turn to the text of the *Scriptum* that takes head on the question of the appointing of ends vis-à-vis the roles of prudence and synderesis.

The *Scriptum* and Capreolus

Book III, Distinction 33, of the *Scriptum*

For Saint Thomas, prudence is about "the means which we gather from the *ends* themselves" (*ST* II-II, q. 47, a. 6, corp.); whatever the ends are,

---

[68] Cajetan commentary on *ST* I-II, q. 66, a. 3: "Prudence directs moral virtue by appointing [*praestitudendo*] the end to it, not first and absolutely, however, but by applying it to a particular matter that arises" (Leonine ed., 6:433 [no. 13]).

[69] See Farrell, *The Ends of the Moral Virtues*, 104. He cites comments of Cajetan on *ST* I-II, q. 58, a. 5 (Leonine ed., 6:378 [no. 8]), and q. 47, a. 6: "The end is appointed to moral virtue by synderesis because the natural reason dictates that in fears and delights—and, similarly, in fearful things and actions—the good of reason ought to be followed" (Leonine ed., 3:354 [no. 73]).

[70] Cajetan commentary on *ST* I-II, q. 66, a. 3: "With the appetite incipiently inclined to these ends—namely, the good of reason in actions, the good of reason in times of fear or boldness, the good of reason amidst delights—one discursively reasons from firm principles of this sort that are fixed in the intellect and incipient in the appetite, by subsuming something less universal (such as to abstain from venereal delights for the sake of defending the republic). . . . Now, this discourse is that which generates prudence" (Leonine ed., 6:433 [no. 12]). This discourse precedes prudence, and thus the prudent man is not reliant solely upon appetite.

What Appoints the End?

prudence does not strictly pertain to them. As we saw in Cajetan, this seems to mean that it relies upon the natural habit of synderesis for those ends and that it does not deliberate about them as if it has some say over them and can simply invent them on its own after having consulted the appetites. We mentioned in the introduction that Denis Bradley referenced *ST* I-II, q. 66, as "one exception" to Thomas's usual deference to "the original Aristotelian dichotomy between wishing for ends and deliberating and choosing (solely) about the means."[71] For Bradley, the *ST* I-II text is an exception to his reiteration of Aristotle's "narrow view of deliberation and choice,"[72] for if prudence can appoint the end, it must be able to deliberate about it. Is this necessarily so?

Nearly everything we have seen thus far has suggested there is no deliberation about the ends appointed by synderesis, since it is not subject to free will.[73] If by saying prudence appoints the end, Thomas meant to suggest there is deliberation about ultimate ends, this would indeed be noteworthy, but given Aquinas's consistency elsewhere, we should not expect such a significant alteration. Actually, Thomas occasionally makes it known when he changes his mind or wishes to add further nuance. In *ST* II-II, for example, he diverged from his own earlier position found in *ST* I-II when he revisited the question of the scope of the gift of understanding. He recalled what he had said earlier and then said it is better to say it applies to both practical and speculative matters, as opposed to only the former.[74] There is no reason we should not expect something similarly clear in this case if he somewhat suddenly decided that prudence is able to deliberate about ends themselves. There must, therefore, be another way of interpreting Aquinas's intention when he says prudence appoints the end. As it turns out, the following *Scriptum*

---

[71] Denis J. M. Bradley, *Aquinas on the Twofold Human Good: Reason and Human Happiness in Aquinas's Moral Science* (Washington, DC: Catholic University of America Press, 1997), 206–7.

[72] Bradley, *Aquinas on the Twofold Human Good*, 207.

[73] *Liberum arbitrium* is distinguished from the judgment of synderesis in *De veritate*, q. 16, a. 1, ad 15: "Judgment is twofold: of universals, which pertains to synderesis and [secondly] of particular doable things—and this is the judgment of choice and pertains to free will [*liberum arbitrium*]. It is clear from this that they are not the same." *Liberum arbitrium* is distinguished from the judgment of conscience in *De veritate*, q. 17, a. 1, ad 4: "The judgment of conscience is different from the judgment of free will [*liberi arbitrii*] because the judgment of conscience consists in pure knowledge, whereas the judgment of free will consists in an application of knowledge to affections—which judgment, indeed, is the judgment of choice."

[74] See *ST* II-II, q. 8, a. 6.

text addresses this issue while also calling to mind the role of natural reason / synderesis:

> For the perfection of moral virtue, three things are necessary. First is the appointing of the end. Second is the inclination to the end appointed. Third is the choice of the means [*ea quae sunt ad finem*]. Now the proximate end of human life is the good of reason in general [*in communi*]. For this reason, Dionysius says that man's evil is to be against reason, and therefore in all the moral virtues, it is intended that passions and actions be reduced to the rectitude of reason. Now rectitude belongs to the natural reason. Accordingly, in this way, the appointing of the end pertains to the natural reason and precedes prudence just as the understanding of principles precedes science. And therefore the Philosopher says in *Ethics* VI that prudence has the ends of the virtues as its principles. But this good of reason is determined inasmuch as the mean is constituted in actions and passions by a fitting commensuration of circumstances, which prudence brings about [*facit*]. Thus the mean of moral virtue, as it is said in *Ethics* II, is according to right reason, which is prudence. And thus prudence in a certain measure appoints the end to the moral virtues and is mixed in with their acts. But the inclination to that end pertains to moral virtue which assents to the good of reason by way of nature. And this inclination to the end is called choice inasmuch as the proximate end is ordered to the ultimate end. And therefore the Philosopher says in *Ethics* II that moral virtue brings about right choice. But the discrimination of those things by which we are able to attain this good of reason in actions and passions is the act of prudence. Accordingly, the appointing of the end precedes the act of prudence and of moral virtue. But the inclination to the end, or the right choice of the proximate end, is principally an act of moral virtue, though it is from prudence as from an origin. Thus the Philosopher says that rectitude of choice is in the other virtues from prudence just as the rectitude in the intention of nature is from the divine wisdom directing nature. And in this way, an act of prudence can even be said to be mixed in with the acts of the other virtues. For, as the natural inclination is from the natural reason, so the inclination of moral virtue is from prudence. Now inasmuch as choice implies the precept of reason about things to be pursued, choice pertains to the means.

But the act of prudence is its own and distinct from the acts of the other virtues.[75]

Though Thomas also grants here that prudence appoints the end to the moral virtues (as he did in *ST* I-II, q. 66, a. 3), there is no indication one prudentially deliberates about ends. Actually, the natural reason is responsible for the natural inclination. Pursuant to that natural inclination, prudence has a guiding power over the inclination of moral virtue and is, in fact, a source of it. It brings about a "fitting commensuration of circumstances" by ensuring there is a "right choice of the proximate end." Accordingly, what Bradley refers to as the "narrow view" of choice remains. Prudence appoints the end inasmuch as it enables one to choose well about proximate ends—which are strictly means. In other words, the appointing of the end by the natural reason (to which rectitude belongs more originally), is prior to deliberation and choice, and its act of appointing precedes both prudence and moral virtue.

---

[75] *In* III *sent.*, dist. 33, q. 2, a. 3, corp.: "Ad perfectionem virtutis moralis tria sunt necessaria. Primum est praestitutio finis; secundum autem est inclinatio ad finem praestitutum; tertium est electio eorum quae sunt ad finem. Finis autem proximus humanae vitae est bonum rationis in communi; unde dicit Dionysius, quod malum hominis est contra rationem esse: et ideo est intentum in omnibus virtutibus moralibus, ut passiones et operationes ad rectitudinem rationis reducantur. Rectitudo autem rationis naturalis est; unde hoc modo praestitutio finis ad naturalem rationem pertinet, et praecedit prudentiam, sicut intellectus principiorum scientiam; et ideo dicit philosophus, 6 Ethic., quod prudentia habet principia fines virtutum. Sed hoc bonum rationis determinatur secundum quod constituitur medium in actionibus et passionibus per debitam commensurationem circumstantiarum, quod facit prudentia. Unde medium virtutis moralis, ut in 2 Ethic. dicitur, est secundum rationem rectam, quae est prudentia; et sic quodammodo prudentia praestituit finem virtutibus moralibus, et ejus actus in earum actibus immiscetur; sed inclinatio in finem illum pertinet ad virtutem moralem quae consentit in bonum rationis per modum naturae: et haec inclinatio in finem dicitur electio, inquantum finis proximus ad finem ultimum ordinatur. Et ideo dicit philosophus, 2 Ethic., quod virtus moralis facit electionem rectam. Sed discretio eorum quibus hoc bonum rationis consequi possumus et in operationibus et in passionibus, est actus prudentiae: unde praestitutio finis praecedit actum prudentiae et virtutis moralis; sed inclinatio in finem, sive recta electio finis proximi, est actus moralis virtutis principaliter, sed prudentiae originaliter. Unde philosophus dicit, quod rectitudo electionis est in aliis virtutibus a prudentia, sicut rectitudo in intentione naturae est ex sapientia divina ordinante naturam: et secundum hoc actus etiam prudentiae immixtus est actibus aliarum virtutum. Sicut enim inclinatio naturalis est a ratione naturali, ita inclinatio virtutis moralis a prudentia; electio autem eorum quae sunt ad finem, secundum quod electio importat praeceptum rationis de his prosequendis. Sed actus prudentiae sibi proprius est, et distinctus ab actibus aliarum virtutum."

Thomas's own explanation and resolution of the difficulty is practically identical to Cajetan's, even though the latter did not seem to be aware of this text. For both of them, the appointing of the end precedes the inclination of the appetite, which prudence must necessarily look to. At the same time, prudence appoints the end to the moral virtues since it is their origin in the sense that it specifies what the commensurate act is in actions and passions given various circumstances; in other words, it appoints the end that is the mean.

Capreolus on the Scriptum

John Capreolus, the fifteenth-century commentator of Aquinas who has been called the "prince of the commentators," quoted the *Scriptum* text in full and then explained its meaning as follows:

> Thus this is what he says. He posits something similar in *ST* II-II 47, q. 6, a. 6, except that he says there that it does not pertain to prudence to appoint the end to the moral virtues, but only those things that are for the end; for the natural reason, which is called synderesis, appoints the end to the moral virtues; and, although the moral virtues tend to the end appointed by natural reason and not by prudence, they are nevertheless helped in this regard by prudence, which prepares the way for them by disposing those things that are for the end. And this last argument seems more probable. But whatever is the case with this, it appears from the foregoing that the habit of prudence is not able to be generated in someone through dictates of the understanding or of reason (from which moral virtue is generated) unless the acts of the appetite concur, as was related above about *ST* I-II, q. 58, a. 5, in the solution to the first objection, where he speaks thus: "Reason, inasmuch as it apprehends the end precedes the appetite of the end; but the appetite for the end precedes reason reasoning for the sake of choosing those things that are for the end; which pertains to prudence";[76] and so on.[77]

---

[76] *ST* I-II, q. 58, a. 5, ad 1: "Reason, inasmuch as it apprehends the end, precedes the appetite for the end, but the appetite for the end precedes discursive reasoning in regard to the choosing of means, which pertains to prudence. Similarly, the understanding of principles is the beginning of reason syllogizing in speculative things."

[77] John Capreolus, O.P., *Defensiones Theologiae, De Novo Editae Cura Et Studio Paban et Pegues*, vol. 5, dist. 36, q. 1 "Simile ponit, 2a 2ae, q. 47, art. 6, nisi quod ibi dicit quod

Although Capreolus and Cajetan are similar, the former takes a stand and says the *ST* II-II, q. 47, text was "more probable." All things considered, this seems the best solution. Although prudence can be said to appoint the end to the moral virtues inasmuch as it presupposes the ends appointed by God, nature, and natural reason, still the ends it appoints are properly speaking the mean between two vicious extremes. In moral matters, the ends are the first principles and there seems no denying that, since the appointing of the end precedes prudence, what most truly appoints the end is synderesis.

The Content of Synderesis

We have seen that, as noble as prudence is, it is subject to the appointing that comes from synderesis. What is it that is appointed though? It is not always clear whether Aquinas has *one* thing in mind, such as the precept to obey reason or pursue the good, or alternatively, it is actually many, such as the prohibition against harming anyone[78] and the principle that "God ought to be obeyed."[79] In book III of the *Scriptum*, Thomas speaks of the prudence as proceeding "to choice and deliberation" from the ends of the other virtues" that are its principles. These ends are said to "preexist in the reason essentially," and so the reason in question seems to be the natural reason known as synderesis.[80] As a consequence, these "ends" too

---

ad prudentiam non pertinet praestituere finem virtutibus moralibus, sed solum de his quae sunt ad finem; finem autem virtutibus moralibus praestituit ratio naturalis, quae dicitur synderesis; et, licet virtutes morales tendant in finem praestitutum a ratione naturali, et non a prudentia, tamen ad hoc juvantur per prudentiam, quae eis viam parat, disponendo ea quae sunt ad finem. Et hoc ultimum videtur probabilius. Quidquid autem sic de hoc, apparet ex praemissis quod habitus prudentiae non potest in aliquo generari per quaecumque dictamina intellectus vel rationis, nisi concurrant actus appetitus, ex quibus generatur virtus moralis; sicut supra allegatum fuit (b) de I-II, q. 58, art 5, in solutione primi, ubi sic dicit: 'Ratio, secundum quod est apprehensiva finis, praecedit appetitus finis; sed appetitus finis praecedit rationem ratiocinantem ad eligendum eaquae sunt ad finem; quod pertinet ad prudentiam, etc." ([Turin: Cattier; 1904], 431).

[78] *ST* I-II, q. 100, a. 5, ad 4: "The natural reason of man judges that harm should be done to no one." See also II-II, q. 49, a. 2, ad 1.

[79] *In* II *sent.*, dist. 39, q. 3, a. 2, corp.: "The first principles, by which reason is directed in practical things, are *per se* known, and error does not occur in regard to these.... Now these naturally known principles about things to be done pertain to synderesis (as, for example, the principle that God ought to be obeyed, and similar things)." See also *De veritate*, q. 16., a. 1, ad 9.

[80] *In* III *sent.*, dist. 33, q. 2, a. 5, ad 6: "Just as the speculative reason proceeds to a

(which are multiple, since "the good of reason is not found in all matters of morality in the same way"[81]) seem to pertain to the content of synderesis. But are there any other ends pertaining to the habit of synderesis?

In the *Scriptum* passage, Thomas seemed to identify the end of the moral virtues as the good of reason and Cajetan speaks of it in these terms frequently.[82] Actually, in the example he gives of a practical syllogism, the first premise he gives is "the good of reason is to be pursued as much in passions as it is in operations,"[83] and he refers to this good of reason as the "beginning of prudence"[84] and the "one end of temperance."[85] He also explains the contention in *ST* II-II, q. 47, that the end is appointed to the moral virtues by prudence in virtue of synderesis dictating "what the good of reason that should be followed is."[86] If we were to prescind from Thomas's assertions elsewhere pertaining to synderesis's content, we might agree with Porter and others that "the end . . . appointed to man according to natural reason" consists of nothing else than that it "dictates to each one that he act according to reason,"[87] Though this conclusion is evidently contrary to the thought of Thomas when considering it as a

---

conclusion from *per se* known principles, so the reason of prudence proceeds to choice and counsel about the means from the end. And, therefore, the ends of the other virtues are said to be the principles of prudence. These ends, though, substantially [*essentialiter*] preexist in the reason because moral virtue tends toward the agreement of the appetite with reason. For this reason, prudence is closest to these ends that reason perfects."

[81] *In* III *sent.*, dist. 33, q. 1, a. 1, qc 1, corp.: "Quia non in omnibus materiis moralibus eodem modo invenitur rationis bonum, ut patet."

[82] Cajetan commentary on *ST* I-II, q. 55, a. 2, says that the "proximate end of moral virtue itself" is "the good of reason in such matter, which is the mean in some matter determined by reason" (Leonine ed., 6:350 [no. 2]).

[83] Cajetan commentary on *ST* I-II, 58, a. 5, corp.: "The first premise is a proposition looking to synderesis; for example, 'the good of reason, as much in passions as in operations, is to be pursued.'" (Leonine ed., 6:378 [no. 8]).

[84] Cajetan commentary on *ST* I-II, 58, a. 5, corp.: "Bonum rationis, quod est principium prudentiae" (Leonine ed., 6:378 [no. 9]).

[85] Cajetan commentary on *ST* I-II, q. 69, a. 2: "The good of reason in the delights of touch is the one end of temperance, and the good of reason in fears and daring acts is the one end of fortitude, and thus of the others. So the good of reason in the whole genus of actions is the unique end of prudence" (Leonine ed., 6:387 [no. 7]).

[86] Cajetan commentary on *ST* II-II, q. 47, a. 6, no. 3: "Virtuti morali finis praestituitur a synderesi: quia naturalis ratio dictat quod in timoribus bonum rationis, et similiter in concupiscentiis, et similiter in ira et operationibus sectandum est" (Leonine ed., 8:354).

[87] *ST* II-II, q. 47, a. 7, corp., does, in fact, say that the end "is appointed to man according to natural reason," since it "dictates to each one that he act according to reason." However, it does not limit the end to this or say that is the only end appointed by synderesis.

whole, it may be helpful to further consider the foundations and implications of such a claim.

For Thomas, synderesis is not open to opposites because it is "determinedly related to one."[88] If we were to apply Ockham's razor here, synderesis would be really reduced to some hard-to-identify principle pertaining to reason in some way. Michael Sherwin speaks of "some cognitive understanding of human flourishing" and happiness,[89] whereas Keenan and Porter speak of following reason. Other options might be the precept to "pursue the perfect good as known by reason."

The first observation to be made, however, is that synderesis can pertain to either the higher or the lower reason:

> Synderesis names neither the higher nor the lower reason, but is related commonly to both. For in the habit itself of universal principles of law, certain things pertaining to eternal concepts [*rationes*] are contained, as, for instance, this principle: that God ought to be obeyed. Some precepts, however, pertain to lower concepts; as, for instance, that one ought to live according to reason.[90]

For this reason, man is exhorted in virtue of his natural reason to turn himself to God as soon as he hits the age of reason. It pertains to the rational creature's nature itself that God ought to be obeyed because there is a twofold law in man, meaning human reason and the eternal law—and the natural law is a participation in the latter that, as one might expect, comes naturally to a rational creature.[91] In a sense, therefore, the natural law is not "something different from the eternal law," because it is "nothing but a certain participation in it."[92] Although Thomas sometimes refers to the

---

[88] *In* III *sent.*, dist. 24, q. 2, a. 3, sc 1: "A rational power is related to opposites. But synderesis is related determinately to one thing because it never errs. Therefore it seems that it is not a power, but a habit."

[89] See Michael Sherwin, *By Knowledge and By Love: Charity and Knowledge in the Moral Theology of Thomas Aquinas* (Washington, DC: Catholic University of America Press, 2005), 19–20.

[90] *De veritate*, q. 16, a. 1, ad 9: "Synderesis neque nominat superiorem rationem neque inferiorem, sed aliquid communiter se habens ad utramque. In ipso enim habitu universalium principiorum iuris continentur quaedam quae pertinent ad rationes aeternas, ut hoc quod est Deo esse obediendum; quaedam vero quae pertinent ad rationes inferiores, utpote secundum rationem esse vivendum."

[91] *ST* I-II, q. 91, a. 2, corp., speaks of the natural law as a participation of the eternal law by the rational creature.

[92] *ST* I-II, q. 91, a. 2, ad 1: "Ratio illa procederet, si lex naturalis esset aliquid diversum a

distinction between the proximate rule that is reason and the "first rule, namely the eternal law, which is as the reason of God"[93] in terms of the natural and supernatural orders,[94] the eternal law can at least in part[95] be known by man naturally, and to the extent that it can be, we might think of that as pertaining to the realm of the "higher reason."

Synderesis consequently pertains to both higher and lower principles. So, when Keenan asserts, "*synderesis* appoints the end of each moral virtue, which ends [*sic*] are . . . to act according to reason,"[96] at the very least, he is not being specific enough, because one of those kinds of reason we naturally know to act according to is the *eternal* reason. In virtue of our rational participation in it, even the commandments themselves are reduced to natural law.

Thomas even refers to the principles of the Decalogue as *per se* known,[97] so there must be more than one principle that is an end appointed by synderesis or natural reason. At the same time, a distinction needs to be made between the certitude one is able to have about the Ten Commandments:

> Every judgment of the practical reason proceeds from certain naturally known principles. . . . It is necessary that all the moral precepts pertain to the law of nature, but in diverse ways. For there are some which the natural reason of any man immediately judges to be done or not to be done, such as "Honor your father and mother," "You shalt not kill," and "You shalt not steal." And these are absolutely of the law of nature. . . . However, there are some that human reason requires divine instruction to make

---

lege aeterna: non autem est nisi quaedam participatio ejus, ut dictum est."
[93] *ST* I-II, q. 71, a. 6, corp.
[94] In *ST* II-II, q. 17, a. 1, corp., the context is the supernatural virtue of hope: "There is a twofold measure of human acts, one of which is proximate and of like kind—namely, reason. The other, though, is the supreme and exceeding measure—namely, God. And therefore every act attaining to reason or to God himself is good."
[95] In *ST* I-II, q. 93, a. 2, Thomas answers the question "whether the eternal law is known by all" in the affirmative. In the body of that article, he says, "every rational creature knows it, to a greater or lesser extent, in its reflection." Nevertheless, we are also "directed in many things that surpass human reason, e.g. in matters of faith" (*ST* I-II, q. 71, a. 6, ad 5). As a consequence, "when human reason falls short, it is necessary to have recourse to the eternal reason," (*ST* I-II, q. 19, a. 4, corp.).
[96] Keenan, "Virtue of Prudence," 260.
[97] *ST* II-II, q. 170, a. 2, ad 1, says this of all Ten Commandments: "The precepts of the Decalogue, which are the first self-evident principles . . ."

judgments about, . . . as "You shall not make to yourself a graven thing, nor the likeness of anything" and "You shall not take the name of the Lord thy God in vain."[98]

On the one hand, this text makes it clear that Aquinas maintains there is more than one principle. On the other, however, one wonders whether any of the Ten Commandments absolutely pertain to indemonstrable naturally known principles known by everyone. In other words, even though the "dictate" of synderesis necessarily moves prudence, since the "natural reason" points out "the ends of human life, which in things to be done are as the naturally known principles in speculative things,"[99] the reality is that someone who has freely developed a habit of turning more toward the good of the sensitive appetites than the good proposed by the natural reason need not be perfectly directed by synderesis, as we will see.

In *ST* I-II, q. 94, a. 2 (among other places), Thomas distinguishes between principles that are *per se* known in themselves and those which are *per se* known to us. In that same article, he speaks of the "order of natural inclinations" corresponding to the "order of the precepts of the natural law."[100] The "natural inclination to the fitting act and end" that is possessed by all creatures is possessed in a special way by the rational creature.[101] This means there is a teleological order written in nature itself and in the way the intellect and will and all the appetites are naturally ordered. Thanks to his nature, man participates in the eternal law in a more perfect way

---

[98] *ST* I-II, q. 100, a. 1, corp.: "Sicut autem omne iudicium rationis speculativae procedit a naturali cognitione primorum principiorum, ita etiam omne iudicium rationis practicae procedit ex quibusdam principiis naturaliter cognitis, ut supra dictum est. . . . Necesse est quod omnia praecepta moralia pertineant ad legem naturae, sed diversimode. Quaedam enim sunt, quae statim per se ratio naturalis cujuslibet hominis dijudicat esse facienda, vel non facienda; sicut: Honora patrem tuum, et matrem; et: Non occides: Non furtum facies: et hujusmodi sunt absolute de lege naturae . . . quaedam vero sunt, ad quae judicanda ratio humana indiget instructione divina, per quam erudimur de divinis: sicut est illud: Non facies tibi sculptile, neque omnem similitudinem: Non assumes nomen Dei tui in vanum."

[99] *ST* II-II, q. 56, a. 1, corp.: "The precepts of the Decalogue, being given to the whole people, are a matter of common knowledge to all as pertaining to the natural reason. Now the ends of human life, which in things to be done are as the naturally known principles in speculative things, especially stand out among the things dictated by the natural reason."

[100] *ST* I-II, q. 94, a. 2, corp.: "Secundum igitur ordinem inclinationum naturalium est ordo praeceptorum legis naturae."

[101] See *ST* I-II, q. 91, a. 2, corp.

simply by dint of being a man because he has reason and will. In virtue of these rational faculties, man's nature is well ordered to universal truths, and some truths can even be said to come naturally to him in some way. Unfortunately, though, the consequence of the Fall is that the order to objective truth has been hindered somewhat and principles that are "naturally known" seem to be less than natural for some. This is not necessarily all that problematic, however, because nature can be expected to procure its effects only "more often than not," and thus need not do so in every instance.[102] "Natural things," in other words, definitively tend to determinate ends only "for the most part"[103] so it is enough that these principles are found in the majority of men. The question remains though: what are these principles?

Thomas says the commandment against stealing is said to be immediately known to the natural reason (otherwise known as synderesis[104]) of every individual[105] because it is *per se nota*,[106] even though he also said someone could reason badly on this point and deem stealing to be licit due to bad customs, inordinate passion, or bad dispositions of nature (he gave the *Germani* as an example, since, despite the fact that stealing is "clearly

---

[102] *ST* I, q. 63, a. 9, corp.: "Natura enim consequitur suum effectum vel semper, vel ut in pluribus."

[103] Thomas frequently speaks of nature in terms of acting "always or for the most part," and thus the natural reason does so as well. I emphasize "for the most part" because that is all we can definitively expect from nature. One place this is clear is in the *SCG* I, ch. 44, no. 8: "Everything that tends in a determinate way to some end either appoints [*praestituit*] that end itself or has it appointed to it by another. Otherwise, it would not tend more toward this end than to that. Now natural things tend toward determined ends. They do not follow after their natural needs by chance, since they would not follow after them always or for the most part, but rarely." Another text is found in the commentary on the *Physics*, in which Thomas says things that come about from nature do not necessarily always come about: "Those things that come about from what is proposed [by the intellect] or from nature come about on account of an end. And those things which come about from an end come about always or frequently" (*In* II *phys.*, lec. 8, no. 8). See also *De veritate*, q. 5, a. 2, corp., which links the notion that natural things can only definitively happen "for the most part" with the appointing of the end: "We see that harmony and usefulness occur in works of nature either always or for the most part. This can not happen by mere chance; it must proceed from an intention of an end." Finally, see also the end of the body of *ST* I, q. 2, a. 3, and q. 63, a. 9, corp.

[104] *ST* II-II, q. 47, a. 6, ad 1: "The natural reason, which is called synderesis, appoints [*praestituit*] the end to the moral virtues."

[105] *ST* I-II, q. 100, a. 1, corp. (see note 98 above and English translation in text there).

[106] Again, *ST* II-II, q. 170, a. 2, ad 1, says this of all the Ten Commandments ("The precepts of the Decalogue, which are the first self-evident principles...").

contrary to the law of nature," they used to think it was morally licit).[107] This "natural habit of the ... universal principles of natural law"[108] can, therefore, become clouded in any individual just as it was historically "clouded through the profusion of sins" which necessitated the revealing of the Decalogue.[109] He similarly teaches that the love of God above all things (even more than himself)[110] is something that is "connatural"[111] to humans and implanted in them naturally, even though there are clearly people who deny God's very existence (and moreover, despite the fact that healing grace is necessary after the Fall in order to love God above all else).[112]

Fallen intellectual creatures can clearly choose in virtue of their free will to reject the Ten Commandments (which are reduced to the natural

---

[107] See *ST* I-II, q. 94, a. 4, corp.

[108] *De veritate*, q. 16, a. 1, corp.: "There is a certain natural habit of the first practical principles, which are the universal principles of natural law."

[109] See *ST* I-II, q. 98, a. 6, corp.

[110] See *ST* I, q. 60, a. 5, sc, which says it pertains to the natural law to love God more than oneself and that man loves God by a natural love (*naturali dilectione*), and even more than and before himself. Evidently, he is referring to integral nature, since I-II, q. 109, a. 4, ad 3, is clear that man cannot fulfill the commandments without healing grace. Besides, q. 109, a. 3, maintains that healing grace is necessary for fallen man to not love his own apparent private good ahead of the common good.

[111] *ST* I-II, q. 109, a. 3, corp.: "To love [*diligere*] God above all things is something connatural to man, and even to whichever creature—not only rational, but irrational—and even to inanimate things according to the manner of love that can belong to each creature." In the reply to the first objection, he adds: "For nature loves God over all things inasmuch as he is the first principle and the end of the natural good." See also I-II, q. 100, a. 3, obj. and ad 1. The objection mentions the two first and principle precepts ("love the Lord your God and love your neighbor"; "Diliges Dominum Deum tuum et Diliges proximum tuum"), and the response says that they are the "common precepts [*communia praecepta*] of the natural law, which are *per se* known to the human reason." Interestingly, it adds that they are *per se* known either by nature *or* by faith. But if, as II-II, q. 2, a. 10, appears to say, the more something is known by the reason, the less it is known by faith, it seems we must conclude (if faith may be necessary) that natural reason is not actually always definitive about the truth of these two precepts, despite the fact that I-II, q. 94, a. 4, corp., speaks of the *communia principia* as equally known to all and I-II, q. 91, a. 3, ad 1, speaks of man's practical reason participating in the eternal law naturally by means of such common principles that, as q. 91, a. 5, ad 3, adds, are common to the perfect and imperfect alike.

[112] *ST* I-II, q. 109, a. 3, corp.: "In the state of integral nature, man did not need the gift of grace superadded to natural goods for the sake of loving God naturally over all things, although he did need the help of God moving him toward this. But in the state of corrupt nature, man needs the help of grace healing nature even for this." This passage may be read in two ways: (1) grace is necessary to do this at all; (2) grace is necessary to possess *the habit* of doing so.

law),[113] and they can even lose sight of the value of keeping them. In the commentary on the *Ethics*, Thomas explains that this especially happens with evil men, for whom "that which is truly best does not appear so . . . because the malice that is opposed to virtue perverts the judgment of the reason and lies about the ends which pertain to practical principles."[114] When synderesis has become clouded by such an interposition of disordered appetite deranging particular judgment, a proximate end that is evil can appear good and the will is apt to move the reason to rationalize. Once people have become accustomed to evil principles, they more readily appoint to themselves bad ends: "The good appoint to themselves good ends; the bad, however, appoint evil ends. . . . As each one is so does the end seem to him."[115] As Thomas explains, that to which the will tends by sinning can be "apprehended as something good and fitting to nature inasmuch as it is fitting in virtue of some sensual delight."[116] In this way, a merely apparent good may be apprehended as a true good and a corrupt habit by which "reason is constrained, lest its dictate issue into choice"[117] can be developed. That this amounts to a clouding of the natural reason is perhaps most clear from the fact that the malicious man is "badly disposed in respect of the *end itself,* which is the principle in matters of action." Since "a defect about the principle is the worst" defect of all, this is no insignificant matter.[118] Nevertheless, even if certain people can lose sight

---

[113] See *ST* I-II, q. 100, a. 1.

[114] *In* VI *eth.*, lec. 10, no. 18: "Malis non appareat id quod vere est optimum, patet per hoc, quod malitia opposita virtuti pervertit iudicium rationis, et facit mentiri circa fines, qui sunt circa practica principia."

[115] *De virtutibus*, q. 1, a. 5, sc to arg. 2: "The good appoint to themselves good ends and evil men appoint evil ends, as it is said in *Ethics* III (as each one is, so does the end seem to him). It is required for the rectitude of the will, then, that there be in it some habit of virtue perfecting it [Boni praestituunt sibi bonos fines, mali vero malos, ut dicitur in III Ethic.: qualis unusquisque est, talis finis videtur ei. Ergo requiritur ad rectitudinem voluntatis, quod sit in ea aliquis habitus virtutis ipsam perficiens]."

[116] See *ST* I-II, q. 6, a. 4, ad 3.

[117] *De veritate*, q. 17, a. 1, ad 4: "And therefore it happens sometimes that the judgment of free will is perverted but not the judgment of conscience—as when someone examines something that is incumbent upon him to do here and now and judges, still speculating through principles, that something is evil (as, for instance, to fornicate with this woman). But when he begins to apply [this judgment] to the act, many circumstances present themselves from all sides as, for instance, the pleasure of fornication, From such a consideration, the reason is bound by concupiscence lest its dictate issue into choice."

[118] *ST* I-II, q. 78, a. 4, corp.: "He who sins out of certain malice is badly disposed in regard to the end itself, which is the beginning in practical things. . . . Now, the defect of principle is the worst of all defects."

of *per se nota* principles due to personal sins or cultural depravity (as with the *Germani*), Thomas manifestly maintains that there are many foundational moral principles that most people naturally grasp in one way or another. There is no other way of explaining the fact that he considers all the precepts of the Decalogue to be known through themselves[119] and argues that the "common first precepts of the law of nature" need no promulgation because the natural reason makes them known.[120]

Nevertheless, we have encountered a number of scholars who think that the end (in the singular) is presented by synderesis solely in terms of a vague push toward the good and think the natural reason is devoid of substantive content. Scott MacDonald refers to such interpreters of Aquinas as holding to a thin foundationalism.[121] They often essentially think synderesis consists solely of the first principle, whether that centers around the good or reason. We have seen Porter and Keenan arguing along these lines, though David Nelson can be added to their number. Farrell and Steven Long have both analyzed Nelson's position, and the former summarizes it as follows:

> Nelson argues that for Aquinas synderesis possesses a thin natural knowledge of our end. Natural reason does not possess any substantial standard of moral judgment. Rather, it is only through deliberation that we discover the secondary natural law precepts, which provide us with some measure of substantial action-guidance.[122]

---

[119] *ST* II-II, q. 170, a. 2, ad 1: "The precepts of the Decalogue . . . are first self-evident principles."

[120] *ST* I-II, q. 100, a. 4, ad 1: "The first common precepts of the natural law are *per se* known to one having reason and do not need promulgation."

[121] Scott MacDonald, "Foundations in Aquinas's Ethics," in *Objectivism, Subjectivism and Relativism in Ethics*, ed. Ellen Frankel Paul, Fred D. Miller Jr., and Jeffrey Paul (Cambridge: Cambridge University Press, 2008), 350–66, at 350: "Commentators often suppose that Aquinas takes this foundationalist account of practical reasoning to license a moral theory, and in particular a theory of natural law, with thick foundations: universal, objective, self-evident, substantive moral principles from which all morality can be derived. But some foundationalisms are thinner than others, and I will argue that Aquinas's foundationalism about practical reasoning is among the thin ones and is thinner than what these interpreters suppose."

[122] Farrell, *The Ends of the Moral Virtues*, 110–11, and Daniel Mark Nelson, *Priority of Prudence: Virtue and Natural Law in Thomas Aquinas and the Implications for Modern Ethics* (University Park: Pennsylvania State University Press, 1992), 91–111. For Long's assessment, see his review of Nelson's *Priority of Prudence* in *Review of Metaphysics* 46,

The consequence is that, for Nelson, matters pertaining to the natural law are really too vague or abstract to be "a source of concrete moral information."[123]

The question that arises is how proponents of a thin foundationalism can square their view with the fact that synderesis moves prudence[124] and with the texts we have encountered speaking of a variety of precepts that are *per se nota* by human reason in virtue of man's rational nature. How would synderesis, an intellectual habit, move prudence if it has no specific and substantial information? Also, how would it make sense for Thomas to say, "the ends of human life are from the dictate of natural reason, which are, in practical things, like the naturally known principles in speculative things,"[125] if there were really only knowledge of one relatively contentless end? Finally, why would Thomas argue that "prudence is not about *ends* but about means"[126] and that the "*ends* of an upright human life are determined"[127] if there were no way of determining those ends besides relying upon appetite or an "athematic"[128] conception of the good?

If prudence were to take as its starting point merely the appetites, this would essentially be reduced to a case of the tail wagging the dog, as it were. There is no doubt that, for Thomas, reason is what is highest in us and we should act in accordance with reason. But if prudence has no cognized and—at least—mostly reliable principles from which to proceed, how would man truly do that which is most proper to him well? There must, then, be some way to have intellectual knowledge about ends. Just as the speculative intellect needs solid principles from which to work, so does the practical intellect.

A clarification is called for here. The fact that synderesis is a *natural* habit does not imply that Thomas subscribes to Kantian *apriorism*. Although Thomas thinks there are naturally known principles, a

---

no. 2 (1992): 413–14. See also Long, "A Note on Jean Porter's *Nature as Reason*," *Nova et Vetera* (English) 6, no. 3 (2008): 681–88.

[123] Nelson, *Priority of Prudence*, 72 (quoted by Long on 413 of his review).

[124] *ST* II-II, q. 47, a. 6, ad 3: "But synderesis moves prudence, as the understanding of principles moves science [Sed synderesis movet prudentiam, sicut intellectus principiorum scientiam]."

[125] *ST* II-II, q. 56, a. 1, corp.: "Praecipue autem sunt de dictamine rationis naturalis fines humanae vitae, qui se habent in agendis, sicut principia naturaliter cognita in speculativis."

[126] *ST* II-II, q. 47, a. 15, corp.: "Prudentia non circa fines, sed circa ea quae sunt ad finem."

[127] *ST* II-II, q. 47, a. 15, corp.: "Fines autem recti humanae vitae sunt determinate" (emphasis added).

[128] See Keenan, *Goodness and Rightness*, 103.

"natural habit, as the understanding of principles, needs its knowledge to be determined through the senses," just as "the habit of faith receives a determination on our part," and in this way, even the "habit of the principles is said to be acquired through sense as regards the distinction of the principles, not as regards the light by which the principles are known."[129] Even the very first principle must, then, be attained by contact with the senses. Just as one does not know the whole is greater than the part until one has experienced a whole and a part, one does not know the good ought to be done unless he has an experience of good things, and so on. Having attained sufficient sensory perception, one begins to further qualify what it means to do good and avoid evil, and thus the principles are distinguished from each other. This does not mean the sense faculty appoints the end, but it is required so that *intellectus* can.

We turn now to how one comes to grasp more particular consequences of the principles. We have seen that synderesis pertains to both the higher and the lower reason. Thomas more precisely explains their relationship by giving an example of a practical syllogism:

> Synderesis administers in this syllogism that premise which is as the major premise; but the higher or lower reason administers the minor, and its consideration is of the act itself; but the consideration of the elicited conclusion is a consideration of conscience. For example: synderesis proposes, "everything bad is to be avoided"; the higher reason assumes, "adultery is bad, because it is prohibited by the law of God," or the lower reason arrives at this conclusion because it is bad for the individual because it is unjust or shameful; but the conclusion, which is "this adultery ought to be avoided," pertains to conscience, and indifferently, whether it be of the present or the past or the future, because conscience murmurs about things that have been done and contradicts things that are to be done. For this reason, conscience is named from being, as it were, with another knowledge [*cum alio scientia*], because universal knowledge is applied to a particular act.[130]

---

[129] *In* III *sent.*, dist. 23, q. 3, a. 2, ad 1: "Naturalis autem habitus, sicut intellectus principiorum, indiget ut cognitio determinetur per sensum, quo acquisitus non indiget: quia dum acquiritur, per actum determinationem recipit. Et similiter oportet quod fidei habitus determinationem recipiat ex parte nostra ... sicut habitus principiorum dicitur acquiri per sensum quantum ad distinctionem principiorum, non quantum ad lumen quo principia cognoscuntur."

[130] *In* II *sent.*, dist. 24, q. 2, a. 4, corp.: "Et quia universalia principia juris ad synderesim

Synderesis is thus distinguished in a sense from the higher and lower reason even though it pertains to them. Just as, in other syllogisms, "as much as with speculative ones as of practical ones, the major premise is *per se* known, as existing in a universal judgment,"[131] here too the universal is indemonstrable and undeniable. At the same time, even if it is not quite "athematic" (to use Keenan's word[132]), it is rather vague. A certain degree of specification is added by the higher and lower reason, though, and the judgments of either of those supply the minor premise. Interestingly, conscience here is said to supply the conclusion by applying universal knowledge so it further specifies what action should be done and, we might say, acts in the manner of an end proposing to the will what ought to be done. If the prudent man intentionally receives that which has been proposed, action ensues.[133]

Conscience is so closely bound up with synderesis that the two are sometimes spoken of as identical.[134] Just as synderesis is inseparably connected to the natural law and to whatever ought to be done or avoided, so "conscience dictates something to be done or avoided ... because it believes it to be against or according to the law of God. For the law is not applied

---

pertinent, rationes autem magis appropriatae ad opus, pertinent ad habitus, quibus ratio superior et inferior distinguuntur; synderesis in hoc syllogismo quasi majorem ministrat, cujus consideratio est actus synderesis; sed minorem ministrat ratio superior vel inferior, et ejus consideratio est ipsius actus; sed consideratio conclusionis elicitae, est consideratio conscientiae. Verbi gratia, synderesis hanc proponit: omne malum est vitandum: ratio superior hanc assumit: adulterium est malum, quia lege Dei prohibitum: sive ratio inferior assumeret illam, quia ei est malum, quia injustum, sive inhonestum: conclusio autem, quae est, adulterium hoc esse vitandum, ad conscientiam pertinet, et indifferenter, sive sit de praesenti vel de praeterito vel futuro: quia conscientia et factis remurmurat, et faciendis contradicit: et inde dicitur conscientia, quasi cum alio scientia, quia scientia universalis ad actum particularem applicatur."

[131] *De veritate*, q. 17, a. 2, corp.: "In utroque syllogismo, tam speculabilium quam operabilium, et maior est per se nota, utpote in universali iudicio existens."

[132] See Keenan, *Goodness and Rightness*, 103.

[133] This, of course, is not intended to suggest that someone who is not prudent cannot follow his conscience, but our focus at this point is on an individual who is virtuous.

[134] *ST* I, q. 79, a. 13, ad 3: "The habits from which conscience is informed, even if they are many, all nevertheless have efficacy from one first habit; namely, the habit of the first principles that is called synderesis. In view of this in particular, this habit is sometimes called conscience." See also *De veritate*, q. 17, a. 1, ad 5: "Conscience is said to be the natural judging power inasmuch as the whole examination or counseling of conscience depends upon the judging power." Aquinas says the natural judging power on which conscience depends is "called synderesis" in *De Veritate*, q. 17, a. 1, ad 5. On this, see also *In* II *sent.*, dist. 39, q. 3, a. 2, ad 2.

to our actions except by means of our conscience."[135] It is called the law of our intellect because it is the judgment of reason deduced from natural law,[136] and its judgment is always binding[137] because of this close connection. In fact, its judgment sometimes shares in the infallibility of synderesis.[138] Two examples Thomas gives of this are the principles "evil should never be done" and "God ought to be loved by me."[139]

Of course, prudence also presupposes things like the Ten Commandments and universal moral precepts in general[140] and applies them to particulars (just as conscience does). There is a difference between the judgments of conscience and prudence, however. Conscience, first of all, is temporally indifferent in the sense that it can pertain to any time period. Related to this, it judges "as yet while speculating through principles."[141] Since it is further removed from the actual act itself, Thomas says it is possible for its judgment not to be influenced by passion, whereas the judgment pertaining to prudence, the free judgment, is in fact able to be corrupted by passion.[142] In the *Summa*, Thomas explains:

---

[135] *Super Rom* 14, lec. 2: "Non enim conscientia dictat aliquid esse faciendum vel vitandum, nisi quia credit hoc esse contra vel secundum legem Dei. Non enim lex nostris actibus applicatur, nisi mediante conscientia nostra."

[136] See *De veritate*, 17, a. 1, ad sc 1.

[137] *De veritate*, 17, a. 4.

[138] *In II sent.*, dist. 39, q. 3, a. 2, ad 2: "Conscience is called the natural judging power not through itself but inasmuch as the virtue of synderesis remains in it—just as the virtue of the principles is preserved in the conclusions. And on the side of conscience that pertains to synderesis, it does not err."

[139] *De veritate*, q. 17, a. 2, corp.: "In certain matters, conscience cannot make a mistake—namely, when that particular to which conscience is applied has a universal judgment about it in synderesis. For as in speculative matters, error does not occur regarding particular conclusions that are directly assumed under universal principles expressed in the same terms—as no one is deceived in the judgment 'this whole is greater than its part' or 'every whole is greater than its part'—so too, conscience does not make a mistake by judging 'I should not love God' or that 'some evil should be done.' For in either a speculative or a practical syllogism, the major term is self-evident inasmuch as it exists in the universal judgment and the minor term, in which the universal judgment is predicated particularly [*in qua idem de seipso praedicatur particulariter*], is also self-evident."

[140] *ST* I-II, q. 100, a. 1, corp., speaks of the moral law in general, though the Ten Commandments were singled out above.

[141] *De veritate*, q. 17, a. 1, ad 4: "Iudicat, quasi adhuc speculando per principia." See the following footnote for further context.

[142] *De veritate*, q. 17, a. 1, ad 4: "It happens sometimes that the judgment of free will is perverted but not the judgment of conscience—as when someone examines something that is incumbent upon him to do here and now and judges, still speculating through principles, that something is evil (as, for instance, to fornicate with this woman). But when he

> Some pleasures, especially overly vehement ones, are contrary to the order of reason, and for this reason, the Philosopher says in *Ethics* VI that bodily pleasures destroy the judgment of prudence, but not the speculative judgment, to which pleasure is not opposed.[143]

Since conscience judges as if while speculating, in the sense that anyone can act contrary to conscience by choosing to do otherwise, conscience is speculative in a sense—just as the prudence's act of judging is sometimes said to be.[144] The only difference is that the judgment of conscience when applying universal principles is not directly dependent upon upright appetite, as the judgment of prudence is; the application of prudence "does not

---

> begins to apply [this judgment] to the act, many circumstances present themselves from all sides as, for instance, the pleasure of fornication. From such a consideration, the reason is bound by concupiscence so that its dictate might not break forth into choice. And thus someone errs in choosing, but not in conscience; rather, he acts against conscience and he is said to do this with an evil conscience inasmuch as the deed is not in keeping with the judgment made from knowledge. And thus is it clear that conscience is not necessarily the same as free will [*liberum arbitrium*]." Although there is legitimate debate on this point, there seems no denying that Thomas distinguished the two acts. Fr. Peter Murphy names the following as those who "regard the two judgments as distinct": H,-D. Noble, Leonard Lehu, Leo Elders, Michel Labourdette, Odon Lottin, and Ralph McInerny. To this list can be added Philippe Delhaye, who refers to the judgment of conscience as one "of liceity" and adds: "But we do not stop there. After this practical conclusion bearing on liceity, there is a second which concerns my concrete action. . . . It is important to insist upon this distinction of the two practical judgments" (*The Christian Conscience*, trans. Charles Quinn [New York: Desclee, 1968], 166–67). The judgment of conscience is always about what ought to be done, and it precedes the actual intention to carry it out. See also Peter Mel Murphy, *Prudence and Conscience in the Light of Veritatis Splendor: A Study on the Necessity of Eubulia, Synesis and Gnome for the Formation of a True and Correct Conscience.* [Rome: Pontificia Universitas Urbaniana, 2012], 58). For McInerny, see ch. 12 of his *Aquinas on Human Action: a Theory of Practice* (Washington, DC: Catholic University of America Press, 2012); for Noble, see H.-D. Noble, O.P., *La Conscience Morale* (Paris: Lethielleux, 1923), 57–58.

[143] *ST* I-II, q. 33, a. 3, corp.: "Quaedam enim delectationes, maxime superexcedentes, sunt contra ordinem rationis, et per hunc modum Philos. dicit. in 6. Ethic. (cap. 5), quod delectationes corporales corrumpunt existimationem prudentiae, non autem existimationem speculativam, cui delectatio non contrariatur."

[144] *ST* I-II, q. 57, a. 6, corp.: "Three acts of reason are found regarding human actions, the first of which is to take counsel, the second of which is to judge, and the third of which is to command. The first two correspond to acts of the speculative intellect." He has the same conclusion II-II, q. 47, a. 8, corp.

come about without rectified appetite"[145] because prudence itself "is not in the reason only, but has something in the appetite."[146]

In *De veritate*, q. 2, a. 8, Saint Thomas speaks of knowledge that is not applied to a work to be done by means of intention (*ad operandum per intentionem applicat*) as "speculative," and in this sense, conscience is speculative and thus not directly able to be corrupted by pleasurable objects. Although the judgment of conscience can certainly be made practical by extension, as Michel Therrien argued, it will not necessarily become so because it is further removed from the actual act.[147] This very fact is the reason someone can "err in choosing and not in conscience."[148]

The consequence of this is that, even if synderesis were to be proven rather "thin" (at least in the sense that a given individual might not have definitive knowledge of the precepts Aquinas generally attributes to it), it would still be able to have significant content in virtue of conscience, which is intimately connected to it. Whereas the application of right reason that is prudence is always in the context of "matters of counsel, in which there is no definite way of attaining the end,"[149] the application of conscience is more abstract and more connected to necessary ends. We might say that it, too, thus acts in the manner of a final cause, whereas prudence acts in the manner of a formal cause according to which the ends appointed by synderesis (and through conscience) are presupposed.

---

[145] *ST* II-II, q. 47, a. 4, corp.: "Applicatio rectae rationis ad opus, quod non fit sine appetitu recto." See also a. 1, ad 3: "The praise of prudence does not consist in consideration alone but in the application to a work, which is the end of the practical reason. And, therefore, if a defect occurs in this, it is most of all contrary to prudence, because just as the end is of greatest import in anything so also the defect that pertains to the end is the worst. Accordingly, the Philosopher goes on to say that prudence is not only with reason [that is, it is not only a rational habit] as art is, because, as was said, it has an application to a work, and this comes about through the will."

[146] *In* VI *eth.*, lec. 7, no. 7: "Prudentia non est in ratione solum, sed habet aliquid in appetitu."

[147] Michel Therrien, "Law, Liberty and Virtue: A Thomistic Defense for the Pedagogical Character of Law" (PhD diss., University of Fribourg, 2007), 54–55: "The judgment of conscience is practical by extension, but does not have motive force, except insofar as we allow it to exercise a determinative influence on our free-decision. Right practical reasoning, therefore, always results from a decision to use and follow our conscience."

[148] *De veritate*, q. 17, a. 1, ad 4: "And thus someone errs in choosing, but not in conscience; rather, he acts against conscience and he is said to do this with an evil conscience inasmuch as the deed is not in keeping with the judgment made from knowledge."

[149] See *ST* II-II, q. 47, a. 2, ad 3.

Proposed Solution

What is it, then, that appoints the end to the moral virtues? Capreolus said the position found in *ST* II-II, q. 47, was "more probable" because, even if prudence appoints on some level, in the end, prudence is subordinate to ends, inasmuch it moves the moral virtues to attain them. As Thomas said in *De virtutibus*, prudence renders actions good while looking to the end, while a habit of the speculative intellect (such as synderesis can be said to be—at least *secundum quid*[150]) renders acts good in a more noble way in virtue of their relationship to the end itself.[151] Considering that synderesis pertains to ends such as the Ten Commandments while prudence pertains to making judgments, deliberating, and commanding about means, it is understandable that Aquinas would say "synderesis moves prudence."[152] As we have seen, Cajetan argues synderesis is "the first of all the things in our mind" because, by means of it, "we naturally judge not only that every good ought to be pursued and every evil fled from and that happiness ought to be desired and misery avoided, but that the good of reason ought to be pursued and the evil opposed to it ought to be shunned."[153] He goes

---

[150] By describing synderesis as *secundum quid* speculative, I have in mind the fact that the judgment prudence presupposes is said to be made or brought about by the "speculative reason" in *ST* II-II, q. 47, a. 8, corp. (see also I-II, q. 57, a. 6). I am, however, also indebted to the work of John Naus, S.J. Though he does not say precisely that, he does say that, when we speak of the first principles "of the practical order had through the habit of synderesis," these principles may represent speculative knowledge inasmuch as "an actual tendency" is not necessarily presupposed (*The Nature of the Practical Intellect according to Saint Thomas Aquinas* (Rome: Libreria Editrice Dell' Universita Gregoriana, 1959], 66–67). He goes on to provide a category of *secundum quid* practical things as opposed to "purely speculative" things, among which he numbers ethics and conscience (167). Although he does not explicitly label synderesis in this way in this text, because conscience is an *applicatio* of synderesis to a particular work, it seems synderesis can also be labeled as *secundum quid* speculative in the sense that one need not necessarily do the good things made known by it. An indication of this is that the Ten Commandments can be broken even though they pertain to the natural law—and synderesis is the habit of the natural law.

[151] *De virtutibus*, q. 1, a. 7, ad 1: "A habit of the speculative intellect is ordered to its own act that it renders perfect and that is a consideration of truth. Now it is not ordered to an exterior act as to an end, but it has the end in its own proper act. But the practical intellect is ordered to an exterior act as to another exterior act.... And thus the habit of the speculative intellect renders its own act good in a more noble way than a habit of the practical intellect because an act of the speculative intellect serves as an end whereas an act of the practical intellect is for an end."

[152] *ST* II-II, q. 47, a. 6, ad 3: "Sed synderesis movet prudentiam, sicut intellectus principiorum scientiam."

[153] Cajetan commentary on *ST* I-II, q. 66, a. 3: "In mente nostra primo omnium est

even further than that in his estimation of the role of synderesis by adding that one judges through it "not only the ultimate end but also the proper ends of the moral virtues."[154] In other words, as Farrell observes, Cajetan suggests it sets the ends for the cardinal virtues by dictating what it means for the appetites to follow the good of reason.[155] This seems to be an accurate assessment of both Aquinas's meaning and the truth of the matter. As Thomas said in the *Scriptum*, both the common and the proximate end ("which is to attain the mean") is appointed to moral virtues by reason.[156] Things that have the "ratio of a common end," though, are "happiness and things of this sort,"[157] whereas the proper end pertains to the appetites' conformity to right reason. As Thomas explains in *ST* II-II:

> The proper end of any given moral virtue is to be conformed to right reason. For temperance intends this lest a man strays from reason on account of his concupiscence and fortitude, similarly, intends this lest it stray from the right judgment of the reason on account of fear or temerity. And this end is appointed [*praestitutus*] to man in accordance with the natural reason.[158]

---

synderesis, qua non solum omne bonum prosequendum et malum fugiendum, felicitatem appetendam et miseriam fugiendam; sed bonum rationis prosequendum et malum oppositum vitandum, iudicamus naturaliter" (Leonine ed., 6:433 [no. 12]).

[154] Cajetan on *ST* I-II, q. 66, a. 3: "Synderesis, then, is in the adjudicating intellect proposing not only the ultimate end but also the proper ends of the moral virtues (whether in the passions or actions). It judges how one should live according to reason" (Leonine ed., 6:433 [no. 12]).

[155] See Farrell, *The Ends of the Moral Virtues*, 104. He cites comments of Cajetan on *ST* I-II, q. 58, a. 5 ("The first premise is a proposition looking to synderesis, for example, 'the good of reason, as much as in passions as in operations, is to be pursued'"; Leonine ed., 6:378 [no. 8]), and on *ST* II-II, q. 47, a. 6 ("The end is appointed to moral virtue by synderesis because the natural reason dictates that in fears and delights—and, similarly, in fearful things and actions—the good of reason ought to be followed"; Leonine ed., 8:354 [no. 3]).

[156] *In* III *sent.*, dist. 33, q. 2, a. 5, corp.: "For virtue, as Cicero says, moves in the manner of nature, which is to say through a certain affective inclination.... it is necessary that the end be appointed to the other moral virtues through reason, not only the general end, but also the proximate end, which is to attain the mean."

[157] *In* II *sent.*, dist. 38, q. 1, a. 2, sc 1: "It is necessary for the end without which there can be no joining with the ultimate end to be intended as a common end. But without charity, happiness and things of this sort, there can be no joining of man's will with the ultimate end that is God. All of these, then, have the notion of a common end."

[158] *ST* II-II, q. 47, a. 7, corp.: "Conformari rationi rectae est finis proprius cujuslibet virtutis moralis: temperantia enim hoc intendit, ne propter concupiscentias homo divertat a ratione: et similiter fortitudo, ne a recto judicio rationis divertat propter timorem, vel

At least in this way, the natural reason can be said to appoint the end to the moral virtues. At the same time, since prudence relies upon and presupposes the right "disposition about ends" that are present in a moral agent due to the moral virtues,[159] it needs to look, at least on some level, to the moral virtues for ends, and those ends, in turn, are appointed by synderesis because, even though they can be perceived by looking to right appetite, they also "preexist in the reason"[160]—which seems to be a reference to the natural reason (synderesis) and even its natural extension in the speculative judgment of conscience. Synderesis, accordingly, moves prudence and does so, in part at least, by directing the moral virtues in regard to foundational principles. We will return to this below.

At the same time, presupposing synderesis and whatever principles we want to include in it—such as "the good is to be done and evil avoided," "God is to be obeyed," "one should act in accordance with reason," "the perfect good should be pursued as perfective," or even whatever follows necessarily from those principles and thus constitutes an end toward which the prudent man directs his actions—we might also say that prudence itself appoints the ends in the sense that the prudent man makes them his own and "providentially" guides his path toward attaining those ends in an optimally perfective manner. As *ST* I-II, q. 91 suggests, he can be providential over himself in this way.[161]

He also should be guided by divine providence, however, and for this, he needs to turn himself to God and rely upon the gracious assistance of the Creator who appoints the ends to nature itself and also graciously enlightens the created intellect so that it might appoint the supernatural end as well. We saw in chapter 1 of the present volume that, just as one cannot rest in anything other than contemplating God as the truly perfect Good, one also cannot rest in merely natural aptitudes. For this

---

audaciam: et hic finis praestitutus est homini secundum naturalem rationem."

[159] See *ST* I-II, q. 57, a. 4, corp.: "It is required for prudence, which is right reason about doable things, that a man be rightly disposed about ends and this comes about through upright appetite. Therefore, moral virtue, through which upright appetite comes about, is required for prudence."

[160] *ST* II-II, q. 47, a. 6, corp.: "The end of the moral virtues is the human good. But the good of the human soul is in keeping with reason, as is clear by Dionysius (in *Divine Names*, ch. 6). It is thus necessary that the ends of the moral virtues preexist in the reason."

[161] *ST* I-II, q. 91, a. 2: "The rational creature is subject to divine providence in a more excellent way than the other creatures, insofar as it is made to share in it by being provident over itself and others. Therefore, the eternal reason, through which it has a natural inclination to its fitting end, is participated in by it."

reason, acquired virtues need to be developed and, more importantly, one needs to remove obstacles to grace, turn to God, and ask for supernatural enlightenment. After the Fall, man's reason was clouded, so all of this becomes especially crucial given the present condition of man. In *De malo*, Thomas says:

> Man would have been created frustrated and in vain if he were not able to attain beatitude.... Lest it be the case that man be created frustrated and in vain since he is born with original sin, from the beginning of the human race, God put forward a remedy for man through which he could be freed from this inanity—the mediator between God and man, Jesus Christ. Through faith in him, the impediment of original sin is able to be taken away.[162]

If man is to be "transformed by the renewal of [his] mind,"[163] he has to have faith. For Thomas, the "two first commandments" pertaining to the respective precepts to love God and to love one's neighbor are "*per se* known to the human reason, either by nature or by faith; and therefore all the precepts of the Decalogue are referred to those two as conclusions are referred to common principles."[164] One might think that the words "by nature or by faith" imply that either one is sufficient, but a few questions later, we learn that "in the state of corrupt nature, man cannot fulfill all the divine commandments without healing grace,"[165] and after that, Thomas adds that even "the natural reason became clouded" after the Fall.[166]

---

[162] *De malo*, q. 5, a. 1, ad 1: "Homo frustra et vane factus esset, si beatitudinem consequi non posset, sicut quaelibet res quae non potest consequi ultimum finem. Unde ne homo frustra et vane factus esset, cum peccato originali nascens, a principio humani generis proposuit Deus homini remedium, per quod ab hac vanitate liberaretur, scilicet ipsum mediatorem Deum et hominem Iesum Christum per cuius fidem impedimentum peccati originalis subtrahi posset."

[163] Rom 12:2: "Do not be conformed to this world, but be transformed by the renewal of your mind [*kai mē suschēmatizesthe tō aiōni toutō, alla metamorphousthe tē anakainōsei tou noos*]." See also Eph 4:23.

[164] *ST* I-II, q. 100, a. 3, ad 1 (see note 47 above).

[165] *ST* I-II, q. 109, a. 4, corp.: "In statu naturae corruptae non potest homo implere omnia mandata divina sine gratia sanante." Similarly, he says that in the fallen state (*statu naturae corruptae*), man needs healing grace to help him love God above all else in I-II, q. 109 a. 3, corp.

[166] *ST* III, q. 70, a. 2, ad 1: "The natural reason became clouded even in regard to sins against nature through the increase of carnal concupiscence." This sentence is specifically speaking about the time period after "the faith of Abraham was diminished."

Grace, then, is necessary both to fulfill the commandments and to acquire certain kinds of knowledge. Regarding the latter, the healing influence of grace is often requisite in a postlapsarian world even to make people recognize—at least habitually—certain truths that would be known naturally in an unfallen world. It is also indispensable to human nature qua nature if man is to come to know his most-high calling to supernatural beatitude[167] because the supernatural virtue of faith is that which "directs the intention for the ultimate end."[168]

Commenting on the letter to the Ephesians (likely writing between 1272 and 1273[169]), Thomas speaks of three things man needs to be just and progress spiritually. The first is the "reason judging about particular things to be done," the second is the "understanding of universal principles, which is synderesis," and the third is the "divine law or God."[170] This suggests an order. Whether the reason judging about particulars is conscience or prudence, this reason should be subject to the first principles that are naturally known and, in turn, to the divine law itself.

Returning to the matter of appointing ends, those that are most properly said to be appointed seem to be remote ends about which there is no need to deliberate. They simply are those things directly pertaining to the perfect good in such a way that they are constitutive of it—in other words, the entire order of ends, from the beatific vision through the entire hierarchy of natural goods. For this reason, synderesis and faith, corresponding respectively to the natural and supernatural end, undeniably appoint the end. We did not discuss charity in great detail because the

---

[167] See Second Vatican Council, *Gaudium et Spes*, §22.

[168] See In II sent., dist. 41, q. 1, a. 2, ad 2. After saying, "fides dirigit intentionem in finem ultimum," he adds, interestingly, that natural reason is "able" to direct to some proximate end. This does not mean, though, that it always actually directs to such an end in a postlapsarian world.

[169] See Jean-Pierre Torrell, *Saint Thomas Aquinas*, vol. 1, *The Person and His Work*, rev. ed., trans. Robert Royal (Washington, DC: Catholic University of America Press, 2005), 250.

[170] *Super Eph* 4, lec. 6: "Three norms are immanent in man whereby he is directed and guided. They are necessary for him to walk justly and prosper spiritually. The first is reason judging about particular things to be done; another is synderesis, which is the understanding of universal principles; the third is the divine law or God. Someone is guided by these three in the way he is related to others by having his action accord with the judgment of reason. This occurs when reason judges in accordance with right understanding, which is synderesis, and when synderesis is ordered according to the divine law. When this happens, an action is good and meritorious."

notion of appointing ends is always linked to the intellect for Thomas,[171] and charity is in the will. One may wonder, though: as the form of the virtues, is charity not able to appoint the end? The answer comes down to the kind of causality it exercises. Thomas never says it appoints the end, but only that it is responsible for the movement toward the end. This must be because charity acts in the manner of an efficient cause.[172] It may move the virtues toward attaining the beatific vision, but even so, it presupposes faith appointing the supernatural end in the manner of a final cause as the first of all the virtues.[173]

Given the appointing that takes place by the habits of synderesis and faith, conscience and prudence can also be said to appoint ends. Since conscience is able to apply knowledge of either habit to particular works in a manner that is binding[174]—and since it precedes the activity of prudence in the sense that prudence pertains to means whereas conscience is intimately related to synderesis[175] and applies its judgments to particulars

---

[171] E.g., *ST* I, q. 18, a. 3, corp.: "Over such animals are those which move themselves even in respect of the end which they appoint themselves [literally, to themselves; *praestituunt sibi*]. This would not occur without reason and intellect, whose domain it is to know the proportion of the end and the means to the end—and the order of one to the other."

[172] *ST* II-II, q. 23, a. 8, ad 1: "Charity is said to be the form of the other virtues, not as an exemplar cause, nor essentially, but more by way of an efficient cause."

[173] *ST* II-II, q. 4, a. 7, corp.: "Since the last end is in the will through hope and charity and in the intellect through faith, it is necessary that faith be the first among the other virtues because natural knowledge is not able to attain God as the object of beatitude." Faith, then, which "directs the intention in respect of the last, supernatural end" (*ST* II-II, q. 10, a. 4, ad 2), needs to make God known as the object of beatitude. In this way, then, we might borrow the language used in *ST* I, q. 48 a.1 ad 4 (and elsewhere) that it acts "in the manner of a final cause, as an end is said to move an efficient cause."

[174] In *Super Rom* 14, lec. 2, Thomas says the law is not applied to our actions except by means of conscience ("Lex nostris actibus applicatur, nisi mediante conscientia nostra"). Conscience, of course, is called the law of our understanding (see *ST* I-II, q. 94, a. 1, obj. 2), and this too seems to imply that it is binding. More to the point, however, are *ST* I-II, q. 19, a. 5, and *De veritate*, q. 17, a. 5, which speak of conscience as binding.

[175] As St. Thomas says in *ST* I, q. 79, a. 13, ad 3, and elsewhere, conscience is in a specific way (*specialiter*) called synderesis because of the close connection between the two. *In* II *sent.*, dist. 39, q. 3, a. 1, ad 1, adds that the power of synderesis is in conscience just as the power of principles is in the conclusion. The same is not said of prudence. The close relationship between the two is also manifested by hundreds of years of agreement among certain commentators. For instance, when Capreolus speaks of a distinction between universal conscience and particular conscience (*Thomistarum Principis: Defensiones Theologiae Divi Thomae Aquinatis De Novo Editae*, 4:450), he seems to imply agreement with Bishop Anthony Fisher, who speaks of synderesis as "Conscience-1," the kind

in a more abstract way than prudence ("as if by speculating")—it seems that conscience can be said to apply the ends more fittingly than prudence can. However, there is a sense in which the perfection of man qua rational consists specifically in being able to appoint ends to himself by means of deliberation. On this level, prudence seems more than anything else to appoint the kind of end the attainment of which would ensure a man has lived according to reason in the fullest sense—that is, in the sense that the appetites themselves become rational by participation and conduce to performing virtuous acts in a manner that is connatural and pleasing to the agent. By enabling man to hylomorphically perform the kind of action that is specific to him qua rational and to do so in the most optimal way, prudence ensures viability for attaining true happiness.

In an effort to proclaim the dignity of prudence, however, we should avoid going to the extreme of making it the final arbiter of moral goodness in the sense that we could prescind from the necessity of adhering to objective moral absolutes that have been cognized either antecedent to the activity of prudence or as a part of its activity. Simon, as we have seen, is read by some as having approached this kind of error when he argued—among other things—that the judgment of prudence, "as reasoned" as it "may be, is ultimately determined not by the intellect but by the inclination of the will."[176] In other words, if we say prudence appoints ends, we should keep in mind that the ends it appoints presuppose the apprehension of other ends that are apprehended either by faith or by natural reason.

For Aquinas, "reason as apprehending the end precedes the appetite for the end."[177] Prudence, which is usually spoken of in terms of means, "implies an order to upright appetite," because the ends of the moral

---

of conscience that pertains to first principles of morality (*Catholic Bioethics for a New Millennium* [New York: Cambridge University Press, 2012], 47–48). Similarly, Petri Labbe, S.J., refers to synderesis as "conscientia universalis" and to conscience as "synderesis singularis" (*Elogia Sacra, Theologica & Philosophica, Regia, Eminentia, Illustria, Historica, Poetica, Miscellanea* [Lipsig: 1686], 172).

[176] Simon, *Definition of Moral Virtue*, 96–97: "To know what I should do here and now, I must rely on the judgment of practical wisdom [prudence]. And this judgment, reasoned as it may be, is ultimately determined not by the intellect but by the inclination of the will." See also Simon, *The Tradition of Natural Law*, ed. Vukan Kuic (New York: Fordham University Press, 1965; repr. 1992), 155–56, where he argues that, *whenever* "specific situations and specific regulations are involved, there is absolutely no possibility of preceding by logical connection" in regard to "particular determinations" of universal norms.

[177] *ST* I-II, q. 58, a. 5, ad 1: "Ratio, secundum quod est apprehensiva finis, praecedit appetitum finis."

virtues are its principles.[178] So, again, the role of the appetites is absolutely crucial even if it can be exaggerated when it is not understood in tandem with (and in subordination to) the kind of reason that apprehends the end and both precedes and specifies it. We have seen that man's end can be spoken of in terms of either the natural reason (and the proportionate end) or faith (and the supernatural end). Whether or not a man is blessed with faith, his happiness will essentially require living in accordance with reason. Aquinas has the sanguine view that the natural ends which are constitutive of this happiness are *"per se nota* to the human reason" and that the "two first commandments," to which all the precepts of the Decalogue are referred, are known "by nature or by faith."[179] In a sense, these precepts "fall under the judgment [*existimationem*] of all, as pertaining to the natural reason," since the "ends of human life" especially pertain to the dictate of natural reason.[180] However, natural reason tends to fall short of even those truths that could be known by one's natural powers alone, and lest such truths be only known by "a few, and after a long time, and with the admixture of many errors,"[181] the gift of faith has been given to man in accordance with God's merciful plan of salvation.

Faith, of course, adds knowledge of the supernatural end, but it is necessary even for knowledge of the natural ends after the Fall. Whenever the natural reason falls short in regard to natural or supernatural ends, faith "directs the intention."[182] Prudence is at work, Thomas says, "in discovering those things that lead to an upright end,"[183] but knowledge of both the

---

[178] *ST* II-II, q. 47, a. 13, ad 2: "Prudence implies an order to upright [*rectum*] appetite. First because the principles of prudence are the ends of practical affairs, in regard to which someone has a correct [*rectam*] judgment through the habits of the moral virtues that make the appetite upright [*rectum*]. Prudence, then, cannot be without the moral virtues."

[179] *ST* I-II, q. 100, a. 3, ad 1 (see note 47 above).

[180] *ST* II-II, q. 56, a. 1, corp.: "The precepts of the Decalogue, being given to the whole people, fall under the judgment [*existimationem*] of all, as pertaining to the natural reason. Now the ends of human life, which in things to be done are as the naturally known principles in speculative things, especially stand out among the things dictated by the natural reason."

[181] *ST* I, q. 1, a. 1, corp.: "Veritas de Deo per rationem investigata, a paucis, et per longum tempus, et cum admixtione multorum errorum homini proveniret."

[182] *In* II *sent.*, dist. 41, q. 1, a. 2, ad 2: "Faith directs the intention to the ultimate end." Similarly, *ST* II-II, q. 10, a. 4, ad 2, tells us that faith "directs the intention in respect of the last, supernatural end."

[183] *In* II *sent.*, dist. 33, q. 1, a. 1, qc 2, ad 2: "Prudence is active in discovering the means that lead to an upright end."

natural and supernatural end and whatever is constitutive of them is also indispensable if the appetites are to be fully in accordance with natural reason or the *ratio Dei*.[184] The understanding of universal first principles (whether natural or supernatural ones) thus appears to precede the activity of prudence. Presupposing the understanding of principles, however, Simon seems correct to say in regard to any particular and contingent good which the reason presents to the will that the inclination of the will (precisely under some specification of reason) is the final arbiter. To cite him once more:

> At the instant when the attraction of a thing good in some respect inclines the mind to utter the proposition "this is good for me," the infinite ambition of the will reverses the perspective. The thing which is good only in a certain respect discloses uncongenial aspects, and the proposition "this is not good for me" fights with its contradictory for the assent of the mind.[185]

As an "inclination following understood form"[186] that "tends toward what has been adjudicated by the intellect,"[187] the will necessarily follows the apprehension of the intellect on the level of specification, but on the level of execution (when actions that are directed toward ultimate ends are put into effect), no finite good proposed by the intellect can compel it (though even aversion is under rational specification).

The "object of the will" is, in fact, "that which is proposed by the reason,"[188] but in cases pertaining to contingent doable things, the "intellect does not bring about some effect except by means of the will."[189] The end,

---

[184] *ST* I-II, q. 71, a. 6, corp.: "Now the rule of the human will is twofold. One is proximate and of the same kind (namely, human reason itself) and the other is the first rule (namely, the eternal law which is, so to speak, the reason of God)."

[185] Simon as quoted in Clifford G. Kossel, "Thomistic Moral Philosophy in the Twentieth Century," in Pope, *Ethics of Aquinas*, 385–411, at 393n75 (from Simon, *Freedom of Choice*, 102–3).

[186] *Quolibet* VI, q. 2, a. 2: "The motion of the will is an inclination following an understood form" ("Motus voluntatis est inclinatio sequens formam intellectam"). See also *CT* I, ch. 1 ("The appetite following the intellect is the will"), and *ST* I, q. 87, a. 4, corp. ("An act of the will is nothing other than a kind of inclination following an understood form").

[187] *ST* I-II, q. 74, a. 7, ad 1: "Voluntas tendit in id quod est ratione iudicatum."

[188] *ST* I-II, q. 19, a. 5, corp.: "Objectum voluntatis est id, quod proponitur a ratione."

[189] *SCG* II, ch. 23, no. 4: "Intellectus autem non agit aliquem effectum nisi mediante voluntate, cuius obiectum est bonum intellectum." See also *De potentia*, q. 6, a. 9, obj.

as a consequence, is merely proposed and not coercively imposed, albeit whatsoever disposition of will is always according to some understanding and judgment. Worded differently, though, the intellect is the "first principle of human acts"[190] that "first and *per se* moves the will,"[191] for an action to actually take place, the will must be involved both in bringing about deliberation and in causing the movement toward the end.

Prudence, Thomas says, "has something in the appetite."[192] In fact, "rectitude of the will belongs to the *ratio* of prudence."[193] Prudence, therefore, seems to be something like an inseparable accident in the process of executing good acts proposed by habits pertaining to the understanding of natural or supernatural first principles.[194] Actually, though, it goes beyond this, because it also focuses in on these principles, as it were, enabling pursuit of them in the most ideal and fitting way. In this sense, prudence can also be said to appoint the end. It applies universal principles to particular contingent acts[195] in addition to applying them to one's affectivity.[196]

That said, it seems best to distinguish the kinds of appointing (*praestituens*) by using a word other than to "appoint" to render the meaning of *praestituere* when we are speaking of prudence. Father Romanus Cessario has led the way in this regard by rendering *praestituere* as "to appoint

---

8: "The intellect is not the beginning of an action except by means of the will." The restriction of this to the realm of the practical is my own. If we are to avoid an infinite regress, there must be some act or acts of the intellect that do not require the consent of the will to be effective, and we have seen in *SCG* that the intellect is first *simpliciter*.

[190] *ST* I-II, q. 90, a. 1: "The rule and measure of human actions is reason, which is the first principle of human actions" (the intellect and the reason, of course, are one power).

[191] *SCG* III, ch. 26, no. 22: "Now that which the fifth argument suggests, that the will is higher than the intellect as moving it, is manifestly false. For the intellect moves the will first and through itself [*per se*]."

[192] *In* VI *eth*., lec. 7, no. 7: "Prudentia non est in ratione solum, sed habet aliquid in appetitu."

[193] *ST* I-II, q. 57, a. 4, corp.: "Rectitudo voluntatis est de ratione prudentiae."

[194] Of course, prudence is not precisely an accident, since concretely adequate acts need to be adequated via prudence.

[195] *ST* II-II, q. 47, a. 1, ad 3: "Prudence is not only with reason as art is [that is, it is not only a rational habit], because, as was said, it has an application to a work, and this comes about through the will."

[196] As *ST* II-II, q. 54, a. 2, corp., says, the right choice of means pertains to prudence. Since *De veritate*, q. 17, a. 1, ad 4, tells us the "judgment of free choice" consists of the "application of knowledge *ad affectionem*," we can conclude that prudence pertains to the application to affectivity.

beforehand" in regard to synderesis and as "to enact" in regard to prudence.[197] In other words, prudence enacts principles already apprehended by the habit of synderesis. An example the Dominican commentator Francisco de Vitoria provides is that synderesis provides the norm "one ought to live temperately" whereas, from that judgment, prudence syllogizes about the manner in which one ought to live temperately: "Whether by drinking wine or water, or by eating such and such, and so on"[198] This is similar to Cajetan's position, which we saw earlier in this chapter. For him, again, synderesis proposes "[not only] the ultimate end, but the proper ends of the moral virtues," since one reasons discursively from principles such as that the good of reason ought to be followed in matters pertaining to passions and practical operations to deciding, thanks to prudence, how to "make use of these principles."[199] In other words, synderesis indicates what the ends of the individual moral virtues are and prudence determines the means of attaining them.

One other Dominican commentator who holds a nearly identical opinion is Jerome Medices (born 1569). In his *Formal Explication of the "Summa theologiae,"* he first observes that prudence merely disposes of the means and does not appoint the ends of the moral virtues, since it "applies universal principles to particular conclusions of doable things." He elaborates:

---

[197] See Romanus Cessario, *Introduction to Moral Theology*, rev. ed. (Washington, DC: Catholic University of America Press, 2013), 130.

[198] Francisco de Vitoria, O.P., *Comentarios a la secunda secundae de Santo Tomas*, vol. 2, *De caritate et prudentia*, II-II, q. 47, a. 7: "Prudence, then, directs the other virtues by appointing [*praestituendo*] the ends. This is not to say that the judgment of prudence is about such an end, but it syllogizes from those principles, as when someone syllogizes from the judgment that one ought to live temperately to the conclusion that he ought to live temperately in a certain way—whether by drinking wine or water, or by eating such and such, and so on" ([Salamanca: Apartado, 1932], 362).

[199] Cajetan commentary on *ST* I-II, q. 66, a. 3: "Synderesis, then, is in the adjudicating intellect proposing not only the ultimate end, but also the proper ends of the moral virtues (whether in the passions or actions). It judges how one should live according to reason" (no. 12). See also Cajetan's commentary on *ST* II-II, q. 47, a. 7: "The end is appointed to moral virtue by synderesis because the natural reason dictates that in fears and delights—and, similarly, in fearful things and actions—the good of reason ought to be followed" (Leonine ed., 8:354 [no. 3]). Commenting on article 8 of the same question, Cajetan says it is necessary to look to prudence to apply principles of action because "it is attributed to prudence to discover the mean, but to synderesis to appoint the end" (Leonine ed., 8:356 [no.1]). For a discussion of this text, see Farrell, *The Ends of the Moral Virtues*, 105.

> Just as the virtue of knowledge does not prove first principles, but presupposes those things that are known by the habit of understanding, so prudence does not appoint the end, but only orders those things that are for the end.

He goes on to argue that, even though "reason appoints [*praestituit*] the end to the appetite," the reason that does this is "the natural reason, which is called synderesis and is a natural habit."[200] The addition of the notion of appointing the end "to the appetite" is striking. Medices's position is also reminiscent of Cajetan's, for if synderesis appoints the ends to the moral virtues (which are in the appetites), it must appoint the ends to the appetites in some way. More importantly, though, it perfectly aligns with Thomas's own position in *ST* II-II, q. 47, a. 6, ad 3: "The end does not pertain to the moral virtues as if they themselves appoint the end, but inasmuch as they tend to the end appointed by the natural reason [Finis non pertinet ad virtutes morales, tamquam ipsae praestituant finem; sed quia tendunt in finem a ratione naturali praestitutum]."

All things considered, the best way of resolving the tension Cajetan observed between our two texts is to admit that, strictly speaking, the end is not appointed by prudence in the sense that it is itself capable of determining ends. It relies upon both rightly ordered appetites and the habit of natural reason known as synderesis (and conscience, to which the latter is so closely connected) to do the appointing that it does. Accordingly, Cessario's distinction between "appointing" and "enacting" seems to most faithfully capture the meaning and intention of Aquinas.

Although the apprehension of ultimate ends comes about due to either faith or synderesis (to which conscience is intimately related), ends such as these seem to precede reason discoursing about the choice of means, which pertains to prudence. Thus, the notions that "the will's movement is independent of and prior to reason's presentation of its object"[201] and that the only practical knowledge one can have is "knowledge by inclination, subjectivity"[202] are ultimately irreconcilable with the remarkably consistent teaching of the Angelic Doctor.

At the same time, we are often led back to what Naus and McInerny

---

[200] Hieronymus (Girolamo) Medices (also known as Hieronymus De Medicis de Camerino), *Formalis explicatio summae theologicae S. Thomae Aquinatis*, vol. 7, *Continens secunda secundae partis, secundum volumen* (Soler Fratres, 1861), 15 (commenting of *ST* II-II, q. 47, a. 6).

[201] Keenan, *Goodness and Rightness*, 47.

[202] Simon, *Definition of Moral Virtue*, 110–11.

fittingly called the "virtuous circle."[203] The intellect is, indeed, ultimately responsible for the appointing of ends, but men are not angels, and must therefore look to the appetites in discerning the most fitting way to attain those ends, presuming they have decided to make them their own. The intellect qua natural reason must be there at the beginning pointing to the principles that are ends in the moral life, and the intellect *qua recta ratio agibilium* must be there deliberating, judging, and commanding. But without the appetites performing a central role, there will be neither execution of anything nor attainment of that which is appointed. The rightly ordered appetites are, in a sense, the middle term that connects universal ends to the particular ones that have been discerned by prudence. Without all of these elements, there would remain something lacking in man's participation in the eternal law.[204] Nevertheless, the intellect or reason, which is the "cause and root of human good," must ultimately be seen as the *sine qua non* for the very existence of the virtuous circle.[205]

---

[203] Ralph McInerny, *Ethica Thomistica: The Moral Philosophy of Thomas Aquinas* (Washington, DC: Catholic University of America Press, 1997), 107; Naus, *Nature of the Practical Intellect*, 157.

[204] One could, of course say the same about an absence of the gifts of the Holy Spirit or the other two theological virtues.

[205] *ST* I-II, q. 66, corp.: "Causa et radix humani boni est ratio." See *ST* I-II, q. 17, a. 1, ad 2 ("Radix libertatis . . . sicut causa, est ratio") and note 49 on page 110 for the identity of intellect and reason.

Conclusion

THROUGHOUT THESE PAGES, we have seen that, for Aquinas, reason has an unmistakably central role in the moral life. Whether we consider prudence (right reason about contingent matters that are able to be done[1]), synderesis (the natural reason[2]), conscience ("the judgment of reason deduced from the natural law"[3]), or even the moral virtues (which "consist in the mean determined by reason"[4]), the appetitive part of man must be subject to the intellective part. As Thomas explains in his work on the virtues, "since having reason is that which makes man to be a man, it is necessary that the good of man be to exist in accordance with reason,"[5] which is found to be nothing if not all-pervasive when it comes to the perfection of the rational animal known as man. As chapter 1 of this volume evinced, even the natural desire for happiness is at least implicitly a desire for "the perfect contemplation of the highest truth."[6] Indeed, Thomas goes so far as to cite Augustine with approval when the latter says that animals bereft of reason cannot be happy.[7] The whole of the moral

---

[1] See: *In* III *de an.*, lec., no. 16; *ST* I, q. 22, a. 2, obj. 1; I-II, q. 57, a. 4, corp.; q. 65, a. 1, corp.; II-II, q. 47, a. 2, sc; q. 47, a. 8, corp.; *Quolibet* XII, q. 15, corp.

[2] *ST* II-II, q. 47, a. 6, ad 1: "Ratio naturalis, quae dicitur synderesis."

[3] *De veritate*, q. 17, a. 1, ad sc 1: "Conscientia dicitur esse lex intellectus nostri quia est iudicium rationis ex lege naturali deductum."

[4] *De virtutibus*, q. 1, a. 13, corp.: "Virtutes morales consistunt in medio determinato per rationem."

[5] *De virtutibus*, q. 1, a. 13, corp.: "Nam cum homo sit homo per hoc quod rationem habet, oportet quod bonum hominis sit secundum rationem esse."

[6] See, *De veritate*, q. 1, a. 5, ad 8, which also says the natural desire is for "the contemplative happiness of which the philosophers spoke."

[7] "Ultimus finis hominum est beatitudo, quam omnes appetunt, ut August. dicit: 'Sed non cadit in animalia expertia rationis, ut beata sint' [*De civitate Dei* 19.1; see also 19.12 and *De Trinitate* 4]; sicut August. dicit in *De diversis quaestionibus* LXXXIII."

life, therefore, from the spark of reason[8] that establishes humans as being made in the image of God[9] to the perfection of the reason that comes from faith, must be imbued by reason. Since "faith directs the intention toward the ultimate end, but the natural reason or prudence is able [only] to direct us to some proximate end,"[10] faith is certainly paramount. The will, in fact, cannot tend toward God with perfect love unless there be right faith about him in the intellect.[11] The more germane point for us in the context of the present work, though, is that, whether we have in mind the natural or supernatural realms, the centrality of the intellect manifestly enjoys privileged instrumentality in the pursuit of beatitude throughout Aquinas's career—as chapter 2 made clear. In fact, the "proper beginning of human actions"[12] is reason, and without it, it is impossible to attain the perfect notion of a moral act.[13]

The complete quote from Augustine is: "An animal which lacks reason lacks knowledge. But no animal which lacks knowledge can be happy. It therefore does not belong to animals lacking reason to be happy"; see, Augustine of Hippo, *Eighty-Three Different Questions*, ed. Hermigild Dressler, trans. David L. Mosher, The Fathers of the Church 70 (Washington, DC: Catholic University of America Press, 1982), 39. Mosher observes here: "It does not follow from this that animals are therefore *unhappy*. Rather, Augustine's point is that both happiness and unhappiness are possible only for rational beings, whereas nonrational beings are incapable of such states."

[8] Thomas sometimes refers to synderesis as the superior *scintilla rationis*, apparently contrasting it with the lower *scintilla rationis* otherwise known as "conscience" (which is itself called a *scintilla*). See, for instance, *De veritate*, q. 17, a. 2, ad 3: "Just as a spark is that which is more pure than fire and that which hovers over a whole fire, synderesis is that which is found to be topmost in the judgment of conscience, and in keeping with this metaphor, synderesis is called the spark of conscience."

[9] *ST* I, q. 93, a. 6, sc: "Esse ergo ad imaginem Dei pertinet solum ad mentem."

[10] *In II sent.*, dist. 41, q. 1, a. 2, ad 2: "Fides dirigit intentionem in finem ultimum; sed ratio naturalis vel prudentia potest dirigere in aliquem finem proximum."

[11] *ST* II-II, q. 4, a. 7, ad 5: "A previous act of the will is required for faith, but not an act of the will informed by charity. But the latter kind of act presupposes faith, because the will is not able to tend toward God with perfect love unless there be right faith about him in the intellect [quia non potest voluntas perfecto amore in Deum tendere, nisi intellectus rectam fidem habeat circa ipsum]."

[12] *ST* I-II, q. 100, a. 1, corp. (post 1270): "Human morals are named in virtue of their order to reason, which is the proper beginning of human actions." *Principium*, of course, could be translated as "principle" as well, but in this case, "beginning" seems to better capture the meaning. See also II-II, q. 157, a. 2, corp., and *De malo*, q. 10, a. 2, ad 1, which calls reason the *proprium et principale activum principium humanorum actuum*.

[13] *De malo*, q. 10, a. 2, corp. (post 1270): ". . . non attingunt perfectam rationem actus moralis, cuius principium est ratio."

Though we never entirely prescinded from man's calling to supernatural beatitude, the focus of the present work was largely on the natural foundation of the moral life known as synderesis and the first principles made known in virtue of it. Accordingly, in chapter 3, we investigated the role of natural reason and found that, as important as the appetites, prudence, and the moral virtues are, synderesis has a kind of priority. This teaching is, in a way, especially evident in the *secunda secundae* of the *Summa theologiae*, in which Thomas says that synderesis appoints the end to the moral virtues (i.e., the end the moral virtues tend toward[14]) while unequivocally denying that role to prudence,[15] and that synderesis / natural reason pertains to the end whereas prudence pertains to the means.[16] The *Scriptum* text that was introduced in the last chapter, however—*In III sent.*, dist. 33, q. 2, a. 3, corp.—is also especially illustrative of the kind of primacy synderesis enjoys. In that early work, Thomas argued the order among the three things necessary for moral virtue is as follows:

1. The appointing of the end;
2. The inclination of the appointed end;
3. The choice of the means.

It is because of this order that natural reason can be said to precede prudence. It is true that the "inclination of moral virtue is from prudence," but since the "natural inclination is from the natural reason," prudence would have no inclinations to perfect if synderesis were not present as that which provides the kind of "appointing of the end" that "precedes the act of prudence." For this reason, the teaching of the *Scriptum* passage is

---

[14] *ST* II-II, q. 47, a. 6, ad 3: "The end does not pertain to the moral virtues as if they themselves appoint the end, but because they tend to the end appointed by the natural reason, to which they are helped by prudence, which prepares the way for them by disposing the means. For this reason, it follows that prudence is more noble than the moral virtues and moves them. But synderesis moves prudence, as the understanding of principles moves the virtue of knowledge [*scientia*]."

[15] *ST* II-II, q. 47, a. 6, ad 1: "The natural reason, which is called synderesis, ... appoints the end to the moral virtues; however, prudence does not."

[16] *ST* II-II, q. 56, a. 1, corp.: "The precepts of the Decalogue, being given to the whole people, fall under the judgment [*existimationem*] of all, as pertaining to the natural reason. Now the ends of human life, which in things to be done are as the naturally known principles in speculative things, especially stand out among the things dictated by the natural reason, as was said above. And, therefore, it was not fitting that some precept directly pertaining to prudence be placed among the precepts of the Decalogue." See also note 14 just above.

essentially identical to that of *ST* II-II, q. 47, a. 6: "Prudence is more noble than the moral virtues and moves them, but synderesis moves prudence."[17]

In all three chapters, then, we discovered that, regardless of which kind of reason we consider, reason enjoys a causal primacy that is coupled with a profound fecundity in Thomas's thought. Inclinations and appetites are doubtless essential. Actually, Thomas sometimes speaks of a twofold beginning (*principium*) of human actions: "the intellect or reason and appetite, for these are the two movers in man."[18] Usually, however, he singles out reason as the interior moving power in man,[19] since it is the *first* principle of human actions[20] in which the "whole root of freedom" is located.[21] The reason for this emphasis is that, in the final analysis, the appetites of rational animals must be subject to reason. Indeed, even the most noble of the appetites—the one known as the *rational* appetite—must be subordinated to it. Given the qualifying adjective "rational" and Thomas's explanation of the will as "nothing other than a certain inclination following an understood form,"[22] it should be no surprise that this appetite must live up to its name. Moreover, since virtue pertains to living in accordance with reason, the lower appetites, too, must participate in reason. In all of this, the indispensability of prudence, which ensures this participation, shines forth. At the same time, this practical virtue that is

---

[17] *ST* II-II, q. 47, a. 6, ad 3: "Prudentia sit nobilior virtutibus moralibus, et moveat eas: sed synderesis movet prudentiam."

[18] *ST* I-II, q. 58, a. 3, corp.: "Human virtue is a certain habit perfecting man for acting well. But the beginning of human acts in man is nothing if not twofold—namely, the intellect or reason and the appetite—for these are the two moving powers in man."

[19] *De malo*, q. 10, a. 2, corp.: "... the perfect notion of a moral act, the principle of which is reason." See also *ST* I-II, q. 68, a. 1, corp.: "In man there is a twofold moving principle. One is reason, which is interior and the other is exterior—namely, God."

[20] *ST* I-II, q. 90, a. 1, corp.: "The rule and measure of human actions is reason, which is the *first* principle of human actions" (emphasis added). See also: I-II, q. 90, a. 2, corp. (which refers to reason as the *principium humanorum actuum*); I-II, q. 18, a. 8, corp. ("... principium actuum humanorum, quod est ratio"); I-II, q. 104, a. 1, ad 3 ("ratio, quae est principium moralium").

[21] *De veritate*, q. 24, a. 2, corp.: "Totius libertatis radix est in ratione constituta."

[22] *ST* I, q. 87, a. 4, corp.: "An act of the will is nothing other than a kind of inclination following an understood form." See also *Quolibet* VI, q. 2, a. 2 ("The motion of the will is an inclination following an understood form"), and *CT* I, ch. 1: ("The appetite following the intellect is the will").

also known as *recta ratio agibilium*[23] and the "charioteer of the virtues"[24] must be both grounded in and informed by the foundational principles of the natural law made known by the natural reason. The latter certainly does not provide all necessary cognitive content in one's approach toward the perfect good, but it does provide the most essential content. If we were ignorant of this truth, we would have no satisfying way of understanding Aquinas when he says prudence applies universal principles to particular works,[25] because we would be unable to provide a cogent explanation of how such universal and objective principles are either known or retained. In sum, without an understanding of synderesis, we would inescapably find ourselves trapped in the realm of the subjective. If, on the other hand, we perceive the need to conform our appetites to right reason regarding both particular and universal goods, we will be well positioned to not only appreciate the profundity of Aquinas's teaching, but also—and more importantly—the freedom to which we are called.

---

[23] *ST* I-II, q. 57, a. 4, corp.: "Et ideo ad prudentiam, quae est recta ratio agibilium." This is the description of prudence that I have translated as either "right reason about doable things" or "right reason about things that can be done."

[24] See: *ST* suppl., q. 2, a. 4, corp.; *In* II *sent.*, dist. 41, q. 1, a. 1, obj. 3; *SCG* III, ch. 35. Prudence is specifically the charioteer or driver of the moral virtues. *De virtutibus*, q. 1, a. 6, corp., says prudence is both *perfectiva* of the moral virtues and "the cause of all the virtues of the appetitive part, which are called moral" ("causa omnium virtutum appetitivae partis, quae dicuntur morales").

[25] See *ST* I-II, q. 76, a. 1, corp., and II-II, q. 47, a. 6, corp.

Acknowledgements

THIS BOOK IS THE RESULT of countless hours of discussion with friends, colleagues, and professors. Some of them aided me in formulating or modifying specific ideas, and others provided me assistance in the work of translation. Ultimately, the number of people to whom I owe thanks exceeds the number to whom I can possibly do justice here. I offer my sincere apologies to anyone I may leave out or whom I cannot thank to the degree that is fitting.

My investigations regarding the relationship between particular actions and intellectually apprehended moral principles began when I was studying under Fr. Robert Nortz. His licentiate thesis, *The Specification of Moral Acts: A Comparative Study of St. Thomas Aquinas and St. Alphonsus de Liguori*, has provided the motivation for nearly all of my work in moral theology since it gets right to the heart of the question of how "right reason" relates to law (whether natural or divine law). I might add that the impetus to evaluate the issue in a way that was faithful to the principles of St. Thomas Aquinas was almost entirely due to Fr. Robert's practically limitless appreciation for Aquinas combined with the same appreciation of Dr. Duane Berquist, another one of my professors during the time of my discernment at Most Holy Trinity Monastery.

With regard to the precise way in which I have come to think about the relationship between the kind of "right reason" known as prudence and its relationship to synderesis (which makes known the natural law), the greatest thanks are due to Steven A. Long, who was my mentor and dissertation director at Ave Maria University. His encouragement to pursue the issue further, his repeated attestation to its importance, and his incisive analysis of the central questions were truly invaluable. His insistence that I publish the results of my research on the matter, moreover, amounted to nothing less than efficient causation. Indeed, the book would simply not be if it were not for his guidance, friendship, and example.

Three other professors and colleagues that I had while at AMU are worthy of mention. First is Dr. Joseph Yarbrough, who is presently teaching at my own institution. His guidance of my translations of a variety of texts pertaining to synderesis from the Commentatorial Tradition was very formative. Without our weekly meetings, often supplemented by the insights of Dr. Andrew Dinan, this book would be lacking in depth, at the very least. Finally, I would be lacking in "right reason" were I to fail to mention Dr. Michael Dauphinais, whose counsel led me to focus on this specific topic and whose encouragement to publish often provided significant motivation.

During the course of turning my dissertation into book form, I also received helpful feedback from many of my colleagues in the Sacra Doctrina Project, and I wish to thank each one of them for their insights, encouragement, and kindness. Fr. Dylan Schrader's assistance in my understanding of some important texts from Thomas de Vio Cajetan—and the best way to translate them—is worthy of particular mention.

Finally, I'd like to thank my wife, Rebecca. Her recognition of the importance of my work and her support in getting it published were nearly as helpful as her enduring love and friendship.

Bibliography

Primary Sources

Aquinas, Thomas. *An Exposition of the "On the Hebdomads" of Boethius*. Translated by Janice L. Schultz and Edward A. Synan. Washington, DC: Catholic University of America Press, 2001.

———. *Disputed Questions of Virtue* [*De virtutibus*]. Translated by Jeffrey Hause and Claudia Murphy. Introduction and commentary by Jeffrey Haus. Indianapolis, IN: Hackett, 2010.

———. *On Love and Charity: Readings from the "Commentary on the Sentences of Peter Lombard."* Translated by Peter A. Kwasniewski, Thomas Bolin, and Joseph Bolin. Washington, DC: Catholic University of America Press, 2008.

———. *The Disputed Questions on Truth* [*De veritate*]. 3 vols. Translated by Robert William Mulligan, S.J. (vol. 1, *Questions I–IX*), James V. McGlynn, S.J.(vol. 2, *Questions X–XX*), and Robert W. Scmidt, S.J. (vol. 3, *Questions XXI–XXIX*). Chicago: Henry Regnery, 1952–1954.

Aristotle. *Aristotle in 23 Volumes*. Volume 20 [Loeb Classical Library 285], *Athenian Constitution, Eudemian Ethics, Virtues and Vices*. Translated by H. Rackham. Cambridge, MA: Harvard University Press, 1981.

———. *Nicomachean Ethics* [Greek]. Edited by J. Bywater. Medford, MA: Perseus Digital Library, 1894.

———. *The Works of Aristotle*. Edited by W. D. Ross. Volume 9, *Nicomachean Ethics* [translated by W. D. Ross], *Great Ethics* [translated by George Stock], *Eudemian Ethics* [translated by J. Solomon], and *On Virtues and Vice* [translated by J. Solomon]. Oxford: Clarendon, 1925.

———. *The Works of Aristotle*. Edited by W. D. Ross. Volume 10, *Politics* [translated by Benjamin Jowett], *Economics* [translated by E. S. Forster], and *Athenian Constitution* [translated by Frederic G. Kenyon]. Oxford: Clarendon, 1921.

Saint Augustine of Hippo. *Confessions*. Edited by Roy J. Deferrari. Translated by Vernon J. Bourke. Fathers of the Church 21. Washington, DC: Catholic University of America Press, 1953.

Damascene, Saint John. *De fide orthodoxa.* Translated by S. D. F. Salmond. In *NPNF2*, 9/2:1–101.

Wheatley, Guillemus. *In de consolatione philosophiae.* corpusthomisticum.org/xbc0.html

Commentatorial Tradition

Báñez, R .P. F. Dominici, O.P. *Commentarii Fr. Dominici Báñez Super Secundam Secundae S. Thomae.* Venice: Minimam Societatem, 1595.

Capreolus, John. *Defensiones theologiae divi Thomae Aquinatis.* Vol. 4. Turin: Alfred Cattier, 1903.

De Bergomo, Petri F. *In Opera Sancti Thomae Aquinatis Index Seu Tabula Aurea Eximii Doctoris F. Petri De Bergomo.* New York: Editiones Paulinae, n.d.

De Vitoria, Francisco. *Comentarios a la secunda secundae de Santo Tomas.* Vol. 2, *De caritate et prudentia.* Salamanca: Apartado, 1932.

John of Saint Thomas. *Cursus philosophicus thomisticus.* New edition. Vol. 2, *Philosophia Naturalis.* Paris: Ludovicus Vives, 1883.

Labbe, Petri, S.J. *Elogia sacra: theologica et philosophica, regia, eminentia, illustria, historica, poetica, miscellanea.* Lipsig: 1686.

Medices, Jerome. *Formalis explicatio summae theologicae S. Thomae Aquinatis.* Vol. 7, *Continens secunda secundae partis secundum volumen.* Soler Fratres, 1861.

Milhet, Arnaldo. *Summa philosophiae angelicae, pars IV: Ethica seu philosophia moralis.* Toulouse: Bernardus Dupuy, 1664.

Secondary Scholarship

Bradley, Denis J. M. *Aquinas on the Twofold Human Good: Reason and Human Happiness in Aquinas's Moral Science.* Washington, DC: Catholic University of America Press, 1997.

———. "Reason and the Natural Law: Flannery's Reconstruction of Aquinas's Moral Theory." *The Thomist* 67, no. 1 (2003): 119–31.

Bratcher, Robert G. Review of *The Poetics of Translation: History, Theory, Practice* by Willis Barnstone. *Critical Review of Books in Religion,* 1994, 79. Atlanta, GA: Society of Biblical Literature Press, 1994.

Cahalan, John C. "Natural Obligation: How Rationally Known Truth Determines Ethical Good and Evil." *The Thomist* 66, no. 2 (2013): 101–32.

Cessario, Romanus, O.P. *Introduction to Moral Theology.* Revised ed. Washington, DC: Catholic University of America Press, 2002.

Cunningham, Francis L. B., ed. *The Christian Life.* Dubuque, IA: Priory, 1959.

Davies, Brian, ed. *The Oxford Handbook of Aquinas.* New York: Oxford University Press, 2012.

Deferrari, Roy J., Inviolata M. Barry, and Ignatius McGuiness. *A Lexicon of Saint Thomas Aquinas Based on the Summa Theologica and Selected Passages of His Other Works.* Baltimore, MD: Catholic University of America Press, 1948.

De Haan, Daniel D. "Moral Perception and the Function of the *Vis Cogitativa* in Thomas Aquinas's Doctrine of Antecedent and Consequent Passions." *Documenti e studi sulla tradizione filosofica medievale* 25 (2014): 289–330.

———. "Perception and the *Vis Cogitativa*: A Thomistic Analysis of Aspectual, Actional, and Affectional Percepts." *American Catholic Philosophical Quarterly* 88, no. 3 (2014): 397–437.

Delhaye, P. *The Christian Conscience*. Translated by Charles Quinn. New York: Desclee, 1968.

Dewan, Lawrence. *Wisdom, Law, and Virtue: Essays in Thomistic Ethics*. New York: Fordham University Press, 2007.

Doherty, Reginald D. *The Judgments of Conscience and Prudence*. River Forest, IL: The Aquinas Library, 1961.

Farrell, Dominic L. C. *The Ends of the Moral Virtues and the First Principles of Practical Reason in Thomas Aquinas*. Rome: Gregorian and Biblical Press, 2012.

Feser, Edward. *Scholastic Metaphysics, A Contemporary Introduction*. Lancaster, UK: Editiones Scholasticae, 2014.

Fisher, Bishop Anthony. *Catholic Bioethics for a New Millennium*. New York: Cambridge University Press, 2012.

Flannery, Kevin, S.J. *Acts Amid Precepts: The Aristotelian Logical Structure of Thomas Aquinas's Moral Theory*. Washington, DC: Catholic University of America Press, 2001.

Fuchs, Josef. "Basic Freedom and Morality." In *Human Values and Christian Morality*, 92–111. Dublin: Gill and Macmillan, 1970.

———. "Good Acts and Good Persons." In *Readings in Moral Theology No. 10: John Paul II and Moral Theology*. Edited by Charles E. Curran and Richard A. McCormick, S.J. New York: Paulist Press, 1998.

Gaine, Simon Francis. *Will There Be Free Will in Heaven? Freedom, Impeccability, and Beatitude*. New York: T&T Clark, 2003.

Gallagher, David M. "The Will and Its Acts (Ia IIae, Qq. 6–17)." In *The Ethics of Aquinas*, edited by Stephen J. Pope, 69–89. Moral Traditions. Washington, DC: Georgetown University Press, 2002.

———." Thomas Aquinas on the Causes of Human Choice." PhD diss., Catholic University of America, 1988.

Graham, Mark. *Josef Fuchs on Natural Law*. Washington, DC: Georgetown University Press, 2002.

Hibbs, Thomas S. "Interpretations of Aquinas's Ethics Since Vatican II." In Pope, *Ethics of Aquinas*, 412–25.

Irwin, Terrence. *The Development of Ethics*. Vol. 1. New York: Oxford University Press, 2011.

Jørgensen, Johannes. *Lourdes*. Translated by Ingebord Lund. London: Longmans and Green, 1914.

Keenan, James. *Goodness and Rightness in Thomas Aquinas's Summa theologiae*. Washington, DC: Georgetown University Press, 1992.

———. "Receiving *Amoris Leatitia*." *Theological Studies* 78, no. 1 (2017): 193–212.

———. "The Virtue of Prudence (IIa IIae, Qq. 47–56)." In Pope, *Ethics of Aquinas*, 259–71.

Kobusch, Theo. "Grace (Ia IIae, Qq. 109–114)." In Pope, *Ethics of Aquinas*, 207–20.

Kossel, Clifford G. "Natural Law and Human Law (Ia IIae, Qq. 90–97)." In Pope, *Ethics of Aquinas*, 169–93.

---. "Thomistic Moral Philosophy in the Twentieth Century." In Pope, *Ethics of Aquinas*, 385–41.
Lauer, Rosemary Zita. "St. Thomas's Theory of Intellectual Causality in Election." *The New Scholasticism* 28, no. 3 (1954): 299–319.
Lonergan, Bernard. *Collected Works of Bernard Lonergan*. Vol. 1, *Grace and Freedom: Operative Grace in the Thought of Thomas Aquinas*. Buffalo: University of Toronto Press, 2013.
Long, Steven. "A Note on Jean Porter's *Nature as Reason*." *Nova et Vetera* (English) 6, no. 3 (2008): 681–88.
---. "Obediential Potency, Human Knowledge and the Natural Desire for God." *International Philosophical Quarterly* 37, no. 1 (1997): 45–63.
---. "On the Possibility of a Purely Natural End for Man." *The Thomist* 64, no. 2 (2000): 211–37.
---. "Perfect Storm: Loss of Nature as Normative Principle." In *What Happened in and to Moral Philosophy in the Twentieth Century?: Philosophical Essays in Honor of Alasdair Macintyre*, edited by Fran O'Rourke, 273–305. Notre Dame, IN: University of Notre Dame Press, 2013.
---. "Pruning the Vine of La Nouvelle Theologie in the Garden of Thomism: Regarding the Thomistic Corrective to 'La Nouvelle Theologie.'" *Angelicum* 93 (2016): 135–56.
---. Review of *The Priority of Prudence: Virtue and Natural Law in Thomas Aquinas and the Implications for Modern Ethics* by Daniel Mark Nelson. *Review of Metaphysics* 46, no. 2 (1992): 413–14.
---. *The Teleological Grammar of the Moral Act*. 2nd ed. Naples, FL: Sapientia, 2015.
MacDonald, Scott. "Foundations in Aquinas's Ethics." In *Objectivism, Subjectivism and Relativism in Ethics*, edited by Ellen Frankel Paul, Fred D. Miller Jr., and Jeffrey Paul, 350–66. Cambridge: Cambridge University Press, 2008.
Maritain, Jacques. *Approaches to God*. Translated by Peter O'Reilly. New York: Harper, 1954.
---. *Man and the State*. Chicago: University of Chicago Press, 1951.
McInerny, Ralph. *Ethica Thomistica: The Moral Philosophy of Thomas Aquinas*. Washington, DC: Catholic University of America Press, 1997.
Müller, Jörn. "*Duplex Beatitudo*: Aristotle's Legacy and Aquinas's Conception of Human Happiness." In *Aquinas and the Nicomachean Ethics*, 52–71. Edited by Tobias Hoffmann, Jörn Müller, and Matthias Perkams. Cambridge: Cambridge University Press, 2013.
Murphy, Peter Mel. *Prudence and Conscience in the Light of Veritatis Splendor: A Study on the Necessity of Eubulia, Synesis and Gnome for the Formation of a True and Correct Conscience*. Rome: Pontificia Universitas Urbaniana, 2012.
Naus, John E. *The Nature of the Practical Intellect according to Saint Thomas Aquinas*. Rome: Libreria Editrice Dell' Universita Gregoriana, 1959.
Oderberg, David S. "The Metaphysical Foundation of Natural Law." In *Natural Moral Law in Contemporary Society*, edited by H. Zaborowski, 44–75. Washington, DC: Catholic University of America Press, 2010.
Oesterle, J. A. *Ethics: The Introduction to Moral Science*. Englewood Cliffs, NJ: Prentice-Hall, 1957).
Pinckaers, Servais, O.P. *The Pinckaers Reader: Renewing Thomistic Moral Theology*. Edited

by John Berkman and Craig Titus. Translated by Sr. Mary Thomas Noble, O.P., et al. Washington, DC: Catholic University of America Press. 2005.

Porter, Jean. *The Recovery of Virtue: The Relevance of Aquinas for Christian Ethics*. Louisville, KY: Westminster / John Knox, 1990.

———. "The Virtue of Justice (IIa IIae, Qq. 58–122)." In Pope, *Ethics of Aquinas*, 272–86.

Reichberg, Gregory M. "The Intellectual Virtues (Ia IIae, Qq. 57–58)." In Pope, *Ethics of Aquinas*, 131–50.

Rhonheimer, Martin. "Nature as Reason: A Thomistic Theory of the Natural Law." *Studies in Christian Ethics* 19, no. 3 (2006): 357–78, at 357.

———. "The Cognitive Structure of the Natural Law and the Truth of Subjectivity." *The Thomist* 67, no. 1 (2003): 1–44.

Royal, E. Peter, "Concerning the Coercion of the Intellect." *Laval théologique et philosophique* 13, no. 1 (1957): 97–111.

Sherwin, Michael S. *By Knowledge and By Love: Charity and Knowledge in the Moral Theology of Thomas Aquinas*. Washington, DC: Catholic University of America Press, 2005.

Simon, Yves. *Practical Knowledge*. Edited by Robert J. Mulvaney. New York: Fordham University Press, 1991.

———. *The Definition of Moral Virtue*. Edited by Vukan Kuic. New York: Fordham University Press, 1986.

———. *The Tradition of Natural Law*. Edited by Vukan Kuic. New York: Fordham University Press, 1965, 1992.

Stöckl, Albert. *Handbook of the History of Philosophy*. Translated by T. A. Finlay. 2nd edition. Vol. 1, *Pre-Scholastic and Scholastic Philosophy*. London: Longmans and Green, 1914.

Therrien, Michel. "Law, Liberty and Virtue: A Thomistic Defense for the Pedagogical Character of Law." PhD diss., University of Fribourg, 2007.

Torrell, Jean-Pierre, O.P. *Saint Thomas Aquinas*. Vol. 1, *The Person and His Work*. Translated by Robert Royal. Revised ed. Washington, DC: Catholic University of America Press, 2005.

Weisheipl, James A., O.P. *Friar Thomas D'Aquino: His Life, Thought, and Works*. Garden City, NY: Doubleday, 1974.

Westberg, Daniel. "Did Aquinas Change His Mind about the Will?" *The Thomist* 58, no. 1 (1994): 41–60.

White, Kevin. "Pleasure, a Supervenient End." In *Aquinas and the Nicomachean Ethics*, 220–38. Edited by Tobias Hoffmann, Jorn Muller, and Matthias Perkams. Cambridge: Cambridge University Press, 2013.

White, Thomas Joseph, O.P. "Review of *The Natural Desire to See God according to St. Thomas Aquinas and His Interpreters* by Lawrence Feingold. *The Thomist* 74, no. 3 (2010): 461–67.

Wieland, George. "Happiness (Ia-IIae, qq. 1–5)." Translated by Grant Kaplan. In Pope, *Ethics of Aquinas*, 57–68.

Yuengert, Andrew. *The Boundaries of Technique: Ordering Positive and Normative Concerns in Economic Research*. New York: Lexington Books, 2004.

Index of Subjects and Names

A

appointing of ends
    tension in texts of Aquinas, 12, 183–84
    Cajetan's resolution, 198–202
    Brady's proposed resolution, 222–34

Aquinas, Thomas
    texts prior to 1270 regarding the primacy of the intellect, 128–168
    texts after 1270 pertaining to the primacy of the intellect and the supposed voluntaristic shift, 169–73

Aristotle
    and contemplation of God as last end, 83–84
    on bodily pleasures destroying the judgment of prudence, 220
    on end as first in practical affairs, 45
    on prudence as moved by appetite, 198
    on the beginning of prudence being "in the moral virtues," 70
    on the beginning of prudence being the end of the virtues, 204
    on the definition of nature, 53n125
    on the definition of virtue, 11n56, 32n14, 55, 55n131, 57n137

Augustine, St., 8
    and stolen pears, 14, 45, 48–49
    on virtue, 12n60, 73n200
    on animals, knowledge, and happiness, 236

B

Báñez
    on the natural determination of the will to the good of reason, 31

Bradley, Denis, 13
    on deliberating about ends, 203, 205
    on free choice and Lottin's theory, 100, 181

C

Cahalan, John
    on Hume, 193n37

Cajetan, 2, 3, 12
    on the two texts in the Summa, 183–202
    on prudence as dependent upon rectitude of both apprehensive and appetitive part, 2n10, 16, 198n54.

Capreolus, John
    on the appointing of the end coming more probably from synderesis than prudence, 206–7

catechism
    and virtue, 60
causes
    final cause
        God as, 79–82
        intellect acting as a, 109–14, 121–23, 129, 134–35, 149, 156n234, 166, 178–79
        primacy of, 36–39;
        subordinated to the last end, 46–47
    on relationship between four causes, 36–38, 78–79
    subordinate final causes, 47
Cessario, Romanus
    on the meaning of "*praestituere*," 19, 26–27, 231, 233
charity, 34n23, 43n69, 58n141, 88–91, 164n272, 223n157, 227, 236n11
conscience, 67–69
    and appointing ends, 227
    and the judgments of the will and reason, 132n147, 203n73
    as particular synderesis (*synderesis particularis*), 227–28n228
    as speculative, 220–21
    the inability of conscience to err at times, 153n219, 219n139
    the syllogism of conscience, 217
    vs. free will / *liberum arbitrium*, 118n92, 152n217

D

Damascene, St. John
    and "the law of our understanding," 23
    on the law of conscience, 96
    on virtues as natural qualities, 53
    on "will as nature" and "will as reason," 23, 51, 118–19

De Haan, Daniel, 110, 123–124
Dewan, Lawrence, 112, 116, 133
    on "autonomy" of the will, 147
    on Keenan's reading of Aquinas, 172
    on priority of intellect, 149, 169n302

E

end
    necessity of having one final end, 39–43
    on the appointing of the end (*see* "Appointing of Ends")
    on the end "by which" vs. "for which," 29
    on the importance of the end, 29–39

F

faith, 34, 87, 89–91, 107, 196n47, 213n111, 217, 225–29, 233, 236
Farrell, Dominic, 3n10, 26, 101n12, 202n69, 215, 223
Feser, Edward
    on relationship among causes, 36–37
Fisher, Bishop Anthony, 227n175
Flannery, Kevin, 99, 116, 121, 180
free will
    and choice, 119n92, 161n259
    and conscience, 118n92
    and *liberum arbitrium*, 117–18, 65n174, 94
    and sin, 158n244, 160, 213–14
    as "indifferently related to choosing well or badly," 167n286
    happiness not subject to, 48n98
    judgment of is different from that of synderesis, 154
    judgment of perverted by concupiscence, 69n191, 214n117, 219n142

judgment of vs. judgment of
    conscience, 67n182, 152n217,
    176n347, 203n73
"names will in relation to choosing,"
    156n236
not a natural habit, 119n94
per se ordered to the good, 163n264
reason as source of, 125n118,
    144n189, 149, 173n331
relationship to reason, 174–81, 186
freedom
    for excellence, 161–63;
    of indifference, 156–60;
    of will (*see* "free will")
Fuchs, Josef, 6–7, 122

G

Gaine, Simon Francis, 38n47
Gaudium et Spes, 1
God
    image of, 50, 96, 96n307, 236
    love of as natural to man, 213n111
good
    "in what does the perfect good
        consist?", 50–97
    on "the perfect good and intellectual
        virtue," 75–78
    on "the perfect good and moral
        virtue," 65–75
    on "the perfect good in relation to
        God," 78–97
    on "the perfect good, nature, and
        synderesis," 50–65
Graham, Mark, 7

H

happiness
    and God, 78–97
    and intellectual virtue, 75–78
    and natural reason, 63

and moral virtue, 65–75
consists in God, 82
general ratio of, 52n120
the end as the perfect good of, 43–49
Hibbs, Thomas, 139
    on Keenan, 6, 150n210
Hoffmann, Tobias, 8

I

intellect
    acting as a final cause, 109–14, 121–
        23, 129, 134–35, 149, 156n234,
        166, 178–80
    as formal cause, 128, 179, 180
    as foundation of freedom, 141
    causality of, 174–81
    estimative/cogitative power or
        passive, 20n88, 72n197, 175,
        177n352
    primacy of intellect over other
        powers, 102, 156n232, 170–71
    specification of intellect, 169n300,
        179
Irwin, Terrence, 26, 101n12

J

John of St. Thomas
    on final causes that are subordinated
        to the last end, 46–47, 91
    on the role of the end, 37
    judgment
        of conscience vs. judgment of free
            will, 67n182, 69n191, 152n217
        of free will vs. judgment of
            synderesis, 91, 119n92

K

Kierkegaard, Soren, 5
Kossel, Clifford, 10n51, 230n185

L

Labbe, Petri, 228n175
Lauer, Rosemary Zita, 101, 108, 116
Lonergan, Bernard, 115, 169n299
Long, Steven, foreword (xv–xxii), 92, 100, 105
 grace and the supernatural end, 49
 happiness as the achievement of the good, 65
 "indefinite more," 92
 on "elicited desire," 35
 on finite goods, 148
 on freedom of the will, 148
 on Nelson's "thin" view regarding the content of synderesis, 215
 on obediential potency, 93, 96
 on ordering of human nature to transcendent end, 49
 on "prior speculum," 16
 on the elicited desire for God, 35
 speculative foundation of practical ordering, 16
Lottin, Odon
 and purported voluntaristic move of Aquinas, 100, 108, 116, 120–21, 149, 170, 180, 220

M

MacDonald, Scott
 on "thin foundationalism," 215
Maritain, Jacques
 and "knowledge by Inclination," 5, 7, 10n5, 22
 on the desire to know the first Cause, 96n306
McInerny, Ralph
 on man's ultimate end, 40
 on the distinct judgments of prudence and conscience, 220n142
 on the virtuous circle, 13, 15, 234
Medices, Jerome, 232–33
Milhet, Arnaldo, 31
Müller, Jörn, 81
Murphy, Peter Mel, 220n142

N

natural reason
 and man's assent to good, 50, 51n111
 as appointing end, 193–202, 111, 179, 189, 205–6, 244
 as "beclouded by sin," 64n171, 214, 255
 as derived from eternal law, 33
 as making humans provident over themselves, 82
 called synderesis, xv note 1, xvi, xix, 12, 21, 23, 31, 32n11, 59, 234
 content of natural reason, 215
 freedom and, 161
 immediate judgments of, 210–11
 natural reason and the Decalogue, 237n16
 prudence vs., 58, 59, 63, 237
Naus, John, 13n68, 68, 139n173, 222n150, 233
Nelson, Daniel Mark, 215

O

obediential potency, 93, 94–97

P

Pinckaers, Servais, 134n155, 163, 181
Porter, Jean, 76, 190–91, 195, 208–9, 215
praestituere, meaning of, 24–27
prudence
 and conscience, 219
 and appointing ends, 227
 as an intellectual virtue, 11–12

as essentially intellectual yet
belonging with moral virtues,
75n208
the second act of and the act of
conscience, 220n142

R

reason, 64–65
as nature, 51, 58, 160n254
as reason, 58, 160
compared to intellect, 110–11
see also right reason
Reichbert, Gregory M., 73n203
Rhonheimer, Martin
on "reason as nature," 51, 130n137
right reason
and the definition of prudence,
239n23
application of, 221
application of different for prudence
and conscience, 221
as cause of virtue, 57n137
as proper end of moral virtue,
201n66, 223
as ruled rule / measured measure,
32n14, 106n33
conformity to, 223
dependence of on naturally known
principles, 17
dependence of on rectitude of
appetitive and apprehensive parts,
198
dependence of right reason about
doable things (prudence) on
moral virtue, 13, 15, 16n74,
199n55, 224n159, 234
moral virtues and, 30
moral virtue as participation in, 188
relationship of to the mean of virtue,
189; 191n23

S

Shakespeare
on reason as large discourse, 65
Sherwin, Michael
on Keenan, 7–8, 127n139, 11
on the judgment of conscience, 68
on the supposed shift in Aquinas's
thought, 128–30
on the will as a passive potency, 117
on understanding, 22
Simon, Yves, xvi, 4–5, 7, 9, 21, 137, 144,
191n24, 228, 230, 233
synderesis (*see also*, natural reason)
and conscience, 32n11, 218
and free will, 118n92
and prudence, 219
and "thin" natural knowledge, 215
as virtue, 199n56
called "natural reason," 12, 23
content of, 207–21
meaning of, 19–24
primacy of, 237
the difference between synderesis,
conscience, and natural law,
32n12

T

Therrien, Michel
on the judgment of conscience, 67,
221

U

understanding (*intellectus*)
two kinds of, 21, 175–78

V

virtue(s)
definition of, 11–12, 32n14, 55,
57, 60n152, 73n200, 76n211,
76n215, 188, 188n16

intellectual, 73–78
natural vs. infused, 22, 23n94,
  60n152, 62, 62n163, 89, 192

W

Weisheipl, James, 116n82
  on dating of the Prima Pars, 120n95
  on Parisian condemnations, 117
Westberg, Daniel, 6, 99, 103, 115
Wheatley, William
  on twofold end, 29–30
White, Kevin, 122
White, Thomas Joseph
  on the elicitation of the natural
    desire for God, 34
will, the
  as following the intellect, 156n232,
    170–71, 230
  as nature (*thelēsis* or simple will), 51
  as nature follows natural reason, 155
  as reason (*boulēsis* or advising will),
    51, 119
  primacy on the level of exercise,
    150–51, 160, 169, 169n300

Y

Yuengert, Andrew, 5